The RA CONTACT

TEACHING THE LAW OF ONE

VOLUME II

Source: Ra, an Humble Messenger of the Law of One
Instrument: Carla L. Rueckert
Questioner: Don Elkins
Scribe: Jim McCarty

Relistening Project: Tobey Wheelock
Production and Editing: Gary Bean and Austin Bridges

The Ra Contact: Teaching the Law of One – Volume 2

Second printing.

ISBN: 978-0-945007-98-2

Published by L/L Research
Box 5195
Louisville, Kentucky 40255-0195, USA
www.llresearch.org
contact@llresearch.org

Cover art by Aaron Maret
Cover photo by Mark Zealor

TABLE OF CONTENTS

INTRODUCTION: VOLUME 2

This book is the second volume in a two-volume set of books titled *The Ra Contact: Teaching the Law of One.* It contains sessions #57–106 of a tuned, telepathic, trance contact with an extraterrestrial group of beings known in Earth's history as those of Ra. This contact was the result of an ongoing experiment in establishing telepathic communication with extraterrestrials, started in 1962. The discussion with Ra took the form of question and answer and lasted from January 15, 1981 through March 15, 1984. Don Elkins served as the questioner; Carla L. Rueckert served as the instrument; and, Jim McCarty, the last living member of this original group, served as the scribe.

Ra indicates that Earth is now in the midst of a graduation of souls into the next evolutionary stage, what they call the fourth density of love and understanding. Ra made contact with our group to give information to the interested spiritual seeker concerning the evolution of mind, body, and spirit. They describe the densities, or dimensions, of light that form our octave of creation and how we move through these densities on our journey back to the One Infinite Creator. Ra teaches us about the nature of the seven energy centers, or chakras, and how we can open our heart center and focus our will upon serving others to achieve this graduation to fourth density.

These books, along with every other publication and transcript produced by L/L Research, are available for free in digital format on our archive website www.llresearch.org. Hardcopy books can also be ordered from our online store.

57.0 **RA** I am Ra. I greet you in the love and in the light of the One Infinite Creator. We communicate now.

57.1 **QUESTIONER** Could you first give me an indication of the instrument's condition, please?

RA I am Ra. This instrument is under a most severe psychic attack. This instrument is bearing up well due to replenished vital energies and a distortion towards a sense of proportion which your peoples call a sense of humor.

This attack is potentially disruptive to this contact for a brief period of your space/time.

57.2 **QUESTIONER** Is there anything in particular that we can do in addition to what we are doing to alleviate this attack?

RA I am Ra. There is nothing you can do to alleviate the attack. The understanding of its mechanism might be of aid.

57.3 **QUESTIONER** Could you tell us its mechanism?

RA I am Ra. The Orion group cannot interfere directly but only through pre-existing distortions of mind/body/spirit complexes.

Thus in this case this entity reached for an heavy object with one hand, and this miscalculated action caused a deformation, or distortion, of the skeletal/muscular structure of one of this instrument's appendages.

Your aid may be helpful in supporting this instrument in the proper care of this distortion, which is equivalent to what you call your post-operative state, when bones are not firmly knit. This instrument needs to be aware of care necessary to avoid such miscalculated actions, and your support in this state of awareness is noted and encouraged.

57.4 **QUESTIONER** Is there anything that we can specifically do to alleviate the problem that is already existing?

RA I am Ra. This information is harmless, thus we share it though it is transient, lacking the principle but only offering a specific transient effect.

The wrist area should be wrapped as in the sprained configuration, as you call this distortion, and what you call a sling may be used on this distorted right side of the body complex for one diurnal period. At that time symptoms, as you call these distortions, shall be reviewed and such repeated until the distortion is alleviated.

The healing work to which each is apprentice may be used as desired.

It is to be noted that a crystal is available.

57.5 **QUESTIONER** Which crystal is that?

RA I am Ra. The flawed but sufficient crystal which rests upon the digit of this instrument's right hand.

57.6 **QUESTIONER** Would you tell me how to use that crystal for this purpose?

RA I am Ra. This is a large question.

You first, as a mind/body/spirit complex, balance and polarize the self, connecting the inner light with the upward spiraling inpourings of the universal light. You have done exercises to regularize the processes involved. Look to them for the preparation of the crystallized being.

Take, then, the crystal, and feel your polarized and potentiated, balanced energy channeled in green-ray healing through your being, going into and activating the crystalline regularity of frozen light, which is the crystal. The crystal will resound with the charged light of incarnative love and light energy and will begin to radiate in specified fashion, beaming, in required light vibrations, healing energy, focused and intensified towards the magnetic field of the mind/body/spirit complex which is to be healed. This entity requesting such healing will then open the armor of the overall violet/red-ray protective vibratory shield.

Thus the inner vibratory fields, from center to center in mind, body, and spirit, may be interrupted and adjusted momentarily, thus offering the one to be healed the opportunity to choose a less distorted inner complex of energy fields and vibratory relationships.

57.7 **QUESTIONER** Should the crystal be held in the right hand of the healer?

RA I am Ra. This is incorrect. There are two recommended configurations.

The first: the chain about the neck to place the crystal in the physical position of the green-ray energy center.

Second: the chain hung from the right hand, out-stretched, wound about the hand in such a way that the crystal may be swung so as to effect sensitive adjustments.

We offer this information realizing that much practice is needed to efficiently use these energies of self. However, each has the capability of doing so, and this information is not information which, if followed accurately, can be deleterious.

57.8 **QUESTIONER** Would an unflawed crystal be considerably more effective than the flawed one that we now have?

RA I am Ra. Without attempting to deem the priorities you may choose, we may note that the regularized or crystallized entity, in its configuration, is as critical as the perfection of the crystal used.

57.9 **QUESTIONER** Does the size, physical size, of the crystal have any relationship to the effectiveness in the healing?

RA I am Ra. In some applications concerning planetary healing, this is a consideration. In working with an individual mind/body/spirit complex the only requirement is that the crystal be in harmony with the crystallized being.

There is, perhaps, a lower limit to the size of what you may call a faceted crystal, for light coming through this crystal needs to be spread the complete width of the spectrum of the one to be healed. It may further be noted that water is a type of crystal which is efficacious also, although not as easy to hang from a chain in your density.

57.10 **QUESTIONER** Placing this end of this pencil sitting on my navel, would the point of it then represent the position where the crystal should hang for proper green ray? Is this position correct?

RA I am Ra. We attempt your measurements. From 2 to 5.4 centimeters towards your heart is optimal.

57.11 **QUESTIONER** Using this piece of wood, then, I would determine the position between the piece of wood [and] my navel, I would determine the position to be approximately the top of the piece of wood. Is this correct?

RA I am Ra. This is correct.

57.12 **QUESTIONER** How does the healing that you just told us about relate to the healing done in the King's Chamber in the Giza pyramid?

RA I am Ra. There are two advantages to doing this working in such a configuration of shapes and dimensions.

Firstly, the disruption, or interruption, of the violet/red armoring, or protective shell, is automatic.

In the second place, the light is configured by the very placement of this position in the seven distinctive color, or energy, vibratory rates, thus allowing the energy through the crystallized being, focused with the crystal, to manipulate with great ease the undisturbed and, shall we say, carefully delineated palette of energies, or colors, both in space/time and in time/space.

Thus the unarmored being may be adjusted rapidly. This is desirable in some cases, especially when the armoring is the largest moiety of the possibility of continued function of body complex activity in this density.[1] The trauma of the interruption of this armoring vibration is then seen to be lessened.

We take this opportunity to pursue our honor/duty, as some of those creating the pyramid shape, to note that it is in no way necessary to use this shape in order to achieve healings, for seniority of vibration has caused the vibratory complexes of mind/body/spirit complexes to be healed to be less vulnerable to the trauma of the interrupted armoring.

Furthermore, as we have said, the powerful effect of the pyramid, with its mandatory disruption of the armoring—if used without the crystallized being, used with the wrong intention, or in the wrong configuration—can result in further distortions of entities which are, perhaps, the equal of some of your chemicals which cause disruptions in the energy fields in like manner.

57.13 **QUESTIONER** Is there currently any use for the pyramid shape at all that is beneficial?

---

[1] In this context, *moiety* can be defined as "part, or portion."

RA I am Ra. This is in the affirmative, if carefully used.

The pyramid may be used for the improvement of the meditative state as long as the shape is such that the entity is in Queen's Chamber position, or entities are in balanced configuration about this central point.

The small pyramid shape, placed beneath a portion of the body complex, may energize this body complex. This should be done for brief periods only, not to exceed 30 of your minutes.

The use of the pyramid to balance planetary energies still functions to a slight extent, but due to earth changes the pyramids are no longer aligned properly for this work.

57.14 **QUESTIONER** What is the aid, or the mechanism of the aid, received for meditation for an entity who would be positioned in the so-called Queen's Chamber position?

RA I am Ra. Consider the polarity of mind/body/spirit complexes. The inner light is that which is your heart of being. Its strength equals your strength of will to seek the light. The position, or balanced position of a group, intensifies the amount of this will, the amount of awareness of the inner light necessary to attract the instreaming light upward, spiraling from the south magnetic pole of being.

Thus this is the place of the initiate, for many extraneous items, or distortions, will leave the entity as it intensifies its seeking so that it may become one with this centralized and purified incoming light.

57.15 **QUESTIONER** Then if a pyramid shape is used, it would seem to me that it would be necessary to make it large enough so that the Queen's Chamber position would be far enough from the King's Chamber position, so that you could use that energy position and not be harmed by the energy position of the King's Chamber position, or any position farther from the Queen's Chamber. Is this correct?

RA I am Ra. In this application a pyramid shape may be smaller if the apex angle is less, thus not allowing the formation of the King's Chamber position. Also efficacious for this application are the following shapes: the silo, the cone, the dome, and the tepee.

57.16 **QUESTIONER** Do these shapes that you just mentioned have any of the effect of the King's Chamber at all, or do they have only the Queen Chamber effect?

RA I am Ra. These shapes have the Queen's Chamber effect. It is to be noted that a strongly crystallized entity is, in effect, a portable King's Chamber position.

57.17 **QUESTIONER** Then are you saying that there is absolutely no need, use, or good in having the King's Chamber effect at this time in our planetary evolution?

RA I am Ra. If those who desired to be healers [were] of a crystallized nature, and were all supplicants those wishing less distortion, the pyramid would be, as always, a carefully designed set of parameters to distribute light and its energy so as to aid in healing catalyst.

However, we found that your peoples are not distorted towards the desire for purity to a great enough extent to be given this powerful and potentially dangerous gift. We, therefore, would suggest it not be used for healing in the traditional, shall we say, King's Chamber configuration which we naïvely gave to your peoples only to see its use grossly distorted and our teachings lost.

57.18 **QUESTIONER** What would be an appropriate apex angle for a tepee shape for our uses?

RA I am Ra. This is at your discretion. The principle of circular, rounded, or peaked shapes is that the center acts as an invisible inductive coil. Thus the energy patterns are spiraling and circular. Thus the choice of the most pleasant configuration is yours. The effect is relatively fixed.

57.19 **QUESTIONER** Is there any variation in the effect with respect to the material of construction, the thickness of the material? Is it simply the geometry of the shape, or is it related to some other factors?

RA I am Ra. The geometry, as you call it, or relationships of these shapes in their configuration is the great consideration. It is well to avoid stannous material, or that of lead or other baser metals.[2] Wood, plastic, glass, and other materials may all be considered to be appropriate.

57.20 **QUESTIONER** If a pyramid shape were placed below the entity, how would this be done? Would this be placed beneath the bed? I'm not quite sure of the arrangement for energizing the entity by "placing it below." Could you tell me how to do that?

RA I am Ra. Your assumption is correct. If the shape is of appropriate size it may be placed directly beneath the cushion of the head or the pallet upon which the body complex rests.

We again caution that the third spiral of upward lining light, that which is emitted from the apex of this shape, is most deleterious to an entity in overdose and should not be used over-long.

57.21 **QUESTIONER** What would the height of one of these pyramids be, approximately, in centimeters, for best functioning?

RA I am Ra. It matters not. Only the proportion of the height of the pyramid from base to apex to the perimeter of the base is at all important.

57.22 **QUESTIONER** What should that proportion be?

RA I am Ra. This proportion should be the 1.16 which you may observe.

57.23 **QUESTIONER** Do you mean that the sum of the four base sides should be 1.16 of the height of the pyramid?

RA I am Ra. This is correct.[3]

57.24 **QUESTIONER** By saying that the Queen's Chamber was the initiatory place, could you tell me what you mean by that?

RA I am Ra. This question is a large one. We cannot describe initiation in its specific sense due to our distortion towards the belief/understanding that the process which we offered so many of your years ago was not a balanced one.

---

2   In this context, *stannous* can be defined as "made of tin."

3   To read a few theories about the befuddling 1.16 ratio, see the Resource Series.

However, you are aware of the concept of initiation and realize that it demands the centering of the being upon the seeking of the Creator. We have hoped to balance this understanding by enunciating the Law of One; that is, that all things are One Creator. Thus, seeking the Creator is done not just in meditation and the work of an adept but in the experiential nexus of each moment.

The initiation of [the] Queen's Chamber has to do with the abandoning of self to such desire to know the Creator in full that the purified instreaming light is drawn, in balanced fashion, through all energy centers, meeting in indigo and opening the gate to intelligent infinity. Thus the entity experiences true life or, as your people call it, resurrection.

57.25 **QUESTIONER** You also mentioned the pyramid was used for learning. Is this the same process, or is there a difference?

RA I am Ra. There is a difference.

57.26 **QUESTIONER** What is the difference?

RA I am Ra. The difference is the presence of other-selves manifesting in space/time and—after some study in time/space—for the purpose of teach/learning. In the system created by us, schools were apart from the pyramid, the experiences being solitary.

57.27 **QUESTIONER** I didn't quite understand what you meant by that. Could you tell me more of what you're talking about?

RA I am Ra. This is a wide subject. Please restate for specificity.

57.28 **QUESTIONER** Did you mean that teachers from your vibration, or density, were able to manifest in the Queen's Chamber to teach those initiates, or did you mean something else?

RA I am Ra. In our system, experiences in the Queen's Chamber position were solitary. In Atlantis and in South America teachers shared the pyramid experiences.

57.29 **QUESTIONER** How did this learning process take place in—learning or teaching—take place in the pyramid?

RA I am Ra. How does teach/learning and learn/teaching ever take place?

57.30 **QUESTIONER** The dangerous pyramid shape for use today would be a four-sided pyramid that was large enough to create the King's Chamber effect. Is that statement correct?

RA I am Ra. This statement is correct with the additional understanding that the 76° apex angle is that characteristic of the powerful shape.

57.31 **QUESTIONER** Then I am assuming that we should not use a pyramid of 76° apex angle under any circumstances. Is this correct?

RA I am Ra. This is at your discretion.

57.32 **QUESTIONER** I will restate the question. I am assuming then that it might be dangerous to use a 76° angle pyramid, and I will ask what angle less than 76° would be roughly the first angle that would not produce this dangerous effect?

RA I am Ra. Your assumption is correct. The lesser angle may be any angle less than 70°.

57.33 **QUESTIONER** Thank you. I want to go on more questioning on the pyramid, but I want to ask a question [*name*] has here. I'll throw it in at this point. Could you please expand on the concept of space/time and time/space and how to get past this, the concept of these things? And at what density level do these concepts no longer affect the individual?

RA I am Ra. This will be the last full query of this working. This instrument has some vital energy left. However, we become concerned with the increasing distortions of the body complex towards pain.

The space/time and time/space concepts are those concepts describing, as mathematically as possible, the relationships of your illusion: that which is seen to that which is unseen. These descriptive terms are clumsy. They, however, suffice for this work.

In the experiences of the mystical search for unity these need never be considered, for they are but part of an illusory system. The seeker seeks the One. This One is to be sought, as we have said, by the balanced and self-accepting self, aware both of its apparent distortions and its total perfection.

Resting in this balanced awareness, the entity then opens the self to the universe, which it is. The light energy of all things may then be attracted by this intense seeking, and wherever the inner seeking meets the attracted cosmic prana, realization of the One takes place.

The purpose of clearing each energy center is to allow that meeting place to occur at the indigo-ray vibration, thus making contact with intelligent infinity and dissolving all illusions. Service-to-others is automatic at the released energy generated by this state of consciousness.

The space/time and time/space distinctions, as you understand them, do not hold sway except in third density. However, fourth, fifth, and to some extent, sixth, work within some system of polarized space/time and time/space.

The calculations necessary to move from one system to another through the dimensions are somewhat difficult. Therefore, we have the most difficulty sharing numerical concepts with you and take this opportunity to repeat our request that you monitor our numbers and query any that seem questionable.

Is there a brief query that we may answer before we leave this instrument?

57.34 **QUESTIONER** Is there anything we can do to make the instrument more comfortable or improve the contact?

RA I am Ra. All is harmonious. We greet you all in joy. The adjustments are satisfactory.

I am Ra. I leave you in the love and in the light of the One Infinite Creator. Go forth, therefore, rejoicing in the power and in the peace of the One Infinite Creator. Adonai.

58.0 **RA** I am Ra. I greet you in the love and in the light of the One Infinite Creator. We communicate now.

58.1 **QUESTIONER** Would you please give me an indication of the instrument's condition?

RA I am Ra. This condition is as previously noted except that the physical distortions mentioned have somewhat increased.

58.2 **QUESTIONER** Could you tell me the cause for the increase of the physical distortion?

RA I am Ra. Physical distortions of this nature are begun, as we have said, due to over-activity of weak, as you call this distortion, portions of the body complex. The worsening is due to the nature of the distortion itself which you call arthritis. Once begun, the distortion will unpredictably remain and unpredictably worsen or lessen.

58.3 **QUESTIONER** We have tried healing with the diamond crystal. I have tried both using the crystal around my neck and dangling it from a chain under my right hand. I think that possibly that to do the best work on the wrist I should dangle the crystal just below my right hand from a distance of just a centimeter or two, holding it directly above the wrist. Is this correct?

RA I am Ra. This would be appropriate if you were practiced at your healing art. To work with a powerful crystal such as you have, while unable to perceive the magnetic flux of the subtle bodies, is perhaps the same as recommending that the beginner, with saw and nail, create the Vatican.

There is great art in the use of the swung crystal. At this point in your development, you would do well to work with the unpowerful crystals in ascertaining, not only the physical major energy centers, but also the physical secondary and tertiary energy centers, and then begin to find the corresponding subtle body energy centers. In this way, you may activate your own inner vision.

58.4 **QUESTIONER** What type of crystal should be used for that?

RA I am Ra. You may use any dangling weight of symmetrical form, for your purpose is not to disturb or manipulate these energy centers but merely to locate them and become aware of what they feel like when in a balanced state and when in an unbalanced, or blocked, state.

58.5 **QUESTIONER** Am I correct in assuming that what I would do would be to dangle a weight approximately two feet below my hand, and place it over the body, and when the weight started moving in a clockwise rotational direction it would indicate an unblocked energy center? Is this correct?

RA I am Ra. The measurement from hand to weight is unimportant and at your discretion. The circular motion shows an unblocked energy center. However, some entities are polarized the reverse of others, and, therefore, it is well to test the form of normal energy spirals before beginning the procedure.

58.6 **QUESTIONER** How would you test?

RA I am Ra. A test is done by first holding the weight over your own hand and observing your particular configuration. Then, using the other-self's hand, repeat the procedure.

58.7 **QUESTIONER** Now in the case of the instrument we are concerned with the healing of the wrists and hands. Would I then test the energy center of the instrument's hand and wrist area? Is this correct?

RA I am Ra. We have given you general information regarding this form of healing and have explicated the instrument's condition. There is a line beyond which information is an intrusion upon the Law of Confusion.

[*There is an 82-second pause between the end of this answer and the beginning of the next question.*]

58.8 **QUESTIONER** I would like to trace the energy patterns and what is actually happening with these patterns and flow of energy in a couple of instances. I will first take the pyramid shape and trace the energy that is focused, somehow, by this shape. I will make a statement and let you correct it.

I think that the pyramid can be in any orientation and provide some focusing of spiraling energy, but the greatest focusing occurs when one side of it is precisely parallel to magnetic north. Is this correct?

RA I am Ra. This is substantially correct, with one addition. If one corner is oriented to the magnetic north, the energy will be enhanced in its focus also.

58.9 **QUESTIONER** Do you mean that if I drew a line through two opposite corners of the pyramid at the base and aimed that at magnetic north—that would be precisely 45° out of the orientation of one side aimed at magnetic north—it would work just as well? Is that what you are saying?

RA I am Ra. It would work much better than if the pyramid shape were quite unaligned. It would not work quite as efficiently as the aforementioned configuration.

58.10 **QUESTIONER** Would the pyramid shape work just as well right side up as upside down, with respect to the surface of the earth, assuming the magnetic alignment was the same in both cases?

RA I am Ra. We do not penetrate your query. The reversed shape of the pyramid reverses the effects of the pyramid. Further, it is difficult to build such a structure, point down. Perhaps we have misinterpreted your query.

58.11 **QUESTIONER** I used this question only to understand the way the pyramid focuses light, not for the purpose of using one. I was just saying if we did build a pyramid point down, would it focus at the Queen's Chamber position, or just below it, the same way as it would if it were point up?

RA I am Ra. It would only work thusly if an entity's polarity were, for some reason, reversed.

58.12 **QUESTIONER** Then the lines of spiraling light energy—do they originate from a position toward the center of the earth and radiate outward from that point?

RA I am Ra. The pyramid shape is a collector which draws the instreaming energy from what you would term the bottom, or base, and allows this energy to spiral upward in a line with the apex of this shape. This is also true if a pyramid shape is upended. The energy is not earth energy, as we understand your question, but is light energy which is omni-present.

58.13 **QUESTIONER** Does it matter if the pyramid is solid or is made of four thin sides, or is there a difference in effect between those two makes?

RA I am Ra. As an energy collector the shape itself is the only requirement. From the standpoint of the practical needs of your body complexes, if one is to house one's self in such a shape, it is well that this shape be solid sided in order to avoid being inundated by outer stimuli.

58.14 QUESTIONER Then if I just used a wire frame that were four pieces of wire and joined at the apex running down to the base, and the pyramid were totally open, this would do the same thing to the spiraling light energy? Is this correct?

RA I am Ra. The concept of the frame as equal to the solid form is correct. However, there are many metals not recommended for use in pyramid shapes designed to aid the meditative process. Those that are recommended are, in your system of barter, what you call expensive. The wood, or other natural materials, or the man-made plastic rods will also be of service.

58.15 QUESTIONER Why is the spiraling light focused by something as open and simple as four wooden rods joined at an apex angle?

RA I am Ra. If you pictured light in the metaphysical sense as water, and the pyramid shape as a funnel, this concept might become self-evident.

58.16 QUESTIONER I can see how a solid-sided pyramid would act as a funnel. It seems to me that using just the four rods joined at the apex angle would be less efficient. Can you tell me how they are equivalent to the solid-sided pyramid?

RA I am Ra. They are unequal in space/time, and we recommend, for practical use, the solid-sided pyramid, or other focusing shape, in order to give your physical bodily complexes respite from outside noise, rain, and other distractions to meditation. However, in time/space one is concerned with the electromagnetic field produced by the shape. An equivalent field is produced by the solid and the open shape. Light is influenced metaphysically by this field rather than by visible shapes.

58.17 QUESTIONER Thank you, that explains it nicely. I apologize for asking so many stupid questions on this, but I am really functioning here with very little knowledge. I do not wish to get into subject matter of no importance. I had assumed that questions about the pyramid were desired by you due to the fact that some danger was involved to some who had misused the pyramid, etc.

I am trying to understand the way light works, and trying to get a grasp of how everything works together, and I was hoping that questions in this area on the pyramid would help me understand the Third Distortion, I'll say, which is Light.

Now, as I understand it, the pyramid shape acts as a funnel, in this way increasing the, I'll say, density of energy so that the individual may have a greater intensity of actually the Third Distortion. Is this correct?

RA I am Ra. In general, this is correct.

58.18 QUESTIONER Then the pure crystalline shape, such as the diamond, you mentioned as being frozen light—it seems that this third-density physical manifestation of light is somehow a window, or focusing mechanism for the Third Distortion in the general sense. Is this correct?

RA I am Ra. This is basically correct. However, it may be noted that only the will of the crystallized entity may cause interdimensional light to flow through this material. The more regularized the entity and the more regularized the crystal, the more profound the effect.

58.19 QUESTIONER There are many people who are now bending metal, doing other things like that by mentally requesting this happen. What is happening in that case? What are they— Can you explain what's happening there?

RA I am Ra. That which occurs in this instance may be likened to the influence of the second spiral of light in a pyramid being used by an entity. As this second spiral ends at the apex, the light may be likened unto a laser beam in the metaphysical sense; and when intelligently directed may cause bending not only in the pyramid, but this is the type of energy which is tapped into by those capable of this focusing of the upward spiraling light. This is made possible through contact in indigo ray with intelligent energy.

58.20 QUESTIONER Why are these people able to do this? They seem to have no training; they just are able to do it.

RA I am Ra. They remember the disciplines necessary for this activity which is merely useful upon other true-color vibratory experiential nexi.

58.21 **QUESTIONER** Then you are saying that this wouldn't be useful in our present density. Will it be useful in fourth-density on this planet in the very near future?

RA I am Ra. The end of such energy focusing is to build, not to destroy, and it does become quite useful as, shall we say, an alternative to third-density building methods.

58.22 **QUESTIONER** Is it also used for healing?

RA I am Ra. No.

58.23 **QUESTIONER** Is there any advantage in attempting to develop these characteristics or being able to bend metal, etc.? What I am trying to say is that, are these characteristics a signpost of the development of an entity, or are they something else? For instance, as an entity develops through his indigo would a signpost of his development be this bending?

RA I am Ra. This will be the last full query of this working.

Let us specify the three spirals of light energy which the pyramid exemplifies. Firstly, the fundamental spiral which is used for study and for healing. Second, the spiral to the apex which is used for building. Thirdly, the spiral spreading from the apex which is used for energizing.

Contact with indigo ray need not necessarily show itself in any certain gift, or guidepost, as you have said. There are some whose indigo energy is that of pure being and never is manifested, yet all are aware of such an entity's progress. Others may teach or share in many ways contact with intelligent energy. Others continue in unmanifested form seeking intelligent infinity.

Thus the manifestation is a lesser signpost than that which is sensed, or intuited, about a mind/body/spirit complex. This violet-ray beingness is far more indicative of true self.

Are there any brief queries or small matters we may clear up, if we can, before we leave this instrument?

58.24 **QUESTIONER** Well, I did have a question on what you meant by the "third spiral." And if that is too long I would just ask if there is anything that we can do to make the instrument more comfortable or improve the contact?

RA I am Ra. We may answer briefly. You may query in more detail if you deem it desirable at another session.

If you picture the candle flame, you may see the third spiral.

This instrument is well balanced. The accoutrements are aligned well. You are conscientious.

I am Ra. I leave you, my friends, in the love and in the light of the One Infinite Creator. Go forth, therefore, rejoicing in the power and the peace of the One Infinite Creator. Adonai.

59.0   RA   I am Ra. I greet you in the love and in the light of the One Infinite Creator. We communicate now.

59.1   QUESTIONER   Could you first tell me the instrument's condition and why she feels so tired?

RA   I am Ra. This instrument's condition is as previously stated. We cannot infringe upon your free will by discussing the latter query.

59.2   QUESTIONER   Would it be any greater protection for the instrument if Jim changed his sitting position to the other side of the bed?

RA   I am Ra. No.

59.3   QUESTIONER   I have a question from Jim that states: "I think I have penetrated the mystery of my lifelong anger at making mistakes. I think I have always been aware subconsciously of my abilities to master new learnings, but my desire to successfully complete my mission on Earth has been energized by the Orion group into irrational and destructive anger when I fail. Could you comment on this observation?"

RA   I am Ra. We would suggest that as this entity is aware of its position as a wanderer, it may also consider what pre-incarnative decisions it undertook to make regarding the personal, or self-oriented, portion of the choosing to be here at this particular time/space. This entity is aware, as stated, that it has great potential, but potential for what? This is the pre-incarnative question.

The work of sixth density is to unify wisdom and compassion. This entity abounds in wisdom. The compassion it is desirous of balancing has, as its antithesis, lack of compassion. In the more conscious being this expresses or manifests itself as lack of compassion for self. We feel this is the sum of suggested concepts for thought which we may offer at this time without infringement.

59.4   QUESTIONER   At the end of the second major cycle there were a few hundred thousand people incarnate on Earth. There are over four billion incarnate today. Were the over four billion people who are incarnate today, were they in the earth planes but not incarnate at that time, or did they come in from elsewhere during the last 25,000-year cycle?

RA I am Ra. There were three basic divisions of origin of these entities.

Firstly and primarily, those of the planetary sphere you call Maldek, having become able to take up third density once again, were gradually loosed from self-imposed limitations of form.

Secondly, there were those of other third-density entrance, or neophytes, whose vibratory patterns matched the Terran experiential nexus. These then filtered in through incarnative processes.

Thirdly, in the past approximate 200 of your years you have experienced much visiting of the wanderers.

It may be noted that all possible opportunities for incarnation are being taken at this time due to your harvesting process and the opportunities which this offers.

59.5 **QUESTIONER** Just to clarify that: could you tell me approximately how many total mind/body/spirit complexes were transferred to Earth at the beginning of this last 75,000 year period?

RA I am Ra. The transfer, as you call it, has been gradual. Over two billion souls are those of Maldek which have successfully made the transition.

Approximately 1.9 billion souls have, from many portions of the creation, entered into this experience at various times. The remainder are those who have experienced the first two cycles upon this sphere or who have come in at some point as wanderers; some wanderers having been in this sphere for many thousands of your years; others having come far more recently.

59.6 **QUESTIONER** I'm trying to understand the three spirals of light in the pyramid shape. I would like to question on each.

The first spiral starts below the Queen's Chamber and ends in the Queen's Chamber? Is that correct?

RA I am Ra. This is incorrect. The first notion of upward spiraling light is as that of the scoop, the light energy being scooped in through the attraction of the pyramid shape through the bottom or base. Thus the first configuration is a semi-spiral.

59.7   QUESTIONER Would this be similar to the vortex you get when you release the water from a bathtub?

RA I am Ra. This is correct except that in the case of this action the cause is gravitic, whereas in the case of the pyramid the vortex is that of upward spiraling light being attracted by the electromagnetic fields engendered by the shape of the pyramid.

59.8   QUESTIONER Then the first spiral after this semi-spiral is the spiral used for study and healing. Relative to the Queen's Chamber position, where does this first spiral begin and end?

RA I am Ra. The spiral which is used for study and healing begins at, or slightly below, the Queen's Chamber position, depending upon your earth and cosmic rhythms. It moves through the King's Chamber position in a sharply delineated form and ends at the point whereby the top approximate third of the pyramid may be seen to be intensifying the energy.

59.9   QUESTIONER Now, the first spiral is obviously different somehow than the second and third spirals since they have different uses and different properties. The second spiral then starts at the end of the first spiral and goes up, I assume, to the apex of the pyramid. Is that correct?

RA I am Ra. This is partially correct. The large spiral is drawn into the vortex of the apex of the pyramid. However, some light energy—which is of the more intense nature of the red, shall we say, end of the spectrum—is spiraled once again, causing an enormous strengthening and focusing of energy which is then of use for building.

59.10   QUESTIONER And then the third spiral radiates from the top of the pyramid. Is this correct?

RA I am Ra. The third complete spiral does so. This is correct. It is well to reckon with the foundation semi-spiral which supplies the prana for all that may be affected by the three following upward spirals of light.

59.11   QUESTIONER Now I am trying to understand what happens in this process. I'll call the first semi-spiral zero position and the other three spirals one, two, and three; the first spiral being study and healing. What change takes place in light from the zero position into the first spiral that makes that first spiral available for healing and study?

RA I am Ra. The prana scooped in by the pyramid shape gains coherence of energetic direction. The term "upward spiraling light" is an indication not of your up and down concept, but an indication of the concept of that which reaches towards the source of love and light.

Thus all light, or prana, is upward spiraling, but its direction, as you understand this term, is unregimented and not useful for work.

59.12 **QUESTIONER** Could I assume, then, that from all points in space light radiates in our illusion outward in a 360° solid angle, and this scoop shape with the pyramid then creates the coherence to this radiation as a focusing mechanism? Is this correct?

RA I am Ra. This is precisely correct.

59.13 **QUESTIONER** Then the first spiral has a different factor of cohesion, you might say, than the second. What is the difference between this first and second spiral?

RA I am Ra. As the light is funneled into what you term the zero position, it reaches the point of turning. This acts as a compression of the light, multiplying tremendously its coherence and organization.

59.14 **QUESTIONER** Then is the coherence and organization multiplied once more at the start of the second spiral? Is there just a doubling effect or an increasing effect?

RA I am Ra. This is difficult to discuss in your language. There is no doubling effect but a transformation across boundaries of dimension so that light, which was working for those using it in space/time–time/space configuration, becomes light working in what you might consider an inter-dimensional time/space–space/time configuration. This causes an apparent diffusion and weakness of the spiraling energy. However, in position two, as you have called it, much work may be done inter-dimensionally.

59.15 **QUESTIONER** In the Giza pyramid there was no chamber at position two. Do you ever make use of position two by putting a chamber in that position, say on other planets or in other pyramids?

RA I am Ra. This position is useful only to those whose abilities are such that they are capable of serving as conductors of this type of focused spiral. One would not wish to attempt to train third-density entities in such disciplines.

59.16 **QUESTIONER** Then the third spiral radiating from the top of the pyramid, you say, is used for energizing. Can you tell me what you mean by "energizing?"

RA I am Ra. The third spiral is extremely full of the positive effects of directed prana, and that which is placed over such a shape will receive shocks energizing the electromagnetic fields. This can be most stimulating in third-density applications of mental and bodily configurations. However, if allowed to be in place over-long such shocks may traumatize the entity.

59.17 **QUESTIONER** Are there any other effects of the pyramid shape beside the spirals that we have just discussed?

RA I am Ra. There are several. However, their uses are limited. The use of the resonating chamber position is one which challenges the ability of an adept to face the self. This is one type of mental test which may be used. It is powerful and quite dangerous.

The outer shell of the pyramid shape contains small vortices of light energy which, in the hands of capable crystallized beings, are useful for various subtle workings upon the healing of invisible bodies affecting the physical body.

Other of these places are those wherein perfect sleep may be obtained and age reversed. These characteristics are not important.

59.18 **QUESTIONER** What position would be the age reversal position?

RA I am Ra. Approximately 5 to 10° above and below the Queen's Chamber position, in ovoid shapes on each face of the four-sided pyramid, extending into the solid shape approximately one-quarter of the way to the Queen's Chamber position.

59.19 **QUESTIONER** In other words, if I went just inside the wall of the pyramid a quarter of the way but still remained three-quarters of the way from the center, at approximately the level above the base of the Queen's Chamber, I would find that position?

RA I am Ra. This is approximately so. You must picture the double teardrop extending in both the plane of the pyramid face and in half towards the Queen's Chamber, extending above and below it. You may see this as the position where the light has been scooped into the spiral and then is expanding again. This position is what you may call a prana vacuum.

59.20 QUESTIONER Why would this reverse aging?

RA I am Ra. Aging is a function of the effects of various electromagnetic fields upon the electromagnetic fields of the mind/body/spirit complex. In this position there is no input or disturbance of the fields, nor is any activity within the electromagnetic field complex of the mind/body/spirit complex allowed full sway. The vacuum sucks any such disturbance away. Thus the entity feels nothing and is suspended.

59.21 QUESTIONER Is the pyramid shape that Jim has constructed in our yard functioning properly? Is it aligned properly and built properly?

RA I am Ra. It is built within good tolerances though not perfect. However, its alignment should be as this resting place for maximum efficacy.

59.22 QUESTIONER Do you mean that one of the base sides should be aligned 20° east of north?

RA I am Ra. That alignment would be efficacious.

59.23 QUESTIONER Previously you stated that one of the base sides should be aligned with magnetic north. Which is better, to align with magnetic north or to align with 20° east of magnetic north?

RA I am Ra. This is at your discretion. The proper alignment for you of this sphere at this time is magnetic north. However, in your query you asked specifically about a structure which has been used by specific entities whose energy vortices are more consonant with the, shall we say, true-color green orientation. This would be the 20° east of north.

There are advantages to each orientation. The effect is stronger at magnetic north and can be felt more clearly. The energy, though weak, coming from the now-distant-but-soon-to-be-paramount direction is more helpful.

The choice is yours. It is the choice between quantity and quality, or wide-band and narrow-band aid in meditation.

59.24 **QUESTIONER** When the planetary axes realign, will they realign 20° east of north to conform to the green vibration?

RA I am Ra. We fear this shall be the last question as this entity rapidly increases its distortion towards what you call pain of the body complex.

There is every indication that this will occur. We cannot speak of certainties but are aware that the grosser, or less dense, materials will be pulled into conformation with the denser and lighter energies which give your Logos its proceedings through the realms of experience.

May we answer any brief queries at this time?

59.25 **QUESTIONER** Only if there is anything that we can do to make the instrument more comfortable or improve the contact?

RA I am Ra. All is well. We are aware that you experience difficulties at this time, but they are not due to your lack of conscientiousness or dedication.

I am Ra. I leave you in the love and in the light of the One Infinite Creator. Go forth, then, rejoicing in the power and the peace of the One Infinite Creator. Adonai.

Session 60

60.0 **RA** I am Ra. I greet you in the love and in the light of the One Infinite Creator. We communicate now.

60.1 **QUESTIONER** Could you first give me an indication of the instrument's condition?

RA I am Ra. It is as previously stated.

60.2 **QUESTIONER** It is my opinion that the best way for the instrument to improve her condition is through periods of meditation followed by periods of contemplation with respect to the condition and its improvement. Could you tell me if I am correct and expand on my thinking?

RA I am Ra. Meditation and contemplation are never untoward activities. However, this activity will in all probability, in our opinion, not significantly alter the predispositions of this instrument which cause the fundamental distortions which we, as well as you, have found disconcerting.

60.3 **QUESTIONER** Can you tell me the best approach for altering, to a more acceptable condition, the distortions that the instrument is experiencing?

RA I am Ra. There is some small amount of work which the instrument may do concerning its pre-incarnative decisions regarding service to the Infinite Creator in this experience. However, the decision to open, without reservation, to the offering of self when service is perceived is such a fundamental choice that it is not open to significant alteration, nor would we wish to interfere with the balancing process which is taking place with this particular entity.

The wisdom and compassion being so balanced by this recapitulation of fourth density is helpful to this particular mind/body/spirit complex. It is not an entity much given to quibbling with the purity with which it carries out that which it feels it is best to do. We may say this due to the instrument's knowledge of itself, which is clear upon this point. However, this very discussion may give rise to a slightly less fully unstopped dedication to service in any one working so that the service may be continued over a greater period of your space/time.

60.4   **QUESTIONER** You are saying then that the physical distortions that the instrument experienced are part of a balancing process? Is this correct?

RA I am Ra. This is incorrect. The physical distortions are a result of the instrument's not accepting fully the limitations, placed prior to incarnation, upon the activities of the entity once it had begun the working. The distortions caused by this working, which are inevitable given the plan chosen by this entity, are limitation and—to a degree consonant with the amount of vital and physical energy expended— weariness due to that which is the equivalent in this instrument of many, many hours of harsh physical labor.

This is why we suggested the instrument's thoughts dwelling upon the possibility of its suggesting to its higher self the possibility of some slight reservation of energy at a working. This instrument, at this time, is quite open until all resources are quite exhausted. This is well, if desired. However, it will, shall we say, shorten the number of workings in what you may call the long run.

60.5   **QUESTIONER** Will spreading the workings out over greater intervals of time so that we have more time between workings help?

RA I am Ra. This you have already done. It is not helpful to your group to become unbalanced by concern for one portion of the work above another. If this instrument is, in your judgment, capable, and if the support group is functioning well, if all is harmonious, and if the questions to be asked have been considered well, the working is well begun. To overly stress the condition of the instrument is as deleterious to the efficiency of this contact as the antithetical behavior was in your past.

60.6   **QUESTIONER** Aside from the workings I am concerned about the physical distortions of the instrument in the area of hands and arms. Is there a, shall we say, mental exercise or something else that the instrument could work on to help to alleviate the extreme problems she has at this time with her hands, etc.?

RA I am Ra. Yes.

60.7   **QUESTIONER** Would this be an exercise of meditation and contemplation upon the alleviation of these problems?

RA I am Ra. No.

60.8   **QUESTIONER** What would she do then in order to alleviate these problems?

RA I am Ra. As we have said, this instrument, feeling that it lacked compassion to balance wisdom, chose an incarnative experience whereby it was, of necessity, placed in situations of accepting self in the absence of other-selves' acceptance, and the acceptance of other-self without expecting a return or energy transfer. This is not an easy program for an incarnation but was deemed proper by this entity.

This entity, therefore, must needs meditate and consciously, moment by moment, accept the self in its limitations which have been placed for the very purpose of bringing this entity to the precise tuning we are using.

Further, having learned to radiate acceptance and love without expecting return, this entity now must balance this by learning to accept the gifts of love and acceptance of others, which this instrument feels some discomfort in accepting. These two balancing workings will aid this entity in the release from the distortion called pain. The limitations are, to a great extent, fixed.

60.9   **QUESTIONER** Is the fact that the instrument already was consciously aware of this the reason that the First Distortion was not in force in making it impossible for you to communicate this to us?

RA I am Ra. This is not only correct for this entity, which has been consciously aware of these learn/teachings for some of your years, but also true of each of the support group. The possibility of some of this information being offered was not there until this session.

60.10   **QUESTIONER** Thank you. When you spoke in the last session of "energizing shocks" coming from the top of the pyramid, did you mean that these came at intervals rather than steadily?

RA I am Ra. These energizing shocks come at discrete intervals but come very, very close together in a properly functioning pyramid shape. In one whose dimensions have gone awry the energy will not be released with regularity, or in quanta, as you may perhaps better understand our meaning.

60.11 **QUESTIONER** The next statement that I make may or may not be enlightening to me in my investigation of the pyramid energy, but it has occurred to me that the so-called effect in the so-called Bermuda Triangle is possibly due to the large pyramid beneath the water which releases this third spiral at discrete and varying intervals, and when other entities, or craft, are in the vicinity of this it creates a situation where they change space/time continuum in some way. Is this correct?

RA I am Ra. Yes.

60.12 **QUESTIONER** Then this third spiral has an energizing effect that, if strong enough, will actually change the space/time continuum. Is there a use, or value, to this type of change?

RA I am Ra. In the hands of one of fifth-density or above this particular energy may be tapped in order to communicate information, love, or light across what you would consider vast distances but which, with this energy, may be considered transdimensional leaps. Also, there is the possibility of travel using this formation of energy.

60.13 **QUESTIONER** Would this travel be the instantaneous type having to do with the . . . not the slingshot effect, but the effect used primarily by sixth-density entities? Or is it the sling-shot effect that you are talking about?

RA I am Ra. The former effect is that of which we speak. You may note that as one learns the, shall we say, understandings or disciplines of the personality each of these configurations of prana is available to the entity without the aid of this shape. One may view the pyramid at Giza as metaphysical training wheels.

60.14 **QUESTIONER** Then is the large underwater pyramid off the Florida coast one of the balancing pyramids that Ra constructed, or some other social memory complex? And if so, which one?

RA I am Ra. That pyramid of which you speak was one whose construction was aided by sixth-density entities of a social memory complex working with Atlanteans prior to our working with the, as you call them, Egyptians.

60.15 **QUESTIONER** You mentioned working with one other group other than the Egyptians. Who were they?

RA I am Ra. These entities were those of South America. We divided our forces to work within these two cultures.

60.16 **QUESTIONER** The pyramid shape, then, as I understand it, was deemed by your social memory complex at that time to be of paramount importance as, shall I say, a physical training aid for spiritual development. At this particular time in the evolution of our planet it seems that you place little or no emphasis on this shape. Is this correct?

RA I am Ra. This is correct. It is our honor/duty to attempt to remove the distortions that the use of this shape has caused in the thinking of your peoples and in the activities of some of your entities. We do not deny that such shapes are efficacious, nor do we withhold the general gist of this efficacy. However, we wish to offer our understanding, limited though it is, that—contrary to our naïve beliefs many thousands of your years ago—the optimum shape for initiation does not exist.

Let us expand upon this point. When we were aided by sixth-density entities during our own third-density experiences, we, being less bellicose in the extreme, found this teaching to be of help. In our naïveté in third density we had not developed the interrelationships of your barter or money system, and power. We were, in fact, a more philosophical third-density planet than your own, and our choices of polarity were much more centered about the, shall we say, understanding of sexual energy transfers and the appropriate relationships between self and other-self.

We spent a much larger portion of our space/time working with the unmanifested being. In this less complex atmosphere it was quite instructive to have this learn/teaching device, and we benefited without the distortions we found occurring among your peoples.

We have recorded these differences meticulously in the Great Record of Creation that such naïveté shall not be necessary again.

At this space/time we may best serve you, we believe, by stating that the pyramid for meditation, along with other rounded and arched, or pointed, circular shapes, is of help to you.

However, it is our observation that due to the complexity of influences upon the unmanifested being at this space/time nexus among your planetary peoples, it is best that the progress of the mind/body/spirit complex take place without, as you call them, training aids—because when using a training aid an entity then takes upon itself the Law of

Responsibility for the quickened or increased rate of learn/teaching. If this greater understanding, if we may use this misnomer, is not put into practice in the moment by moment experience of the entity, then the usefulness of the training aid becomes negative.

60.17 **QUESTIONER** Thank you. I don't know if this question will result in any usable direction, but I think I must ask it. What was the Ark of the Covenant, and what was its use?

RA I am Ra. The Ark of the Covenant was that place wherein those things most holy, according to the understanding of the one called Moishe, [were] placed. The article placed therein has been called by your peoples two tablets called the Ten Commandments. There were not two tablets. There was one writing in scroll. This was placed along with the most carefully written accounts by various entities of their beliefs concerning the creation by the One Creator.

This Ark was designed to constitute the place wherefrom the priests, as you call those distorted towards the desire to serve their brothers, could draw their power and feel the presence of the One Creator. However, it is to be noted that this entire arrangement was designed, not by the one known to the Confederation as Yahweh, but rather was designed by negative entities preferring this method of creating an elite called the Sons of Levi.

60.18 **QUESTIONER** Was this a device for communication then? You said they also drew power from it. What type of power? How did this work?

RA I am Ra. This was charged by means of the materials with which it was built being given an electromagnetic field. It became an object of power in this way. And, to those whose faith became that untarnished by unrighteousness or separation, this power, designed for negativity, became positive, and is so to those truly in harmony with the experience of service to this day.

Thus the negative forces were partially successful, but the positively oriented Moishe, as this entity was called, gave to your planetary peoples the possibility of a path to the One Infinite Creator which is completely positive.

This is in common with each of your orthodox religious systems which have all become somewhat mixed in orientation yet offer a pure path to the One Creator which is seen by the pure seeker.

60.19 **QUESTIONER** Where is the Ark of the Covenant now? Where is it located?

RA I am Ra. We refrain from answering this query due to the fact that it does still exist and is not that which we would infringe upon your peoples by locating.

60.20 **QUESTIONER** Thank you. In trying to understand the energies—creative energies—it has occurred to me that I really do not understand why unusable heat is generated as our earth moves from third into fourth density. I know it has to do with disharmony between the vibrations of third and fourth density, but why this would show up as a physical heating within the earth is beyond me. Can you enlighten me on that?

RA I am Ra. The concepts are somewhat difficult to penetrate in your language. However, we shall attempt to speak to the subject.

If an entity is not in harmony with its circumstances it feels a burning within. The temperature of the physical vehicle does not yet rise, only the heat of the temper or the tears, as we may describe this disharmony. However, if an entity persists for a long period of your space/time in feeling this emotive heat and disharmony, the entire body complex will begin to resonate to this disharmony, and the disharmony will then show up as the cancer or other degenerative distortions from what you call health.

When an entire planetary system of peoples and cultures repeatedly experiences disharmony on a great scale, the earth under the feet of these entities shall begin to resonate with this disharmony. Due to the nature of the physical vehicle, disharmony shows up as a blockage of growth or an uncontrolled growth, since the primary function of a mind/body/spirit complex's bodily complex is growth and maintenance.

In the case of your planet, the purpose of the planet is the maintenance of orbit and the proper location or orientation with regards to other cosmic influences. In order to have this occurring properly the interior of your sphere is hot, in your physical terms. Thus, instead of uncontrolled growth you begin to experience uncontrolled heat and its expansive consequences.

60.21 **QUESTIONER** Is the earth solid all the way through from one side to the other?

RA I am Ra. You may say that your sphere is of an honey-comb nature. The center is, however, solid if you would so call that which is molten.

60.22 **QUESTIONER** And the honey-comb nature—are there third-density incarnate entities living in the honey-combed areas? Is this correct?

RA I am Ra. This was at one time correct. This is not correct at this present space/time.

60.23 **QUESTIONER** And there are no— Are there any inner civilizations or entities living in these areas that are some of the other-than-physically incarnate who do come and materialize on the earth's surface at times?

RA I am Ra. As we have noted, there are some which do as you say. Further, there are some inner plane entities of this planet which prefer to do some materialization into third-density visible in these areas. There are also bases, shall we say, in these areas of those from elsewhere, both positive and negative. There are abandoned cities.

60.24 **QUESTIONER** What are these bases used for by those from elsewhere?

RA I am Ra. These bases are used for the work of materialization of needed equipment for communication with third-density entities and for resting places for some equipment which you might call small craft. These are used for surveillance when it is requested by entities. Thus some of the, shall we say, teachers of the Confederation speak partially through these surveillance instruments along computerized lines, and when information is desired and those requesting it are of the proper vibratory level, the Confederation entity itself will then speak.

60.25 **QUESTIONER** Am I to understand then that the Confederation entity needs communication equipment and craft to communicate with the third-density incarnate entity requesting the information?

RA I am Ra. This is incorrect. However, many of your peoples request the same basic information in enormous repetition, and for a social memory complex to speak ad infinitum about the need to meditate is a waste of the considerable abilities of such social memory complexes.

Thus, some entities have had approved by the Council of Saturn the placement and maintenance of these message-givers for those whose needs are simple, thus reserving the abilities of the Confederation members for those already meditating and absorbing information, which are then ready for additional information.

60.26 **QUESTIONER** There has been, for the past 30 years, a lot of information and a lot of confusion, and in fact, I would say the Law of Confusion has been [*chuckles*] working overtime, to make a small joke, in bringing information for spiritual catalysis to groups requesting it. And we know that both the positively and the negatively oriented social memory complexes have been adding to this information as they can. This has led to somewhat of a condition of apathy in a lot of cases with respect to the information by many who are truly seeking but have been thwarted by a condition of what I might call spiritual entropy in this information.

Can you comment on this and the mechanisms of alleviating these problems?

RA I am Ra. We can comment on this.

60.27 **QUESTIONER** Only if you deem it to be of importance I would request a comment. If you feel it unimportant we'll skip it.

RA I am Ra. This information is significant, to some degree, as it bears upon our own mission at this time.

We of the Confederation are at the call of those upon your planet. If the call, though sincere, is fairly low in consciousness of the, shall we say, system whereby spiritual evolution may be precipitated, then we may only offer that information useful to that particular caller. This is the basic difficulty. Entities receive the basic information about the Original Thought and the means—that is, meditation and service to others— whereby this Original Thought may be obtained.

Please note that, as Confederation members, we are speaking for positively oriented entities. We believe the Orion group has precisely the same difficulty.

Once this basic information is received it is not put into practice in the heart and in the life experience but, instead, rattles about within the mind-complex distortions as would a building block which has lost its place and simply rolls from side to side uselessly, yet still the entity calls. Therefore, the same basic information is repeated. Ultimately the entity decides that it is weary of this repetitive information. However, if an entity puts into practice that which it is given, it will not find repetition except when needed.

60.28 **QUESTIONER** Thank you. Are the chakras or bodily energy centers related to, or do they operate like, the pyramid energy funnel?

RA I am Ra. No.

60.29 **QUESTIONER** Was there a purpose for mummification having to do with anything other than bodily burial?

RA I am Ra. Much as we would like to speak to you of this distortion of our designs in constructing the pyramid, we can say very little, for the intent was quite mixed; and the uses, though many felt them to be positive, were of a non-positive order of generation. We cannot speak upon this subject without infringing upon some basic energy balances between the positive and negative forces upon your planet. It may be said that those offering themselves felt they were offering themselves in service to others.

60.30 **QUESTIONER** What civilization was it that helped Ra using the pyramid shape while Ra was in third density?

RA I am Ra. Your people have a fondness for the naming. These entities have begun their travel back to the Creator and are no longer experiencing time.

60.31 **QUESTIONER** The instrument wished to know, when using the pendulum for discovering energy centers, if the back and forth motion meant anything rather than the circular motion?

RA I am Ra. This shall have to be the final question although this entity is still providing us with energy. It is experiencing the distortion towards pain.

The rotations having been discussed,[1] we shall simply say that the weak back and forth motion indicates a partial blockage, although not a complete blockage. The strong back and forth motion indicates the reverse of blockage which is over-stimulation of a chakra, or energy

---

[1] Discussed in 58.5.

center, which is occurring in order to attempt to balance some difficulty in body, or mind, complex activity. This condition is not helpful to the entity as it is unbalanced.

Are there any brief queries before we leave this instrument?

60.32 **QUESTIONER** Only is there anything that we can do to make the instrument more comfortable or to improve the contact?

RA I am Ra. Be merry, my friends. All is well, and your conscientiousness is to be recommended.

We leave you in the love and the light of the One Infinite Creator. Rejoice, then, and go forth in the peace and in the glory of the One Infinite Creator. I am Ra. Adonai.

SESSION 61

61.0   **RA** I am Ra. I greet you, my friends, in the love and in the light of the Infinite Creator. We communicate now.

61.1   **QUESTIONER** Could you give me an indication of the instrument's condition?

RA I am Ra. This instrument's vital energies are improving. The physical-complex distortions are quite marked at this space/time, and there is a decrease in physical-complex energies.

61.2   **QUESTIONER** Is there anything in particular that the instrument could do to improve the physical condition?

RA I am Ra. This instrument has two factors affecting its bodily distortions. This is in common with all those which, by seniority of vibration, have reached the green-ray level of vibratory consciousness complexes.

The first is the given instreamings which vary from cycle to cycle in predictable manner. In this particular entity the cyclical complexes at this space/time nexus are not favorable for the physical energy levels.

The second ramification of condition is that which we might call the degree of mental efficiency in use of catalyst provided for the learning of programmed lessons, in particular, and the lessons of love, in general.

This instrument, unlike some entities, has some further distortion due to the use of pre-incarnative conditions.

61.3   **QUESTIONER** Can you expand on what you meant by the "cycling instreamings of energy?"

RA I am Ra. There are four types of cycles which are those given in the moment of entry into incarnation. There are, in addition, more cosmic and less regularized inpourings which, from time to time, affect a sensitized mind/body/spirit complex. The four rhythms are, to some extent, known among your peoples and are called biorhythms.

There is a fourth cycle which we may call the cycle of gateway of magic of the adept or of the spirit. This is a cycle which is completed in approximately eighteen of your diurnal cycles.

The cosmic patterns are also a function of the moment of incarnative entrance and have to do with your satellite you call the moon, your planets of this galaxy, the galactic sun, and in some cases the instreamings from the major galactic points of energy flow.[1]

61.4   **QUESTIONER** Would it be helpful to plot the cycles for the instrument and attempt to have these sessions at the most favorable points with respect to the cycle?

RA I am Ra. To that specific query we have no response.

It may be noted that the three in this triad bring in this energy pattern which is Ra. Thus each energy input of the triad is of note.

We may say that while these information systems are interesting they are in sway only insofar as the entity or entities involved have not made totally efficient use of catalyst, and, therefore, instead of accepting the, shall we say, negative or retrograde moments or periods without undue notice, have the distortion towards the retaining of these distortions in order to work out the unused catalyst.

It is to be noted that psychic attack continues upon this entity although it is only effective at this time in physical distortions towards discomfort.

We may suggest that it is always of some interest to observe the road map, both of the cycles and of the planetary and other cosmic influences, in that one may see certain wide roads or possibilities. However, we remind that this group is an unit.

61.5   **QUESTIONER** Is there some way that we could, as a unit, then, do something to reduce the effect of the psychic attack on the instrument and optimize the communicative opportunity?

RA I am Ra. We have given you the information concerning that which aids this particular mind/body/spirit complex. We can speak no further. It is our opinion, which we humbly offer, that each is in remarkable

---

[1] To see a graph depicted the 18-day adept cycle, see the Resource Series. Also, to see a tool for charting the other biorhythms, go to www.bring4th.org/biorhythms/

harmony with each for this particular third-density illusion at this space/time nexus.

61.6 **QUESTIONER** I want to ask a few questions Jim had here about the healing exercises. The first is, in the healing exercise concerning the body, what do you mean by the disciplines of the body having to do with the balance between love and wisdom in the use of the body in its natural functions?

RA I am Ra. We shall speak more briefly than usual due to this instrument's use of the transferred energy. We, therefore, request further queries if our reply is not sufficient.

The body complex has natural functions. Many of these have to do with the unmanifested self and are normally not subject to the need for balancing.

There are natural functions which have to do with other-self. Among these are touching, loving, the sexual life, and those times when the company of another is craved to combat the type of loneliness which is the natural function of the body, as opposed to those types of loneliness which are of the mind/emotion complex or of the spirit.

When these natural functions may be observed in the daily life they may be examined in order that the love of self and love of other-self versus the wisdom regarding the use of natural functions may be observed. There are many fantasies and stray thoughts which may be examined in most of your peoples in this balancing process.

Equally to be balanced is the withdrawal from the need for these natural functions with regard to other-self. On the one hand there is an excess of love. It must be determined whether this is love of self or other-self or both. On the other hand there is an over-balance towards wisdom.

It is well to know the body complex so that it is an ally, balanced and ready to be clearly used as a tool; for each bodily function may be used in higher and higher, if you will, complexes of energy with other-self.

No matter what the behavior, the important balancing is the understanding of each interaction on this level with other-selves, so that whether the balance may be love/wisdom or wisdom/love, the other-self is seen by the self in a balanced configuration, and the self is, thus, freed for further work.

61.7 **QUESTIONER** Second question: could you give an example of how feelings affect portions of the body and the sensations of the body?

RA I am Ra. It is nearly impossible to speak generally of these mechanisms, for each entity of proper seniority has its own programming. Of the less aware entities we may say that the connection will often seem random as the higher self continues producing catalyst until a bias occurs. In each programmed individual the sensitivities are far more active, and, as we have said, that catalyst not used fully by the mind and spirit is given to the body.

Thus you may see in this entity the numbing of the arms and the hands signifying this entity's failure to surrender to the loss of control over the life. Thus, this drama is enacted in the physical-distortion complex.

In the questioner we may see the desire not to be carrying the load it carries given as physical manifestation of the soreness of those muscles for carrying used. That which is truly needed to be carried is a pre-incarnative responsibility which seems highly inconvenient.

In the case of the scribe we see a weariness and numbness of feelings ensuing from lack of using catalyst designed to sensitize this entity to quite significant influxes of unfamiliar distortion complexes of the mental/emotional and spiritual level. As the numbness removes itself from the higher, or more responsive, complexes, the bodily-complex distortions will vanish. This is true also of the other examples.

We would note at this time that the totally efficient use of catalyst upon your plane is extremely rare.

61.8 **QUESTIONER** Could you tell me how you are able to give us information like this with respect to the First Distortion, or Law of Confusion?

RA I am Ra. Each of those is already aware of this information.

Any other reader may extract the heart of meaning from this discussion without interest as to the examples' sources. If each was not fully aware of these answers we could not speak.

It is interesting that in many of your queries you ask for confirmation, rather than information. This is acceptable to us.

61.9 **QUESTIONER** This brings out the point of the purpose for the physical incarnation, I believe. And that is to reach a conviction through your own thought processes as to a solution to problems and understandings in a totally unbiased, or totally free, situation with no proof at all or anything that you would consider proof—proof being a very poor word in itself. Can you expand on my concept?

RA I am Ra. Your opinion is an eloquent one, although somewhat confused in its connections between the freedom expressed by subjective knowing and the freedom expressed by subjective acceptance. There is a significant distinction between the two.

This is not a dimension of knowing, even subjectively, due to the lack of overview of cosmic and other inpourings which affect each and every situation which produces catalyst. The subjective acceptance of that which is at the moment and the finding of love within that moment is the greater freedom.

That known as the subjective knowing without proof is, in some degree, a poor friend, for there will be anomalies no matter how much information is garnered due to the distortions which form third density.

61.10 **QUESTIONER** OK. The third question I have here is, could you give examples of bodily polarity?

RA I am Ra. Within the body there are many polarities which relate to the balancing of the energy centers of the various bodies of the unmanifested entity. It is well to explore these polarities for work in healing.

Each entity is, of course, a potential polarized portion of an other-self.

61.11 **QUESTIONER** It says here it would seem the proper balancing exercises for all the sensations of the body would be some form of inactivity such as meditation or contemplation. Is this correct?

RA I am Ra. This is largely incorrect. The balancing requires a meditative state in order for the work to be done. However, the balancing of sensation has to do with an analysis of the sensation with especial respect to any unbalanced leaning between the love and the wisdom, or the positive and the negative. Then whatever is lacking in the balanced sensation is, as in all balancing, allowed to come into the being after the sensation is remembered and recalled in such detail as to overwhelm the senses.

61.12 **QUESTIONER** Could you tell me why it is important for the appurtenances, and other things, to be so carefully aligned with respect to the instrument, and why just a small ruffle in the sheet by the instrument causes a problem with the reception of Ra?

RA I am Ra. We may attempt an explanation. This contact is narrow-band. The instrument is highly sensitive. Thus we have good entry into it and can use it to an increasingly satisfactory level.

However, the trance condition is, shall we say, not one which is without toll upon this instrument. Therefore, the area above the entrance into the physical complex of this instrument must be kept clear to avoid discomfort to the instrument, especially as it re-enters the body complex.

The appurtenances give to the instrument sensory input and mental visualization which aid in the trance beginning. The careful alignment of these is important for the energizing group in that it is a reminder to that support group that it is time for a working.

The ritualistic behaviors are triggers for many energies of the support group. You may have noticed more energy being used in workings as the number has increased due to the long-term, shall we say, effect of such ritualistic actions.

This would not aid another group as it was designed for this particular system of mind/body/spirit complexes and especially the instrument.

There is enough energy transferred for one more long query. We do not wish to deplete this instrument.

61.13 **QUESTIONER** OK, then I will ask this one. Could you tell us the purpose of the frontal lobes of the brain and the conditions necessary for their activation?

RA I am Ra. The frontal lobes of the brain will, shall we say, have much more use in fourth density.

The primary mental/emotive condition of this large area of the so-called brain is joy, or love, in its creative sense. Thus, the energies which we have discussed in relationship to the pyramids—all of the healing, the learning, the building, and the energizing—are to be found in this area. This is the area tapped by the adept. This is the area which, working through the trunk and root of mind, makes contact with intelligent energy and, through this gateway, intelligent infinity.

Are there any queries before we leave this instrument?

61.14 **QUESTIONER** Only is there anything we can do to make the instrument more comfortable or improve the contact?

RA I am Ra. This instrument is somewhat distorted, but each is doing well. You are conscientious. We thank you for continuing to observe the alignments and request that, on each level, you continue to be this fastidious as this will maintain the contact.

I am Ra. I leave you in the love and the light of the One Infinite Creator. Go forth, my friends, rejoicing in the power and the peace of the One Infinite Creator. Adonai.

SESSION 62

62.0 **RA** I am Ra. I greet you in the love and in the light of the One Infinite Creator.

Before we begin may we request that a circle be walked about this instrument, and let then each of the supporting group expel breath forcibly, approximately two and one-half feet above the instrument's head, the circle then again being walked about the instrument.

[*This was done as directed.*]

I am Ra. We appreciate your kind cooperation. Please recheck the alignment of perpendicularity, and we will begin.

[*This was done as directed.*]

I am Ra. We communicate now.

62.1 **QUESTIONER** Could you tell me what was wrong, or what caused the necessity for the re-walking of the circle and the purpose of the expelling of breath?

RA I am Ra. This instrument was under specific psychic attack at the time of the beginning of the working. There was a slight irregularity in the words verbalized by your sound complex vibratory mechanisms in the protective walking of the circle. Into this opening came this entity and began to work upon the instrument, now in trance state, as you would call it. This instrument was being quite adversely affected in physical-complex distortions.

Thus the circle was properly walked. The breath of righteousness expelled the thought-form, and the circle again walked.

62.2 **QUESTIONER** What was the nature of the thought-form or its affiliation?

RA I am Ra. This thought-form was of Orion affiliation.

62.3 **QUESTIONER** Was the attack successful in creating any further distortion of the instrument's physical complex?

RA I am Ra. This is correct.

62.4 **QUESTIONER** What is the nature of this distortion?

RA This thought-form sought to put an end to this instrument's incarnation by working with the renal distortions which—although corrected upon time/space—are vulnerable to one which knows the way to separate time/space molding and space/time distortions which are being unmolded, vulnerable as before the, shall we say, healing.

62.5 **QUESTIONER** What detrimental effect has been done?

RA I am Ra. There will be some discomfort. However, we were fortunate in that this instrument was very open to us and well-tuned. Had we not been able to reach this instrument and instruct you, the instrument's physical vehicle would soon be unviable.

62.6 **QUESTIONER** Will there be any lasting effect from this attack as far as the instrument's physical vehicle is concerned?

RA I am Ra. This is difficult to say. We are of the opinion that no lasting harm, or distortion, will occur.

The healer was strong, and the bonds taking effect in the remolding of these renal distortions were effective.

It is at this point a question of two forms of the leavings of what you may call a spell or a magic working—the healer's distortions versus the attempt at Orion distortions: the healer's distortions full of love, the Orion distortions also pure in separation. It seems that all is well except for some possible discomfort which shall be attended if persistent.

62.7 **QUESTIONER** Was the opening that was made in the protective circle planned to be made by the Orion entity? Was it a specific planned attempt to make an opening, or was this something that just happened by accident?

RA I am Ra. This entity was, as your people put it, looking for a target of opportunity. The missed word was a chance occurrence and not a planned one.

We might suggest in the, shall we say, future, as you measure space/time, as you begin a working be aware that this instrument is likely being watched for any opportunity. Thus if the circle is walked with some imperfection it is well to immediately repeat. The expelling of breath is also appropriate, always to the left.

62.8 **QUESTIONER** Would you expand on what you just said about the expelling of breath? I wasn't quite sure what you meant.

RA I am Ra. The repetition of that performed well at this working is advisable if the circle is walked in less than the appropriate configuration.

62.9 **QUESTIONER** But you mentioned the expelling of the breath to the left, I believe. Would you tell me what you meant by that?

RA I am Ra. It is as you have just accomplished, the breath being sent above the instrument's head from its right side to its left.

62.10 **QUESTIONER** Is there anything we can do for the instrument after she comes out of trance to help her recover from this attack?

RA I am Ra. There is little to be done. You may watch to see if distortions persist and see that the appropriate healers are brought into contact with this mind/body/spirit complex in the event that difficulty persists. It may not. This battle is even now being accomplished. Each may counsel the instrument to continue its work as outlined previously.

62.11 **QUESTIONER** Who would the appropriate healers be, and how would we bring them in contact with the instrument?

RA I am Ra. There are four. The difficulty being at all noticed as bodily distortion, the one known as Don and the one known as Jim may work upon the instrument's bodily complex by means of the practices which are developing in each entity. Given persistence of distortion, the one known as Stuart shall be seen. Given the continued difficulty past the point of one of your cycles called the fortnight, the one known as Douglas shall be seen.

62.12 **QUESTIONER** Does the instrument know who these people are, Stuart and Douglas? I don't know who they are.

RA I am Ra. This is correct.

62.13 **QUESTIONER** Is that the sum total of what we can do to aid the instrument?

RA I am Ra. This is correct. We may note that the harmonies and loving social intercourse which prevails habitually in this group create a favorable environment for each of you to do your work.

62.14 **QUESTIONER** What priority, shall I say, does the Orion group place upon the reduction of effectiveness, or elimination of effectiveness, of this group with respect to activities on planet Earth at this time? Can you tell me that?

RA I am Ra. This group, as all positive channels and supporting groups, is a greatly high priority with the Orion group. This instrument's bodily distortions are its most easily unbound, or unloosed, distortion dissolving the mind/body/spirit complex if the Orion group is successful—this particular group having learned to be without serious chinks, may we say, in mind and spirit complex vibratory patterns. In other channels other chinks may be more in evidence.

62.15 **QUESTIONER** I'll make this statement, and you correct me. The Orion group has as an objective the bringing of service-to-self polarized entities to harvest, as great a harvest as possible. This harvest will build their potential, or their ability to do work in consciousness, as given by the distortion of the Law of One called the Law of Squares or Doubling. Is this correct?

RA I am Ra. This is correct.

62.16 **QUESTIONER** Are there other groups of those who are on the service-to-self path joined with those from the Orion constellation? For instance, those of Southern Cross, are they presently working for the same type of harvest with respect to Earth?

RA I am Ra. These you mention of Southern Cross are members of the Orion group. It is not, shall we say, according to understood wording that a group from various galaxies should be named by one. However, those planetary social memory complexes of the so-called Orion constellation have the upper hand and thus rule the other members. You must recall that in negative thinking there is always the pecking order, shall we say, and the power against power in separation.

62.17 **QUESTIONER** By creating as large a harvest as possible of negatively oriented entities from Earth, then, the social memory complex of the Orion group gains in strength. Am I correct in assuming this strength then is in the total strength of the complex, the pecking order remaining approximately the same, and those at the top gaining in strength with respect to the total strength of the social memory complex? Is this correct?

RA I am Ra. This is correct. To the stronger go the greater shares of polarity.

62.18 **QUESTIONER** Then what do the ones at the top of the pecking order of the Orion group— Well, let me first ask this: Are we talking about the fourth-density group now?

RA I am Ra. There are fourth and a few fifth-density members of the Orion group.

62.19 **QUESTIONER** Then is the top of the pecking order fifth-density?

RA I am Ra. This is correct.

62.20 **QUESTIONER** What is the objective—what does the, shall we say, the leader, the one at the very top of the pecking order in fifth-density Orion, have as an objective? I would like to understand his philosophy with respect to his objectives and plans for what we might call the future or his future?

RA I am Ra. This thinking will not be so strange to you. Therefore, we may speak through the densities as your planet has some negatively oriented action in sway at this space/time nexus.

The early fifth-density negative entity, if oriented towards maintaining cohesion as a social memory complex, may, in its free will, determine that the path to wisdom lies in the manipulation, in exquisite propriety, of all other-selves. It, then, by virtue of its abilities in wisdom, is able to be the leader of fourth-density beings which are upon the road to wisdom by exploring the dimensions of love of self and understanding of self. These fifth-density entities see the creation as that which shall be put in order.

Dealing with a plane such as this third density at this harvesting it will see the mechanism of the call more clearly and have much less distortion towards plunder, or manipulation by thoughts which are given to negatively oriented entities—although in allowing this to occur and sending less wise entities to do this work, any successes redound to the leaders.

The fifth density sees the difficulties posed by the light and in this way directs entities of this vibration to the seeking of targets of opportunity such as this one. If fourth-density temptations, shall we say, towards distortion of ego, etc., are not successful, the fifth-density entity then thinks in terms of the removal of light.

62.21 **QUESTIONER** When the Orion entity who waits us, seeking the opportunity to attack, is with us here, can you describe his method of coming here, what he looks like, and how he waits? I know that this isn't too important, but it might give me a little insight into what we are talking about.

RA I am Ra. Fifth-density entities are very light beings although they do have the type of physical vehicle which you understand. Fifth-density entities are very fair to look upon in your standard of beauty.

The thought is what is sent, for a fifth-density entity is likely to have mastered this technique or discipline. There is little or no means of perceiving such an entity, for unlike fourth-density negative entities the fifth-density entity walks with light feet.

This instrument was aware of extreme coldness in the past diurnal cycle and spent much more time than your normal attitudes would imagine to be appropriate in what seemed to each of you an extremely warm climate. This was not perceived by the instrument, but the drop in subjective temperature is a sign of presence of a negative, or non-positive, or draining entity.

This instrument did mention a feeling of discomfort but was nourished by this group and was able to dismiss it. Had it not been for a random mishap, all would have been well, for you have learned to live in love and light and do not neglect to remember the One Infinite Creator.

62.22 **QUESTIONER** Then it was a fifth-density entity that made this particular attack on the instrument today?

RA I am Ra. This is correct.

62.23 **QUESTIONER** Isn't this unusual that a fifth-density then would bother to do this rather than sending a fourth-density servant, shall I say?

RA I am Ra. This is correct. Nearly all positive channels and groups may be lessened in their positivity, or rendered quite useless, by what we may call the temptations offered by the fourth-density negative thought-forms. They may suggest many distortions towards specific information, towards the aggrandizement of the self, towards the flowering of the organization in some political, social, or fiscal way.

These distortions remove the focus from the One Infinite Source of love and light, of which we are all messengers, humble and knowing that we, of ourselves, are but the tiniest portion of the Creator, a small part of a magnificent entirety of infinite intelligence.

62.24 **QUESTIONER** Is there something that the instrument could do or we could do for the instrument to eliminate the problem she has as she continually experiences the cold feeling of these attacks?

RA I am Ra. Yes.

62.25 **QUESTIONER** Would you tell me what we could do?

RA I am Ra. You could cease in your attempts to be channels for the love and the light of the One Infinite Creator.

62.26 **QUESTIONER** Have I missed anything now that we can do at all to aid the instrument during, before, or after a session, or at any time?

RA I am Ra. The love and devotion of this group misses nothing. Be at peace. There is some toll for this work. This instrument embraces this, or we could not speak.

Rest, then, in that peace and love, and do as you will, as you wish, as you feel. Let there be an end to worry when this is accomplished. The great healer of distortions is love.

62.27 **QUESTIONER** I have a question that I couldn't properly answer last night. It was asked by Morris. It has to do with the vibrations of the densities. I understand that first density is composed of core atomic vibrations that are in the red spectrum, second in the orange, etc. Am I to understand that the core vibrations of our planet are still in the red and that second-density beings are still in the orange at this time/space, or space/time, right now? And that each density as it exists on our planet at this time has a different core vibration, or is this incorrect?

RA I am Ra. This is precisely correct.

62.28 **QUESTIONER** Then as the fourth-density vibrations come in, this means that the planet can support entities of fourth-density core vibration. Will the planet then still be first-density core vibration, and will there be second-density entities on it with second-density vibrations, and will there be third-density entities with third-density vibrations?

RA I am Ra. This will be the last full query of this working. There is energy, but the distortions of the instrument suggest to us it would be well to shorten this working, with your permission.

62.29 **QUESTIONER** Yes.

RA You must see the Earth, as you call it, as being seven Earths. There is red, orange, yellow, and there will soon be a completed green-color vibratory locus for fourth-density entities which they will call Earth. During the fourth-density experience, due to the lack of development of fourth-density entities, the third-density planetary sphere is not useful for habitation since the early fourth-density entity will not know, precisely, how to maintain the illusion that fourth density cannot be seen or determined from any instrumentation available to any third density.

Thus in fourth density the red, orange, and green energy nexi of your planet will be activated while the yellow is in potentiation, along with the blue and the indigo.

May we ask at this time if there be any brief queries?

62.30 **QUESTIONER** Is there anything that we can do to make the instrument more comfortable or improve the contact?

RA All is well. You have been most conscientious.

I am Ra. I leave you, my friends, in the glory of the love and the light of the One Infinite Creator. Go forth, then, rejoicing in the power and the peace of the One Infinite Creator. Adonai.

SESSION 63

JULY 18, 1981

63.0 **RA** I am Ra. I greet you in the love and in the light of the One Infinite Creator. We communicate now.

63.1 **QUESTIONER** Could you give me an indication of the condition of the instrument?

RA I am Ra. This instrument's vital energies are at the distortion which is normal for this mind/body/spirit complex. The body complex is distorted due to psychic attack in the area of the kidneys and urinary tract. There is also distortion continuing due to the distortion called arthritis.

You may expect this psychic attack to be constant, as this instrument has been under observation by negatively oriented force for some time.

63.2 **QUESTIONER** Was the original problem with the kidneys some 25 years ago caused by psychic attack?[1]

RA I am Ra. This is only partially correct. There were psychic attack components to the death of this body at that space/time. However, the guiding vibratory complex in this event was the will of the instrument. This instrument desired to leave this plane of existence as it did not feel it could be of service.

63.3 **QUESTIONER** You are saying that the instrument itself then created the kidney problem at that time?

RA I am Ra. The instrument's desire to leave this density lowered the defenses of an already predisposed weak body complex, and an allergic reaction was so intensified as to cause the complications which distorted the body complex towards unviability.

The will of the instrument, when it found that there was, indeed, work to be done in service, was again the guiding factor, or complex of vibratory patterns, which kept the body complex from surrendering to dissolution of the ties which cause the vitality of life.

---

[1] This is in reference to a near-death experience Carla had at 13 years old. See 106.4 for more information.

63.4   **QUESTIONER** Is the necessity for the instrument to go to the bathroom several times before a session due to the psychic attack?

RA I am Ra. In general this is incorrect. The instrument is eliminating from the body complex the distortion leavings of the material which we use for contact. This occurs variably, sometimes beginning before contact, other workings this occurring after the contact.

In this particular working, this entity is experiencing the aforementioned difficulties causing the intensification of that particular distortion/condition.

63.5   **QUESTIONER** I know that you have already answered this question, but I feel it my duty now to ask it each time in case there is some new development, and that is, is there anything that we can do, that we aren't doing, to lessen the effectiveness of the psychic attack upon the instrument?

RA I am Ra. Continue in love, and praise, and thanksgiving to the Creator. Examine previous material. Love is the great protector.

63.6   **QUESTIONER** Could you give me a definition of vital energy?

RA I am Ra. Vital energy is the complex of energy levels of mind, body, and spirit. Unlike physical energy, it requires the integrated complexes vibrating in an useful manner.

The faculty of will can, to a variable extent, replace missing vital energy, and this has occurred in past workings, as you measure time, in this instrument. This is not recommended. At this time, however, the vital energies are well-nourished in mind and spirit, although the physical energy level is, in and of itself, low at this time.

63.7   **QUESTIONER** Would I be correct in guessing that vital energy is a function of the awareness, or bias, of the entity with respect to its polarity, or general unity, with the Creator or creation?

RA I am Ra. In a nonspecific sense we may affirm the correctness of your statement. The vital energy may be seen to be that deep love of life or life experiences, such as the beauty of creation, and the appreciation of other-selves, and the distortions of your co-Creators' making which are of beauty.

Without this vital energy the least distorted physical complex will fail and perish. With this love, or vital energy, or élan, the entity may continue though the physical complex is greatly distorted.

63.8 **QUESTIONER** From last session, I would like to continue with a few questions about the fact that in fourth density, red, orange, and green energies will be activated; yellow, blue, etc., being in potentiation. Right now you say we have green energies activated. They have been activated for the last 45 years. I am wondering about the transition through this period, so that the green is totally activated, and the yellow is in potentiation. What will we lose as the yellow goes from activation into potentiation, and what will we gain as the green comes into total activation, and what is that process?

RA I am Ra. It is misleading to speak of gains and losses when dealing with the subject of the cycle's ending and the green-ray cycle beginning upon your sphere. It is to be kept in the forefront of the faculties of intelligence that there is One Creation in which there is no loss. There are progressive cycles for experiential use by entities. We may now address your query.

As the green-ray cycle or the density of love and understanding begins to take shape the yellow-ray plane or Earth, which you now enjoy in your dance, will cease to be inhabited for some period of your space/time as the space/time necessary for fourth-density entities to learn their ability to shield their density from that of third is learned. After this period there will come a time when third density may again cycle on the yellow-ray sphere.

Meanwhile there is another sphere, congruent to a great extent with yellow ray, forming. This fourth-density sphere coexists with first, second, and third. It is of a denser nature due to the rotational core atomic aspects of its material. We have discussed this subject with you.[2]

The fourth-density entities which incarnate at this space/time are fourth density, in the view of experience, but are incarnating in less dense vehicles due to desire to experience and aid in the birth of fourth density upon this plane.

---

[2] Discussed in 27.16, 40.5, and 62.27–29.

You may note that fourth-density entities have a great abundance of compassion.

63.9 **QUESTIONER** Now, at present we have, in third-density incarnation on this plane, those third-density entities of the planet Earth who have been here for some number of incarnations who will graduate in the three-way split: either positive polarity remaining for fourth-density experience on this plane; the negative polarity harvestable going to another planet; and the rest unharvestable third density going to another third-density planet. In addition to these entities, I am assuming that we have here already some entities harvestable from other third-density planets who have come here and incarnated in third-density form to make the transition with this planet into fourth density, plus wanderers.

Is this correct?

RA I am Ra. This is correct except we may note a small point. The positively oriented harvested entities will remain in this planetary influence but not upon this plane.

63.10 **QUESTIONER** Now, we have I believe, if I remember correctly— I think you said there were 600 million wanderers, approximately. Am I correct in that memory?

RA I am Ra. This is approximately correct. There is some excess to that amount.[3]

63.11 **QUESTIONER** Does that number include the harvestable third density who are coming to this planet for the fourth-density experience?

RA I am Ra. No.

63.12 **QUESTIONER** Approximately how many are here now who have come from other planets who are third density harvestable for fourth-density experience?

RA I am Ra. This is a recent, shall we say, phenomenon, and the number is not yet in excess of 35,000 entities.

---

[3] The correct number in 1981 was somewhat in excess of 60 million. Ra and Don corrected their mistake in session 64.3.

63.13 **QUESTIONER** Now these entities incarnate into a third-density vibratory body. I am trying to understand how this transition takes place from third to fourth density. I will take the example of one of these entities of which we are speaking who is now in a third-density body. He will grow older, and then will it be necessary that he die from the third-density physical body and reincarnate in a fourth-density body for that transition?

RA I am Ra. These entities are those incarnating with what you may call a double body in activation. It will be noted that the entities birthing these fourth-density entities experience a great feeling of, shall we say, the connection and the use of spiritual energies during pregnancy. This is due to the necessity for manifesting the double body.

This transitional body is one which will be, shall we say, able to appreciate fourth-density vibratory complexes, as the instreaming increases, without the accompanying disruption of the third-density body. If a third-density entity were, shall we say, electrically aware of fourth-density in full, the third-density electrical fields would fail due to incompatibility.

To answer your query about death, these entities will die according to third-density necessities.

63.14 **QUESTIONER** You are saying, then, that for the transition from third to fourth density for one of the entities with doubly activated bodies, in order to make the transition, the third-density body will go through the process of what we call death. Is this correct?

RA I am Ra. The third and fourth, combination, density's body will die according to the necessity of third-density mind/body/spirit-complex distortions.

We may respond to the heart of your questioning by noting that the purpose of such combined activation of mind/body/spirit complexes is that such entities, to some extent, consciously are aware of those fourth-density understandings which third density is unable to remember due to the forgetting. Thus fourth-density experience may be begun with the added attraction, to an entity oriented towards service to others, of dwelling in a troubled third-density environment and offering its love and compassion.

63.15 **QUESTIONER** Would the purpose in transitioning to Earth prior to the complete changeover then be for the experience to be gained here during the harvesting process?

RA I am Ra. This is correct. These entities are not wanderers in the sense that this planetary sphere is their fourth-density home planet. However, the experience of this service is earned only by those harvested third-density entities which have demonstrated a great deal of orientation towards service to others. It is a privilege to be allowed this early an incarnation as there is much experiential catalyst in service to other-selves at this harvesting.

63.16 **QUESTIONER** There are many children now who demonstrate the ability to bend metal mentally which is a fourth-density phenomenon. Would most of these children, then, be this type of entity of which we speak?

RA I am Ra. This is correct.

63.17 **QUESTIONER** Is the reason that they can do this and the fifth- and sixth-density wanderers who are here cannot do it the fact that they have the fourth-density body in activation?

RA I am Ra. This is correct. Wanderers are third-density activated in mind/body/spirit and are subject to the forgetting which can only be penetrated with disciplined meditation and working.

63.18 **QUESTIONER** I am assuming that the reason for this is that, first, since the entities of harvestable third density who have very recently come here, they're coming here late enough so that they will not affect the, shall I say, polarization through their teachings. They are not infringing on the First Distortion because they are children now, and they won't be old enough to really affect any of the polarization until the transition is well into transition.

However, the wanderers—who came here and are older and have a greater ability to affect polarization—must do that affecting as a function of their ability to penetrate the forgetting process in order to be within the First Distortion. Is this correct?

RA I am Ra. This is quite correct.

63.19 **QUESTIONER** It would seem to me that some of the harvestable third-density entities are, however, relatively old since I know of some individuals who can bend metal who are over 50 years old and some over 30. Would there be other entities who can bend metal for other reasons than having dual-activated bodies?

RA I am Ra. This is correct. Any entity who, by accident or by careful design, penetrates intelligent energy's gateway may use the shaping powers of this energy.

63.20 **QUESTIONER** OK. Now as this transition continues into fourth-density activation, in order to inhabit this fourth-density sphere, it will be necessary for all third-density physical bodies to go through the process which we refer to as death. Is this correct?

RA I am Ra. This is correct.

63.21 **QUESTIONER** Now, are there any inhabitants at this time of this fourth-density sphere who have already gone through this process? Is it now being populated?

RA I am Ra. This is correct only in the very, shall we say, recent past.

63.22 **QUESTIONER** I would assume this population is from other planets since the harvesting has not occurred yet on this planet. It is from planets where the harvesting has already occurred. Is this correct?

RA I am Ra. This is correct.

63.23 **QUESTIONER** Then are these entities visible to us? Could I see one of them? Would he walk upon our surface?

RA I am Ra. We have discussed this. These entities are in dual bodies at this time.

63.24 **QUESTIONER** Sorry I am so stupid on this, but this particular concept is very difficult for me to understand. It is something that I'm afraid requires some rather dumb questions on my part to fully understand. I don't think I'll ever fully understand, but [*inaudible*] even get a grasp of it.

Then as the fourth-density sphere is activated there is heat energy being generated. I assume this heat energy is generated in the third-density sphere only. Is this correct?

RA I am Ra. This is quite correct. The experiential distortions of each dimension are discrete.

63.25 **QUESTIONER** Then at some time in the future the fourth-density sphere will be fully activated. What is the difference between full activation and partial activation for this sphere?

RA I am Ra. At this time the cosmic influxes are conducive to true-color green core particles being formed and material of this nature thus being formed. However, there is a mixture of the yellow-ray and green-ray environments at this time necessitating the birthing of transitional mind/body/spirit complex types of energy distortions.

At full activation of the true-color green density of love, the planetary sphere will be solid and inhabitable upon its own, and the birthing that takes place will have been transformed through the process of time, shall we say, to the appropriate type of vehicle to appreciate in full the fourth-density planetary environment. At this nexus the green-ray environment exists to a far greater extent in time/space than in space/time.

63.26 **QUESTIONER** Could you describe the difference that you are speaking of with respect to time/space and space/time?

RA I am Ra. For the sake of your understanding we will use the working definition of inner planes. There is a great deal of subtlety invested in this sound vibration complex, but it, by itself, will perhaps fulfill your present need.

63.27 **QUESTIONER** I will make this statement, and you correct me. What we have is, as our planet is spiraled by the spiraling action of the entire major galaxy, as the big wheel in the sky turns, and our planetary system spirals into the new position, the fourth-density vibrations become more and more pronounced. These atomic core vibrations begin to create, more and more completely, the green— That is the green core vibrations complete more and more completely the fourth-density sphere and the fourth-density bodily complexes for inhabitation of that sphere. Is this correct?

RA I am Ra. This is partially correct. To be corrected is the concept of the creation of green-ray density bodily complexes. This creation will be gradual and will take place beginning with your third-density type of physical vehicle and, through the means of bisexual reproduction, become, by evolutionary processes, the fourth-density body complexes.

63.28 **QUESTIONER** Then are these entities of which we spoke, the third-density harvestable who have been transferred, are they the ones who then will, by bisexual reproduction, create the fourth-density complexes that are necessary?

RA I am Ra. The influxes of true-color green energy complexes will more and more create the conditions in which the atomic structure of cells of bodily complexes is that of the density of love. The mind/body/spirit complexes inhabiting these physical vehicles will be, and to some extent are, those of whom you spoke, and, as harvest is completed, the harvested entities of this planetary influence.

63.29 **QUESTIONER** Is there a clock-like face, shall I say, associated with the entire major galaxy of many billions of stars so that, as it revolves, it carries all of these stars and planetary systems through transitions from density to density? Is this how it works?

RA I am Ra. You are perceptive. You may see a three-dimensional clock face, or spiral of endlessness, which is planned by the Logos for this purpose.

63.30 **QUESTIONER** I understand that the Logos did not plan for the heating effect that occurs in our third-density transition into fourth. Is this correct?

RA I am Ra. This is correct except for the condition of free will which is, of course, planned by the Logos as It, Itself, is a creature of free will. In this climate an infinity of events or conditions may occur. They cannot be said to be planned by the Logos but can be said to have been freely allowed.

63.31 **QUESTIONER** It would seem to me the heating effect that takes place on the planet is analogous to a disease in the body and would have as a root cause the same, or analogous, mental configuration. Is this correct?

RA I am Ra. This is correct except that the spiritual configuration as well as mental biases of your peoples has been responsible for these distortions of the body complex of your planetary sphere.

[*There is a 39-second pause between the end of this answer and the beginning of the next question.*]

63.32 **QUESTIONER** When the third density goes out of activation and into potentiation, that will leave us with a planet that is first, second, and fourth density. At that time there will be no activated third-density vibrations on this planet. Am I correct in assuming that all third-density vibrations on this planet now are those vibrations that compose the bodily complexes of entities such as us, and that that is the sum total of third-density vibrations on this planet at this time?

RA I am Ra. This will be the last full query of this working. This instrument has energy left due to transfer, but there is discomfort. We do not wish to deplete this instrument. May we say that this instrument seems in better configuration, despite attack, than previous workings.

To answer your query, this is incorrect only in that in addition to the mind/body/spirit complexes of third density there are the artifacts, thought-forms, and feelings which these co-Creators have produced. This is third density.

May we answer any brief queries as we leave this instrument?

63.33 **QUESTIONER** Is there anything that we can do to make the instrument more comfortable or improve the contact?

RA I am Ra. You are conscientious. All is well.

We leave you now, my friends, in the glory of the love and the light of the One Infinite Creator. Go forth, then, rejoicing in the power and the peace of the Infinite Creator. Adonai.

SESSION 64

JULY 26, 1981

64.0   RA   I am Ra. I greet you in the love and in the light of the One Infinite Creator. We communicate now.

64.1   QUESTIONER Could you first tell me the condition of the instrument?

RA   I am Ra. It is as previously stated with the exception of a transitory distortion lessening the free flow of vital energy.

64.2   QUESTIONER Can you tell what the transitory distortion is?

RA   I am Ra. This is marginal information.

64.3   QUESTIONER Then we won't question on it.

I would like to ask first about a mistake I believe that I might have made in the last session[1] on the number of wanderers on Earth today. Did I make an error?

RA   I am Ra. You and Ra made an error. The appropriate number of your ciphers is one less than previously stated.[2]

64.4   QUESTIONER Thank you. Could you explain the basic principles behind the ritual which we perform to initiate the contact and what I would call the basic white magical rituals—principles of protection and other principles? Could you please do this?

RA   I am Ra. Due to your avenue of question we perceive the appropriateness of inclusion of the cause of this instrument's transitory vital-energy distortion. The cause is a bias towards the yearning for expression of devotion to the One Creator in group worship.[3]

This entity was yearning for this protection both consciously in that it

---

[1]   Session 63.10.

[2]   In this context, *cipher* means zero, as in "0." Meaning that 600 million should have been 60 million in 63.10.

[3]   This was the only session with Ra that was ever held on a Sunday when Carla would normally be singing sacred music in the choir at church.

responds to the accoutrements of this expression, the ritual, the colors and their meanings as given by the distortion system of what you call the church, the song of praise, and the combined prayers of thanksgiving, and, most of all, that which may be seen to be most centrally magical: the intake of that food which is not of this dimension, but has been transmuted into metaphysical nourishment in what this distortion of expression calls the Holy Communion.

The subconscious reason, it being the stronger for this yearning, was the awareness that such expression is—when appreciated by an entity as the transmutation into the presence of the One Creator—a great protection of the entity as it moves in the path of service to others.

The principle behind any ritual of the white magical nature is to so configure the stimuli which reach down into the trunk of mind that this arrangement causes the generation of disciplined and purified emotion, or love, which then may be both protection and the key to the gateway to intelligent infinity.

64.5   **QUESTIONER** Can you tell me why the slight error made in the ritual starting this communication two sessions ago allowed the intrusion of one Orion-affiliated entity?

RA I am Ra. This contact is narrow-band and its preconditions precise. The other-self offering its service in the negative path also is possessed of the skill of the swordsman. You deal in this contact with, shall we say, forces of great intensity poured into a vessel as delicate as a snowflake and as crystalline.

The smallest of lapses may disturb the regularity of this pattern of energies which forms the channel for these transmissions.

We may note, for your information, that our pause was due to the necessity of being quite sure that the mind/body/spirit complex of the instrument was safely in the proper light configuration or density before we dealt with the situation. Far better would it be to allow the shell to become unviable than to allow the mind/body/spirit complex to be, shall we say, misplaced.

64.6   **QUESTIONER** Could you describe or tell me of rituals or technique used by Ra in seeking in the direction of service?

RA I am Ra. To speak of that which sixth-density social memory complexes labor within in order to advance is at best misprision of plain communication, for much is lost in transmission of concept from density to density, and the discussion of sixth density is inevitably distorted greatly.[4]

However, we shall attempt to speak to your query, for it is an helpful one in that it allows us to express once again the total unity of creation. We seek the Creator upon a level of shared experience to which you are not privy, and rather than surrounding ourselves in light, we have become light. Our understanding is that there is no other material except light. Our rituals, as you may call them, are an infinitely subtle continuation of the balancing processes which you are now beginning to experience.

We seek now without polarity. Thus we do not invoke any power from without, for our search has become internalized as we become light/love and love/light. These are the balances we seek, the balances between compassion and wisdom which, more and more, allow our understanding of experience to be informed that we may come closer to the unity with the One Creator which we so joyfully seek.

Your rituals at your level of progress contain the concept of polarization, and this is most central at your particular space/time.

We may answer further if you have specific queries.

64.7 QUESTIONER Would it be helpful if Ra were to describe the techniques used while Ra was in third density to evolve in mind, body, and spirit?

RA I am Ra. This query lies beyond the Law of Confusion.

64.8 QUESTIONER What about fourth-density experience of Ra? Would that also lie beyond the Law of Confusion?

RA I am Ra. This is correct. Let us express a thought. Ra is not elite. To speak of our specific experiences to a group which honors us is to guide to the point of a specific advising. Our work was that of your peoples, of experiencing the catalyst of joys and sorrows. Our circumstances were somewhat more harmonious.

---

4 In this context, *misprision* can be defined as meaning "neglect or wrong performance of official duty" or "misunderstanding or mistake."

Let it be said that any entity or group may create the most splendid harmony in any outer atmosphere. Ra's experiences are no more than your own. Yours is the dance at this space/time in third-density harvest.

64.9 **QUESTIONER** The question was brought up recently having to do with possible records left near, in, or under the Great Pyramid at Giza. I have no idea whether this would be of benefit. I will just ask if there is any benefit in investigating in this area?

RA I am Ra. We apologize for seeming to be so shy of information. However, any words upon this particular subject create the possibility of infringement upon free will.

64.10 **QUESTIONER** In a previous session[5] you mentioned the gateway of magic for the adept occurring in eighteen-day cycles. Could you expand on that information please?

RA I am Ra. The mind/body/spirit complex is born under a series of influences, both lunar, planetary, cosmic, and in some cases, karmic. The moment of the birthing into this illusion begins the cycles we have mentioned.

The spiritual, or adept's, cycle is an eighteen-day cycle and operates with the qualities of the sine wave. Thus there are a few excellent days on the positive side of the curve, that being the first nine days of the cycle—precisely the fourth, the fifth, and the sixth—when workings are most appropriately undertaken, given that the entity is still without total conscious control of its mind/body/spirit distortion/reality.

The most interesting portion of this information, like that of each cycle, is the noting of the critical point wherein, passing from the ninth to the tenth and from the eighteenth to the first days, the adept will experience some difficulty, especially when there is a transition occurring in another cycle at the same time.

At the nadir of each cycle the adept will be at its least powerful but will not be open to difficulties in nearly the degree that it experiences at critical times.

---

5 61.3.

64.11 **QUESTIONER** Then, to find the cycles, we would take the instant of birth and the emerging of the infant from the mother into this density and start the cycle at that instant and continue it through the life. Is this correct?

RA I am Ra. This is mostly correct. It is not necessary to identify the instant of birthing. The diurnal cycle upon which this event occurs is satisfactory for all but the most fine workings.

64.12 **QUESTIONER** Now, am I correct in assuming that whatever magic the adept would perform would be more successful or, shall we say, more to his design than that performed at less opportune times in the cycle?

RA I am Ra. This cycle is an helpful tool to the adept, but, as we said, as the adept becomes more balanced, the workings designed will be dependent less and less upon these cycles of opportunity and more and more even in their efficacy.

64.13 **QUESTIONER** I have no ability to judge at what point, at what level of abilities the adept would reach this point of being, shall we say, independent of the cyclical action. Can you give me an indication of what level of "adeptness" that would be necessary to be so independent?

RA I am Ra. We are fettered from speaking specifically due to this group's work, for to speak would seem to be to judge. However, we may say that you may consider this cycle in the same light as the so-called astrological balances within your group; that is, they are interesting but not critical.

64.14 **QUESTIONER** Thank you. I read that recent research has indicated that the normal sleep cycle for entities on this planet occurs one hour later each diurnal period, so that we have a 25-hour cycle instead of a 24. Is this correct, and if so, why is this?

RA I am Ra. This is in some cases correct. The planetary influences from which those of Mars experience memory have some effect upon these third-density physical bodily complexes. This race has given its genetic material to many bodies upon your plane.

64.15 **QUESTIONER** Thank you. Ra mentioned the ones Stuart and Douglas in a recent session.[6] These are members of what we call our medical

---

6   Mentioned in 62.11.

profession. What is the value, overall value, shall I say, of modern medical techniques in alleviating bodily distortions with respect to the purpose for these distortions and what we might call karma and other effects?

RA I am Ra. This query is convoluted. However, we shall make some observations in lieu of attempting one coherent answer, for that which is allopathic among your healing practices is somewhat two-sided.

Firstly, you must see the possibility/probability that each and every allopathic healer is, in fact, an healer. Within your cultural nexus this training is considered the appropriate means of perfecting the healing ability.

In the most basic sense, any allopathic healer may be seen to, perhaps, be one whose desire is service to others in alleviation of bodily-complex and mental/emotional-complex distortions so that the entity to be healed may experience further catalyst over a longer period of what you call the life. This is a great service to others, when appropriate, due to the accumulation of distortions toward wisdom and love which can be created through the use of the space/time continuum of your illusion.

In observing the allopathic concept of the body complex as the machine, we may note the symptomology of a societal complex seemingly dedicated to the most intransigent desire for the distortions of distraction, anonymity, and sleep.[7] This is the result, rather than the cause, of societal thinking upon your plane.

In turn this mechanical concept of the body complex has created the continuing proliferation of distortions towards what you would call ill-health due to the strong chemicals used to control, and hide, bodily distortions. There is a realization among many of your peoples that there are more efficacious systems of healing, not excluding the allopathic, but also including the many other avenues of healing.

64.16 **QUESTIONER** Let us assume that a bodily distortion occurs within a particular entity who then has a choice of seeking allopathic aid or experiencing the catalyst of the distortion and not seeking correction of

---

[7] In this context, *intransigent* may be defined as "characterized by refusal or unwillingness to compromise, or to change one's views, or to abandon a(n often extreme) position or attitude."

the distortion. Can you comment on the two possibilities for this entity and his analysis of each path?

RA I am Ra. If the entity is polarized towards service to others, analysis properly proceeds along the lines of consideration of which path offers the most opportunity for service to others.

For the negatively polarized entity the antithesis is the case.

For the unpolarized entity the considerations are random and, most likely, in the direction of the distortion towards comfort.

64.17 **QUESTIONER** Dr. Monroe,[8] I understand, brought a four-toed Bigfoot cast by here the other day. Could you tell me which form of Bigfoot that cast was?

RA I am Ra. We can.

64.18 **QUESTIONER** I know it is totally unimportant, but as a service to Dr. Monroe I thought that I should ask that.

RA I am Ra. This entity was one of a small group of thought-forms.

64.19 **QUESTIONER** He also asked (and I know this is unimportant) why there were no Bigfoot remains found, that is, after the Bigfoot entities had died on our surface. He had asked why there had never been any remains of these entities found. Could you answer this for him? It's just of no importance, but just as a service to him I ask it.

RA I am Ra. You may suggest that exploration of the caves which underlie some of the western coastal mountain regions of your continent will one day offer such remains. They will not be generally understood if this culture survives in its present form long enough, in your time measurement, for this probability/possibility vortex to occur.

There is enough energy for one more full query at this time.

64.20 **QUESTIONER** In the healing exercises, when you say "examine the sensations of the body," do you mean those sensations available to the body via the five senses? Or in relation to the natural functions of the

---

[8] Dr. Burt Monroe was the head of the biology department at the University of Louisville.

body such as touching, loving, sexual sharing, and company? Or are you speaking of something else altogether?

RA I am Ra. The questioner may perceive its body complex at this moment. It is experiencing sensations. Most of these sensations, or in this case nearly all of them, are transient and without interest. However, the body is the creature of the mind. Certain sensations carry importance due to the charge or power which is felt by the mind upon the experience of this sensation.

For instance, at this space/time nexus one sensation is carrying a powerful charge and may be examined. This is the sensation of what you call the distortion towards discomfort due to the cramped position of the body complex during this working. In balancing you would then explore this sensation. Why is this sensation powerful? Because it was chosen in order that the entity might be of service to others in energizing this contact.

Each sensation that leaves the aftertaste of meaning upon the mind, that leaves the taste within the memory, shall be examined. These are the sensations of which we speak.

May we answer any brief queries before we leave this instrument?

64.21 **QUESTIONER** Is there anything that we could do to make the instrument more comfortable or improve the contact?

RA I am Ra. Continue to consider the alignments. You are conscientious and aware of the means of caring for the instrument in its present distortions having to do with the wrists and hands. As always, love is the greatest protection.

I am Ra. I leave you, my friends, in the glorious love and joyful light of the Infinite Creator. Go forth, then, rejoicing in the power and in the peace of the One Infinite Creator. Adonai.

SESSION 65

65.0 **RA** I am Ra. I greet you in the love and in the light of the One Infinite Creator. We communicate now.

65.1 **QUESTIONER** Could you first please give us an indication of the instrument's condition and the level of vital and physical energies?

RA I am Ra. This instrument's vital energies are as previously stated. The physical energies are greatly distorted towards weakness at this space/time due to the distortion complexes symptomatic of that which you call the arthritic condition. The level of psychic attack is constant but is being dealt with by this instrument in such a way as to eliminate serious difficulties due to its fidelity and that of the support group.

65.2 **QUESTIONER** I may be re-covering a little ground already covered in previous questioning today, but I am trying to get a clearer picture of some things that I don't understand and possibly develop a plan of my own for activity in the future.

I have the impression that in the near future the seeking will increase by many who now are incarnate in the physical on this planet. Their seeking will increase because they will become more aware of the creation as it is, opposed, I might say, to the creation of man. Their orientation and their thinking will, by catalyst of a unique nature, be reoriented to thinking of the more basic concepts, shall I say. Is this correct?

RA I am Ra. The generalities of expression can never be completely correct. However, we may note that when faced with a hole in the curtain, an entity's eyes may well peer for the first time through the window beyond. This tendency is probable given the possibility/probability vortices active within your space/time and time/space continua at this nexus.

65.3 **QUESTIONER** I have assumed that the reason that so many wanderers, and those harvested third-density entities who have been transferred here, find it a privilege and an exceptionally beneficial time to be incarnate upon this planet is that the effect that I just spoke of gives them the opportunity to be more fully of service because of the increased seeking. Is this, in general, correct?

RA I am Ra. This is the intention which wanderers had prior to incarnation. There are many wanderers whose dysfunction with regard to the planetary ways of your peoples have caused, to some extent, a condition of being caught up in a configuration of mind complex activity which, to the corresponding extent, may prohibit the intended service.

65.4 **QUESTIONER** I noticed that you are speaking more slowly than usual. Is there a reason for this?

RA I am Ra. This instrument is somewhat weak and, although strong in vital energy and well able to function at this time, is somewhat more fragile than the usual condition we find. We may note a continuing bearing of the physical distortion called pain which has a weakening effect upon physical energy. In order to use the considerable store of available energy without harming the instrument we are attempting to channel even more narrow-band than is our wont.

65.5 **QUESTIONER** Thank you. Now, have I properly analyzed the condition that creates the possibility of greater service as follows: One, seniority by vibration of incarnation has greatly polarized those upon the surface now, and the influx of wanderers has greatly increased the mental configuration, I might say, toward things of a more spiritual nature. This, I would assume, would be one of the factors creating a better atmosphere for service. Is this correct?

RA I am Ra. This is correct.

65.6 **QUESTIONER** Would the coming changes as we progress into fourth density—I'm speaking of changes not only in the physical third-density planet due to the heating effect but also the changes that are heralding fourth-density vibrations, such as the ability of people to perform what we term paranormal activities—I'm assuming that both of these are also and will act as catalyst to create a greater seeking. Is this correct?

RA I am Ra. This is partially correct. The paranormal events occurring are not designed to increase seeking but are manifestations of those whose vibratory configuration enables these entities to contact the gateway to intelligent infinity. These entities capable of paranormal service may determine to be of such service on a conscious level. This, however, is a function of the entity and its free will and not the paranormal ability.

The correct portion of your statements is the greater opportunity for service due to the many changes which will offer many challenges, difficulties, and seeming distresses within your illusion to many who then will seek to understand, if we may use this misnomer, the reason for the malfunctioning of the physical rhythms of their planet.

Moreover, there exist probability/possibility vortices which spiral towards your bellicose actions. Many of these vortices are not of the nuclear war but of the less annihilatory but more lengthy so-called conventional war. This situation, if formed in your illusion, would offer many opportunities for seeking and for service.

65.7   **QUESTIONER** How would conventional warfare offer the opportunities for seeking and service?

RA I am Ra. The possibility/probabilities exist for situations in which great portions of your continent and the globe in general might be involved in the type of warfare which you might liken to guerrilla warfare. The ideal of freedom from the so-called invading force of either the controlled fascism or the equally controlled social common ownership of all things would stimulate great quantities of contemplation upon the great polarization implicit in the contrast between freedom and control.

In this scenario, which is being considered at this time/space nexus, the idea of obliterating valuable sites and personnel would not be considered an useful one. Other weapons would be used which do not destroy as your nuclear arms would.

In this ongoing struggle the light of freedom would burn within the mind/body/spirit complexes capable of such polarization. Lacking the opportunity for overt expression of the love of freedom, the seeking for inner knowledge would take root, aided by those of the Brothers and Sisters of Sorrow which remember their calling upon this sphere.

65.8   **QUESTIONER** Are you saying then that this possible condition of war would be much more greatly spread across the surface of the globe than anything we have experienced in the past and, therefore, touch a larger percentage of the population in this form of catalyst?

RA I am Ra. This is correct. There are those now experimenting with one of the major weapons of this scenario, that is the so-called psychotronic group of devices, which are being experimentally used to cause such alterations in wind and weather as will result in eventual famine. If this program is not countered and proves experimentally satisfactory, the methods in this scenario would be made public. There would then be what those whom you call Russians hope to be a bloodless invasion of their personnel in this and every land deemed valuable. However, the peoples of your culture have little propensity for bloodless surrender.

65.9   **QUESTIONER** We would seem to have dual catalysts operating, and the question is which one is going to act first. The prophecies, I will call them, made by Edgar Cayce indicated many earth changes, and I am wondering about the mechanics of describing what we call the future.

Ra, it has been stated, is not a part of time, and yet we concern ourselves with probability/possibility vortices. It is very difficult for me to understand how the mechanism of prophecy operates. What is the value of a prophecy such as Cayce made with respect to earth changes? With respect to all of these scenarios?

RA I am Ra. Consider the shopper entering the store to purchase food with which to furnish the table for the time period you call a week. Some stores have some items, others a variant set of offerings. We speak of these possibility/probability vortices, when asked, with the understanding that such are as a can, jar, or portion of goods in your store.

It is unknown to us, as we scan your time/space, whether your peoples will shop hither or yon. We can only name some of the items available for the choosing. The, shall we say, record which the one you call Edgar read from is useful in that same manner. There is less knowledge in this material of other possibility/probability vortices and more attention paid to the strongest vortex.

We see the same vortex, but also see many others. Edgar's material could be likened unto one hundred boxes of your cold cereal, another vortex likened unto three, or six, or fifty of another product which is eaten by your peoples for breakfast. That you will breakfast is close to certain. The menu is your own choosing.

The value of prophecy must be realized to be only that of expressing possibilities. Moreover, it must be, in our humble opinion, carefully taken into consideration that any time/space viewing—whether by one of your time/space, or by one such as we who view the time/space from a dimension, shall we say, exterior to it—will have a quite difficult time expressing time measurement values. Thus prophecy given in specific terms is more interesting for the content, or type, of possibility predicted than for the space/time nexus of its supposed occurrence.

65.10 **QUESTIONER** So we have the distinct possibility of two different types of catalyst creating an atmosphere of seeking that is greater than that which we experience at present. There will be much confusion, especially in the scenario of earth changes, simply because there have been many predictions of these changes by many groups giving various and sundry reasons for the changes. Can you comment on the effectiveness of this type of catalyst and the rather wide pre-knowledge of the coming changes, but also the rather wide variation in, shall I say, explanation for these changes?

RA I am Ra. Given the amount of strength of the possibility/probability vortex which posits the expression by the planet itself of the difficult birthing of the planetary self into fourth density, it would be greatly surprising were not many which have some access to space/time[1] able to perceive this vortex. The amount of this cold cereal in the grocery, to use our previous analogy, is disproportionately large. Each which prophesies does so from an unique level, position, or vibratory configuration. Thus biases and distortions will accompany much prophecy.

65.11 **QUESTIONER** Well, this entire scenario over the next, shall I say, twenty years seems to be aimed at producing an increase in seeking and an increase in the awareness of the natural creation, but also a terrific amount of confusion. Was it the pre-incarnative objective of many of the wanderers to attempt to reduce this confusion?

RA I am Ra. It was the aim of wanderers to serve the entities of this planet in whatever way was requested, and it was also the aim of wanderers that their vibratory patterns might lighten the planetary vibration as a whole, thus ameliorating[2] the effects of planetary

---

[1] In light of the fact that in 65.9 and elsewhere Ra called the activity of prophecy one of viewing "time/space," Ra presumably meant to say "time/space" here.

[2] In this context, *ameliorate* may be defined as "to make or become better, more bearable, or more satisfactory; improve."

disharmony and palliating[3] any results of this disharmony.

Specific intentions such as aiding in a situation not yet manifest are not the aim of wanderers. Light and love go where they are sought and needed, and their direction is not planned aforetimes.

65.12 **QUESTIONER** Then each of the wanderers here acts as a function of the biases he has developed in any way he sees fit to communicate—or simply be in his polarity—to aid the total consciousness of the planet.

Is there any, shall I say, more physical way that he aids in— What I mean is, do his vibrations somehow add to the process, just as electrical polarity or charging a battery or something? Does that also aid the planet, just the physical presence of the wanderers?

RA I am Ra. This is correct, and the mechanism is precisely as you state. We intended this meaning in the second portion of our previous answer.

You may at this time note that as with any entities, each wanderer has its unique abilities, biases, and specialties, so that from each portion of each density represented among the wanderers comes an array of pre-incarnative talents which then may be expressed upon this plane which you now experience; so that each wanderer, in offering itself before incarnation, has some special service to offer in addition to the doubling effect of planetary love and light and the basic function of serving as beacon or shepherd.

Thus there are those of fifth density whose abilities to express wisdom are great. There are fourth- and sixth-density wanderers whose ability to serve as, shall we say, passive radiators or broadcasters of love and love/light are immense. There are many others whose talents brought into this density are quite varied.

Thus wanderers have three basic functions once the forgetting is penetrated, the first two being basic, the tertiary one being unique to that particular mind/body/spirit complex.

We may note at this point while you ponder the possibility/probability

---

3   In this context, *palliating* may defined as "to reduce the violence of (a disease)," or "to ease (symptoms) without curing the underlying disease," or "to moderate the intensity."

vortices, that although you have many, many items which cause distress and thus offer seeking and service opportunities, there is always one container in that store of peace, love, light, and joy. This vortex may be very small, but to turn one's back upon it is to forget the infinite possibilities of the present moment. Could your planet polarize towards harmony in one fine, strong moment of inspiration? Yes, my friends. It is not probable; but it is ever possible.

65.13   **QUESTIONER** How common in the universe is a mixed harvest for a planet of both positively and negatively oriented mind/body/spirit complexes?

RA I am Ra. Among planetary harvests which yield an harvest of mind/body/spirit complexes: approximately 10% are negative; approximately 60% are positive; and approximately 30% are mixed with nearly all harvest being positive.

In the event of mixed harvest it is almost unknown for the majority of the harvest to be negative. When a planet moves strongly towards the negative there is almost no opportunity for harvestable positive polarization.

65.14   **QUESTIONER** Can you tell me why there is almost no opportunity in that case?

RA The ability to polarize positively requires a certain degree of self-determination.

65.15   **QUESTIONER** Then as these final days of the cycle transpire, if the harvest were to occur now, today, it would have a certain number harvested positively and negatively, and a certain number of repeaters. I am going to assume that because of the catalyst which will be experienced between now and the actual harvesting time these numbers of harvestable entities will increase.

Generally speaking, not particularly with respect to this planet, but with respect to general experience, shall we say, in harvesting, how big an increase in harvestable entities can you logically assume will occur because of the catalyst that occurs in the final period such as this one? Or am I making a mistake in assuming that other planets have added catalyst at the end of a harvesting period when they have a mixed harvest?

RA I am Ra. In the event of mixed harvest there is nearly always disharmony and, therefore, added catalyst in the form of your so-called "earth changes." In this assumption you are correct.

It is the Confederation's desire to serve those who may, indeed, seek more intensely because of this added catalyst. We do not choose to attempt to project the success of added numbers to the harvest, for this would not be appropriate. We are servants. If we are called, we shall serve with all our strength. To count the numbers is without virtue.

65.16 **QUESTIONER** Now the added catalyst at the end of the cycle is a function specifically of the orientation of the consciousness that inhabits the planet. The consciousness has provided the catalyst for itself in orienting its thinking in the way it has oriented it, thus acting upon itself the same as catalyst of bodily pain and disease act upon the single mind/body/spirit complex. I made this analogy once before but reiterate it at this time to clarify my own thinking in seeing the planetary entity as somewhat of a single entity made up of billions of mind/body/spirit complexes. Is my viewpoint correct?

RA I am Ra. You are quite correct.

65.17 **QUESTIONER** Then we deal with an entity that has not yet formed a social memory but is yet an entity, just as one of us can be called a single entity. Can we continue this observation of the, shall I say, conglomerate entity through the galactic entity, or shall I say, small planetary system type of entity? Let me try to phrase it this way. Could I look at a single sun in its planetary system as an entity and then look at a major galaxy with its billions of stars as an entity? Can I continue this extrapolation in this way?

RA I am Ra. You can but not within the framework of third-density space/time.

Let us attempt to speak upon this interesting subject. In your space/time you and your peoples are the parents of that which is in the womb. The earth, as you call it, is ready to be born, and the delivery is not going smoothly. When this entity has become born it will be instinct with the social memory complex of its parents which have become fourth-density positive. In this density there is a broader view.

You may begin to see your relationship to the Logos, or sun, with which you are most intimately associated. This is not the relationship of parent to child but of Creator (that is Logos) to Creator (that is the mind/body/spirit complex as Logos).

When this realization occurs you may then widen the field of "eyeshot," if you will, infinitely recognizing parts of the Logos throughout the One Infinite Creation and feeling—with the roots of mind informing the intuition—the parents aiding their planets in evolution in reaches vast and unknown in the creation, for this process occurs many, many times in the evolution of the creation as an whole.

65.18 **QUESTIONER** The wanderer goes through the forgetting process. You mentioned that those who have both third- and fourth-density bodies activated now do not have the forgetting that the wanderer has. I was just wondering if, say, a sixth-density wanderer were here with a third-density body activated, would he have gone through a forgetting that was in sections, shall I say, with a forgetting of fourth, fifth, and sixth densities? And if he were to have his fourth-density body activated, he would have a partial additional memory? And then another partial if his fifth were activated? And then the full memory if he had the sixth activated? Does this make any sense?

RA I am Ra. No.

65.19 **QUESTIONER** [*chuckles*] Thank you. The forgetting process was puzzling me because you said that the fourth-density activated people, who were here who had been harvestable, did not have the same forgetting problem. Could you tell me why the wanderer loses his memory?

RA I am Ra. The reason is twofold:

First, the genetic properties of the connection between the mind/body/spirit complex and the cellular structure of the body is different for third density than for third/fourth density.

Secondly, the free will of third-density entities needs be preserved. Thus wanderers volunteer for third-density genetic, or DNA, connections to the mind/body/spirit complex.

The forgetting process can be penetrated to the extent of the wanderer remembering what it is, and why it is upon the planetary sphere. However, it would be an infringement if wanderers penetrated the forgetting so far as to activate the more dense bodies and, thus, be able to live, shall we say, in a god-like manner. This would not be proper for those who have chosen to serve.

The new fourth-density entities which are becoming able to demonstrate various newer abilities are doing so as a result of the present experience, not as a result of memory. There are always a few exceptions, and we ask your forgiveness for constant barrages of over-generalization.

65.20 **QUESTIONER** I don't know if this question is related to what I am trying to get at or not, but I'll ask it and see. You mentioned in speaking of the pyramids that the resonating chamber was used so that the adept could meet the self. Would you explain what you meant by that?

RA I am Ra. One meets the self in the center, or deeps, of the being. The so-called resonating chamber may be likened unto the symbology of the burial and resurrection of the body wherein the entity dies to self, and, through this confrontation of apparent loss and realization of essential gain, is transmuted into a new and risen being.

65.21 **QUESTIONER** Could I make the analogy of, in this apparent death, losing the desires that are the illusory, common desires of third density, and gaining the desires of total service to others?

RA I am Ra. You are perceptive. This was the purpose and intent of this chamber as well as forming a necessary portion of the King's Chamber position's effectiveness.

65.22 **QUESTIONER** Can you tell me what this chamber did to the entity to create this awareness in him?

RA I am Ra. This chamber worked upon the mind and the body. The mind was affected by sensory deprivation and the archetypical reactions to being buried alive with no possibility of extricating the self. The body was affected both by the mind configuration, and by the electrical and piezoelectrical properties of the materials which were used in the construction of the resonating chamber.

This will be the last full query of this working. May we ask if there are any brief queries at this time?

65.23 **QUESTIONER** Is there anything that we can do to make the instrument more comfortable or improve the contact?

RA I am Ra. We feel that the instrument is well supported, and that all is well. We caution each regarding this instrument's distortions towards pain, for it dislikes sharing these expressions, but as support group, this instrument subconsciously accepts each entity's aid. All is in alignment. You are conscientious. We thank you for this.

I am Ra. I leave you, my friends, rejoicing in the love and the light of the One Infinite Creator. Go forth, therefore, glorying in the power and in the peace of the One Infinite Creator. Adonai.

SESSION 66

AUGUST 12, 1981

66.0 **RA** I am Ra. I greet you in the love and in the light of the One Infinite Creator. We communicate now.

66.1 **QUESTIONER** Could you give me an indication of the instrument's condition?

RA I am Ra. The vital energies are somewhat depleted at this time but not seriously so. The physical energy level is extremely low. Otherwise, it is as previously stated.

66.2 **QUESTIONER** Is there anything that we can do, staying within the First Distortion, to seek aid from the Confederation in order to alleviate the instrument's physical problems?

RA I am Ra. No.

66.3 **QUESTIONER** Can you tell me the most appropriate method for attempting to alleviate the instrument's physical problems?

RA I am Ra. The basic material has been covered before concerning the nurturing of this instrument. We recapitulate: the exercise according to ability, not to exceed appropriate parameters, the nutrition, the social intercourse with companions, the sexual activity in green ray or above and, in general, the sharing of the distortions of this group's individual experiences in an helpful, loving manner.

These things are being accomplished with what we consider great harmony, given the density in which you dance. The specific attention and activities, with which those with physical-complex distortions may alleviate these distortions, are known to this instrument.

Finally, it is well for this instrument to continue the practices it has lately begun.

66.4 **QUESTIONER** Which practices are those?

RA I am Ra. These practices concern exercises which we have outlined previously. We may say that the variety of experiences which this entity seeks is helpful, as we have said before, but as this instrument works in these practices the distortion seems less mandatory.

66.5   **QUESTIONER** I would like to investigate the mechanism of healing using the crystallized healer. I am going to make a statement, and I would appreciate it if you would correct my thinking.

It seems to me that once the healer has become properly balanced and unblocked with respect to energy centers, it is possible for him to act in some way as a collector and focuser of light the same way that, or analogous to the way that a pyramid works, taking or collecting light through the left hand and emitting it through the right. This then, somehow, penetrating the first and seventh chakra envelope, vibratory envelope, you might say, of the body and allowing for the realignment of energy centers of the entity to be healed.

I'm quite sure that I'm not exactly correct on this and possibly considerably off. Could you rearrange my thinking so that it makes sense?

RA I am Ra. You are correct in your assumption that the crystallized healer is analogous to the pyramidal action of the King's Chamber position. There are a few adjustments we might suggest.

Firstly, the energy which is used is brought into the field complex of the healer by the outstretched hand used in a polarized sense. However, this energy circulates through the various points of energy to the base of the spine and, to a certain extent, the feet; thus coming through the main energy centers of the healer, spiraling through the feet, turning at the red energy center towards a spiral at the yellow energy center, and passing through the green energy center in a microcosm of the King's Chamber energy configuration of prana. This then continuing for the third spiral through the blue energy center and being sent therefrom through the gateway back to intelligent infinity.

It is from the green center that the healing prana moves into the polarized healing right hand and therefrom to the one to be healed.

We may note that there are some who use the yellow-ray configuration to transfer energy, and this may be done, but the effects are questionable— and, with regard to the relationship between the healer, the healing energy, and the seeker, questionable due to the propensity for the seeker to continue requiring such energy transfers without any true healing taking place in the absence of the healer due to the lack of penetration of the armoring shell of which you spoke.

66.6 **QUESTIONER** Now, a wanderer who has an origin from fifth or sixth density can attempt such a healing and have little or no results. This indicates to me that there is some function of the activated body, since the— Can you tell me what the wanderer has lost, and why it is necessary for him to regain certain balances and abilities to perfect his healing ability?

RA I am Ra. You may see the wanderer as the infant attempting to verbalize the sound complexes of your peoples. The memory of the ability to communicate is within the infant's undeveloped mind complex, but the ability to practice or manifest this, called speech, is not immediately forthcoming due to the limitations of the mind/body/spirit complex it has chosen to be a part of in this experience.

So it is with the wanderer which, remembering the ease with which adjustments can be made in the home density, yet still, having entered third density, cannot manifest that memory due to the limitations of the chosen experience. The chances of a wanderer being able to heal in third density are only more than those native to this density because the desire to serve may be stronger and this method of service chosen.

66.7 **QUESTIONER** What about the ones with the dual—not the wanderers—but the harvested and dual-activated third- and fourth-density-body entities? Are they able to heal using the techniques that we have discussed?

RA I am Ra. In many cases this is so, but as beginners of fourth density the desire may not be present.

66.8 **QUESTIONER** I'm assuming, then, that we have a wanderer with the desire attempting to learn the techniques of healing while, shall I say, trapped in third density. He then, it seems to me, is primarily concerned with the balancing and unblocking of energy centers. Am I correct in this assumption?

RA I am Ra. This is correct. Only insofar as the healer has become balanced may it be a channel for the balancing of an other-self. The healing is first practiced upon the self, if we may say this in another way.

66.9 **QUESTIONER** Now as the healer approaches an other-self to do the healing we have a situation where the other-self has, through programming of catalyst, possibly created a condition which is viewed as a condition needing healing. What is the situation, and what are the ramifications of the healer acting upon a condition of programmed catalyst to bring about healing?

Am I correct in assuming that in doing this healing, the programmed catalyst is useful to the one to be healed in that the one to be healed then becomes aware of what it wished to become aware of in programming the catalyst? Is this correct?

RA I am Ra. Your thinking cannot be said to be completely incorrect but shows a rigidity which is not apparent in the flow of the experiential use of catalyst.

The role of the healer is to offer an opportunity for realignment, or aid in realignment, of either energy centers or some connection between the energies of mind and body, spirit and mind, or spirit and body. This latter is very rare.

The seeker will then have the reciprocal opportunity to accept a novel view of the self, a variant arrangement of patterns of energy influx. If the entity, at any level, desires to remain in the configuration of distortion which seems to need healing, it will do so. If, upon the other hand, the seeker chooses the novel configuration, it is done through free will.

This is one great difficulty with other forms of energy transfer in that they do not carry through the process of free will as this process is not native to yellow ray.

66.10 **QUESTIONER** What is the difference, philosophically, between a mind/body/spirit complex healing itself through mental, shall I say, configuration or it being healed by an healer?

RA I am Ra. You have a misconception. The healer does not heal. The crystallized healer is a channel for intelligent energy which offers an opportunity to an entity that it might heal itself.

In no case is there an other description of healing. Therefore, there is no difference as long as the healer never approaches one whose request for aid has not come to it previously. This is also true of the more conventional healers of your culture, and if these healers could but fully realize that they are responsible only for offering the opportunity of healing, and not for the healing, many of these entities would feel an enormous load of misconceived responsibility fall from them.

66.11 **QUESTIONER** Then in seeking healing a mind/body/spirit complex would then be seeking in some cases a source of gathered and focused light energy. This source could be another mind/body/spirit complex sufficiently crystallized for this purpose, or the pyramid shape, or possibly something else. Is this correct?

RA I am Ra. These are some of the ways an entity may seek healing. Yes.

66.12 **QUESTIONER** Could you tell me the other ways that the entity could seek healing?

RA I am Ra. Perhaps the greatest healer is within the self and may be tapped with continued meditation, as we have suggested.

The many forms of healing available to your peoples—each have virtue and may be deemed appropriate by any seeker who wishes to alter the physical-complex distortions or some connection between the various portions of the mind/body/spirit complex thereby.

66.13 **QUESTIONER** I have observed many activities known as psychic surgery in the area of the Philippine Islands. It was my assumption that these healers are providing what I would call a training aid, or a way of creating a reconfiguration of the mind of the patient to be healed, as the relatively naïve patient observes the action of the healer in seeing the materialized blood, etc., then reconfigures the roots of mind to believe, you might say, the healing is done and, therefore, heals himself. Is this analysis that I made correct?

RA I am Ra. This is correct. We may speak slightly further upon this type of opportunity.

There are times when the malcondition to be altered is without emotional, mental, or spiritual interest to the entity and is merely that which has, perhaps by chance genetic arrangement, occurred. In these cases that which is apparently dematerialized will remain dematerialized and may be observed as so by any observer.

The malcondition which has an emotional, mental, or spiritual charge is likely not to remain dematerialized in the sense of the showing of the objective referent to an observer. However, if the opportunity has been taken by the seeker, the apparent malcondition of the physical complex will be at variance with the actual health, as you call this distortion, of the seeker; and the lack of experiencing the distortions which the objective referent would suggest still held sway.

For instance, in this instrument the removal of three small cysts was the removal of material having no interest to the entity. Thus these growths remained dematerialized after the so-called psychic surgery experience.

In other psychic surgery the kidneys of this instrument were carefully offered a new configuration of beingness which the entity embraced. However, this particular portion of the mind/body/spirit complex carried a great deal of emotional, mental, and spiritual charge due to this distorted functioning being the cause of great illness, in a certain configuration of events, which culminated in this entity's conscious decision to be of service. Therefore, any objective scanning of this entity's renal complex would indicate the rather extreme dysfunctional aspect which it showed previous to the psychic surgery experience, as you call it.

The key is not in the continuation of the dematerialization of distortion to the eye of the beholder but, rather, lies in the choosing of the newly materialized configuration which exists in time/space.

66.14 **QUESTIONER** Would you explain that last comment about the configuration in time/space?

RA I am Ra. Healing is done in the time/space portion of the mind/body/spirit complex, is adopted by the form-making, or etheric, body and is then given to the space/time physical illusion for use in the activated yellow-ray mind/body/spirit complex. It is the adoption of the configuration which you call health by the etheric body in time/space which is the key to what you call health, not any event which occurs in space/time.

In this process you may see the transdimensional aspect of what you call will, for it is the will, the seeking, the desire of the entity which causes the indigo body to use the novel configuration and to reform the body which exists in space/time. This is done in an instant and may be said to operate without regard to time.

We may note that in the healing of very young children there is often an apparent healing by the healer in which the young entity has no part.

This is never so, for the mind/body/spirit complex in time/space is always capable of willing the distortions it chooses for experience no matter what the apparent age, as you call it, of the entity.

66.15 **QUESTIONER** Is this desire and will that operates through to the time/space section a function only of the entity who is healed, or is it also the function of the healer, the crystallized healer?

RA I am Ra. May we take this opportunity to say that this is the activity of the Creator. To specifically answer your query, the crystallized healer has no will. It offers an opportunity without attachment to the outcome, for it is aware that all is one, and that the Creator is knowing Itself.

66.16 **QUESTIONER** Then the desire must be strong within the mind/body/spirit complex who seeks healing to be healed in order for the healing to occur? Is this correct?

RA I am Ra. This is correct on one level or another. An entity may not consciously seek healing and yet subconsciously be aware of the need to experience the new set of distortions which result from healing. Similarly an entity may consciously desire healing greatly but within the being, at some level, find some cause whereby certain configurations which seem quite distorted are, in fact, at that level, considered appropriate.

66.17 **QUESTIONER** I assume that the reason for assuming the distortions appropriate would be that these distortions would aid the entity in its reaching its ultimate objective, which is a movement along the path of evolution in the desired polarity. Is this correct?

RA I am Ra. This is correct.

66.18 **QUESTIONER** Then in the case of an entity who becomes aware of its polarization with respect to service to others, it might find a paradoxical situation in the case where it was unable to fully serve because of distortions chosen to reach that understanding which it has reached. At this point it would seem that the entity who was aware of the mechanism might, through meditation, understand the necessary mental configuration for alleviating the physical distortion so that it could be of greater service to others at this particular nexus. Am I correct in this thinking?

RA I am Ra. You are correct although we might note that there are often complex reasons for the programming of a distorted physical complex pattern. In any case, meditation is always an aid to knowing the self.

66.19 **QUESTIONER** Is a vertical positioning of the spine useful or helpful in the meditative procedure?

RA I am Ra. It is somewhat helpful.

66.20 **QUESTIONER** I have a written question, two of them actually. The first is would you please list the polarities within the body which are related to the balancing of the energy centers of the various bodies of the unmanifested entity?

RA I am Ra. In this question there lies a great deal of thought which we appreciate. It is possible that the question itself may serve to aid meditations upon this particular subject. Each unmanifested self is unique. The basic polarities have to do with the balanced vibratory rates and relationships between the first three energy centers and, to a lesser extent, each of the other energy centers.

May we answer more specifically?

66.21 **QUESTIONER** Possibly in the next session we will expand on that.

I would like to ask the second question. What are the structure and contents of the archetypical mind, and how does the archetypical mind function in informing the intuition and conscious mind of an individual mind/body/spirit complex?

RA I am Ra. You must realize that we offered these concepts to you so that you might grow in your own knowledge of the self through the consideration of them. We would prefer, especially for this latter query, to listen to the observations upon this subject which the student of these exercises may make and then suggest further avenues of the refinement of these inquiries. We feel we might be of more aid in this way.

66.22 **QUESTIONER** You mentioned that an energizing spiral is emitted from the top of any pyramid, and that you could benefit by placing this under the head for a period of thirty minutes or less. Can you tell me how this third spiral is helpful, and what help it gives the entity who is receiving it?

RA I am Ra. There are substances which you may ingest which cause the physical vehicle to experience distortions towards an increase of energy.

These substances are crude, working rather roughly upon the body complex, increasing the flow of adrenaline.

The vibration offered by the energizing spiral of the pyramid is such that each cell, both in space/time and in time/space, is charged as if hooked to your electricity. The keenness of mind, the physical and sexual energy of body, and the attunement of will of spirit are all touched by this energizing influence. It may be used in any of these ways.

It is possible to over-charge a battery, and this is the cause of our cautioning any who use such pyramidal energies to remove the pyramid after a charge has been received.

66.23 **QUESTIONER** Is there a best material, or optimal size, for the small pyramid to go beneath the head?

RA I am Ra. Given that the proportions are such as to develop the spirals in the Giza pyramid, the most appropriate size for use beneath the head is an overall height small enough to make placing it under the cushion of the head a comfortable thing.

66.24 **QUESTIONER** There's no best material?

RA I am Ra. There are better materials which are, in your system of barter, quite dear. They are not that much better than substances which we have mentioned before.[1] The only incorrect substances would be the baser metals.

66.25 **QUESTIONER** Now, you mentioned the problems with the action in the King's Chamber of the Giza-type pyramid. I am assuming if we used the same geometrical configuration that is used at the pyramid at Giza, this would be perfectly all right for the pyramid placed beneath the head since we wouldn't be using the King's Chamber radiations but only the third spiral from the top. And I'm also asking would it be better to use a 60° apex angle than the larger apex angle? Would it provide a better energy source?

RA I am Ra. For energy through the apex angle, the Giza pyramid offers an excellent model. Simply be sure the pyramid is so small that there is no

---

[1]   Mentioned before in 57.19 and 58.14.

entity small enough to crawl inside it.

66.26 **QUESTIONER** I assume that this energy, then, this spiraling light energy, is somehow absorbed by the energy field of the body. Is this somehow connected to the indigo energy center? Am I correct in this guess?

RA I am Ra. This is incorrect. The properties of this energy are such as to move within the field of the physical complex and irradiate each cell of the space/time body and, as this is done, irradiate also the time/space equivalent which is closely aligned with the space/time yellow-ray body. This is not a function of the etheric body or of free will. This is a radiation much like your sun's rays. Thus it should be used with care.

66.27 **QUESTIONER** How many applications of thirty minutes or less during a diurnal period would be appropriate?

RA I am Ra. In most cases, no more than one. In a few cases, especially where the energy will be used for spiritual work, experimentation with two shorter periods might be possible, but any feeling of sudden weariness would be a sure sign that the entity had been over-radiated.

66.28 **QUESTIONER** Can this energy help in any way as far as healing of physical distortions?

RA I am Ra. There is no application for direct healing using this energy, although if used in conjunction with meditation it may offer to a certain percentage of entities some aid in meditation. In most cases it is most helpful in alleviating weariness and in the stimulation of physical or sexual activity.

66.29 **QUESTIONER** In a transition from third to fourth density we have two other possibilities other than the type that we are experiencing now. We have the possibility of a totally positively polarized harvest, and the possibility of a totally negatively polarized harvest that, I understand, have occurred elsewhere in the universe many times. When there is a totally negatively polarized harvest, when a whole planet, that is, has negatively polarized and makes the transition from third to fourth density, does the planet have the experience of the distortion of disease that this planet now experiences prior to that transition?

RA I am Ra. You are perceptive. The negative harvest is one of intense disharmony, and the planet will express this.

66.30 **QUESTIONER** The planet has a certain set of conditions prior to transition into fourth density, that is in late third density, and then the conditions are different in early fourth density. Could you give me an example of a negatively polarized planet and the conditions in late third density and early fourth density, so that I can see how they change?

RA I am Ra. The vibrations from third to fourth density change on a negatively oriented planet precisely as they do upon a positively oriented planet. With fourth-density negative comes many abilities and possibilities of which you are familiar. The fourth density is more dense, and it is far more difficult to hide the true vibrations of the mind/body/spirit complex. This enables fourth-density negatives, as well as positives, the chance to form social memory complexes. It enables negatively oriented entities the opportunity for a different set of parameters with which to show their power over others and to be of service to the self. The conditions are the same as far as the vibrations are concerned.

66.31 **QUESTIONER** I was concerned about the amount of physical distortions, disease, and that sort of thing in third-density negative just before harvest and in fourth-density negative just after harvest or in transition. What are the conditions of the physical problems, disease, etc., at late third-density negative?

RA I am Ra. Each planetary experience is unique. The problems, shall we say, of bellicose actions are more likely to be of pressing concern to late third-density negative entities than the earth's reactions to negativity of the planetary mind, for it is often by such warlike attitudes on a global scale that the necessary negative polarization is achieved.

As fourth density occurs there is a new planet and new physical vehicle system gradually expressing itself, and the parameters of bellicose actions become those of thought rather than manifested weapons.

66.32 **QUESTIONER** Well then is physical disease and illness, as we know it on this planet, rather widespread on a third-density negative planet just before harvest into fourth-density negative?

RA I am Ra. Physical-complex distortions of which you speak are likely to be less found as fourth-density negative begins to be a probable choice of harvest due to the extreme interest in the self which characterizes the harvestable third-density negative entity. Much more care is taken of the physical body as well as much more discipline being offered to the self mentally. This is an orientation of great self-interest and self-discipline.

There are still instances of the types of disease which are associated with the mind-complex distortions of negative emotions such as anger. However, in an harvestable entity these emotional distortions are much more likely to be used as catalyst in an expressive and destructive sense as regards the object of anger.

66.33   **QUESTIONER** I am trying to understand the way that disease and bodily distortions are generated with respect to polarities, both positive and negative. It seems that they are generated in some way to create the split or polarization, that they have a function in creating the original polarization that occurs in third-density. Is this correct?

RA I am Ra. This is not precisely correct. Distortions of the bodily or mental complex are those distortions found in beings which have need of experiences which aid in polarization. These polarizations may be those of entities which have already chosen the path or polarization to be followed.

It is more likely for positively oriented individuals to be experiencing distortions within the physical complex due to the lack of consuming interest in the self and the emphasis on service to others.

Moreover, in an unpolarized entity catalyst of the physical distortion nature will be generated at random. The hopeful result is, as you say, the original choice of polarity. Oftentimes this choice is not made, but the catalyst continues to be generated.

In the negatively oriented individual the physical body is likely to be more carefully tended and the mind disciplined against physical distortions.

66.34   **QUESTIONER** This planet, to me, seems to be what I would call a cesspool of distortions. This includes all diseases and malfunctions of the physical body in general. It would seem to me that, on the average, this planet would be very, very high on the list if we just took the overall amount of these problems. Am I . . . is my feeling correct in this assumption?

RA I am Ra. We will review previous material.[2]

Catalyst is offered to the entity. If it is not used by the mind complex it will then filter through to the body complex and manifest as some form of physical distortion. The more efficient the use of catalyst, the less physical distortion to be found.

There are, in the case of those you call wanderers, not only a congenital difficulty in dealing with the third-density vibratory patterns, but also a recollection, however dim, that these distortions are not necessary or usual in the home vibration.

We over-generalize as always, for there are many cases of pre-incarnative decisions which result in physical or mental limitations and distortions, but we feel that you are addressing the question of widespread distortions towards misery of one form or another.

Indeed, on some third-density planetary spheres catalyst has been used more efficiently. In the case of your planetary sphere there is much inefficient use of catalyst and, therefore, much physical distortion.

We have enough energy available for one query at this time.

66.35 QUESTIONER Then I will ask if there is anything that we can do to make the instrument more comfortable or improve the contact?

RA I am Ra. Continue as always in love. All is well. You are conscientious.

I am Ra. I leave you in the love and in the light of the One Infinite Creator. Go forth, rejoicing in the power and the peace of the One Infinite Creator. Adonai.

---

[2] Originally covered in 61.7.

67.0   **RA** I am Ra and I greet you in the love and in the light of the One Infinite Creator. I communicate now.

67.1   **QUESTIONER** Could you first give us the instrument's condition, please?

RA I am Ra. The vital energies are more closely aligned with the amount of distortion normal to this entity than previous asking showed. The physical complex energy levels are somewhat less strong than at the previous asking. The psychic attack component is exceptionally strong at this particular nexus.

67.2   **QUESTIONER** Can you describe what you call the psychic attack component and tell me why it is strong at this particular time?

RA I am Ra. We shall elect not to retrace previously given information but, rather, elect to note that the psychic attack upon this instrument is at a constant level as long as it continues in this particular service.

Variations towards the distortion of intensity of attack occur due to the opportunities presented by the entity in any weakness. At this particular nexus the entity has been dealing with the distortion which you call pain for some time, as you call this measurement, and this has a cumulatively weakening effect upon physical energy levels. This creates a particularly favorable target of opportunity, and the entity of which we have previously spoken has taken this opportunity to attempt to be of service in its own way.

It is fortunate for the ongoing vitality of this contact that the instrument is a strong-willed entity with little tendency towards the distortion called among your peoples, hysteria, since the dizzying effects of this attack have been constant and at times disruptive for several of your diurnal periods.

However, this particular entity is adapting well to the situation without undue distortions towards fear. Thus the psychic attack is not successful but does have some draining influence upon the instrument.

67.3   **QUESTIONER** I will ask if I am correct in this analysis. We would consider that the entity making this so-called attack is offering its service with respect to its distortion in our polarized condition now so that we may more fully appreciate its polarity, and we are appreciative and thank this entity for its attempt to serve our One Creator in bringing to us knowledge in, shall I say, a more complete sense. Is this correct?

RA I am Ra. There is no correctness or incorrectness to your statement. It is an expression of a positively polarized and balanced view of negatively polarized actions which has the effect of debilitating the strength of the negatively polarized actions.

67.4 **QUESTIONER** We would welcome the services of the entity who uses, and I will use the misnomer, you might say, of attack, since I do not consider this an attack but an offering of service, and we welcome this offering of service—but we would be able, I believe, to make more full use of the service if it were not physically disabling the instrument in a minor way. For with a greater physical ability she would be able to more appreciate the service. We would greatly appreciate it if the service was carried on in some manner which we could welcome in even greater love than at present. This, I assume, would be some service that would not include the dizzying effect.

I am trying to understand the mechanism of this service by the entity that seems to be constantly with us, and I am trying to understand the origin of this entity and the mechanism of greeting us. I will make a statement that is probably not only incorrect but is a function of my extreme limitation in understanding the other densities and how they work.

I am guessing that this particular entity is a member of the Orion Confederation and is possibly, or possibly not, incarnate in a body of the appropriate density, which I assume is the fifth, and by mental discipline he has been able to project a portion if not all of his consciousness to our coordinates, you might say, here, and it is possibly one of the seven bodies that make up his mind/body/spirit complex. Is any of this correct, and can you tell me what is correct or incorrect about that statement?

RA I am Ra. The statement is substantially correct.

67.5 **QUESTIONER** Would you rather not give me information as to the specifics of my statement?

RA I am Ra. We did not perceive a query in further detail. Please re-question.

67.6   **QUESTIONER** Which body, with respect to the colors, does the entity use to travel to us?

RA I am Ra. This query is not particularly simple to answer due to the transdimensional nature, not only of space/time to time/space, but from density to density. The time/space light or fifth-density body is used while the space/time fifth-density body remains in fifth density. The assumption that the consciousness is projected thereby is correct. The assumption that this conscious vehicle, attached to the space/time fifth-density physical complex, is that vehicle which works in this particular service is correct.

67.7   **QUESTIONER** I undoubtedly will ask several very uninformed and poor questions. However, I was trying to understand certain concepts having to do with the illusion, I shall say, of the polarization that seems to exist at certain density levels in the creation and how can the mechanism of interaction of consciousness— It is a very difficult subject for me and therefore I ask your forgiveness for my poor questions, but it seems to me that the fifth-density entity is attracted in some way to our group by the polarization of this group which acts, somehow, as a beacon to the entity. Am I correct?

RA I am Ra. This is, in substance, correct, but the efforts of this entity are put forward only reluctantly. The usual attempts upon positively oriented entities, or groups of entities, are made, as we have said, by minions of the fifth-density Orion leaders; these are fourth-density. The normal gambit of such fourth-density attack is the tempting of the entity or group of entities away from total polarization towards service to others and toward the aggrandizement of self, or of social organizations with which the self identifies.

In the case of this particular group, each was given a full range of temptations to cease being of service to each other and to the One Infinite Creator. Each entity declined these choices and, instead, continued with no significant deviations from the desire for a purely other-self service orientation.

At this point one of the fifth-density entities over-seeing such detuning processes determined that it would be necessary to terminate the group by what you might call magical means, as you understand ritual magic. We have previously discussed the potential for the removal of one of this group by such attack and have noted that, by far, the most vulnerable is the instrument due to its pre-incarnative physical-complex distortions.

67.8 **QUESTIONER** In order for this group to be fully in service to the Creator, since we recognize this fifth-density entity as the Creator, we must also attempt to serve, in any way we can, this entity. Is it possible for you to communicate to us the desires of this entity, if there are any, in addition to simply ceasing the reception and dissemination of that which you provide for us?

RA I am Ra. This entity has two desires. The first, and foremost, is to, shall we say, misplace one or more of this group in a negative orientation so that it may choose to be of service along the path of service to self. The objective which must precede this is the termination of the physical complex viability of one of this group while the mind/body/spirit complex is within a controllable configuration.

May we say that although we of Ra have limited understanding, it is our belief that sending this entity love and light, which each of the group is doing, is the most helpful catalyst which the group may offer to this entity.

67.9 **QUESTIONER** We find a— I'm sorry, continue if you wish to continue with it.

RA I am Ra. We were about to note that this entity has been as neutralized as possible, in our estimation, by this love offering, and thus its continued presence is, perhaps, the understandable limit for each polarity of the various views of service which each may render to the other.

67.10 **QUESTIONER** We have a paradoxical situation in that in order to fully serve the Creator at this level in the polarized section, you might say, of the creation, we have requests from those whom we serve in this density for Ra's information. In fact, I just had one by telephone a short while ago. However, we have requests from, in this particular case, another density not to disseminate this information. We have the Creator, in fact, requesting two seemingly opposite activities of this group.

It would be very helpful if we could reach a condition of full, total, complete service in such a way that we were, by every thought and activity, serving the Creator to the very best of our ability. Is it possible for you to solve, or possible for the fifth-density entity who offers its service to solve, the paradox that I have observed?

RA I am Ra. It is quite possible.

67.11 **QUESTIONER** Then how could we solve this paradox?

RA I am Ra. Consider, if you will, that you have no ability not to serve the Creator since all is the Creator. In your individual growth patterns appear the basic third-density choice. Further, there are overlaid memories of the positive polarizations of your home density. Thus your particular orientation is strongly polarized towards service to others and has attained wisdom as well as compassion.

You do not have merely two opposite requests for service. You will find an infinite array of contradictory requests for information, or lack of information from this source if you listen carefully to those whose voices you may hear. This is all one voice to which you resonate upon a certain frequency. This frequency determines your choice of service to the One Creator. As it happens this group's vibratory patterns and those of Ra are compatible and enable us to speak through this instrument with your support. This is a function of free will.

A portion, seemingly, of the Creator rejoices at your choice to question us regarding the evolution of spirit. A seemingly separate portion would wish for multitudinous answers to a great range of queries of a specific nature. Another seemingly separate group of your peoples would wish this correspondence through this instrument to cease, feeling it to be of a negative nature. Upon the many other planes of existence there are those whose every fiber rejoices at your service and those, such as the entity of whom you have been speaking, which wish only to terminate the life upon the third-density plane of this instrument. All are the Creator. There is one vast panoply of biases and distortions, colors and hues, in an unending pattern.

In the case of those with whom you, as entities and as a group, are not in resonance, you wish them love, light, peace, joy, and bid them well. No more than this can you do, for your portion of the Creator is as it is, and your experience and offering of experience, to be valuable, needs be more and more a perfect representation of who you truly are.

Could you, then, serve a negative entity by offering the instrument's life? It is unlikely that you would find this a true service.

Thus you may see, in many cases, the loving balance being achieved: the love being offered, light being sent, and the service of the service-to-self oriented entity gratefully acknowledged while being rejected as not being useful in your journey at this time. Thus you serve One Creator without paradox.

67.12 **QUESTIONER** This particular entity is able to create, with its service, a dizzying effect on the instrument. Could you describe the mechanics of such a service?

RA I am Ra. This instrument, in the small times of its incarnation, had the distortion in the area of the otic complex of many infections which caused great difficulties at this small age, as you would call it. The scars of these distortions remain, and, indeed, that which you call the sinus system remains distorted. Thus the entity works with these distortions to produce a loss of the balance and a slight lack of ability to use the optic apparatus.

67.13 **QUESTIONER** I was wondering about the magical, shall I say, principles behind the fifth-density entity giving this service and his ability to give it. Why is he able to utilize these particular physical distortions from a philosophical or magical point of view?

RA I am Ra. This entity is able to, shall we say, penetrate in time/space configuration the field of this particular entity. It has moved through the quarantine without any vehicle and, thus, has been more able to escape detection by the net of the Guardians.

This is the great virtue of the magical working whereby consciousness is sent forth, essentially without vehicle, as light. The light would work instantly upon an untuned individual by suggestion; that is, the stepping out in front of the traffic because the suggestion is that there is no traffic. This entity, as each in this group, is enough disciplined in the ways of love and light that it is not suggestible to any great extent.

However, there is a predisposition of the physical complex which this entity is making maximal use of as regards the instrument, hoping, for instance, by means of increasing dizziness to cause the instrument to fall or to, indeed, walk in front of your traffic because of impaired vision.

The magical principles, shall we say, may be loosely translated into your system of magic whereby symbols are used and traced and visualized in order to develop the power of the light.

67.14   **QUESTIONER** Do you mean then that this fifth-density entity visualizes certain symbols? I am assuming that these symbols are of a nature where their continued use would have some power or charge. Am I correct?

RA I am Ra. You are correct. In fifth density light is as visible a tool as your pencil's writing.

67.15   **QUESTIONER** Then am I correct in assuming this entity configures the light into symbology, that is what we would call a physical presence? Is this correct?

RA I am Ra. This is incorrect. The light is used to create a sufficient purity of environment for the entity to place its consciousness in a carefully created light vehicle which then uses the tools of light to do its working. The will and presence are those of the entity doing the working.

67.16   **QUESTIONER** Are you familiar with a book that the instrument and I wrote approximately twelve years ago called *The Crucifixion Of Esmerelda Sweetwater*, in particular the banishing ritual used to bring the entities to Earth?

RA I am Ra. This is correct.

67.17   **QUESTIONER** Were there any incorrectnesses in our writing with respect to the way this was performed?

RA I am Ra. The incorrectnesses occurred only due to the difficulty an author would have in describing the length of training necessary to enable the ones known in that particular writing as Theodore and Pablo in the necessary disciplines.

67.18   **QUESTIONER** It has seemed to me that that book has, somehow, in its entirety, been a link to many of those whom we have met since we wrote it and to many of the activities we have experienced. Is this correct?

RA I am Ra. This is quite so.

67.19   **QUESTIONER** I will ask about that in a later session—since I don't want to get off the track—because it has something to do with the mechanics of time, which I am very puzzled about.

But I would ask then: the fifth-density entity in coming here to offer us service, as you mentioned, penetrated the quarantine. Was this done through one of the windows, or was this because of his, shall I say, magical ability?

RA I am Ra. This was done through a very slight window which less magically oriented entities or groups could not have used to advantage.

67.20 **QUESTIONER** Now, the main point of this line of questioning has to do with the First Distortion and the fact that this window existed. Was this, shall I say, a portion of the random window effect? And are we experiencing the same type of balancing in receiving the offerings of this entity as the planet in general receives because of the window effect?

RA I am Ra. This is precisely correct. As the planetary sphere accepts more highly evolved positive entities or groups with information to offer, the same opportunity must be offered to similarly wise negatively oriented entities or groups.

67.21 **QUESTIONER** Then we experience in this seeming difficulty the, what I would call, effect of the wisdom of the First Distortion, and for that reason must fully accept the wisdom of that which we experience. This is my personal view. Is it congruent with Ra's?

RA I am Ra. In our view we would perhaps go further in expressing appreciation of this opportunity. This is an intensive opportunity in that it is quite markèd in its effects, both actual and potential, and as it affects the instrument's distortions towards pain and other difficulties, such as the dizziness, it enables the instrument to continuously choose to serve others and to serve the Creator.

Similarly it offers a continual opportunity for each in the group to express support under more distorted, or difficult, circumstances of the other-self experiencing the brunt, shall we say, of this attack, thus being able to demonstrate the love and light of the Infinite Creator; and, furthermore, choosing working by working to continue to serve as messengers for this information which we attempt to offer and to serve the Creator thereby.

Thus the opportunities are quite noticeable as well as the distortions caused by this circumstance.

67.22 QUESTIONER Thank you. Is this so-called attack offered to myself and Jim as well as the instrument?

RA I am Ra. This is correct

67.23 QUESTIONER I personally have felt no effect that I am aware of. Is it possible for you to tell me how we are offered this service?

RA I am Ra. The questioner has been offered the service of doubting the self and of becoming disheartened over various distortions of the personal nature. This entity has not chosen to use these opportunities, and the Orion entity has basically ceased to be interested in maintaining constant surveillance of this entity.

The scribe is under constant surveillance and has been offered numerous opportunities for the intensification of the mental/emotional distortions and, in some cases, the connection matrices between mental/emotional complexes and the physical complex counterpart. As this entity has become aware of these attacks it has become much less pervious to them.

This is the particular cause of the great intensification and constancy of the surveillance of the instrument, for it is the weak link due to factors beyond its control within this incarnation.

67.24 QUESTIONER Is it within the First Distortion to tell me why the instrument experienced so many physical distortions during the new times of its incarnation?

RA I am Ra. This is correct.

67.25 QUESTIONER In that case can you answer me as to why the instrument experienced so much during its early years?

RA I am Ra. We were affirming the correctness of your assumption that such answers would be breaking the Way of Confusion. It is not appropriate for such answers to be laid out as a table spread for dinner. It is appropriate that the complexes of opportunity involved be contemplated.

67.26 QUESTIONER Then there is no other service that we can at this time offer that fifth-density entity of the Orion group who is so constantly with us. As I see it now there is nothing that we can do for him from your point of view? Is this correct?

RA I am Ra. This is correct. There is great humor in your attempt to be of polarized service to the opposite polarity. There is a natural difficulty in doing so since what you consider service is considered by this entity non-service. As you send this entity love and light and wish it well it loses its polarity and needs to regroup. Thus it would not consider your service as such.

On the other hand, if you allowed it to be of service by removing this instrument from your midst, you might, perhaps, perceive this as not being of service.

You have here a balanced and polarized view of the Creator: two services offered, mutually rejected, and in a state of equilibrium in which free will is preserved and each allowed to go upon its own path of experiencing the One Infinite Creator.

67.27 QUESTIONER Thank you. In closing that part of the discussion I would just say that if there is anything that we can do that is within our ability—and I understand that there are many things such as the ones that you just mentioned that are not within our ability—that we could do for this particular entity, if you would in the future communicate its requests to us, we will at least consider them because we would like to serve in every respect. Is this agreeable to you?

RA I am Ra. We perceive that we have not been able to clarify your service versus its desire for service. You need, in our humble opinion, to look at the humor of the situation and relinquish your desire to serve where no service is requested. The magnet will attract or repel. Glory in the strength of your polarization, and allow others of opposite polarity to similarly do so, seeing the great humor of this polarity and its complications in view of the unification in sixth density of these two paths.

67.28 QUESTIONER Thank you very much. I have a statement here that I will quickly read and have you comment on the accuracy or inaccuracy. In general, the archetypical mind is a representation of facets of the One Infinite Creator.[1]

---

[1] Here, Don is reading a question provided by Jim. Don mistakenly read this portion as "one infinite creation." Ra seems to have responded to Jim's original wording, so it has been corrected to "One Infinite Creator" per Jim's request.

The Father archetype corresponds to the male or positive aspect of electromagnetic energy and is active, creative, and radiant, as is our local sun. The Mother archetype corresponds to the female or negative aspect of electromagnetic energy and is receptive or magnetic as is our earth as it receives the sun's rays and brings forth life via third-density fertility. The Prodigal Son or the Fool archetype corresponds to every entity who seems to have strayed from unity and seeks to return to the One Infinite Creator. The Devil archetype represents the illusion of the material world and the appearance of evil but is more accurately the provider of catalyst for the growth of each entity within the third-density illusion.

The Magician, Saint, Healer, or Adept corresponds to the higher self and, because of the balance within its energy centers, pierces the illusion to contact intelligent infinity and, thereby, demonstrates mastery of the catalyst of third density. The archetype of Death symbolizes the transition of an entity from the yellow-ray body to the green-ray body either temporarily between incarnations or, more permanently, at harvest.

Each archetype presents an aspect of the One Infinite Creation to teach the individual mind/body/spirit complex according to the calling, or the electromagnetic configuration of mind, of the entity. Teaching is done via the intuition. With proper seeking, or mind configuration, the power of will uses the spirit as a shuttle to contact the appropriate archetypical aspect necessary for the teach/learning.

In the same way each of the other informers of intuition are contacted. They are hierarchical and proceed from the entity's own subconscious mind to group, or planetary mind, to guides, to higher self, to archetypical mind, to cosmic mind or intelligent infinity. Each is contacted by the spirit serving as shuttle according to the harmonized electromagnetic configuration of the seeker's mind and the information sought.

Will you please comment on the accuracy of these observations and correct any errors or fill in any omissions?

RA I am Ra. The entity has been using transferred energy for most of this session due to its depleted physical levels. We shall begin this rather complex answer, which is interesting, but do not expect to finish it. Those portions which we do not respond to we ask that you re-question us upon at a working in your future.

67.29 **QUESTIONER** Perhaps it would be better to start the next session with the answer to this question. Would that be appropriate or is the energy already fixed?

RA I am Ra. The energy is, as always, allotted. The choice, as always, is yours.

67.30 **QUESTIONER** In that case, continue.

RA I am Ra. Perhaps the first item which we shall address is the concept of the spirit used as a shuttle between the roots and the trunk of mind. This is a misapprehension, and we shall allow the questioner to consider the function of the spirit further, for in working with the mind we are working within one complex and have not yet attempted to penetrate intelligent infinity.

It is well said that archetypes are portions of the One Infinite Creator or aspects of its face. It is, however, far better to realize that the archetypes, while constant in the complex of generative energies offered, do not give the same yield of these complexes to any two seekers. Each seeker will experience each archetype in the characteristics within the complex of the archetype which are most important to it.

An example of this would be the observation of the questioner that the Fool is described in such and such a way. One great aspect of this archetype is the aspect of faith, the walking into space without regard for what is to come next. This is, of course, foolish but is part of the characteristic of the spiritual neophyte. That this aspect was not seen may be pondered by the questioner.

At this time we shall again request that the query be restated at the next working, and we shall, at this time, cease using this instrument. Before we leave may we ask if there may be any short questions?[2]

67.31 **QUESTIONER** Only if there is anything that we can do to make the instrument more comfortable or to improve the contact?

---

[2] To read a comprehensive study of the archetypes as depicted by Ra, see the Resource Series.

RA I am Ra. Continue, my friends, in the strength of harmony, love, and light. All is well. The alignments are appreciated for their careful placement.

I am Ra. I leave you now, my friends, in the glory of the love and the light of the Infinite Creator. Go forth, then, rejoicing in the power and the peace of the One Infinite Creator. Adonai.

68.0 RA I am Ra. I greet you in the love and in the light of the One Infinite Creator. We communicate now.

68.1 QUESTIONER Could you first please give me an indication of the instrument's condition?

RA I am Ra. This instrument's physical energies are depleted completely. The remainder is as previously stated.

68.2 QUESTIONER With the physical energies depleted completely should I continue with the session? I'm not sure exactly what that means.

RA I am Ra. We have available transferred energy which is due to the service offered by two of this group and, therefore, we are able to continue. Were it not for this transferred energy the instrument, whose will is strong, would have depleted its vital energies by willing the available resources.

Thus if there is no transfer of energy, and if the instrument seems depleted to the extent it now is, it is well to refrain from using the instrument. If there is energy transferred, this service may be accepted without damage to the distortion of normal vital energy.

We may note that the physical energy has been exhausted, not due to the distortion toward pain, although this is great at this space/time, but primarily due to the cumulative effects of continual experience of this distortion.

68.3 QUESTIONER Would you recommend a greater rest period between the end of this session and the next session? Would that help the instrument?

RA I am Ra. We might suggest, as always, that the support group watch the instrument with care and make the decision based upon observation. It is not within our capacity to specifically recommend a future decision. We would note that our previous recommendation of one working on alternate diurnal periods did not take into account the fragility of the instrument, and thus we would ask your forgiveness for this suggestion.

At this nexus our distortion is towards a flexible scheduling of workings based upon, as we said, the support group's decisions concerning the instrument. We would again note that there is a fine line between the care of the instrument for continued use, which we find acceptable, and the proper understanding, if you will excuse this misnomer, of the entire group's need to work in service.

Thus, if the instrument's condition is truly marginal, by all means let more rest occur between workings. However, if there is desire for the working, and the instrument is at all able, in your careful opinion, it is, shall we say, a well done action for this group to work. We cannot be more precise, for this contact is a function of your free will.

68.4   **QUESTIONER** The primary reason that we considered it important to have this session today is that I might not be around for a while, and I had a pressing question about what happened Sunday night when, apparently, the instrument was slipping into a trance state during one of the normal meetings,[1] and I would like to question you on this. Can you give me information about what happened?

RA I am Ra. We can.

68.5   **QUESTIONER** Would you tell me what happened in that case?

RA I am Ra. We have instructed this instrument to refrain from calling us unless it is within this set of circumscribed circumstances. In the event of which you speak this instrument was asked a question which pertained to what you have been calling *The Ra Material*. This instrument was providing the voice for our brothers and sisters of the wisdom density known to you as Latwii.

This instrument thought to itself, "I do not know this answer. I wish I were channeling Ra." The ones of Latwii found themselves in the position of being approached by the Orion entity, which seeks to be of service in its own way. The instrument began to prepare for Ra contact. Latwii knew that if this was completed the Orion entity would have an opportunity which Latwii wished to avoid.

It is fortunate for this instrument, firstly, that Latwii is of fifth density and able to deal with that particular vibratory complex which the Orion

---

[1]   This refers to the channeling of August 16, 1981.

entity was manifesting; and, secondly, that there were those in the support group at that time which sent great amounts of support to the instrument in this crux.

Thus what occurred was the ones of Latwii never let go of this instrument, although this came perilously close to breaking the Way of Confusion. It continued to hold its connection with the mind/body/spirit complex of the instrument and to generate information through it even as the instrument began to slip out of its physical vehicle.

The act of continued communication caused the entity to be unable to grasp the instrument's mind/body/spirit complex, and after but a small measure of your space/time, Latwii recovered the now completely amalgamated instrument and gave it continued communication to steady it during the transition back into integration.

68.6 **QUESTIONER** Could you tell me what the plan of the fifth-density negatively oriented entity was, and how it would have accomplished it, and what the results would have been if it had worked?

RA I am Ra. The plan, which is ongoing, was to take the mind/body/spirit complex while it was separated from its yellow-body physical-complex shell, to then place this mind/body/spirit complex within the negative portions of your time/space. The shell would then become that of the unknowing, unconscious entity and could be, shall we say, worked upon to cause malfunction which would end in coma and then in what you call the death of the body.

At this point the higher self of the instrument would have the choice of leaving the mind/body/spirit complex in negative sp— we correct— time/space, or of allowing incarnation in space/time of equivalent vibration and polarity distortions. Thus this entity would become a negatively polarized entity without the advantage of native negative polarization. It would find a long path to the Creator under these circumstances although the path would inevitably end well.

68.7 **QUESTIONER** Then you are saying that if this fifth-density negative entity is successful in its attempts to transfer the mind/body/spirit complex, when that complex is in what we call the trance state, to negatively polarized time/space, then the higher self has no choice but to allow incarnation in negatively polarized space/time? Is that correct?

RA I am Ra. This is incorrect. The higher self could allow the mind/body/spirit complex to remain in time/space. However, it is unlikely that the higher self would do so indefinitely due to its distortion towards the belief that the function of the mind/body/spirit complex is to experience and learn from other-selves, thus experiencing the Creator. A highly polarized positive mind/body/spirit complex surrounded by negative portions of space/time[2] will experience only darkness, for, like the magnet, there is no, shall we say, likeness. Thus a barrier is automatically formed.

68.8 **QUESTIONER** Let me be sure that I understand you. Is that darkness experienced in negative space/time, or in negative time/space?

RA I am Ra. Negative time/space.

68.9 **QUESTIONER** Incarnation in negative space/time, then, in a condition like that would result in incarnation into which density level for, let us take as an example, the instrument?

RA I am Ra. The answer to this query violates the First Distortion.

68.10 **QUESTIONER** OK, let's not take the instrument then as an example. Let's say that this was done to a wanderer of sixth density. If this answer violates the First Distortion, don't answer. But let's say a sixth-density wanderer had this happen and went into negative time/space. Would that be a sixth-density negative time/space, and would he incarnate into sixth-density negative space/time?

RA I am Ra. Your assumption is correct. The strength of the polarization would be matched as far as possible. In some positive sixth-density wanderers the approximation would not quite be complete due to the paucity of negative sixth-density energy fields of the equivalent strength.

68.11 **QUESTIONER** Is the reason that this could be done the fact that the wanderer's mind/body/spirit complex extracted in what we call the trance state, leaving the third-density physical, in this state the wanderer does not have the full capability or capability to magically defend itself? Is this correct?

---

2 Don's follow-up question and Ra's answer to it (68.8) appear to indicate that Ra meant to say time/space here.

RA I am Ra. In the case of this instrument, this is correct. This is also correct when applied, almost without exception, to those instruments working in trance which have not consciously experienced magical training in time/space in the, shall we say, present incarnation. The entities of your density capable of magical defense in this situation are extremely rare.

68.12 **QUESTIONER** It would seem to me that since I can't imagine anything . . . anything worse, shall I say, than this particular result, other than possibly the total disintegration of the mind/body/spirit complex due to nuclear bomb, that it would be very advisable to seek out the magical training and defense for this situation. Could Ra, and would Ra, instruct in this type of magical defense?

RA I am Ra. This request lies beyond the First Distortion. The entity seeking magical ability must do so in a certain manner. We may give instructions of a general nature. This we have already done. The instrument has begun the process of balancing the self. This is a lengthy process.

To take an entity before it is ready and offer it the scepter of magical power is to infringe in an unbalanced manner. We may suggest with some asperity[3] that the instrument never call upon Ra in any way while unprotected by the configuration which is at this time present.

68.13 **QUESTIONER** We have been speaking almost precisely of the portion of the *Esmerelda Sweetwater* book which we wrote having to do with Trostrick's misplacement of the space girl's mind/body/spirit complex. What is the significance of that work that we did with respect to our lives? It has been confusing to me for some time how that meshes in. Can you tell me that?

RA I am Ra. We scan each and find we may speak.

68.14 **QUESTIONER** Would you please do so now?

RA I am Ra. We confirm the following which is already, shall we say, supposed or hypothesized.

---

[3] In this context, *asperity* can be defined as "rigor" or "sharpness of temper."

When the commitment was made between two of this group to work for the betterment of the planetary sphere, this commitment activated a possibility/probability vortex of some strength. The experience of generating this volume was unusual in that it was visualized as if watching the moving picture.

Time had become available in its present-moment form. The scenario of the volume went smoothly until the ending of the volume. You could not end the volume, and the ending was not visualized as [was] the entire body of the material but [instead] was written or authored.

This is due to the action of free will in all of the creation. However, the volume contains a view of significant events, both symbolically and specifically, which you saw under the influence of the magnetic attraction which was released when the commitment was made and full memory of the dedication of this, what you may call, mission restored.[4]

68.15   QUESTIONER We have a situation with which I am concerned having to do with the understanding, I shall say (poor word of course), completely the . . . This activity occurs due to polarity . . . I think that it is important for me to investigate the techniques, if they are within the First Distortion, of the fifth-density negative entity who wishes to displace the mind/body/spirit complexes of this group. Am I within the First Distortion in asking you to describe how this entity goes about this working?

RA I am Ra. You are.

68.16   QUESTIONER Well how does the fifth-density entity go about this working from the very start of his being alerted to the fact that we exist. How does that occur? Can you please trace the steps that he involves himself in? Please.

RA I am Ra. The entity becomes aware of power. This power has the capacity of energizing those which may be available for harvest. This entity is desirous of disabling this power source. It sends its legions. Temptations are offered. They are ignored or rejected. The power source

---

4   To read a more in-depth account of the ways in which Don and Carla's book was prophetic, see the Resource Series.

persists and, indeed, improves its inner connections of harmony and love of service.

The entity determines that it must needs attempt the disabling itself. By means of projection it enters the vicinity of this power source. It assesses the situation. It is bound by the First Distortion but may take advantage of any free-will distortion. The free-will, pre-incarnative distortions of the instrument with regards to the physical vehicle seem the most promising target. Any distortion away from service to others is also appropriate.

When the instrument leaves its physical vehicle it does so freely. Thus the misplacement of the mind/body/spirit complex of the instrument would not be a violation of its free will if it followed the entity freely. This is the process.

We are aware of your pressing desire to know how to become impervious, as a group, to any influences such as this. The processes which you seek are a matter of your free choice. You are aware of the principles of magical work. We cannot speak to advise, but can only suggest, as we have before, that it would be appropriate for this group to embark upon such a path as a group, but not individually, for obvious reasons.

68.17 **QUESTIONER** I am interested in how the First Distortion applies to the negatively polarized entity misplacing the mind/body/spirit complex. Why is the negatively polarized entity followed to the place of negative time/space? Why would one of us freely follow the entity?

RA I am Ra. The positive polarity sees love in all things. The negative polarity is clever.

68.18 **QUESTIONER** Then I am assuming if the negative polarity used any other approach that did not use the free will of the other-self he would lose magical polarization and power. This is correct, isn't it?

RA I am Ra. This is correct.

The transferred energy grows low. We wish to close. Are there any short queries before we leave this instrument?

68.19 **QUESTIONER** Only is there anything that we can do to make the instrument more comfortable or improve the contact?

RA I am Ra. You are conscientious. We realize your necessity for these queries. All is well, my friends.

We thank you and leave you in the love and in the light of the One Infinite Creator. Go forth, therefore, rejoicing in the power and in the peace of the One Infinite Creator. Adonai.

SESSION 69

69.0   **RA** I am Ra. I greet you in the love and in the light of the One Infinite Creator.

Before we proceed, may we make a small request for future workings. At this particular working there is some slight interference with the contact due to the hair of the instrument. We may suggest the combing of this antenna-like material into a more orderly configuration prior to the working.

We communicate now.

69.1   **QUESTIONER** Could you first please give me the condition of the instrument?

RA I am Ra. It is as previously stated.

69.2   **QUESTIONER** Do you mean that the physical energy is completely depleted?

RA I am Ra. This is correct, although we have physical energy transferred and available for this working.

69.3   **QUESTIONER** Thank you. A question I didn't get to ask the previous session which I will be forced to continue at this time: is the trance state the only condition from which a mind/body/spirit positive entity may be lured by a negative adept to a negative time/space configuration?

RA I am Ra. This is a misperceived concept. The mind/body/spirit complex which freely leaves the third-density physical complex is vulnerable when the appropriate protection is not at hand. You may perceive carefully that very few entities which choose to leave their physical complexes are doing work of such a nature as to attract the polarized attention of negatively oriented entities. The danger to most in trance state, as you term the physical complex being left, is the touching of the physical complex in such a manner as to attract the mind/body/spirit complex back thereunto, or to damage the means by which that which you call ectoplasm is being recalled.

This instrument is an anomaly in that it is well that the instrument not be touched, or artificial light thrown upon it, while in the trance state. However, the ectoplasmic activity is interiorized. The main difficulty, as you are aware, is then the previously discussed negative removal of the entity under its free will.

That this can happen only in the trance state is not completely certain, but it is highly probable that in an other out-of-body experience, such as death, the entity here examined would, as most positively polarized entities, have a great deal of protection from comrades, guides, and portions of the self which would be aware of the transfer you call the physical death.

69.4   **QUESTIONER** Then you are saying that the protective friends, I will call them, would be available in every condition except for what we call the trance state which seems to be anomalistic with respect to the others. Is this correct?

RA I am Ra. This is correct.

69.5   **QUESTIONER** Why is this trance state, as we call it, different? Why are there not protective entities available in this particular state?

RA I am Ra. The uniqueness of this situation is not the lack of friends, for this, as all entities, has its guides or angelic presences and, due to polarization, teachers and friends also. The unique characteristic of the workings, which the social memory complex Ra and your group have begun, is the intent to serve others with the highest attempt at near purity which we as comrades may achieve.

This has alerted a much more determined friend of negative polarity which is interested in removing this particular opportunity.

We may say once again two notes: Firstly, we searched long to find an appropriate channel or instrument and an appropriate support group. If this opportunity is ended we shall be grateful for that which has been done, but the possibility/probability vortices indicating the location of this configuration again are slight. Secondly, we thank you, for we know what you sacrifice in order to do that which you, as a group, wish to do.

We will not deplete this instrument insofar as we are able. We have attempted to speak of how the instrument may deplete itself through too great a dedication to the working. All these things and all else we have said has been heard. We are thankful. In the present situation we express thanks to the entities who call themselves Latwii.

69.6 **QUESTIONER** Do I understand, then, that death, whether it is by natural means, or accidental death, or suicide—all deaths of this type would create the same after-death condition which would avail an entity to its protection from friends? Is this correct?

RA I am Ra. We presume you mean to inquire whether in the death experience, no matter what the cause, the negative friends are not able to remove an entity. This is correct largely because the entity without the attachment to the space/time physical complex is far more aware and without the gullibility which is somewhat the hallmark of those who love wholeheartedly.

However, the death, if natural, would undoubtedly be the more harmonious; the death by murder being confused and the entity needing some time/space in which to get its bearings, so to speak; the death by suicide causing the necessity for much healing work and, shall we say, the making of a dedication to the third density for the renewed opportunity of learning the lessons set by the higher self.

69.7 **QUESTIONER** Is this also true of unconscious conditions due to accident, or medical anesthetic, or drugs?

RA I am Ra. Given that the entity is not attempting to be of service in this particular way which is proceeding now, the entities of negative orientation would not find it possible to remove the mind/body/spirit. The unique characteristic, as we have said, which is, shall we say, dangerous, is the willing of the mind/body/spirit complex outward from the physical complex of third density for the purpose of service to others. In any other situation this circumstance would not be in effect.

69.8 **QUESTIONER** Would this be a function of the balancing action under the First Distortion?

RA I am Ra. Your query is somewhat opaque. Please restate for specificity.

69.9 **QUESTIONER** I was just guessing that since the mind/body/spirit complex is willed from the third-density body for a particular duty of service to others, that this then would create a situation primarily with respect to the First Distortion where the opportunity for balancing this service by the negative service would be available and, therefore, shall I say, magically possible for the intrusion of the other polarization. Is this thinking at all correct?

RA I am Ra. No. The free will of the instrument is, indeed, a necessary part of the opportunity afforded the Orion group. However, this free will and the First Distortion applies only to the instrument. The entire hope of the Orion group is to infringe upon free will without losing polarity. Thus this group, if represented by a wise entity, attempts to be clever.

69.10 **QUESTIONER** Now, has a wanderer ever been so infringed upon by, shall I say, a negative adept or whoever and then placed in negative time/space?

RA I am Ra. This is correct.

69.11 **QUESTIONER** Can you tell me of the situation that the wanderer finds itself in, and why the path back cannot be the simple moving back into the same value of positive time/space?

RA I am Ra. The path back revolves, firstly, about the higher self's reluctance to enter negative space/time. This may be a significant part of the length of that path.

Secondly, when a positively oriented entity incarnates in a thoroughly negative environment it must needs learn/teach the lessons of the love of self thus becoming one with its other-selves.

When this has been accomplished the entity may then choose to release the potential difference and change polarities.

However, the process of learning the accumulated lessons of love of self may be quite lengthy. Also the entity, in learning these lessons, may lose much positive orientation during the process, and the choice of reversing polarities may be delayed until the mid-sixth density. All of this is, in your way of measurement, time-consuming, although the end result is well.

69.12 **QUESTIONER** Is it possible to tell me, roughly, how many wanderers that have come to this planet within this master cycle have experienced this displacement into a negative time/space? Just wondering if there have been many.

RA I am Ra. We can note the number of such occurrences. There has been only one. We cannot, due to the Law of Confusion, discuss the entity.

69.13 **QUESTIONER** You said the higher self is reluctant to enter negative space/time. Is that correct?

RA I am Ra. The incarnative process involves being incarnated from time/space to space/time. This is correct.

69.14 **QUESTIONER** Then the positively polarized entity (I will make this statement and see if I am correct), when first moved into time/space of a negative polarization, experiences nothing but darkness. Then, on incarnation into negative space/time by the higher self, it experiences a negative space/time environment with negatively polarized other-selves. Is this correct?

RA I am Ra. This is correct.

69.15 **QUESTIONER** It would seem to me that this would be an extremely difficult situation for the positively polarized entity, and the learning process would be extremely traumatic. Is this correct?

RA I am Ra. Let us say that the positively polarized individual makes a poor student of the love of self and thus spends much more time, if you will, than those native to that pattern of vibrations.

69.16 **QUESTIONER** Is there no process or way by which the entity, once misplaced, and . . . I am assuming this misplacement must be a function of his free will in some way. Is this correct?

RA I am Ra. This is absolutely correct.

69.17 **QUESTIONER** Now, this is a point that I find quite confusing to me.

It is a function of the free will of the positively polarized entity to move into negatively polarized time/space. However, it is also a function of his lack of understanding of what he is doing. I am sure if the entity had full understanding of what he was doing that he would not do it. It is a function of his negatively polarized other-self creating a situation by which he is, shall I say, lured to that configuration.

What is the principle with respect to the First Distortion that allows this to occur since we have two portions of the Creator, each of equal value, or equal potential, shall I say, but oppositely polarized, and we have this situation resulting. Could you tell me the philosophical principle behind this particular act?

RA I am Ra. There are two important points in this regard. Firstly, we may note the situation wherein an entity gets a road map which is poorly marked and, in fact, is quite incorrect. The entity sets out to its destination. It wishes only to reach the point of destination but, becoming confused by the faulty authority and not knowing the territory through which it drives, it becomes hopelessly lost.

Free will does not mean that there will be no circumstances when calculations will be awry. This is so in all aspects of the life experience. Although there are no mistakes, there are surprises.

Secondly, that which we and you do in workings such as this carries a magical charge, if you would use this much misunderstood term. Perhaps we may say, a metaphysical power. Those who do work of power are available for communication to and from entities of roughly similar power.

It is fortunate that the Orion entity does not have the native power of this group. However, it is quite disciplined, whereas this group lacks the finesse equivalent to its power. Each is working in consciousness, but the group has not begun a work as a group. The individual work is helpful, for the group is mutually an aid, one to another.

[*There is a 48-second pause between the end of this answer and the beginning of the next question.*]

69.18 QUESTIONER This instrument performs services on Sunday night channeling other members of the Confederation. We are reluctant to continue this because of the possibility of her slipping into trance and being offered the services of the negatively polarized adept. Are there any safeguards to create a situation where she cannot go into trance other than at a protected working such as this one?

RA I am Ra. There are three. Firstly, the instrument must needs improve the disciplined subconscious taboo against requesting Ra. This would involve daily conscious and serious thought. The second safeguard is the refraining from the opening of the instrument to questions and answers for the present. The third is quite gross in its appearance but suffices to keep the instrument in its physical complex. The hand may be held.

69.19 **QUESTIONER** Then you are saying just by holding the instrument's hand during the channeling sessions that this would prevent trance?

RA I am Ra. This would prevent those levels of meditation which necessarily precede trance. Also in the event that, unlikely as it might seem, the entity grew able to leave the physical complex, the auric infringement and tactile pressure would cause the mind/body/spirit complex to refrain from leaving.

69.20 **QUESTIONER** We keep bringing up points out of the *Esmerelda Sweetwater* book, that being one particularly in the book. I was wondering, in that we were attempting to retrieve the space girl's mind/body/spirit complex from what must have been negative time/space, as it was placed there by the magician Trostrick: was the scenario of Trostrick's actions working with the space girl—and in Esmerelda Sweetwater's magical ritual that she designed to help retrieve the space girl's mind/body/spirit complex—were both of these techniques approximately reasonable? Or were there any errors in the design of these magical techniques?

RA I am Ra. There were no errors. We only remind each that this particular character imaged forth by you was an experienced adept.

69.21 **QUESTIONER** You mean the character Trostrick?

RA I am Ra. This is incorrect. We referred to Esmerelda, as this imagined entity was called.

We may note that long practice at the art which each intuits here would be helpful. We cannot speak of methodology, for the infringement would be most great. However, to speak of group efforts is, as we scan each, merely confirmation of what is known. Therefore, this we may do.

We have the available energy for one fairly brief query.

69.22 **QUESTIONER** There are many techniques and ways of practicing so-called white magical arts. Are rituals designed by a particular group for their own particular use just as good, or possibly better, than those that have been practiced by groups such as the Order of the Golden Dawn and other magical groups?

RA I am Ra. Although we are unable to speak with precision on this query, we may note some gratification that the questioner has penetrated some of the gist of a formidable system of service and discipline.

I am Ra. May we thank you again, my friends, for your conscientiousness. All is well. We leave you rejoicing in the power and the peace of the One Infinite Creator. Go forth with joy. Adonai.

Session 70

70.0　**RA** I am Ra. I greet you in the love and in the light of the One Infinite Creator. We communicate now.

70.1　**QUESTIONER** Could you please give me an indication of the condition of the instrument?

RA I am Ra. We are gratified to say that it is as previously stated.

70.2　**QUESTIONER** Why do you say you are gratified to say that?

RA I am Ra. We say this due to a sense of gratitude at the elements which have enabled this instrument to maintain, against great odds, its vital energy at normal vibratory strength. As long as this complex of energies is satisfactory we may use this instrument without depletion regardless of the distortions previously mentioned.

70.3　**QUESTIONER** The instrument has complained of intensive psychic attack for the past diurnal period, approximately. Is there a reason for the intensification of this at this time?

RA I am Ra. Yes.

70.4　**QUESTIONER** Can you tell me what this reason is, please?

RA I am Ra. The cause is that with which you are intimately involved; that is, the cause is the intensive seeking for what you may call enlightenment. This seeking upon your parts has not abated but intensified.

In the general case, pain—as you call this distortion, and the various exaggerations of this distortion by psychic attack—would, after the depletion of physical complex energy, begin the depletion of vital energy.

This instrument guards its vital energy due to previous errors upon its part. Its subconscious will, which is preternaturally strong for this density, has put a ward upon this energy complex. Thus the Orion visitor strives with more and more intensity to disturb this vital energy as this group intensifies its dedication to service through enlightenment.

70.5   **QUESTIONER** I have an extra little question that I want to throw in at this time. Is regressive hypnosis of an individual to reveal to them memories of previous incarnations a service or a disservice to them?

RA I am Ra. We scan your query and find you shall apply the answer to your future. This causes us to be concerned with the First Distortion. However, the query is also general and contains an opportunity for us to express a significant point. Therefore, we shall speak.

There is an infinite range of possibility of service/disservice in the situation of time-regression hypnosis, as you term this means of aiding memory. It has nothing to do with the hypnotist. It has only to do with the use which the entity so hypnotized makes of the information so gleaned. If the hypnotist desires to serve, and if such a service is performed only upon sincere request, the hypnotist is attempting to be of service.

70.6   **QUESTIONER** In the last session Ra stated that "the path back from sixth-density negative time/space revolves, firstly, about the higher self's reluctance to enter negative time/space."[1] Could you explain the higher self's position with respect to positive and negative time/space, and why it is so reluctant to enter negative time/space that it is necessary for the mind/body/spirit complex to incarnate in negative space/time to find its path back?

RA I am Ra. In brief, you have answered your own query. Please question further for more precise information.

70.7   **QUESTIONER** Why is the higher self reluctant to enter negative time/space?

RA I am Ra. The higher self is reluctant to allow its mind/body/spirit complex to enter negative time/space for the same basic reason an entity of your societal complex would be reluctant to enter a prison.

70.8   **QUESTIONER** What I am trying to understand here is more about the higher self and its relationship with the mind/body/spirit complex. Does the higher self have a sixth-density mind/body/spirit complex that is a

---

[1] The passage quoted is located in 69.11. Though Don quotes Ra as saying "negative time/space," Ra actually said "negative space/time." Due to this discrepancy, the subsequent conversation in this session may have become confused.

separate unit from the mind/body/spirit complex that is, in this case, displaced to negative time/space?

RA I am Ra. This is correct. The higher self is the entity of mid-sixth density which, turning back, offers this service to its self.

70.9 **QUESTIONER** I think I have an erroneous concept of the mind/body/spirit complex (for instance, that I represent here in this density) and my higher self. The concept probably comes from my concept of space and time. I am going to try to unscramble it.

The way I see it right now is that I am existing in two different locations, here and in mid-sixth density, simultaneously. Is this correct?

RA I am Ra. You are existing at all levels simultaneously. It is specifically correct that your higher self is you in mid-sixth density and, in your way of measuring what you know of as time, your higher self is your self in your future.

70.10 **QUESTIONER** Am I correct in assuming that all of the mind/body/spirit complexes that exist in the levels below mid-sixth density have a higher self in mid-sixth density? Is this correct?

RA I am Ra. This is correct.

70.11 **QUESTIONER** Would an analogy for this situation be that the individual's higher self is manipulating to some extent, shall I say, the mind/body/spirit complex that is its analog, you might say, to move it through the lower densities for purposes of gaining experience, and then finally transferring that experience or amalgamating it, you might say, in mid-sixth density with the higher self?

RA I am Ra. This is incorrect. The higher self does not manipulate its past selves. It protects when possible and guides when asked, but the force of free will is paramount. The seeming contradictions of determinism and free will melt when it is accepted that there is such a thing as true simultaneity. The higher self is the end result of all the development experienced by the mind/body/spirit complex to that point.

70.12 **QUESTIONER** Then what we are looking at is a long path of experience through the densities up to mid-sixth density which is a function totally of free will and results in the awareness of the higher self in mid-sixth density. But since time is illusory and there is a, shall I say, unification of time and space, or an eradication of what we think of as time, then all of this experience that results in the higher self—the cause of evolvement through the densities—is existing *while the evolvement takes place*, since it's all simultaneous. Is this correct?

RA I am Ra. We refrain from speaking of correctness due to our understanding of the immense difficulty of absorbing the concepts of metaphysical existence. In time/space, which is precisely as much of your self as is space/time, all times are simultaneous just as in your geography your cities and villages are all functioning, bustling, and alive with entities going about their business at once. So it is in time/space with the self.

70.13 **QUESTIONER** The higher self existing in mid-sixth density seems to be at the point where the negative and positive paths of experience merge into one. Is there a reason for this?

RA I am Ra. We have covered this material previously.[2]

70.14 **QUESTIONER** Oh yes. Sorry about that. It slipped my mind. Now, if a positive entity is displaced to negative time/space, I understand that the higher self is reluctant to enter the negative time/space. And for some reason this makes it necessary for the mind/body/spirit complex to incarnate in negative space/time. Why is it necessary for this incarnation in negative space/time?

RA I am Ra. Firstly, let us remove the concept of reluctance from the equation and then, secondly, address your query more to the point.

Each time/space is an analog of a particular sort, or vibration, of space/time. When a negative time/space is entered by an entity, the next experience will be that of the appropriate space/time. This is normally done by the form-making body of a mind/body/spirit complex which places the entity in the proper time/space for incarnation.

70.15 **QUESTIONER** I think to try and clear up this point I'm going to ask a few questions that are related that will possibly enable me to understand this better, because I am really confused about this, and I think it is a very important point in understanding the creation and the Creator in general,

---

2   Covered previously in 33.20, 36.12, 36.15, and 43.14.

you might say. If a wanderer of fourth, fifth, or sixth density dies from this third-density state in which we presently find ourselves, does he then find himself in third-density time/space after death?

RA I am Ra. This will depend upon the plan which has been approved by the Council of Nine. Some wanderers offer themselves for but one incarnation, while others offer themselves for varying lengths of your time up to and including the last two cycles of 25,000 years. If the agreed-upon mission is complete the wanderer's mind/body/spirit complex will go to the home vibration.

70.16 QUESTIONER Have there been any wanderers on this planet for the past 50,000 years now?

RA I am Ra. There have been a few. There have been many more which chose to join this last cycle of 25,000 years and many, many more which have come for harvest.

70.17 QUESTIONER Now here is the point of my confusion. If, after physical death, a wanderer would return to his home planet, shall I say, why cannot the same entity be extracted from negative time/space to the home planet rather than incarnating in negative space/time?

RA I am Ra. As we stated, the position in negative time/space, of which we previously were speaking, is that position which is pre-incarnative. After the death of the physical complex in yellow-ray activation, the mind/body/spirit complex moves to a far different portion of time/space in which the indigo body will allow much healing and review to take place before any movement is made towards another incarnative experience.

I perceive a basic miscalculation upon your part in that time/space is no more homogenous than space/time. It is as complex and complete a system of illusions, dances, and pattern as is space/time, and has as structured a system of what you may call natural laws.

70.18 QUESTIONER I'll ask this question to inform me a little bit about what you just stated. When you came to this planet in craft 18,000 and 11,000 years ago, these craft have been called, I believe, bell craft, and were photographed by George Adamski. If I am correct these craft looked somewhat like a bell; they had portholes around the upper portions; and they had three hemispheres at 120° apart underneath. Is this correct?

RA I am Ra. This is correct.

70.19 **QUESTIONER** Were these constructed in time/space or space/time?

RA I am Ra. We ask your persistent patience, for our answer must be complex.

A construct of thought was formed in time/space. This portion of time/space is that which approaches the speed of light. In time/space, at this approach, the conditions are such that time becomes infinite and mass ceases so that one which is able to skim the, shall we say, boundary strength of this time/space is able to become placed where it will.

When we were where we wished to be, we then clothed the construct of light with that which would appear as the crystal bell. This was formed through the boundary into space/time. Thus there were two constructs: the time/space (or immaterial) construct, and the space/time (or materialized) construct.

70.20 **QUESTIONER** Now was there a reason for the particular shape you chose, in particular a reason for the three hemispheres on the bottom?

RA I am Ra. It seemed an aesthetically pleasing form and one well suited to those limited uses which we must needs make of your space/time motivating requirements.

70.21 **QUESTIONER** Was there a principle of motivation contained within the three hemispheres on the bottom, or were they just aesthetic, or were they landing gear?

RA I am Ra. These were aesthetic and part of a system of propulsion. These hemispheres were not landing gear.

70.22 **QUESTIONER** I am sorry to ask such stupid questions, but I am trying to determine something about space/time, time/space, and, you might say, this very difficult area of the mechanism of evolution. I think it is central to the understanding of our evolution. However, I am not sure of this, and I may be wasting my time. Could Ra comment on whether I am wasting my time in this particular [*chuckles*] investigation or whether it would be fruitful?

RA I am Ra. Since the concepts of space/time, or physics, and time/space, or metaphysics, are mechanical, they are not central to the spiritual evolution of the mind/body/spirit complex. The study of love and light is far more productive in its motion towards unity in those entities pondering such concepts. However, this material is, shall we say, of some small interest and is harmless.

70.23 **QUESTIONER** I was asking these questions primarily to understand or to build a base for an attempt to get a little bit of enlightenment on the way that time/space and space/time are related to the evolution of the mind/body/spirit complex so that I could better understand the techniques, you might say, of that evolution.

For instance, you stated that "the potential difference may be released and polarities changed after an entity has learned/taught the lessons of love of self"—if the entity is a positive entity that has found itself in negative time/space and then had to incarnate in negative space/time. And what I was trying to do was build a base for attempting to understand, or at least get a slight understanding of, what you meant by this statement: that potential difference may be released and polarities changed after the above step.

I am very interested in knowing, if placed in a negative time/space, why it is necessary to incarnate in negative space/time and learn/teach love of self and develop, I guess, a sixth-density level of polarity before you can release that potential difference. I was trying to build a little foothold, or platform, from which to make that more apparent. Could you speak on that subject, please?

RA I am Ra. This will be the last full query of this working.

The entity which incarnates into negative space/time will not find it possible to maintain any significant positive polarity as negativity, when pure, is a type of gravity well, shall we say, pulling all into it. Thus the entity, while remembering its learned and preferred polarity, must needs make use of the catalyst given and recapitulate the lessons of service to self in order to build up enough polarity in order to cause the potential to occur for reversal.

There is much in this line of questioning which is somewhat muddled. May we, at this point, allow the questioner to rephrase the question or to turn the direction of query more towards that which is the heart of its concern.

70.24 **QUESTIONER** I will, at the next session, then attempt to turn more toward the heart. I was attempting in this session to get at a point that I thought was central to the evolution of spirit, but I seem to have gone awry. I'm sorry for that. It is sometimes very, very difficult for me to question wisely in these areas.

I will just ask if there is anything that we can do to benefit the contact or make the instrument more comfortable?

RA I am Ra. You are most conscientious, and the alignments are especially good. We thank you, my friends, and have been glad to speak with you. We are attempting to be of the greatest aid to you by taking care not to deplete this instrument. Thus, although a reserve remains we will attempt from this working onward to keep this reserve, for this instrument has arranged its subconscious to accept this configuration.

I am Ra. You are all doing well, my friends. We leave you in the love and in the light of the One Infinite Creator. Go forth, therefore, rejoicing and glorying in the power and in the peace of the One Infinite Creator. Adonai.

SESSION 71

71.0 **RA** I am Ra and I greet you in the love and in the light of the One Infinite Creator. We communicate now.

71.1 **QUESTIONER** Could you first please give me the condition of the instrument?

RA I am Ra. It is as previously stated with the exception of a slight improvement in the vital-energy distortions. One may note to the support group, without infringement, that it is well to aid the instrument in the reminders that, while physical-complex distortions remain as they are, it is not advisable to use the increased vital energies for physical complex activities, as this will take a somewhat harsh toll.

[*There is a 57-second pause between the end of this answer and the beginning of the next question.*]

71.2 **QUESTIONER** I have several different questions. In this session I hope to establish, by searching around with several different types of questions, a point of entry into an investigation that will be fruitful. I would first ask, is it possible to increase polarity without increasing harvestability?

RA I am Ra. The connection between polarization and harvestability is most important in third-density harvest. In this density an increase in the serving of others, or the serving of self, will almost inevitably increase the ability of an entity to enjoy an higher intensity of light. Thus, in this density, we may say, it is hardly possible to polarize without increasing in harvestability.

71.3 **QUESTIONER** This would probably be possible in the higher densities such as the fifth density. Is this correct?

RA I am Ra. In fifth-density harvest, polarization has very little to do with harvestability.

71.4 **QUESTIONER** Would you explain the concept of working with the unmanifested being in third density to create the evolution?

RA I am Ra. This is a many-layered question, and which stria we wish to expose is questionable.[1] Please restate giving any further depth of information requested, if possible.

71.5 **QUESTIONER** Define, please, the unmanifested being.

RA I am Ra. We may see that you wish to pursue the deeper stratum of information. We shall, therefore, answer in a certain way which does not exhaust the query but is designed to move beneath the outer teachings somewhat.

The unmanifested being is, as we have said, that being which exists and does its work without reference to, or aid from, other-selves. To move into this concept you may see the inevitable connection between the unmanifested self and the metaphysical, or time/space, analog of the space/time self. The activities of meditation, contemplation, and what may be called the internal balancing of thoughts and reactions are those activities of the unmanifested self more closely aligned with the metaphysical self.

71.6 **QUESTIONER** As an entity goes through the death process in third density and finds itself in time/space, it finds itself in a different set of circumstances. Would you please describe the properties or circumstances of time/space and then the process of healing of incarnative experiences that some entities encounter?

RA I am Ra. Although this query is difficult to answer adequately due to the limitations of your space/time sound vibration complexes, we shall respond to the best of our ability.

The hallmark of time/space is the inequity between time and space. In your space/time the spatial orientation of material causes a tangible framework for illusion. In time/space the inequity is upon the shoulders of that property known to you as time. This property renders entities and experiences intangible in a relative sense. In your framework each particle, or core vibration, moves at a velocity which approaches what you call the speed of light from the direction of supraluminal velocities.

Thus the time/space, or metaphysical, experience is that which is very

---

1   In this context, *stria* can be defined as "a number of parallel features or layers."

finely tuned and, although an analog of space/time, lacking in its tangible characteristics. In these metaphysical planes there is a great deal of what you call time which is used to review and re-review the biases and learn/teachings of a prior, as you would call it, space/time incarnation.

The extreme fluidity of these regions makes it possible for much to be penetrated which must needs be absorbed before the process of healing of an entity may be accomplished. Each entity is located in a somewhat immobile state, much as you are located in space/time in a somewhat immobile state in time. In this immobile space the entity has been placed by the form-maker and higher self so that it may be in the proper configuration for learn/teaching that which it has received in the space/time incarnation.

Depending upon this time/space locus there will be certain helpers which assist in this healing process. The process involves seeing in full the experience, seeing it against the backdrop of the mind/body/spirit complex total experience, forgiving the self for all missteps as regards the missed guideposts during the incarnation and, finally, the careful assessment of the next necessities for learning. This is done entirely by the higher self until an entity has become conscious in space/time of the process and means of spiritual evolution, at which time the entity will consciously take part in all decisions.

71.7 **QUESTIONER** Is the process in positive time/space identical with the process in negative time/space for this healing?

RA I am Ra. The process in space/time of the forgiveness and acceptance is much like that in time/space in that the qualities of the process are analogous. However, while in space/time it is not possible to determine the course of events beyond the incarnation but only to correct present imbalances. In time/space, upon the other hand, it is not possible to correct any unbalanced actions but rather to perceive the imbalances and, thusly, forgive the self for that which is.

The decisions then are made to set up the possibility/probabilities of correcting these imbalances in what you call future space/time experiences.

The advantage of time/space is that of the fluidity of the grand overview. The advantage of space/time is that, working in darkness with a tiny candle, one may correct imbalances.

71.8 **QUESTIONER** If an entity has chosen the negative polarization are the processes of healing and review similar for the negative path?

RA I am Ra. This is correct.

71.9 **QUESTIONER** Are the processes that we are talking about processes that occur on many planets in our Milky Way Galaxy, or do they occur on all planets, or what percentage?

RA I am Ra. These processes occur upon all planets which have given birth to sub-Logoi such as yourselves. The percentage of inhabited planets is approximately 10%.

71.10 **QUESTIONER** What percentage of stars, roughly, have planetary systems?

RA I am Ra. This is unimportant information but harmless. Approximately 32% of stars have planets as you know them, while another 6% have some sort of clustering material which upon some densities might be inhabitable.

71.11 **QUESTIONER** Well, this would tell me that roughly 3% of all stars have inhabited planets, which would just give a, shall I say, mind-boggling idea of the number of entities which— I assume, then, this process of evolution is in use throughout the known universe. Is this correct?

RA I am Ra. This octave of infinite knowledge of the One Creator is as it is throughout the One Infinite Creation, with variations programmed by sub-Logoi of what you call major galaxies and minor galaxies. These variations are not significant but may be compared to various regions of geographical location sporting various ways of pronouncing the same sound vibration complex or concept.

71.12 **QUESTIONER** Then it seems to me from this that the sub-Logos such as our sun uses free will to modify only slightly a much more general idea of created evolution so that the general plan of created evolution, which seems then to be uniform throughout the One Infinite Creation, is for this process of the sub-Logoi to grow through the densities and, under the First Distortion, find their way back to the Original Thought. Is this correct?

RA I am Ra. This is correct.

71.13 **QUESTIONER** Then each entity is on a path that leads to the one destination. This is like many, many roads which travel through many, many places but eventually merge into one large center. Is this correct?

RA I am Ra. This is correct but somewhat wanting in depth of description. More applicable would be the thought that each entity contains within it all of the densities and sub-densities of the octave so that in each entity, no matter whither its choices lead it, its great internal blueprint is one with all others. Thusly its experiences will fall into the patterns of the journey back to the original Logos. This is done through free will, but the materials from which choices can be made are one blueprint.

71.14 **QUESTIONER** You have made the statement that pure negativity acts as a gravity well pulling all into it. I was wondering, first, if pure positivity has precisely the same effect? Could you answer that please?

RA I am Ra. This is incorrect. Positivity has a much weaker effect due to the strong element of recognition of free will in any positivity approaching purity. Thus, although the negatively oriented entity may find it difficult to polarize negatively in the midst of such resounding harmony, it will not find it impossible.

Upon the other hand, the negative polarization is one which does not accept the concept of the free will of other-selves. Thusly in a social complex whose negativity approaches purity the pull upon other-selves is constant. A positively oriented entity in such a situation would desire for other-selves to have their free will and, thusly, would find itself removed from its ability to exercise its own free will, for the free will of negatively oriented entities is bent upon conquest.

71.15 **QUESTIONER** Could you please comment on the accuracy of this statement? I'm going to generally talk about the concept of magic and first define it as the ability to create changes in consciousness at will. Is this an acceptable definition?

RA I am Ra. This definition is acceptable in that it places upon the adept the burden it shall bear. It may be better understood by referring back to an earlier query, in your measurement, within this working having to do with the unmanifested self. In magic one is working with one's unmanifested self in body, in mind, and in spirit; the mixture depending upon the nature of the working.

These workings are facilitated by the enhancement of the activation of the indigo-ray energy center. The indigo-ray energy center is fed, as are all energy centers, by experience, but far more than the others is fed by what we have called the disciplines of the personality.

71.16   **QUESTIONER** I will state that the objective of a white magical ritual is to create a change in consciousness of a group. Is this correct?

RA I am Ra. Not necessarily. It is possible for what you term white magic to be worked for the purpose of altering only the self, or the place of working. This is done in the knowledge that to aid the self in polarization towards love and light is to aid the planetary vibration.

71.17   **QUESTIONER** The change in consciousness should result in a greater distortion towards service to others, toward unity with all, and toward knowing in order to serve. Is this correct, and are there any other desired results?

RA I am Ra. These are commendable phrases. The heart of white magic is the experience of the joy of union with the Creator. This joy will, of necessity, radiate throughout the life experience of the positive adept. It is for this reason that sexual magic is not restricted solely to the negatively oriented polarizing adepts, but, when most carefully used, has its place in high magic as it, when correctly pursued, joins body, mind, and spirit with the One Infinite Creator.

Any purpose which you may frame should, we suggest, take into consideration this basic union with the One Infinite Creator, for this union will result in service to others of necessity.

71.18   **QUESTIONER** There are, shall I say, certain rules of white magic. I will read these few that I have written, and I would like for you to comment on the philosophical basis or reasoning behind these and add to this list any of importance that I have neglected. First, a special place of working preferably constructed by the practitioners; second, a signal or key such as a ring to summon the magical personality; third, special clothing worn only for the workings; fourth, a specific time of day; fifth, a series of ritual sound vibratory complexes designed to create the desired mental distortion; sixth, a group objective for each session. Would you comment on this list, please?

RA I am Ra. To comment upon this list is to play the mechanic which views the instruments of the orchestra and adjusts and tunes the instruments. You will note these are mechanical details. The art does not lie herein.

The one item of least import is what you call the time of day. This is important in those experiential nexi wherein the entities search for the metaphysical experience without conscious control over the search. The repetition of workings gives this search structure. In this particular group the structure is available without the need for inevitable sameness of times of working. We may note that this regularity is always helpful.

71.19 **QUESTIONER** You stated in a previous session that Ra searched for some time to find a group such as this one. I would assume that this search was for the purpose of communicating the Law of One. Is this correct?

RA I am Ra. This is partially correct. We also, as we have said, wished to attempt to make reparation for distortions of this law set in motion by our naïve actions of your past.

71.20 **QUESTIONER** Can you tell me if we have covered the necessary material to this point to, if published, make the necessary reparations for the naïve actions?

RA I am Ra. We mean no disrespect for your service, but we do not expect to make full reparations for these distortions. We may, however, offer our thoughts in the attempt. The attempt is far more important to us than the completeness of the result. The nature of your language is such that what is distorted cannot, to our knowledge, be fully undistorted but only illuminated somewhat.

71.21 **QUESTIONER** When you say you searched for this group, what do you mean? What was your process of search? I ask this question to understand more the illusion of time and space.

RA I am Ra. Consider the process of one who sees the spectrograph of some complex of elements. It is a complex paint sample, let us say for ease of description. We of Ra knew the needed elements for communication which had any chance of enduring. We compared our color chip to many individuals and groups over a long span of your time. Your spectrograph matches our sample.

In response to your desire to see the relationship betwixt space/time and time/space, may we say that we conducted this search in time/space, for in this illusion one may quite readily see entities as vibratory complexes and groups as harmonics within vibratory complexes.

[*There is a 33-second pause between the end of this answer and the beginning of the next question.*]

71.22 **QUESTIONER** I see the most important product of this communication being a vehicle of partial enlightenment for those incarnate now who have become aware of their part in their own evolutionary process. Am I correct in this assumption?

RA I am Ra. You are correct. We may note that this is the goal of all artifacts and experiences which entities may come into contact with and is not only the property of Ra or this contact.

We find that this instrument has neglected to continue to remind its self of the need for holding some portion of energy back for reserve. This is recommended as a portion of the inner program to be reinstated as it will lengthen the number of workings we may have. This is acceptable to us. The transferred energy grows quite, quite low. We must leave you shortly. Is there a brief query at this time?

71.23 **QUESTIONER** Is there anything that we can do to improve the contact or make the instrument more comfortable?

RA I am Ra. You are conscientious. Remain most fastidious about the alignments of the appurtenances. We thank you.

I am Ra. I leave you in the love and in the glorious light of the Infinite Creator. Go forth, therefore, rejoicing in the power and in the peace of the One Infinite Creator. Adonai.

SESSION 72

72.0 RA I am Ra. I greet you in the love and in the light of the One Infinite Creator. We communicate now.

72.1 QUESTIONER Could you first give me an indication of the instrument's condition, please?

RA I am Ra. This instrument's physical-energy distortions are as previously stated. The vital energy level has become distorted from normal levels, somewhat downward, due to the distortion in this instrument's mind complex activity that it has been responsible for the, shall we say, difficulties in achieving the appropriate configuration for this contact.

72.2 QUESTIONER Was the banishing ritual that we performed of any effect in purifying the place of working and screening from influences that we do not wish?

RA I am Ra. This is quite correct.

72.3 QUESTIONER Can you tell me what I can do to improve the effectiveness of the ritual?

RA I am Ra. No.

72.4 QUESTIONER Can you tell me what caused the instrument to become in a condition toward unconsciousness during the last two meditations prior to this one to such an extent that we discontinued them?

RA I am Ra. We can.

72.5 QUESTIONER Would you please tell me that?

RA I am Ra. The entity which greets this instrument from the Orion group first attempted to cause the mind/body/spirit complex, which you may call spirit, to leave the physical complex of yellow ray in the deluded belief that it was preparing for the Ra contact. You are familiar with this tactic and its consequences. The instrument, with no pause upon feeling this greeting, called for the grounding within the physical complex by requesting that the hand be held.

Thus the greatest aim of the Orion entity was not achieved. However, it discovered that those present were not capable of distinguishing between unconsciousness, with the mind/body/spirit intact, and the trance state in which the mind/body/spirit complex is not present.

Therefore, it applied to the fullest extent the greeting which causes the dizziness and, in meditation without protection, caused in this instrument simple unconsciousness as in what you would call fainting or vertigo. The Orion entity consequently used this tactic to stop the Ra contact from having the opportunity to be accomplished.

72.6   **QUESTIONER** The instrument has scheduled an operation on her hand next month. If a general anesthetic is used to create the unconscious state will this or any other parameters of the operation allow for any inroads by the Orion entities?

RA I am Ra. It is extremely improbable due to the necessity for the intention of the mind/body/spirit complex, when departing the yellow-ray physical complex, to be serving the Creator in the most specific fashion. The attitude of one approaching such an experience as you describe would not be approaching the unconscious state with such an attitude.

72.7   **QUESTIONER** We have here, I believe, a very important principle with respect to the Law of One. You have stated that the attitude of the individual is of paramount importance for the Orion entity to be able to be effective. Would you please explain how this mechanism works with respect to the Law of One, and why the attitude of the entity is of paramount importance, and why this allows for action by the Orion entity?

RA I am Ra. The Law of Confusion, or Free Will, is utterly paramount in the workings of the infinite creation. That which is intended has as much intensity of attraction to the polar opposite as the intensity of the intention or desire.

Thus those whose desires are shallow or transitory experience only ephemeral configurations of what might be called the magical circumstance. There is a turning point, a fulcrum which swings as a mind/body/spirit complex tunes its will to service. If this will and desire is for service to others, the corresponding polarity will be activated.

In the circumstance of this group there are three such wills acting as one with the instrument in the, shall we say, central position of fidelity to service. This is as it must be for the balance of the working and the continuance of the contact. Our vibratory complex is one-pointed in these workings also, and our will to serve is also of some degree of purity. This has created the attraction of the polar opposite which you experience.

We may note that such a configuration of free will, one-pointed in service to others, also has the potential for the alerting of a great mass of light strength. This positive light strength, however, operates also under free will, and must be invoked.

We could not speak to this and shall not guide you, for the nature of this contact is such that the purity of your free will must, above all things, be preserved. Thus you wend your way through experiences discovering those biases which may be helpful.

[*There is a 30-second pause between the end of this answer and the beginning of the next question.*]

72.8   **QUESTIONER** The negatively oriented entities who contact us and others on this planet are limited by the First Distortion. They have obviously been limited by the banishing ritual just performed. Could you describe, with respect to free will, how they limit themselves in order to work within the First Distortion? And how the banishing ritual itself works?

RA I am Ra. This query has several portions. Firstly, those of negative polarity do not operate with respect to free will unless it is necessary. They call themselves and will infringe whenever they feel it possible.

Secondly, they are limited by the great Law of Confusion in that, for the most part, they are unable to enter this planetary sphere of influence and are able to use the windows of time/space distortion only insofar as there is some calling to balance the positive calling. Once they are here, their desire is conquest.

Thirdly, in the instance of this instrument's being removed permanently from this space/time, it is necessary to allow the instrument to leave its yellow-ray physical complex of its free will. Thus trickery has been attempted.

The use of the light forms being generated is such as to cause such entities to discover a wall through which they cannot pass. This is due to the energy complexes of the light beings and aspects of the One Infinite Creator invoked and evoked in the building of the wall of light.

72.9   QUESTIONER Everything that we experience with respect to this contact— our distortion toward knowledge in order to serve, the Orion entity's distortion toward the attempt to reduce the effectiveness of this service— all of this is a result of the First Distortion, as I see it, in creating totally free atmosphere for the Creator to become more knowledgeable of Itself through the interplay of Its portions, one with respect to another. Is my view correct with respect to what I just said?

RA   I am Ra. Yes.

72.10   QUESTIONER In the last session you mentioned that if the instrument used any of the increased vital energy that she experiences now for physical activity she would pay a "harsh toll." Could you tell me the nature of that harsh toll, and why it would be experienced?

RA   I am Ra. The physical energy level is a measure of the amount of available energy of the body complex of a mind/body/spirit complex. The vital energy measurement is one which expresses the amount of energy of being of the mind/body/spirit complex.

This entity has great distortions in the direction of mind complex activity, spirit complex activity, and that great conduit to the Creator, the will. Therefore, this instrument's vital energy, even in the absence of any physical reserve measurable, is quite substantial.

However, the use of this energy of will, mind, and spirit for the things of the physical complex causes a far greater distortion in the lessening of the vital energy than would the use of this energy for those things which are in the deepest desires and will of the mind/body/spirit complex. In this entity these desires are for service to the Creator. This entity sees all service as service to the Creator, and this is why we have cautioned the support group and the instrument itself in this regard. All services are not equal in depth of distortion. The over-use of this vital energy is, to be literal, the rapid removal of life force.

72.11 **QUESTIONER** You mentioned that the large amount of light is available. Could I by, or this group, by proper ritual, use this for recharging the vital energy of the instrument?

RA I am Ra. This is correct. However, we caution against any working which raises up any personality; rather it is well to be fastidious in your working.

72.12 **QUESTIONER** Could you explain what you mean by "raises up any personality?"

RA I am Ra. Clues, we may offer. Explanation is infringement. We can only ask that you realize that all are One.

72.13 **QUESTIONER** We have included "Shin" in the banishing ritual, "Yod Heh Vau Heh" to make it "Yod Heh Shin Vau Heh." Is this helpful?

RA I am Ra. This is helpful especially to the instrument whose distortions vibrate greatly in congruency with this sound vibration complex.

72.14 **QUESTIONER** We will in the future have group meditations as our Sunday night meditations. I am concerned in . . . protection for the instrument if she is once more a channel in these. Is there an optimum time, or limiting amount of time, for the banishing ritual to be effective? Or if we continually, daily, purify the place of working that we use for the Sunday night meditation with the banishing ritual, would this carry over for long periods of time, or must the ritual be done immediately prior to the meditations?

RA I am Ra. Your former assumption is more nearly correct.

72.15 **QUESTIONER** Is there any danger in the Sunday night meditations, with the precautions we are taking, of the instrument being led away by the Orion entity?

RA I am Ra. The opportunities for the Orion entity are completely dependent upon the instrument's condition of awareness and readiness. We would suggest that this instrument is still too much the neophyte to open itself to questions since that is the format used by Ra. As the instrument grows in awareness this precaution may become unnecessary.

72.16 **QUESTIONER** Is it possible to over-energize the instrument with sexual energy transfers?

RA I am Ra. No.

72.17 **QUESTIONER** Why is there no protection at the floor, or bottom, of the banishing ritual, and should there be?

RA I am Ra. This will be the last full query of this working.

The development of the psychic greeting is possible only through the energy centers starting from a station which you might call within the violet ray, moving through the adept's energy center and therefrom towards the target of opportunity. Depending upon the vibratory nature and purpose of greeting, be it positive or negative, the entity will be energized, or blocked, in the desired way.

We of Ra approach this instrument in narrow-band contact through violet ray. Others might pierce down through this ray to any energy center. We, for instance, make great use of this instrument's blue-ray energy center as we are attempting to communicate our distortion-understandings of the Law of One.

The entity of Orion pierces the same violet ray and moves to two places to attempt most of its non-physical opportunities. It activates the green-ray energy center while further blocking indigo-ray energy center. This combination causes confusion in the instrument and subsequent over-activity in unwise proportions in physical complex workings. It simply seeks out the distortions pre-incarnatively programmed and developed in incarnative state.

The energies of life itself, being the One Infinite Creator, flow from the south pole of the body, seen in its magnetic form. Thus only the Creator may, through the feet, enter the energy shell of the body to any effect. The effects of the adept are those from the upper direction, and thus the building of the wall of light is quite propitious.[1]

May we ask if there are any shorter queries at this time?

72.18 **QUESTIONER** I would just ask if there is anything that we can do to make the instrument more comfortable or improve the contact?

RA I am Ra. This instrument has some increased distortion in the region

---

[1] In this context, *propitious* can be defined as "favorable."

of the neck. Some attention here might provide greater comfort. All is well, my friends. The forbearance and patience observed by Ra are commendable. Continue in this fastidiousness of purpose and care for the appropriate configurations for contact, and our continuance of contact will continue to be possible. This is acceptable to us.

I am Ra. I leave you, my friends, glorying in the love and the light of the One Infinite Creator. Go forth, then, rejoicing in the power and in the peace of the One Infinite Creator. Adonai.

73.0   RA I am Ra. I greet you in the love and in the light of the One Infinite Creator. We communicate now.

73.1   QUESTIONER Could you please give me an indication of the instrument's condition?

RA I am Ra. It is as previously stated with the exception of the vital energy level which is distorted more nearly towards that which is normal for this entity.

73.2   QUESTIONER Has the banishing ritual that we have performed been helpful for this contact?

RA I am Ra. The ritual described has gained with each working in making efficacious the purity of contact needed, not only for the Ra contact, but for any working of the adept.

73.3   QUESTIONER Thank you. We would like to thank Ra at this time for the opportunity to be of service to those on this sphere who would like to have the information that we gain here in this [*inaudible*].

You stated that free will, one-pointed in service to others, had the potential of alerting a great mass of light strength. I assume that the same holds precisely true for the service-to-self polarity. Is this correct?

RA I am Ra. This is incorrect but subtly so. In invocation and evocation of what may be termed negative entities or qualities, the expression alerts the positively oriented equivalent. However, those upon the service-to-others path wait to be called and can only send love.

73.4   QUESTIONER What I was trying to get at was that this alerting of light strength is, as I see it, a process that must be totally a function of free will, as you say. And as the desire, and will, and purity of desire of the adept or operator increases, the alerting of light strength increases. Is this part of it the same for both positive and negative potentials, and am I correct with this statement?

RA I am Ra. To avoid confusion we shall simply restate for clarity your correct assumption.

Those who are upon the service-to-others path may call upon the light strength in direct proportion to the strength and purity of their will to serve. Those upon the service-to-self path may call upon the dark strength in direct proportion to the strength and purity of their will to serve.

73.5 **QUESTIONER** I will undoubtedly make many errors in my statements today because what I am going to do is try to guess at how this works and let you correct me.

In considering the exercise of the Middle Pillar I have thought it to be wrong in that the adept sees or visualizes light moving downward from the crown chakra down to the feet. Ra has stated that the Creator enters from the feet and moves upward, and that this spiraling light enters from the feet and moves upward. It seems to me that an adept alerting light strength, in visualizing the use of this, would visualize it entering in the direction of the feet and energizing first the red energy center and moving upward through the energy centers in that fashion. Is this correct?

RA I am Ra. No.

73.6 **QUESTIONER** Could you tell me how I am wrong in that statement?

RA I am Ra. Yes.

73.7 **QUESTIONER** Would you please do that?

RA I am Ra. There are two concepts with which you deal. The first is the great way of the development of the light in the microcosmic mind/body/spirit. It is assumed that an adept will have its energy centers functioning smoothly and in a balanced manner, to its best effort, before a magical working.

All magical workings are based upon evocation and/or invocation. The first invocation of any magical working is that invocation of the magical personality, as you are familiar with this term. In the working of which you speak, the first station is the beginning of the invocation of this magical personality which is invoked by the motion of putting on something. Since you do not have an item of apparel or talisman, the gesture which you have made is appropriate.

The second station is the evocation of the great cross of life. This is an extension of the magical personality to become the Creator.

Again, all invocations and evocations are drawn through the violet energy center. This may then be continued towards whatever energy centers are desired to be used.

73.8 **QUESTIONER** Then will you speak of the difference between the spiraling light that enters through the feet and the light invoked through the crown chakra?

RA I am Ra. The action of the upward spiraling light drawn by the will to meet the inner light of the One Infinite Creator may be likened to the beating of the heart and the movement of the muscles surrounding the lungs and all the other functions of the parasympathetic nervous system. The calling of the adept may be likened to those nerve and muscle actions over which the mind/body/spirit complex has conscious control.

73.9 **QUESTIONER** Previously you stated[1]—I believe I'm correct in saying this— that where the two directions meet you have a measure, let us say, of the development of any particular mind/body/spirit complex. Am I correct?

RA I am Ra. This is correct.

73.10 **QUESTIONER** In invoking the alerted light, then, it would seem to me that the visualization of the invocation would be dependent upon what the use was to be of the light. The use could be for healing, could be for communication, or it could be for the general awareness, you might say, of the creation and the Creator. Would you please speak on this process and my correctness in making this assumption?

RA I am Ra. We shall offer some thoughts, though it is doubtful that we may exhaust this subject. Each visualization, regardless of the point of the working, begins with some work within the indigo ray. As you may be aware, the ritual which you have begun is completely working within the indigo ray. This is well, for it is the gateway. From this beginning, light may be invoked for communication or for healing.

You may note that in the ritual which we offered you to properly begin the Ra workings the first focus is upon the Creator.

We would further note a point which is both subtile and of some

---

1 Previously stated in 49.5–6.

interest.[2] The upward spiraling light developed in its path by the will, and ultimately reaching an high place of mating with the inward fire of the One Creator, still is only preparation for the work upon the mind/body/spirit which may be done by the adept. There is some crystallization of the energy centers used during each working so that the magician becomes, more and more, that which it seeks.

More importantly, the time/space mind/body/spirit analog, which is evoked as the magical personality, has its only opportunity to gain rapidly from the experience of the catalytic action available to the third-density space/time mind/body/spirit. Thus the adept is aiding the Creator greatly by offering great catalyst to a greater portion of the creation which is identified as the mind/body/spirit totality of an entity.

73.11 **QUESTIONER** Desire and will are key factors in the process. Is this correct?

RA I am Ra. We would add one quality. In the magical personality desire, will, and polarity are the keys.

73.12 **QUESTIONER** I would then assume that the many so-called evangelists which we have in our society at present, many have great desire and very great will, and possibly great polarity. It seems to me that in some cases that there is a lack of information, or awareness, that creates a less-than-effective working in the magical sense. Am I correct in this analysis?

RA I am Ra. You are partially correct. In examining the polarity of a service-to-others working, the free will must be seen as paramount. Those entities of which you speak are attempting to generate positive changes in consciousness while abridging free will. This causes the blockage of the magical nature of the working except in those cases wherein an entity freely desires to accept the working of the evangelist, as you have called it.

73.13 **QUESTIONER** What was the orientation with respect to this type of communication for the one known as Jesus of Nazareth?

RA I am Ra. You may have read some of this entity's workings. It offered itself as teacher to those mind/body/spirit complexes which gathered to hear, and even then spoke as through a veil so as to leave room for those not wishing to hear. When this entity was asked to heal, it oft times did

---

[2] In this context, *subtile* can be defined as "fine, or delicate."

so, always ending the working with two admonitions: firstly, that the entity healed had been healed by its faith, that is, its ability to allow and accept changes through the violet ray into the gateway of intelligent energy; secondly, saying always, "Tell no one." These are the workings which attempt a maximal quality of free will while maintaining fidelity to the positive purity of the working.

73.14 **QUESTIONER** An observation of the working itself by another entity would seem to me to partially abridge free will in that a seemingly magical occurrence had taken place as a result of the working of an adept. This could be extended to any phenomenon which is other than normally acceptable. Could you speak on this paradox that is immediately the problem of anyone doing healing?

RA I am Ra. We are humble messengers of the Law of One. To us there are no paradoxes. The workings which seem magical and, therefore, seem to infringe upon free will do not, in themselves, do so, for the distortions of perception are as many as the witnesses, and each witness sees what it desires to see.

Infringement upon free will occurs in this circumstance only if the entity doing the working ascribes the authorship of this event to its self or its own skills. Those who state that no working comes from it but only through it is [not] infringing upon free will.[3]

73.15 **QUESTIONER** You said that if the entity says that no working comes from it but only through it, it is also infringing. Is that correct?

RA I am Ra. This is incorrect. We said that in that event there is no infringement.

73.16 **QUESTIONER** The one known as Jesus accumulated twelve disciples. What was his purpose in having these disciples with him?

RA I am Ra. What is the purpose of teach/learning if there be no learn/teachers? Those drawn to this entity were accepted by this entity without regard for any outcome. This entity accepted the honor/duty

---

[3] Ra originally said: "Those who state that no working comes from it but only through it is infringing upon free will." The error was corrected in the next Q&A, 73.15, and identified as an error caused by pain flare in 74.2.

placed upon it by its nature and its sense that to speak was its mission.

[*There is a 43-second pause between the end of this answer and the beginning of the next question.*]

73.17 **QUESTIONER** In the exercise of the fire, then, I assume that the healer would be working with the same energy that we spoke of as entering through the crown chakra. Is this correct?

RA I am Ra. This is correct with some additional notation necessary for your thought in continuing this line of study. When the magical personality has been seated in the green-ray energy center for healing work, the energy then may be seen to be the crystalline center through which body energy is channeled. Thus this particular form of healing uses both the energy of the adept and the energy of the upward spiraling light.

As the green-ray center becomes more brilliant—and we would note this brilliance does not imply over-activation but, rather, crystallization—the energy of the green-ray center of the body complex spirals twice: firstly, clockwise from the green-ray energy center to the right shoulder, through the head, the right elbow, down through the solar plexus, and to the left hand. This sweeps all the body complex energy into a channel which then rotates the great circle clockwise again from right—we correct this instrument—from the left to the feet, to the right hand, to the crown, to the left hand, and so forth.[4]

Thus the in-coming body energy, crystallized, regularized, and channeled by the adept's personality, reaching to the green-ray energy center, may then pour out the combined energies of the adept which is incarnate, thus offering the service of healing to an entity requesting that service. This basic situation is accomplished as well when there is an entity which is working through a channel to heal.

73.18 **QUESTIONER** Could you tell me how this transfer of light, I believe it would be, would affect the patient to be healed?

---

4 In 74.19, Ra offered a correction to 73.17 saying: "In the exercise of the fire you may see the initial spiral clockwise from the green-ray energy center, through the shoulders and head, then through the elbows, then to the left hand. The channel had been corrected before the remainder of this answer was completed."

RA I am Ra. The effect is that of polarization. The entity may or may not accept any percentage of this polarized life-energy which is being offered. In the occasion of the laying on of hands, this energy is more specifically channeled, and the opportunity for acceptance of this energy similarly more specific.

It may be seen that the King's Chamber effect is not attempted in this form of working but, rather, the addition to one whose energies are low the opportunity for the building up of those energies. Many of your distortions called illnesses may be aided by such means.

73.19 **QUESTIONER** I'll make a general statement which you can correct. The way I see the overall picture of healer and patient is that the one to be healed has, because of a blockage in one of the energy centers or more—but we will just consider one particular problem—because of this energy center blockage, the upward spiraling light that creates one of the seven bodies has been blocked from the maintenance of that body, and this has resulted in a distortion from the perfection of that body that we call disease, or a bodily anomaly, which is other than perfect.

The healer, having suitably configured its energy centers, is able to channel light, the downward pouring light, through its properly configured energy situation to the one to be healed. If the one to be healed has the mental configuration of acceptance of this light, the light then enters the physical complex and re-configures the distortion that was created by the original blockage. I am sure that I have made some mistakes in that. Would you please correct them?

RA I am Ra. Your mistakes were small. We would not, at this time, attempt a great deal of refinement of that statement as there is preliminary material which will undoubtedly come forward. We may say that there are various forms of healing. In many, only the energy of the adept is used. In the exercise of fire some physical complex energy is also channeled.

We might note further that when the one wishing to be healed, though sincere, remains unhealed, as you call this distortion, you may consider pre-incarnative choices; and your more helpful aid to such an entity may be the suggestion that it meditate upon the affirmative uses of whatever limitations it might experience. We would also note that in these cases the indigo-ray workings are often of aid.

Other than these notes we do not wish to further comment upon your statement at this working.

73.20 **QUESTIONER** It seems to me that the primary thing of importance for those on the service-to-others path is the development of an attitude which I can only describe as vibration. This attitude would be developed through meditation, ritual, and a developing appreciation for the creation or Creator which results in a state of mind that can only by me be expressed as an increase in vibration or oneness with all. Could you expand and correct that statement?

RA I am Ra. We shall not correct this statement but shall expand upon it by suggesting that to those qualities you may add the living day by day, and moment by moment, for the true adept lives more and more as it is.

73.21 **QUESTIONER** Thank you. Could you tell me of the number of possible energy transfers between two or more mind/body/spirit complexes? Is it very large, or are there few [*inaudible*]?

RA I am Ra. The number is infinite, for is not each mind/body/spirit complex unique?

73.22 **QUESTIONER** Could you define this statement "energy transfer between two mind/body/spirit complexes?"

RA I am Ra. This will be the last full query of this working. This entity still has transferred energy available, but we find rapidly increasing distortions towards pain in the neck, the dorsal area, and the wrists and manual appendages.

The physical energy transfer may be done numerous ways.

We shall give two examples. Each begins with some sense of the self as Creator or in some way the magical personality being invoked. This may be consciously or unconsciously done. Firstly, that exercise of which we have spoken called the exercise of fire: this is, though physical energy transfer, not that which is deeply involved in the body complex combinations. Thusly the transfer is subtle and each transfer unique in what is offered and what is accepted. At this point we may note that this is the cause for the infinite array of possible energy transfers.

The second energy transfer of which we would speak is the sexual energy transfer. This takes place upon a non-magical level by all those entities which vibrate green ray active.

It is possible, as in the case of this instrument which dedicates itself to the service of the One Infinite Creator, to further refine this energy transfer. When the other-self also dedicates itself in service to the One Infinite Creator, the transfer is doubled. Then the amount of energy transferred is dependent only upon the amount of polarized sexual energy created and released. There are refinements from this point onward leading to the realm of the high sexual magic.

In the realm of the mental bodies there are variations of mental energy transferred. This is, again, dependent upon the knowledge sought and the knowledge offered. The most common mental energy transfer is that of the teacher and the pupil. The amount of energy is dependent upon the quality of this offering upon the part of the teacher as regards the purity of the desire to serve and the quality of information offered and, upon the part of the student, the purity of the desire to learn and the quality of the mind vibratory complex which receives knowledge.

Another form of mental energy transfer is that of the listener and the speaker. When the speaker is experiencing mental/emotional-complex distortions towards anguish, sorrow, or other mental pain, from what we have said before, you may perhaps garner knowledge of the variations possible in this transfer.

The spiritual energy transfers are at the heart of all energy transfers, as a knowledge of self and other-self as Creator is paramount, and this is spiritual work. The varieties of spiritual energy transfer include those things of which we have spoken this day as we spoke upon the subject of the adept.

Are there any brief queries before we leave this working?

73.23 **QUESTIONER** Only if there is anything we can do to improve the comfort of the instrument or the contact, and secondly, is there anything that you wish not published in today's session?

RA I am Ra. We call your attention to two items. Firstly, it is well that the candle which spirals 10° each working be never allowed to gutter, as this would cause imbalance in the alignment of the appurtenances in their protective role for this instrument. Secondly, we might suggest attention to the neck area so that the cushion upon which it is supported be more comfortable. This difficulty has abbreviated many workings.

We thank you, my friends, for your conscientiousness and your fastidiousness with regard to these appurtenances which, as our workings proceed, seems to be increasing. Secondly, your decisions are completely your own as to that material which you may wish published from this working.

I am Ra. I leave you glorying in the love and in the light of the One Infinite Creator. Go forth, then, rejoicing in the power and in the peace of the One Infinite Creator. Adonai.

SESSION 74

74.0 **RA** I am Ra. I greet you in the love and in the light of the One Infinite Creator. We communicate now.

74.1 **QUESTIONER** Could you first please give me the condition of the instrument?

RA I am Ra. It is as previously stated.

74.2 **QUESTIONER** Before I get to new material, last session there seems to have been a small error that I corrected then having to do with the statement, "no working comes from it but only through it." Was this an error in transmission? Or what caused this problem?

RA I am Ra. This instrument, while fully open to our narrow-band contact, at times experiences a sudden strengthening of the distortion which you call pain. This weakens the contact momentarily. This type of increased distortion has been occurring in this instrument's bodily complex with more frequency in the time period which you may term the previous fortnight. Although it is not normally a phenomenon which causes difficulties in transmission, it did so twice in the previous working. Both times it was necessary to correct or rectify the contact.

74.3 **QUESTIONER** Could you please describe the trance state as I am somewhat confused with respect to how, when in trance, pain can affect the instrument since I was of the opinion that there would be no feeling of pain of the bodily complex in the trance state?

RA I am Ra. This is correct. The instrument has no awareness of this or other sensations. However, we of Ra use the yellow-ray activated physical complex as a channel through which to speak. As the mind/body/spirit complex of the instrument leaves this physical shell in our keeping it is finely adjusted to our contact.

However, the distortion which you call pain, when sufficiently severe, mitigates against proper contact, and—when the increased distortion is violent—can cause the tuning of the channel to waver. This tuning must then be corrected which we may do as the instrument offers us this opportunity freely.

74.4 **QUESTIONER** In a previous session there was a question on the archetypical mind that was not fully answered. I would like to continue with the answer to that question. Could you please continue with that, or would it be necessary for me to read the entire question over again?

RA I am Ra. As a general practice it is well to vibrate the query at the same space/time as the answer is desired. However, in this case it is acceptable to us that a note be inserted at this point in your recording of these sound vibratory complexes referring to the location of the query in previous workings.[1]

The query, though thoughtful, is in some degree falling short of the realization of the nature of the archetypical mind. We may not teach/learn for any other to the extent that we become learn/teachers. Therefore, we shall make some general notations upon this interesting subject and allow the questioner to consider and further refine any queries.

The archetypical mind may be defined as that mind which is peculiar to the Logos of this planetary sphere. Thusly, unlike the great cosmic all-mind, it contains the material which it pleased the Logos to offer as refinements to the great cosmic beingness. The archetypical mind, then, is that which contains all facets which may affect mind or experience.

The Magician was named as a significant archetype. However, it was not recognized that this portion of the archetypical mind represents not a portion of the deep subconscious, but the conscious mind and, more especially, the will. The archetype called by some the High Priestess, then, is the corresponding intuitive, or subconscious faculty.

Let us observe the entity as it is in relationship to the archetypical mind. You may consider the possibilities of utilizing the correspondences between the mind/body/spirit in microcosm and the archetypical mind/body/spirit closely approaching the Creator.

For instance, in your ritual performed to purify this place you use the term *"Ve Geburah."* It is a correct assumption that this is a portion or aspect of the One Infinite Creator. However, there are various correspondences with the archetypical mind which may be more and

---

[1] This may be found in 67.28.

more refined by the adept. *"Ve Geburah"* is the correspondence of Michael, of Mars, of the positive, of maleness. *"Ve Gedulah"* has correspondences to Jupiter, to femaleness, to the negative, to that portion of the Tree of Life concerned with Auriel.

We could go forward with more and more refinements of these two entries into the archetypical mind. We could discuss color correspondences, relationships with other archetypes, and so forth. This is the work of the adept, not the teach/learner.

We may only suggest that there are systems of study which may address themselves to the aspects of the archetypical mind, and it is well to choose one and study carefully. It is more nearly well if the adept go beyond whatever has been written and make such correspondences that the archetype can be called upon at will.

[There is a 34-second pause between the end of this answer and the beginning of the next question.]

74.5   **QUESTIONER** I have a question here that I am going to answer and let you correct. I see that the disciplines of the personality feed the indigo-ray energy center and affect the power of the white magician by unblocking the lower energy centers and allowing for a free flow of the upward spiraling light to reach the indigo center. Is this correct?

RA I am Ra. No.

74.6   **QUESTIONER** Would you please correct me?

RA I am Ra. The indigo center is indeed most important for the work of the adept. However, it cannot, no matter how crystallized, correct to any extent whatsoever imbalances or blockages in other energy centers. They must needs be cleared seriatim from red upwards.[2]

74.7   **QUESTIONER** I'm not sure if I understand this. The question is, "How do disciplines of the personality feed the indigo-ray energy center and affect the power of the white magician?"[3] Does that question make sense?

---

[2] In this context, *seriatim* can be defined as "point by point, one after another in a series."

[3] The question asked in 74.5 and then clarified in 74.7 was the scribe's.

RA I am Ra. Yes.

74.8 **QUESTIONER** Would you answer it please?

RA I am Ra. We would be happy to answer this query. We understood the previous query as being of other import.

The indigo ray is the ray of the adept. A great deal of the answer you seek is in this sentence. There is an identification between the crystallization of that energy center and the improvement of the working of the mind/body/spirit as it begins to transcend space/time balancing and to enter the combined realms of space/time and time/space.

74.9 **QUESTIONER** Let me see if I have a wrong opinion here of the effect of disciplines of the personality. I was assuming that a discipline of the personality to, shall we say, have a balanced attitude toward a single fellow entity would properly clear and balance, to some extent, the orange-ray energy center. Is this correct?

RA I am Ra. We cannot say that you speak incorrectly but merely less-than-completely. The disciplined personality, when faced with an other-self, has all centers balanced according to its unique balance. Thusly the other-self looks in a mirror seeing itself.

74.10 **QUESTIONER** Now, the disciplines of the personality I see as the paramount work of any who have become consciously aware of the process of evolution. Am I correct on that statement?

RA I am Ra. Quite.

74.11 **QUESTIONER** Now, what I am trying to get at is how these disciplines affect the energy centers and the power, shall I say, of the white magician. Could you . . . will you tell me how that works?

RA I am Ra. The heart of the discipline of the personality is threefold:

One, know yourself.
Two, accept yourself.
Three, become the Creator.

The third step is that step which, when accomplished, renders one the most humble servant of all, transparent in personality and completely able to know and accept other-selves.

In relation to the pursuit of the magical working, the continuing discipline of the personality involves the adept in knowing itself, accepting itself, and thus clearing the path towards the great indigo gateway to the Creator. To become the Creator is to become all that there is. There is, then, no personality in the sense with which the adept begins its learn/teaching. As the consciousness of the indigo ray becomes more crystalline, more work may be done; more may be expressed from intelligent infinity.

74.12 **QUESTIONER** You stated that a working of service to others has the potential of alerting a great mass of light strength. Could you describe just exactly how this works and what the uses of this would be?

RA I am Ra. There are sound vibratory complexes which act much like the dialing of your telephone. When they are appropriately vibrated with accompanying will and concentration, it is as though many upon your metaphysical or inner planes received a telephone call. This call they answer by their attention to your working.

74.13 **QUESTIONER** There are many of these. The ones most obvious in our society are those used in the church rather than those used by the magical adept. What is the difference in the effect of those used, say, in the church, in our various churches, and those specifically magical incantations used by the adept?

RA I am Ra. If all in your churches were adepts consciously full of will, of seeking, of concentration, of conscious knowledge of the calling, there would be no difference. The efficacy of the calling is a function of the magical qualities of those who call; that is, their desire to seek the altered state of consciousness desired.

74.14 **QUESTIONER** In selecting a protective ritual we finally agreed upon the Banishing Ritual of the Lesser Pentagram. I assume that these sound vibratory complexes are the type you speak for the alerting of those on the inner planes. Is this correct?

RA I am Ra. This is correct.

74.15 **QUESTIONER** If we had constructed a ritual of our own with words used for the first time in the sequence of protection, what would have been the relative merit of this with respect to the ritual that we chose?

RA I am Ra. It would be less. In constructing ritual it is well to study the body of written work which is available, for names of positive, or service-to-others, power are available.

74.16 **QUESTIONER** I will make an analogy to the loudness of ringing of the telephone in using the ritual as the efficiency of the practitioners using the ritual. Now, I see several things affecting the efficiency of the ritual: first, the desire of the practitioners to serve, their ability to invoke the magical personality, their ability to visualize while performing the ritual. And let me ask you as to the relative importance of those items and how each may be intensified?

RA I am Ra. This query borders upon over-specificity. It is most important for the adept to feel its own growth as teach/learner.

We may only say that you correctly surmise the paramount import of the magical personality. This is a study in itself. With the appropriate emotional will, polarity, and purity, work may be done with or without proper sound vibration complexes. However, there is no need for the blunt instrument when the scalpel is available.

74.17 **QUESTIONER** I assume that the reason that the rituals that have been used previously are of effect is that these words have built a bias in consciousness of those who have worked in these areas so that those who are of the distortion of mind that we seek will respond to the imprint in consciousness of these series of words. Is this correct?

RA I am Ra. This is, to a great extent, correct. The exception is the sounding of some of what you call your Hebrew and some of what you call your Sanskrit vowels. These sound vibration complexes have power before time and space and represent configurations of light which built all that there is.

74.18 **QUESTIONER** Why do these sounds have this property?

RA I am Ra. The correspondence in vibratory complex is mathematical.

At this time we have enough transferred energy for one full query.

74.19 **QUESTIONER** How did the users of these sounds, Sanskrit and Hebrew, determine what these sounds were?

RA I am Ra. In the case of the Hebrew that entity known as Yahweh aided this knowledge through impression upon the material of genetic coding which became language, as you call it.

In the case of Sanskrit the sound vibrations are pure due to the lack of previous, what you call, alphabet, or letter-naming. Thus the sound vibration complexes seemed to fall into place as from the Logos. This was a more, shall we say, natural or unaided situation or process.

We would at this time make note of the incident in the previous working where our contact was incorrectly placed for a short period and was then corrected. In the exercise of the fire you may see the initial spiral clockwise from the green-ray energy center, through the shoulders and head, then through the elbows, then to the left hand. The channel had been corrected before the remainder of this answer was completed.

Is there a brief query at this time?

74.20 **QUESTIONER** Is there anything that we can do to make the instrument more comfortable or improve the contact?

RA I am Ra. All is well. The instrument continues in some pain, as you call this distortion. The neck area remains most distorted although the changes have been, to a small degree, helpful. The alignments are good.

We would leave you now, my friends, in the love and in the light of the One Infinite Creator. Go forth, then, glorying and rejoicing in the power and in the peace of the One Infinite Creator. Adonai.

75.0   **RA** I am Ra. I greet you in the love and in the light of the One Infinite Creator. We communicate now.

75.1   **QUESTIONER** Could you first please give me the condition of the instrument?

RA I am Ra. It is as previously stated with some slight lessening of the reserve of vital energy due to mental/emotional distortions regarding what you call the future.

75.2   **QUESTIONER** I felt that this session was advisable before the instrument has her hospital experience. She wished to ask a few questions, if possible, about those.

First, is there anything that the instrument or we might do to improve the hospital experience or to aid the instrument in any way with respect to this?

RA I am Ra. Yes. There are ways of aiding the mental/emotional state of this entity with the notation that this is so only for this entity or one of like distortions. There is also a general thing which may be accomplished to improve the location which is called the hospital.

The first aiding has to do with the vibration of the ritual with which this entity is most familiar and which this entity has long used to distort its perception of the One Infinite Creator. This is an helpful thing at any point in the diurnal period but is especially helpful as your sun body removes itself from your local sight.

The general improvement of the place of the performance of the ritual of the purification of the place is known. We may note that the distortion towards love, as you call this spiritual/emotional complex which is felt by each for this entity, will be of aid whether this is expressed or unmanifest, as there is no protection greater than love.

75.3   **QUESTIONER** Do you mean that it would be valuable to perform the Banishing Ritual of the Lesser Pentagram in the room that she will be occupying in the hospital?

RA I am Ra. This is correct.

75.4 **QUESTIONER** I was wondering about the operating room. That might be very difficult. Would it be helpful there?

RA I am Ra. This is correct. We may note that it is always helpful. Therefore, it is not easy to posit a query to which you would not receive the answer which we offer. This does not indicate that it is essential to purify a place. The power of visualization may aid in your support where you cannot intrude in your physical form.

75.5 **QUESTIONER** I see the way to do this as a visualization of the operating room and a visualization of the three of us performing the banishing ritual in the room as we perform it in another location. Is this the correct procedure?

RA I am Ra. This is one correct method of achieving your desired configuration.

75.6 **QUESTIONER** Is there a better method than that?

RA I am Ra. There are better methods for those more practiced. For this group, this method is well.

75.7 **QUESTIONER** I would assume those more practiced would leave their physical bodies and, in the other body, enter the room and practice the banishing ritual. Is this what you mean?

RA I am Ra. This is correct.

75.8 **QUESTIONER** The instrument would like to know if she can meditate in the hospital without someone holding her hand, and would this be a safe practice?

RA I am Ra. We might suggest that the instrument may pray with safety but only meditate with another entity's tactile protection.

75.9 **QUESTIONER** The instrument would like to know what she can do to improve the condition of her back, as she says it could be a problem for the operation.

RA I am Ra. As we scan the physical complex we find several factors contributing to one general distortion experienced by the instrument. Two of these distortions have been diagnosed; one has not; nor will the entity be willing to accept the chemicals sufficient to cause cessation of this distortion you call pain.

In general we may say that the sole modality addressing itself specifically to all three contributing distortions, which is not now being used, is that of the warmed water which is moved with gentle force repeatedly against the entire physical complex while the physical vehicle is seated. This would be of some aid, if practiced daily, after the exercise period.

75.10 **QUESTIONER** Did the exercise of the fire that was just performed before the session help the instrument?

RA I am Ra. There was some slight physical aid to the instrument. This will enlarge itself as the practitioner learns/teaches its healing art. Further, there is distortion in the mental/emotional complex which feeds the vital energy towards comfort due to support which tends to build up the level of vital energy as this entity is a sensitive instrument.

75.11 **QUESTIONER** Was the exercise of fire properly done?

RA I am Ra. The baton is well visualized. The conductor will learn to hear the entire score of the great music of its art.

75.12 **QUESTIONER** I assume that if this can be fully accomplished today that exercise would result in total healing of the distortions of the instrument to such an extent that operations would be unnecessary. Is this correct?

RA I am Ra. No.

75.13 **QUESTIONER** What else is necessary, the instrument's acceptance?

RA I am Ra. This is correct, the case with this instrument being delicate, since it must totally accept much which the limitations it now experiences cause to occur involuntarily. This is a pre-incarnative choice.

75.14 **QUESTIONER** The instrument would like to know why twice at the "Benedictus" portion of the music that she practices did she experience what she believes to be a psychic attack?[1]

---

[1] Jim writes: "In this question Don gives the impression by his question that this psychic greeting occurred in a rehearsal or 'practice' of J. S. Bach's 'Mass in B Minor.' However, I recall this occurring during a performance of this piece with the Louisville Bach Society. After 36 years I still have the memory of what I

RA I am Ra. This is not a minor query. We shall first remove the notations which are minor. In the vibrating, which you call singing, of the portion of what this instrument hallows as the Mass, which immediately precedes that which is the chink called the "Hosanna," there is an amount of physical exertion required that is exhausting to any entity. This portion of which we speak is termed the "Sanctus." We come now to the matter of interest.

When the entity Jehoshua[2] decided to return to the location called Jerusalem for the holy days of its people, it turned from work mixing love and wisdom and embraced martyrdom, which is the work of love without wisdom.

The "Hosanna," as it is termed, and the following "Benedictus," is that which is the written summation of what was shouted as Jehoshua came into the place of its martyrdom. The general acceptance of this shout—"Hosanna to the son of David! Hosanna in the highest! Blessed is he who comes in the name of the Lord!"—by that which is called the church has been a misstatement of occurrence which has been, perhaps, unfortunate, for it is more distorted than much of the so-called Mass.

There were two factions present to greet Jehoshua, firstly, a small group of those which hoped for an earthly king. However, Jehoshua rode upon an ass stating by its very demeanor that it was no earthly king, and wished no fight with Roman or Sadducee.

The greater number were those which had been instructed by rabbi and elder to make jest of this entity, for those of the hierarchy feared this entity who seemed to be one of them, giving respect to their laws, and then, in their eyes, betraying those time-honored laws and taking the people with it.

The chink, for this instrument, is this subtle situation which echoes down

thought after Carla told Don and me about the psychic greeting that she experienced while singing in the chorus. I thought to myself then that if I had wanted to help Carla while she was being psychically greeted, I would have to have jumped out of my balcony seat at the Louisville School of Music and landed on the stage in the middle of the performance. That is why I believe that this psychic greeting occurred during an actual performance and not in a 'practice' or rehearsal."

2   Ra refers to an entity, Jehoshua, who Ra previously identified as the biblical Jesus.

through your space/time. And, more than this, the place the "Hosanna" holds as the harbinger of that turning to martyrdom.

We may speak only generally here. The instrument did not experience the full force of the greeting which it correctly identified during the "Hosanna" due to the intense concentration necessary to vibrate its portion of that composition. However, the "Benedictus" in this particular rendition of these words is vibrated by one entity. Thus, the instrument relaxed its concentration and was immediately open to the fuller greeting.

75.15 **QUESTIONER** The chink then, as I understand it, was originally created by the decision of Jesus to take the path of martyrdom? Is this correct?

RA I am Ra. This is, in relation to this instrument, quite correct. It is aware of certain over-balances towards love, even to martyrdom but has not yet, to any significant degree, balanced these distortions. We do not imply that this course of unbridled compassion has any fault but affirm its perfection. It is an example of love which has served as beacon to many.

For those who seek further, the consequences of martyrdom must be considered, for in martyrdom lies the end of the opportunity, in the density of the martyr, to offer love and light. Each entity must seek its deepest path.

75.16 **QUESTIONER** Let me see if I understand, then, how the Orion group finds a chink in this distortion. The entity identifying, or having a distortion of any amount toward martyrdom is then open by its free will to the aid of the Orion group to make it a martyr. Am I correct?

RA I am Ra. You are correct only in the quite specialized position in which the instrument finds itself; that is, of being involved in and dedicated to work which is magical, or extremely polarized, in nature. This group entered this work with polarity but virtual innocence as to the magical nature of this polarity it is beginning to discover.

75.17 **QUESTIONER** How was the Orion entity able to act through this linkage of the "Hosanna?" Was this simply because of the mental distortion of the instrument at this period of time, because of that suggested by the music? Or was it a more physical, or more metaphysical link from the time of Christ?

RA I am Ra. Firstly, the latter supposition is false: this entity is not linked with the entity, Jehoshua. Secondly, there is a most unique circumstance. There is an entity which has attracted the attention of an Orion light being. This is extremely rare.

This entity has an intense devotion to the teachings and example of the one it calls Jesus. This entity then vibrates in song a most demanding version, called *The Mass in B Minor*, by Bach, of this exemplary votive complex of sound vibrations. The entity is consciously identifying with each part of this Mass. Only thusly was the chink made available.

As you can see, it is not an ordinary occurrence and would not have happened had any ingredient been left out: exhaustion, bias in belief complexes, attention from an Orion entity, and the metaphysical nature of that particular set of words.

75.18 QUESTIONER What was the Orion entity's objective with respect to the entity you spoke of who, in a demanding manner, sings the Mass?

RA I am Ra. The Orion entity wishes to remove the instrument.

75.19 QUESTIONER Is this a fourth- or a fifth-density entity?

RA I am Ra. This instrument is being greeted by a fifth-density entity which has lost some polarity due to its lack of dictatorship over the disposition of the instrument's mind/body/spirit or its yellow-ray activated physical complex.

75.20 QUESTIONER You are speaking of this other person now that is singing the Mass? This is correct?

RA I am Ra. No.

75.21 QUESTIONER I think there was a little miscommunication here. The other person who sings the Mass who helped in creating this chink you said was also greeted by an Orion entity, and my question was what density was that entity that greets the person who sings the Mass?

RA I am Ra. We did not speak of any entity but the instrument.

75.22 QUESTIONER OK. I misunderstood. I thought you were speaking of someone else in the singing group who had been the one you were speaking of [regarding] the identification with the singing. The entire time we were speaking, then, we were speaking only of the instrument, Carla? Is this correct?

RA I am Ra. This is correct.

75.23 **QUESTIONER** I am sorry for the confusion. Sometimes, as you say, sound vibration complexes are not very adequate, and I'm sorry.

You made the statement in a previous session that the true adept lives more and more as it is. Will you explain and expand upon that statement?

RA I am Ra. Each entity is the Creator. The entity, as it becomes more and more conscious of its self, gradually comes to the turning point at which it determines to seek either in service to others or in service to self. The seeker becomes the adept when it has balanced, with minimal adequacy, the energy centers red, orange, yellow, and blue, with the addition of the green for the positive, thus moving into indigo work.

The adept then begins to do less of the preliminary, or outer, work having to do with function, and begins to effect the inner work which has to do with being. As the adept becomes a more and more consciously crystallized entity it gradually manifests more and more of that which it always has been since before time: that is, the One Infinite Creator.

75.24 **QUESTIONER** The answer to this question probably has to do with our distorted view of time, but I see wanderers in this density who have come from fifth or sixth density— It seems to me that they should already be of a relatively high degree of adeptness and must follow a slightly or somewhat different path back to the adeptness that they previously had in a higher density and get as close to it as they can in third density. Is this correct?

RA I am Ra. Your query is less than perfectly focused. We shall address the subject in general.

There are many wanderers whom you may call adepts who do no conscious work in the present incarnation. It is a matter of attention. One may be a fine catcher of your game sphere, but if the eye is not turned as this sphere is tossed, then perchance it will pass the entity by. If it turned its eyes upon the sphere, catching would be easy.

In the case of wanderers which seek to recapitulate the degree of adeptness which each had acquired previous to this life experience, we may note that, even after the forgetting process has been penetrated, there is still the yellow-ray activated body which does not respond as does the adept which is of a green- or blue-ray activated body. Thusly, you may see the inevitability of frustrations and confusion due to the inherent difficulties of manipulating the finer forces of consciousness through the chemical apparatus of the yellow-ray activated body.

75.25   **QUESTIONER** You probably can't answer this, but are there any suggestions you could give with respect to the instrument's coming hospital experience that could be of benefit for her?

RA I am Ra. We may make one suggestion and leave the remainder with the Creator. It is well for each to realize its self as the Creator. Thusly each may support each including the support of self by humble love of self as Creator.

75.26   **QUESTIONER** You spoke in a previous session about certain Hebrew and Sanskrit sound vibratory complexes being powerful because they were mathematically related to that which was the creation. Could you expand on this understanding, please, as to how these are linked?

RA I am Ra. As we previously stated[3] the linkage is mathematical or that of the ratio. You may consider it musical. There are those whose mind complex activities would attempt to resolve this mathematical ratio, but at present the coloration of the intoned vowel is part of the vibration which cannot be accurately measured. However, it is equivalent to types of rotation of your primary material particles.

75.27   **QUESTIONER** If these sounds are precisely vibrated then what effect or use would they have with respect to the purposes of the adept?

RA I am Ra. You may consider the concept of sympathetic resonance. When certain sounds are correctly vibrated, the creation sings.

75.28   **QUESTIONER** Would these sounds, then, be of a musical nature in that there would be a musical arrangement of many different sound vibrations, or would this apply to just one single note? Or which would it apply more to?

---

3   Previously stated in 74.17–19.

RA I am Ra. This query is not easily answered. In some cases only the intoned vowel has effect. In other cases, most notably Sanskrit combinations, the selection of harmonic intervals is also of resonant nature.

75.29 **QUESTIONER** Then would the adept use this resonant quality to become more one with the creation and, therefore, attain his objective in that way?

RA I am Ra. It would, perhaps, be more accurate to state that in this circumstance the creation becomes more and more contained within the practitioner. The balance of your query is correct.

75.30 **QUESTIONER** Could you tell me the musical name of the notes to be intoned that are of this quality?

RA I am Ra. We may not.

75.31 **QUESTIONER** I didn't think that you could, but I thought it wouldn't hurt to ask.

Then I assume that these must be sought out and determined by empirical observation of their effect by the seeker. Is this correct?

RA I am Ra. This is partially correct. As your seeking continues, there will be added to empirical data that acuity of sensibility which continued working in the ways of the adept offers.

75.32 **QUESTIONER** The three aspects of the magical personality are stated to be power, love, and wisdom. Is this correct, and are these the only primary aspects of the magical personality?

RA I am Ra. The three aspects of the magical personality—power, love, and wisdom—are so called in order that attention be paid to each aspect in developing the basic tool of the adept: that is, its self.

It is by no means a personality of three aspects. It is a being of unity, being of sixth density, and equivalent to what you call your higher self and, at the same time, is a personality enormously rich in variety of experience and subtlety of emotion.

The three aspects are given that the neophyte not abuse the tools of its trade but, rather, approach those tools balanced in the center of love and wisdom and thus seeking power in order to serve.

75.33 **QUESTIONER** You mentioned in an earlier session that the hair was an antenna. Could you expand on that statement as to how that works?

RA I am Ra. It is difficult to so do due to the metaphysical nature of this antenna-effect. Your physics are concerned with measurements in your physical complex of experience. The metaphysical nature of the contact of those in time/space is such that the hair, as it has significant length, becomes as a type of electrical battery which stays charged and tuned and is then able to aid contact, even when there are small anomalies in the contact.

75.34 **QUESTIONER** Well, is there an optimum length of hair for this aid?

RA I am Ra. There is no outer limit on length but the, shall we say, inner limit is approximately four to four-and-one-half inches depending upon the strength of the contact and the nature of the instrument.

75.35 **QUESTIONER** May anyone in third density accomplish some degree of healing if they have the proper will, desire, and polarity, or is there a minimal balance of the energy centers of the healer that is also necessary?

RA I am Ra. Any entity may, at any time, instantaneously clear and balance its energy centers. Thus in many cases those normally quite blocked, weakened, and distorted may, through love and strength of will, become healers momentarily. To be a healer by nature one must indeed train its self in the disciplines of the personality.

75.36 **QUESTIONER** How does the use of the magical ritual of invoking the magical personality aid the mind/body/spirit complex totality? Could you expand on the answer you gave in the last session with respect to that?

RA I am Ra. When the magical personality is properly and efficaciously invoked, the self has invoked its higher self. Thus a bridge betwixt space/time and time/space is made, and the sixth-density magical personality experiences directly the third-density catalyst for the duration of the working.

It is most central to deliberately take off the magical personality after the working in order that the higher self resume its appropriate configuration as analog to the space/time mind/body/spirit.

75.37 **QUESTIONER** Then you are saying that the act, the signal, or the key for the invoking of the magical personality—which is the putting something on, or a gesture—should be as carefully . . . you should as carefully take that something off or reverse the gesture, perhaps at the end of the invocation. Is this correct?

RA I am Ra. This is correct. It should be fastidiously accomplished either in mind or by gesture as well, if this is of significant aid.

75.38 QUESTIONER Now the invocation of the magical personality is not necessarily effective for the neophyte. Is there a point at which there is a definite quantum change, and that magical personality does then reside? Or can it be done in small degrees, or percentages, of magical personality as the neophyte becomes more adept?

RA I am Ra. The latter is correct.

75.39 QUESTIONER Then is it correct that a good sequence for developing the invocation of the magical personality are alternate meditations, first on power, then a meditation on love, and then a meditation on wisdom, and to continue cycling that way? Is that an appropriate technique?

RA I am Ra. This is indeed an appropriate technique. In this particular group there is an additional aid in that each entity manifests one of these qualities in a manner which approaches the archetype. Thusly visualization may be personalized and much love and support within the group generated.

[There is a 48-second pause between the end of this answer and the beginning of the next question.]

75.40 QUESTIONER Is the exercise of fire the best for the instrument, or is there anything better that we could do other than, of course, the things that you have already suggested to aid the instrument?

RA I am Ra. Continue as you are at present. We cannot speak of the future as we may then affect it, but there is a great probability/possibility if you follow the path which you now tread that more efficacious methods for the entire group will be established.

This instrument begins to show rapid distortion towards increase of pain. We, therefore, would offer time for any brief queries before we leave this working.

75.41 **QUESTIONER** Is there anything that we can do to make the instrument more comfortable or improve the contact?

RA I am Ra. You are conscientious. The alignments are well.

I am Ra. I leave you, my friends, in the love and the light of the One Infinite Creator. Go forth, therefore, rejoicing in the power and peace of the One Infinite Creator. Adonai.

SESSION 76

76.0   **RA** I am Ra. I greet you in the love and in the light of the One Infinite Creator. We communicate now.

76.1   **QUESTIONER** Could you first please give me an indication of the condition of the instrument?

RA I am Ra. This instrument is in a state of physical complex bankruptcy which has existed for some of the measure you call time. The vital energies are normal with a strong spiritual complex counterpart and will lending substance to the mind/body/spirit complex energy levels.

76.2   **QUESTIONER** Will our continued communication with Ra be deleterious to the physical energies of the instrument?

RA I am Ra. We may answer in two modes. Firstly, if the instrument were thusly dedicated to this use with no transfer of energy of physical complex nature, it would begin to call upon the vital energy itself, and this, done in any substantive measure, is actively deleterious to a mind/body/spirit complex if that complex wishes further experience in the illusion which it now distorts.

Secondly, if care is taken, firstly, to monitor the outer parameters of the instrument, then to transfer physical energy by sexual transfer, by magical protection, and, lastly, by the energetic displacements of thought-forms energizing the instrument during contact, there is no difficulty in that there is no worsening of the instrument's mind/body/spirit-complex distortions of strength/weakness.

It is to be noted that the instrument, by dedicating itself to this service, attracts greetings of which you are aware. These are inconvenient but, with care taken, need not be lastingly deleterious either to the instrument or the contact.

76.3   **QUESTIONER** Of the three things you mentioned that we could do for the instrument's benefit, would you clarify the last one? I didn't quite understand that.

RA I am Ra. As the entity which you are allows its being to empathize with another being, so then it may choose to share with the other-self those energies which may be salubrious to the other-self.[1] The mechanism of these energy transfers is the thought or, more precisely, the thought-form, for any thought is a form, or symbol, or thing that is an object seen in time/space reference.

76.4   QUESTIONER Has our use of the Banishing Ritual of the Lesser Pentagram been of any value, and what is its effect?

RA I am Ra. This group's use of the Banishing Ritual of the Lesser Pentagram has been increasingly efficacious. Its effect is purification, cleansing, and protection of the place of working.

The efficacy of this ritual is only beginning to be, shall we say, at the lower limits of the truly magical. In doing the working, those aspiring to adepthood have done the equivalent of beginning the schoolwork, many grades ahead.

For the intelligent student this is not to be discouraged; rather to be encouraged is the homework, the reading, the writing, the arithmetic, as you might metaphorically call the elementary steps towards the study of being.

It is the being that informs the working, not the working that informs the being. Therefore, we may leave you to the work you have begun.

76.5   QUESTIONER Would it be beneficial for us to perform the banishing ritual more in this room?

RA I am Ra. It is beneficial to regularly work in this place.

76.6   QUESTIONER Sorry we have had such a long delay between the last session and this one. It couldn't be helped, I guess. Could you please tell me the origin of the tarot?

RA I am Ra. The origin of this system of study and divination is twofold: firstly, there is that influence which, coming in a distorted fashion from those who were priests attempting to teach the Law of One in Egypt, gave form to the understanding, if you will pardon the misnomer, which they

---

1   In this context, *salubrious* can be defined as "favorable to health or well-being."

had received. These forms were then made a regular portion of the learn/teachings of an initiate.

The second influence is that of those entities in the lands you call Ur, Chaldea, and Mesopotamia who, from old, had received the, shall we say, data for which they called having to do with the heavens.

Thusly we find two methods of divination being melded into one with uneven results; the, as you call it, astrology and the form being combined to suggest what you might call the correspondences which are typical of the distortions you may see as attempts to view archetypes.

76.7 **QUESTIONER** Then am I correct in assuming that the priests in Egypt, in attempting to convert knowledge that they had received initially from Ra into understandable symbology, constructed and initiated the concept of the tarot? Is this correct?

RA I am Ra. This is correct with the addition of the Sumerian influence.

76.8 **QUESTIONER** Were Ra's teachings focusing on the archetypes for this Logos and the methods of achieving a very close approach to the archetypical configuration? Is this correct?

RA I am Ra. This is correct without being true. We of Ra are humble messengers of the Law of One. We seek to teach/learn this single law.

During the space/time of the Egyptian teach/learning we worked to bring the mind complex, the body complex, and the spirit complex into an initiated state in which the entity could contact intelligent energy and so become teach/learner itself that healing and the fruits of study could be offered to all.

The study of the roots of mind is a portion of the vivification of the mind complex and, as we have noted, the thorough study of the portion of the roots of mind called archetypical is an interesting and necessary portion of the process as a whole.

76.9 **QUESTIONER** Is there, in Ra's opinion, any present-day value for the reuse of the tarot as an aid in the evolutionary process?

RA I am Ra. We shall repeat information.[2] It is appropriate to study one form of constructed and organized distortion of the archetypical mind in depth in order to arrive at the position of being able to become and to experience archetypes at will. You have three basic choices:

You may choose astrology—the twelve signs, as you call these portions of your planet's energy web, and what has been called the ten planets.

You may choose the tarot with its twenty-two so-called Major Arcana.

You may choose the study of the so-called Tree of Life with its ten Sephiroth and the twenty-two relationships between the stations.

It is well to investigate each discipline, not as a dilettante, but as one who seeks the touchstone, one who wishes to feel the pull of the magnet. One of these studies will be more attractive to the seeker. Let the seeker then investigate the archetypical mind using, basically, one of these three disciplines.

After a period of study, the discipline mastered sufficiently, the seeker may then complete the more important step: that is, the moving beyond the written in order to express in an unique fashion its understanding, if you may again pardon the noun, of the archetypical mind.

76.10 **QUESTIONER** Would I be correct in saying that our local Logos, in acting as co-Creator, distorted to some extent, for the purposes of experience, that which we experience here? And that the archetypes of this particular Logos are somewhat unique with respect to the rest of the creation—but are, of course, related to the all in that they are part of it, but are, I can only say, a unique part—and that the systems of study that we have just talked about would not translate quickly or easily in other parts of the creation. This is a very difficult question to state. Could you clear that up for me?

RA I am Ra. We may draw from the welter of statement which you offer the question we believe you ask.[3] Please re-question if we have mistaken your query.

The archetypical mind is that mind which is peculiar to the Logos under

---

[2] Originally given in 74.4.

[3] In this context, *welter* can be defined as "a confused mass or jumble."

which influence you are at this space/time distorting your experiences. There is no other Logos the archetypical mind of which would be the same, any more than the stars would appear the same from another planet in another galaxy. You may correctly infer that the closer Logoi are indeed closer in archetypes.

76.11 **QUESTIONER** Then, since Ra evolved initially on Venus, Ra is of the same archetypical origin as that which we experience here. Is this correct?

RA I am Ra. This is correct.

76.12 **QUESTIONER** But I am assuming that the concepts of the tarot and the magical concepts of the Tree of Life, etc., were not in use by Ra. I suspect, possibly, some form of astrology was a previous Ra concept. This is just a guess. Am I correct?

RA I am Ra. To express Ra's methods of study of the archetypical mind under the system of distortions which we enjoyed would be to skew your own judgment of that which is appropriate for the system of distortions forming the conditions in which you learn/teach. Therefore, we must invoke the Law of Confusion.

76.13 **QUESTIONER** I'm going to ask some questions now that may be a little off-center of what we are trying to do. I'm not sure because I'm trying to, with these questions, unscramble something that I consider to be very basic to what we are doing. Please forgive my lack of ability in questioning since this is a difficult concept for me.

Could you give me an idea of the length of the first and second density that occurred for this planet?

RA I am Ra. There is no method of estimation of the time/space before timelessness gave way in your first density. To the beginnings of your time, the measurement would be vast, and yet this vastness is meaningless. Upon the entry into the constructed space/time your first density spanned a bridge of space/time and time/space of, perhaps, two billion of your years.

Second density is more easily estimated and represents your longest density in terms of the span of space/time. We may estimate that time as approximately 4.6 billion years. These approximations are exceedingly rough due to the somewhat uneven development which is characteristic of creations which are built upon the foundation stone of Free Will.

76.14   QUESTIONER Did you state that second density was 4.6 billion? B, b-i-l? Is that correct?

RA   I am Ra. This is correct.

76.15   QUESTIONER Then we have a third density that is, comparatively speaking, the twinkling of an eye, the snap of a finger in time compared to the others. Why does the third density cycle so extremely rapidly compared to first and second?

RA   I am Ra. The third density is a choice.

76.16   QUESTIONER Third density, then, it appears, is, compared to the rest of the densities—all of them—nothing but a uniquely short period of what we consider to be time and is then for the purpose of this choice.

Is this correct?

RA   I am Ra. This is precisely correct. The prelude to choice must encompass the laying of the foundation, the establishment of the illusion and the viability of that which can be made spiritually viable. The remainder of the densities is continuous refining of the choice. This also is greatly lengthened, as you would use the term.

The choice is, as you put it, the work of a moment, but is the axis upon which the creation turns.

76.17   QUESTIONER Is this third-density choice the same throughout all of the creation of which you are aware?

RA   I am Ra. We are aware of creations in which third density is lengthier and more space/time is given to the choosing. However, the proportions remain the same, the dimensions all being somewhat etiolated and weakened by the Logos to have a variant experience of the Creator. [4] This creation is seen by us to be quite vivid.

76.18   QUESTIONER I didn't understand what you meant by "seen to you as being quite vivid." What do you mean?

---

4   In this context, *etiolated* can be defined as "weakened; no longer at full strength" or "made pale or thin."

RA I am Ra. This creation is somewhat more condensed by its Logos than some other Logoi have chosen. Thus each experience of the Creator by the Creator in this system of distortions is, relatively speaking, more bright or, as we said, vivid.

76.19 QUESTIONER I am assuming that on entering into third density, for this planet, disease did not exist in any form. Is this correct?

RA I am Ra. This is incorrect.

76.20 QUESTIONER What was the form of disease, and why did this exist at beginning third density?

RA I am Ra. Firstly, that which you speak of as disease is a functional portion of the body complex which offers the body complex the opportunity to cease viability. This is a desirable body complex function.

The second portion of the answer has to do with second-density other-selves of a microscopic, as you would call it, size, which have in some forms long-existed, and perform their service by aiding the physical body complex in its function of ceasing viability at the appropriate space/time.

76.21 QUESTIONER What I am trying to understand is the difference between the plan of the Logos for these second-density entities and the generation of what I would guess to be a more-or-less runaway array of feedback to create various physical problems that act as catalyst in our present third-density condition. Could you give me an indication of that; of whether my thinking is anywhere near right on that?

RA I am Ra. This instrument's physical body complex is becoming more distorted towards pain. We shall, therefore, speak to this subject as our last full query of this working.

Your query contains some internal confusion which causes the answer to be, perhaps, more general than desired. We invite refinements of the query.

The Logos planned for entities of mind/body/spirit complex to gain experience until the amount of experience was sufficient for an incarnation. This varied only slightly from second-density entities whose mind/body complexes existed for the purpose of experiencing growth and seeking consciousness.

As the third density upon your planet proceeded, as has been discussed, the need for the physical body complex to cease became more rapidly approached due to intensified, and more rapidly gained, catalyst. This catalyst was not being properly assimilated. Therefore, the, shall we say, lifetimes needed to be shorter that learning might continue to occur with the proper rhythm and increment. Thus more and more opportunities have been offered, as your density has progressed, for disease.

May we ask if there are further brief queries before we close?

76.22 **QUESTIONER** I had one that is totally, possibly, of no value. You don't have to expand on it, but there is a crystal skull in the possession of a woman near Toronto that may be of some value in investigating these communications with Ra since I think, possibly, this had some origin from Ra. Can you tell me anything about that?

And then, finally, is there anything that we could do to improve the contact or to make the instrument more comfortable?

RA I am Ra. Although your query is one which uncovers interesting material we cannot answer due to the potential an answer may have for affecting your actions.

The appurtenances are carefully placed and requisite care taken. We are appreciative. All is well.

I am Ra. I leave you, my friends, in the love and the light of the One Infinite Creator. Go forth, therefore, glorying and rejoicing in the power and in the peace of the One Infinite Creator. Adonai.

SESSION 77

77.0 **RA** I am Ra. I greet you in the love and in the light of the One Infinite Creator. We communicate now.

77.1 **QUESTIONER** Could you first please give me an indication of the condition of the instrument?

RA I am Ra. It is as previously stated.

77.2 **QUESTIONER** Was the instrument under attack just prior to this session?

RA I am Ra. This is correct.

77.3 **QUESTIONER** Is there anything that we could do to help protect the instrument from these attacks prior to the session?

RA I am Ra. This is correct.

77.4 **QUESTIONER** What could we do?

RA I am Ra. Your group could refrain from continuing this contact.

77.5 **QUESTIONER** Is that the only thing we could do?

RA I am Ra. That is the only thing you could do which you are not already attempting with a whole heart.

77.6 **QUESTIONER** I have three questions that the instrument asked me to ask that I'll get out of the way first. She wants to know if the preparation for her hospital experience could be improved for the next experience.

RA I am Ra. All was done well with one exception. The instrument was instructed to spend space/time contemplating itself as the Creator. This, done in a more determined fashion, would be beneficial at times when the mind complex is weakened by severe assaults upon the distortions of the body complex towards pain. There is no necessity for negative thought-forms, regardless of pain distortions.

The elimination of such creates the lack of possibility for negative elementals, and other negative entities, to use these thought-forms to create the worsening of the mind complex deviation from the normal distortions of cheerfulness/anxiety.

77.7   **QUESTIONER** The instrument would also like to know if the, what we call, tuning could be improved during times when we do not communicate with Ra, for that communication.

RA I am Ra. That which has been stated in regard to the latter question will suffice to point the way for the present query.

77.8   **QUESTIONER** Finally, she wishes to know why several days ago her heart rate went up to 115 per minute, and then she had extreme pain in her stomach. "Was that an Orion greeting?" it says.[1]

RA I am Ra. Although this experience was energized by the Orion group, the events mentioned, as well as others more serious, were proximally caused by the ingestion of certain foodstuffs in what you call your tablet form.

77.9   **QUESTIONER** Can you tell me what these tablets were, specifically?

RA I am Ra. We examine this query for the Law of Confusion and find ourselves close to the boundary, but acceptably so.

The substance which caused the bodily reaction of the heartbeat was called Pituitone by those which manufacture it. That which caused the difficulty which seemed to be cramping of the lower abdominal musculature, but was in fact more organic in nature, was a substance called Spleentone.

This instrument has a physical body complex of complicated balances which afford it physical existence. Were the view taken that certain functions and chemicals found in the healthy, as you call it, body complex are lacking in this one, and, therefore, simply must be replenished, the intake of the many substances which this instrument began would be appropriate. However, this particular physical vehicle has, for approximately twenty-five of your years, been vital due to the spirit, the mind, and the will being harmoniously dedicated to fulfilling the service it chose to offer.

---

[1]   Don is reading Carla's questions.

Therefore, physical healing techniques are inappropriate whereas mental and spiritual healing techniques are beneficial.

77.10 **QUESTIONER** Is there any technique which we could do that we have not been doing that would be beneficial for the instrument in this case?

RA I am Ra. We might suggest, without facetiousness, two. Firstly, let the instrument remove the possibility of further ingestion of this group of foodstuffs.

Secondly, each of the group may become aware of the will to a greater extent. We cannot instruct upon this but merely indicate, as we have previously,[2] that it is a vital key to the evolution of the mind/body/spirit complex.

77.11 **QUESTIONER** Thank you. I would like to go back to the plan of this Logos for Its creation and examine the philosophical basis that is the foundation for what was created in this local creation and the philosophy of the plan for experience. I am assuming that I am correct in stating that the foundation for this, as we have stated many times before, is the First Distortion. After that, what was the plan in a philosophical sense?

RA I am Ra. We cannot reply due to a needed portion of your query which has been omitted; that is, do we speak of this particular Logos?

77.12 **QUESTIONER** That is correct. I am asking with respect to this particular sub-Logos, our sun, in creating the experience of its planetary system and those sub-Logoi of it.

RA I am Ra. This query has substance. We shall begin by turning to an observation of a series of concept complexes of which you are familiar as the tarot.

The philosophy was to create a foundation, first of mind, then of body, and then of spiritual complex. Those concept complexes you call the tarot lie, then, in three groups of seven: the mind cycle, one through seven; the physical complex cycle, eight through fourteen; the spiritual complex cycle, fifteen through twenty-one. The last concept complex may best be termed The Choice.

---

[2] Indicated previously in 28.14, 41.18, 43.8, 52.7, 52.2, and 54.29.

Upon the foundation of transformation of each complex, with free will guided by the root concepts offered in these cycles, the Logos offered this density the basic architecture of a building and constructing and synthesizing of data culminating in The Choice.

77.13   **QUESTIONER** Then for me to condense your statement, I see it meaning that there are seven basic philosophical foundations for mental experience, seven for bodily, seven for spiritual, and that these produce the polarization that we experience some time during the third-density cycle. This may be very poorly stated on my part. Am I close to correct?

RA I am Ra. You are correct in that you perceive the content of our prior statement with accuracy. You are incorrect in that you have no mention of the, shall we say, location of all of these concept complexes; that is, they exist within the roots of the mind, and it is from this resource that their guiding influence and leitmotifs may be traced.[3] You may further note that each foundation is, itself, not single but a complex of concepts.

Furthermore, there are relationships betwixt mind, body, and spirit of the same location in octave—for instance, one, eight, fifteen—and relationships within each octave which are helpful in the pursuit of The Choice by the mind/body/spirit complex.

The Logos under which these foundations stand is one of free will. Thusly the foundations may be seen to have unique facets and relationships for each mind/body/spirit complex. Only twenty-two, The Choice, is relatively fixed and single.

77.14   **QUESTIONER** I am probably having a problem with the concept of time since it appears that the Logos was aware of the polarization choice. It seems that this choice for polarization at the end of third density is an important philosophical plan for the experience past third density. Am I correct in assuming that this process is a process to create the proper, or the desired, experience that will take place in the creation after third density is complete?

RA I am Ra. These philosophical foundations are those of third density.

---

3   In this context, *leitmotif* can be defined as "an element that is frequently repeated in a work and often serves as a guiding or central theme or element within the work."

Above this density there remains the recognition of the architecture of the Logos but without the veils which are so integral a part of the process of making the choice in third density.

77.15 **QUESTIONER** The specific question that I had was that it seems to me that the choice was planned to create intense polarization past third density so that experience would be intense past third density. Is this correct?

RA I am Ra. Given that our interpretation of your sound vibration complexes is appropriate, this is incorrect. The intensity of fourth density is that of the refining of the rough-hewn sculpture. This is, indeed, in its own way, quite intense, causing the mind/body/spirit complex to move ever inward and onward in its quest for fuller expression.

However, in third density the statue is forged in the fire. This is a type of intensity which is not the property of fourth, fifth, sixth, or seventh densities.

77.16 **QUESTIONER** What I am really attempting to understand, since all of these twenty-one philosophical bases result in the twenty-second, which is The Choice, is why this choice is so important; why the Logos, it seems, puts so much emphasis on this choice; and what function that choice of polarity is, precisely, in the evolution or the experience of that which is created by the Logos?

RA I am Ra. The polarization, or choosing, of each mind/body/spirit is necessary for harvestability from third density. The higher densities do their work due to the polarity gained in this choice.

77.17 **QUESTIONER** Now, would it be possible for this work of our density to be performed if all of the sub-Logoi chose the same polarity in any particular expression or evolution of a Logos? Let us make the assumption that our sun created nothing but, through the First Distortion, there was no product except positive polarity. Would work then be done in fourth density and higher as a function only of this positive polarization evolving from our original creation of sub-Logoi?

RA I am Ra. Elements of this query illustrate the reason I was unable to answer your previous question without knowledge of the Logos involved.

To turn to your question, there were Logoi which chose to set the plan for the activation of mind/body/spirit complexes through each true-color body without recourse to the prior application of free will. It is, to our knowledge, only in an absence of free will that the conditions of which you speak obtain. In such a procession of densities you find an extraordinarily long, as you measure time, third density; likewise, fourth density. Then, as the entities begin to see the Creator, there is a very rapid, as you measure time, procession towards the eighth density. This is due to the fact that one who knows not, cares not.

Let us illustrate by observing the relative harmony and unchanging quality of existence in one of your, as you call it, primitive tribes. The entities have the concepts of lawful and taboo, but the law is inexorable and all events occur as predestined. There is no concept of right and wrong, good or bad. It is a culture in monochrome. In this context you may see the one you call Lucifer as the true light-bringer in that the knowledge of good and evil both precipitated the mind/body/spirits of this Logos from the Edenic conditions of constant contentment but also provided the impetus to move, to work, and to learn.

Those Logoi whose creations have been set up without free will have not, in the feeling of those Logoi, given the Creator the quality and variety of experience of Itself as have those Logoi which have incorporated free will as paramount. Thusly you find those Logoi moving through the timeless states at what you would see as a later space/time to choose the free will character when elucidating the foundations of each Logos.

77.18   **QUESTIONER** I guess, under the First Distortion, it was the free will of the Logos to choose to evolve without free will. Is this correct?

RA I am Ra. This is correct.

77.19   **QUESTIONER** Do the Logoi that choose this type of evolution choose both the service-to-self and the service-to-others path for different Logoi, or do they choose just one of the paths?

RA I am Ra. Those, what you would call, early Logoi which chose lack-of-free-will foundations, to all extents with no exceptions founded Logoi of the service-to-others path. The, shall we say, saga of polarity, its consequences and limits, were unimagined until experienced.

77.20   **QUESTIONER** In other words you are saying that originally the Logoi that did not choose this free will path did not choose it simply because they had not conceived of it. And later Logoi, extending the First Distortion farther down through their evolution, experienced it as an outcropping or growth from that extension of the First Distortion. Am I correct in saying that?

RA I am Ra. Yes.

77.21 **QUESTIONER** Then did this particular Logos that we experience plan for this polarity and know all about it prior to its plan? That I suspect is what happened.

RA I am Ra. This is quite correct.

77.22 **QUESTIONER** In that case, you would have, as a Logos, you would have the advantage of selecting the form of acceleration, I might say, of spiritual evolution by planning for what we call the major archetypical philosophical foundation and planning these as a function of the polarity that would be gained in third density. Is this correct?

RA I am Ra. This is exquisitely correct.

77.23 **QUESTIONER** In that case, it seems that a thorough knowledge of the precise nature of these philosophical foundations would be of primary importance to the study of evolution of mind, body, and spirit, and I would like to carefully go through each of the basic twenty-one, starting with the mind, if this is agreeable with Ra.

RA I am Ra. This is agreeable with two requests which must be made.

Firstly, that an attempt be made to state the student's grasp of each archetype. We may then comment. We cannot teach/learn to the extent of learn/teaching.

Secondly, we request that it be constantly kept before the mind, as the candle before the eye, that each mind/body/spirit complex shall, and should, and indeed must perceive each archetype, if you use this convenient term, in its own way.

Therefore, you may see that precision is not the goal; rather, quality of general concept complex perception is the goal.

77.24 **QUESTIONER** Now, there are several general concepts that I would like to be sure that we have clear before going into this process, and I will certainly adhere to the requests that you have just stated.

When our Logos designed this particular evolution of experience It decided to use the system of which we spoke creating, or allowing for, polarization through total free will. How is this different from the Logos that does not do this? I see the Logos creating the possibility of increase in vibration through the densities.

Let me ask first: How are the densities provided for and set up by the Logos, if you can answer this?

RA I am Ra. This shall be the last full query of this working. The psychic attack upon this instrument has, shall we say, left scars which must be tended, in our own opinion, in order to maintain the instrument.

Let us observe your second density. Many come more rapidly to third density than others not because of an innate efficiency of catalysis but because of unusual opportunities for investment. In just such a way those of fourth density may invest third, those of fifth density may invest fourth.

When fifth density has been obtained the process takes upon itself a momentum based upon the characteristics of wisdom when applied to circumstance. The Logos Itself, then, in these instances provides investment opportunities, if you wish to use that term.

May we enquire if there are any brief queries at this space/time?

77.25 **QUESTIONER** Is there anything that we can do after this contact to increase the instrument's comfort as related to the psychic attack, or is there anything we can do to make the instrument more comfortable or improve the contact in this present situation?

RA I am Ra. The faculties of healing which each has commenced energizing may be used. The entity may be encouraged to remain motionless for a period. As it will not appreciate this, we suggest the proper discussion.

The physical appurtenance called the censer was just a degree off, this having no deeper meaning. We do ask, for reasons having to do with the physical comfort of the instrument, that you continue in your careful efforts at alignment. You are conscientious. All is well.

We leave you, my friends, in the glorious love and light of the One Creator. Go forth, therefore, rejoicing in the power and in the peace of the One Infinite Creator. I am Ra. Adonai.

SESSION 78

78.0   **RA** I am Ra. I greet you in the love and in the light of the One Infinite Creator. We communicate now.

78.1   **QUESTIONER** Was there some problem with the ritual performed that it was necessary to perform it twice?

RA I am Ra. There was a misstep which created a momentary lapse of concentration. This was not well.

78.2   **QUESTIONER** What was the misstep?

RA I am Ra. It was a missed footing.

78.3   **QUESTIONER** Did this have any detrimental effect on the instrument?

RA I am Ra. Very little. The instrument felt the presence it has come to associate with cold and spoke. The instrument did the appropriate thing.

78.4   **QUESTIONER** Could you tell me the condition of the instrument?

RA I am Ra. The physical complex is as previously stated. There is some slight loss of vital energy. The basic complex distortions are similar to your previous asking.

78.5   **QUESTIONER** The instrument would like for me to ask if there is any problem with her kidneys?

RA I am Ra. This query is more complex than its brevity certifies. The physical complex renal system of this instrument is much damaged. The time/space equivalent which rules the body complex is without flaw.

There was a serious question, due to psychic attack, as to whether the spiritual healing of this system would endure. It did so but has the need to be re-enforced by affirmation of the ascendancy of the spiritual over the apparent or visible.

When this instrument began ingesting substances designed to heal in a physical sense, among other things the renal complex, this instrument was ceasing the affirmation of healing. Due to this, again, the healing was weakened. This is of some profound distortion, and it would be well for the instrument to absorb these concepts.

We ask your forgiveness for offering information which may abridge free will, but the dedication of the instrument is such that it would persevere regardless of its condition, if possible. Thusly we offer this information that it may persevere with a fuller distortion towards comfort.

78.6   QUESTIONER What was the experience that caused the healing of the time/space kidney?

RA I am Ra. This experience was the healing of self by self with the catalyst of the spiritual healer whom you call Pachita.

78.7   QUESTIONER Thank you. In utilizing the energetic displacements of thought-forms energizing the instrument during contact most efficiently, what specifically could we do?

RA I am Ra. Each of the support group has an excess of love and light to offer the instrument during the working. Already each sends to the instrument love, light, and thoughts of strength of the physical, mental, and spiritual configurations. These sendings are forms. You may refine these sendings until the fullest manifestations of love and light are sent into the energy web of this entity which functions as instrument. Your exact sending is, in order to be most potent, the creature of your own making.

78.8   QUESTIONER OK. Thank you. I am going to go back to an earlier time, if you could call it that, in the evolution to try to establish a very fundamental base for some of the concepts that seem to be the foundation of everything that we experience here, so that we can more fully examine the basis of our evolution.

I am guessing that in our Milky Way Galaxy (that is, the major galaxy with billions of stars that we find ourselves in) that the progress of evolution was from the center outward toward the rim, and that in the early evolution of this galaxy the First Distortion was not extended down past the sub-Logos simply because it was not thought of, or not conceived, and that this extension of the First Distortion, which created the polarization that we experience, was something that occurred at what we would call a later time, or as the evolution progressed outward from the center of the galaxy. Am I in any way correct with this statement?

RA I am Ra. You are correct.

78.9 **QUESTIONER** Now, we have the First, Second, and Third Distortions of Free Will, Love, and Light. Am I correct in assuming that the central core of this major galaxy began to form with the Third Distortion? That was the origin of our Milky Way Galaxy?

RA I am Ra. In the most basic or teleological sense you are incorrect as the One Infinite Creator is all that there is.[1] In an undistorted seed-form you are correct in seeing the first manifestation visible to the eye of the body complex which you inhabit as the Third Distortion, Light, or to use a technical term, limitless light.

78.10 **QUESTIONER** Now, I realize that we are on very difficult ground, you might say, for precise terminology here, since it is totally displaced from our system of coordinates for evaluation in our present system of language.

These early Logoi that formed in the center of the galaxy wished, I assume, to create a system of experience for the One Creator. Did they then start with no previous experience or information about how to do this? This is difficult to ask.

RA I am Ra. At the beginning of this creation or, as you may call it, octave, there were those things known which were the harvest of the preceding octave. About the preceding creation we know as little as we do of the octave to come. However, we are aware of those pieces of gathered concept which were the tools which the Creator had in the knowing of the self.

These tools were of two kinds.[2] Firstly, there was an awareness of the efficiency for experience of mind, body, and spirit. Secondly, there was an awareness of the most efficacious nature or, if you will, Significator of Mind, Body, and Spirit. Thirdly, there was the awareness of two aspects of mind, of body, and of spirit that the Significator could use to balance all catalyst. You may call these two the Matrix and the Potentiator.

---

[1] Teleology is the philosophical attempt to describe things in terms of their apparent purpose, directive principle, or goal.

[2] Ra mentions "two kinds" and then lists three. Over the years the scribe has joked that Ra could not count beyond one.

78.11   QUESTIONER Could you elaborate please on the nature and quality of the Matrix and the Potentiator?

RA I am Ra. In the mind complex the Matrix may be described as consciousness. It has been called the Magician. It is to be noted that, of itself, consciousness is unmoved. The Potentiator of consciousness is the unconscious. This encompasses a vast realm of potential in the mind.

In the body the Matrix may be seen as Balanced Working or Even Functioning. Note that here the Matrix is always active with no means of being inactive. The Potentiator of the body complex, then, may be called Wisdom, for it is only through judgment that the unceasing activities and proclivities of the body complex may be experienced in useful modes.

The Matrix of the Spirit is what you may call the Night of the Soul, or Primeval Darkness. Again we have that which is not capable of movement or work. The potential power of this extremely receptive Matrix is such that the Potentiator may be seen as Lightning. In your archetypical system called the tarot this has been refined into the concept complex of the Lightning Struck Tower. However, the original Potentiator was light in its sudden and fiery form; that is, the lightning itself.

78.12   QUESTIONER Would you elucidate with respect to the Significator you spoke of?

RA I am Ra. The original Significators may undifferentiatedly be termed the mind, the body, and the spirit.

78.13   QUESTIONER Then we have, at the beginning of this galactic evolution, an archetypical mind that is the product of the previous octave which this galaxy then uses and acts upon under the First Distortion of Free Will to evolve the total experience of this galaxy. Is this correct?

RA I am Ra. This is quite correct.

78.14   QUESTIONER But, in doing this, there was at the center of the galaxy the lack of knowledge, or the lack of concept of possibility of extending the First Distortion so as to allow for what we have experienced as polarity. Was there any concept of polarity carried through from the previous octave in the sense of service-to-others or service-to-self polarity?

RA I am Ra. There was polarity in the sense of the mover and the moved. There was no polarity in the sense of service to self and service to others.

78.15 **QUESTIONER** Then the first experiences, as you say, were in monochrome. Now, was the concept of the seven densities of vibration with the evolutionary process taking place in the discrete densities—was that carried through from the previous octave?

RA I am Ra. To the limits of our knowledge, which are narrow, the ways of the octave are without time; that is, there are seven densities in each creation infinitely.

78.16 **QUESTIONER** I am assuming that the central suns of our galaxy, in starting the evolutionary process in this galaxy, provided for, in their plans, the refinement of consciousness through the densities just as we experience it here. However, they did not conceive of the polarization of consciousness with respect to service to self and service to others. Is this correct, then?

RA I am Ra. This is correct.

78.17 **QUESTIONER** Why do the densities have the qualities that they have? You have named the densities with respect to their qualities, this density being that of . . . the next, the fourth density being that of love, etc. Can you tell me why these qualities exist in that form? Is it possible to answer this question at all?

RA I am Ra. It is possible.

78.18 **QUESTIONER** Would you please answer that?

RA I am Ra. The nature of the vibratory range peculiar to each quantum of the octave is such that the characteristics of it may be described with the same certainty with which you perceive a color with your optical apparatus if it is functioning properly.

78.19 **QUESTIONER** So the original, the first evolution then was planned by the Logos, but the First Distortion was not extended to the product. At some point this First Distortion was extended, and the first service-to-self polarity emerged. Is this correct, and if so could you tell me the history of this process and emergence?

RA I am Ra. As proem let me state that the Logoi always conceived of themselves as offering free will to the sub-Logoi in their care. The sub-Logoi had freedom to experience and experiment with consciousness, the experiences of the body, and the illumination of the spirit. That having been said, we shall speak to the point of your query.

The first Logos to instill what you now see as free will in the full sense in its sub-Logoi came to this creation due to contemplation in-depth of the concepts, or possibilities of conceptualizations, of what we have called the significators. The Logos posited the possibility of the mind, the body, and the spirit as being complex. In order for the significator to be what it is not, it then must be granted the free will of the Creator. This set in motion a quite lengthy, in your terms, series of Logoi improving or distilling this seed thought. The key was the significator becoming a complex.

78.20 QUESTIONER Then our particular Logos, when it created Its own particular creation, was at some point far down the evolutionary spiral of the experiment with the significator becoming what it was not or, in effect, creating the polarity that we strive for in third density and, therefore was, I am assuming, primarily concerned in the design of the archetypes, in designing them in such a way so as they would create the acceleration of this polarization. Is this in any way correct?

RA I am Ra. We would only comment briefly. It is generally correct. You may fruitfully view each Logos and its design as the Creator experiencing Itself.

The seed concept of the Significator being a complex introduces two things: firstly, the Creator against Creator in one sub-Logos in what you may call dynamic tension; secondly, the concept of free will, once having been made fuller by its extension into the sub-Logoi known as mind/body/spirit complexes, creates and re-creates and continues to create as a function of its very nature.

78.21 QUESTIONER You stated previously that The Choice that is made in this density, third density, is the axis upon which the creation turns.[3] Could you expand on your reason for making that statement?

RA I am Ra. This is a statement of the nature of creation as we speak to you.

---

3 Previously stated in 76.16.

78.22 **QUESTIONER** I did not understand that. Could you say that in a different way?

RA I am Ra. As you have noted, the creation of which your Logos is a part is a protean entity which grows and learns upon a macrocosmic scale.[4] The Logos is not a part of time. All that is learned from experience in an octave is, therefore, the harvest of that Logos and is, further, the nature of that Logos.

The original Logos' experience was, viewed in space/time, small; Its experience now, more.

Therefore, we say, as we now speak to you at this space/time, the nature of creation is as we have described. This does not deny the process by which this nature has been achieved but merely ratifies the product.

78.23 **QUESTIONER** After third density, in our experience, social memory complexes are polarized positively and negatively. Is the interaction between social memory complexes of opposite polarity equivalent, but on a magnified scale, to the interaction between mind/body/spirit complexes of opposite polarity? Is this how experience is gained as a function of polarity difference at the fourth and fifth densities?

RA I am Ra. No.

78.24 **QUESTIONER** This is a hard question just to ask, but what is the function or what is the value experientially of the formation of positive and negative social memory complexes, of the separation of the polarities at that point, rather than the allowing for the mixing of mind/body/spirit complexes of opposite polarity at the higher densities?

RA I am Ra. The purpose of polarity is to develop the potential to do work. This is the great characteristic of those, shall we say, experiments which have evolved since the concept of The Choice was appreciated. Work is done far more efficiently and with greater purity, intensity, and variety by the voluntary searching of mind/body/spirit complexes for the lessons of third and fourth densities.

---

[4] In this context, *protean* can be defined as "tending or able to change frequently or easily" or "able to do many different things; versatile."

The action of fifth density is, viewed in space/time, the same with or without polarity. However, viewed in time/space, the experiences of wisdom are greatly enlarged and deepened due, again, to the voluntary nature of polarized mind/body/spirit action.

78.25   **QUESTIONER** Then you are saying as a result of the polarization in consciousness that has occurred later in the galactic evolution, that the experiences are much more, shall I say, profound or deeper along the two paths. Are these experiences independent of the other path, or must there be action across the potentiated difference between the positive and negative polarity? Or is it possible to have this experience simply because of the single polarity? This is difficult to ask.

RA I am Ra. We would agree. We shall attempt to pluck the gist of your query from the surrounding verbiage.

The fourth and fifth densities are quite independent, the positive polarity functioning with no need of negative and vice-versa.

It is to be noted that in attempting to sway third-density mind/body/spirit complexes in choosing polarity there evolves a good bit of interaction between the two polarities.

In sixth density, the density of unity, the positive and negative paths must needs take in each other, for all now must be seen as love/light and light/love. This is not difficult for the positive polarity which sends love and light to all other-selves. It is difficult enough for service-to-self polarized entities that, at some point, the negative polarity is abandoned.

78.26   **QUESTIONER** The choice of polarity being the unique circumstance, shall I say, for the archetypical basis for the evolution of consciousness in our particular experience indicates to me that we have arrived, through a long process of the Creator knowing Itself, we've arrived at a position of present or maximum efficiency for the design of a process of experience. That design for maximum efficiency is in the roots of consciousness and is the archetypical mind and is a product of everything that has gone before. There are, unquestionably, relatively pure archetypical concepts for the seven concepts for mind, body, and spirit. I feel that the language that we have for these is somewhat inadequate.

However, we will continue to attempt to understand—and that is a poor word also—the foundation for this, and I am hoping that I have laid the foundation with some degree of accuracy in attempting to set a background for the development of the archetypes of our Logos. Have I left out anything or made any errors, or could you make any comments on my attempt to lay a background for the construction that our Logos used for the archetypes?

RA I am Ra. Your queries are thoughtful.

78.27 QUESTIONER Are they accurate, or have I made mistakes?

RA I am Ra. There are no mistakes.

78.28 QUESTIONER Let me put it this way. Have I made missteps in my analysis of what has led to the construction of the archetypes that we experience?

RA I am Ra. We may share with you the observation that judgment is no part of interaction between mind/body/spirit complexes. We have attempted to answer each query as fully as your language and the extent of your previous information allow. We may suggest that if, in perusing this present material, you have further queries refining any concept, these queries may be asked, and again we shall attempt adequate rejoinders.

78.29 QUESTIONER I understand your limitations in answering that. Thank you.

Could you tell me how, in first density, wind and fire teach earth and water?

RA I am Ra. You may see the air and [fire]⁵ of that which is chaos as literally illuminating and forming the formless, for earth and water were, in the timeless state, unformed.

As the active principles of fire and air blow and burn incandescently about that which nurtures that which is to come, the water learns to become sea, lake, and river, offering the opportunity for viable life. The earth learns to be shaped, thus offering the opportunity for viable life.

78.30 QUESTIONER Are the seven archetypes for mind a function of, or related to, the seven densities that are to be experienced in the octave?

RA I am Ra. The relationship is tangential in that no congruency may be

---

5   Ra actually said "air and water" but presumably meant "air and fire."

seen. However, the progress through the archetypes has some of the characteristics of the progress through the densities. These relationships may be viewed without being, shall we say, pasted one upon the other.

78.31 QUESTIONER How about the seven bodily energy centers? Are they related to archetypes in some way?

RA I am Ra. The same may be said of these. It is informative to view the relationships but stifling to insist upon the limitations of congruency. Recall at all times, if you would use this term, that the archetypes are a portion of the resources of the mind complex.

78.32 QUESTIONER Then is there any relationship between the archetypes and the planets of our solar system?

RA I am Ra. This is not a simple query. Properly, the archetypes have some relationship to the planets. However, this relationship is not one which can be expressed in your language. This, however, has not halted those among your people who have become adepts from attempting to name and describe these relationships.

To most purely understand, if we may use this misnomer, the archetypes it is well to view the concepts which make up each archetype and reserve the study of planets and other correspondences for meditation.

78.33 QUESTIONER It just seemed to me that since the planets were an outgrowth of the Logos, and since the archetypical mind was the foundation for the experience, that the planets of this Logos would be in some way related. We will certainly follow your suggestion.

I have been trying to get a foothold into an undistorted doorway, you might say, into the archetypical mind. It seems to me that everything that I have read having to do with archetypes is, to some degree or another, distorted by those who have written, and the fact that our language is not really capable of description.

You have spoken of the Magician as a basic archetype, and that this seems to have been carried through from the previous octave. Would this then be, if there is an order, the first archetypical concept of this Logos?

RA I am Ra. We would first respond to your confusion as regards the various writings upon the archetypical mind.

You may well consider the very informative difference between a thing in itself and its relationships or functions. There is much study of archetype which is actually the study of functions, relationships, and correspondences. The study of planets, for instance, is an example of archetype seen as function. However, the archetypes are, first and most profoundly, things in themselves, and the pondering of them and their purest relationships with each other should be the most useful foundation for the study of the archetypical mind.

We now address your query as to the archetype which is the Matrix of the Mind. As to its name, the name of Magician is understandable when you consider that consciousness is the great foundation, mystery, and revelation which makes this particular density possible. The self-conscious entity is full of the magic of that which is to come. It may be considered first, for the mind is the first of the complexes to be developed by the student of spiritual evolution.

78.34 **QUESTIONER** Would the archetype then that has been called the High Priestess, which represents the intuition, be properly the second of the archetypes?

RA I am Ra. This is correct. You see here the recapitulation of the beginning knowledge of this Logos; that is, Matrix and Potentiator. The unconscious is, indeed, what may be poetically described as High Priestess, for it is the Potentiator of the Mind, and as potentiator for the mind is that principle which potentiates all experience.

78.35 **QUESTIONER** Then for the third archetype would the Empress be correct and be related to disciplined meditation?

RA I am Ra. I perceive a mind complex intention of a query but was aware only of sound vibratory statement. Please re-question.

78.36 **QUESTIONER** I was asking if the third archetype was the Empress, and was it correct to say that this archetype had to do with disciplined meditation?

RA I am Ra. The third archetype may broadly be grasped as the Catalyst of the Mind. Thus it takes in far more than disciplined meditation. However, it is certainly through this faculty that catalyst is most efficiently used.

The Archetype, Three, is perhaps confusedly called Empress, although the intention of this nomer is the understanding that it represents the unconscious, or female, portion of the mind complex being first, shall we say, used or ennobled by the male or conscious portion of the mind. Thus the noble name.

78.37 **QUESTIONER** The fourth archetype, called the Emperor, seems to have to do with the experience of other-selves and the green-ray energy center with respect to other-selves. Is this correct?

RA I am Ra. This is perceptive. The broad name for Archetype Four may be the Experience of the Mind. In the tarot you find the name of Emperor. Again this implies nobility, and in this case we may see the suggestion that it is only through the catalyst which has been processed by the potentiated consciousness that experience may ensue. Thusly is the conscious mind ennobled by the use of the vast resources of the unconscious mind.

This instrument's dorsal side grows stiff, and the instrument tires. We welcome one more query.

78.38 **QUESTIONER** I would like to ask the reason for this session having been longer than most previous sessions, and also if there is anything we can do to make the instrument more comfortable or improve the contact?

RA I am Ra. This instrument was given far more than the, shall we say, usual amount of transferred energy. There is a limit to the amount of energy of this type which may with safety be used when the instrument is itself without physical reserves. This is inevitably due to the various distortions such as we mentioned previously in this working having to do with growing dorsal discomfort.

The alignments are fastidious. We appreciate your conscientiousness. In order to enhance the comfort of the instrument it might be suggested that careful manipulation of the dorsal area be accomplished before a working.

It is also suggested that, due to the attempt at psychic attack, this instrument will require warmth along the right side of the physical complex. There has been some infringement, but it should not be long-lasting. It is, however, well to swaddle this instrument sufficiently to ward off any manifestation of this cold in physical form.

I am Ra. I leave you, my friends, in the love and in the light of the One Infinite Creator. Go forth, therefore, merrily rejoicing in the power and in the peace of the One Infinite Creator. Adonai.

79.0 **RA** I am Ra. I greet you in the love and in the light of the One Infinite Creator. We communicate now.

79.1 **QUESTIONER** Could you first please give me the condition of the instrument?

RA I am Ra. It is as previously stated.

79.2 **QUESTIONER** The instrument would like to ask: is there any danger in receiving too much transferred energy with the instrument in her present condition?

RA I am Ra. No.

79.3 **QUESTIONER** She would also like to ask if the very large energy transfer of last session was a sexual transfer in total?

RA I am Ra. This is correct.

79.4 **QUESTIONER** In that case, she would like to know the function of the energy transfer during the session.

RA I am Ra. The function of this energy transfer is a most helpful one in that it serves to strengthen the shuttle through which the instreaming contact is received.

The contact itself will monitor the condition of the instrument and cease communication when the distortions of the instrument begin to fluctuate towards the distortions of weakness or pain. However, while the contact is ongoing, the strength of the channel through which this contact flows may be aided by the energy transfer of which you spoke.

79.5 **QUESTIONER** We have been ending our banishing ritual prior to the session here by a gesture that relieves us of the magical personality. I was just wondering if we should omit that gesture—so as to maintain the magical personality while performing the Circle of One—and then only relinquish the magical personality, either after that has formed or after the session? Which would be more appropriate?

RA I am Ra. The practice of magical workings demands the most rigorous honesty. If your estimate of your ability is that you can sustain the magical personality throughout this working, it is well. As long as you have some doubt, it is inadvisable.

In any case it is appropriate for this instrument to return its magical personality rather than carry this persona into the trance state, for it does not have the requisite magical skill to function in this circumstance and would be far more vulnerable than if the waking personality is offered as channel. This working is, indeed, magical in nature in the basic sense. However, it is inappropriate to move more quickly than one's feet may walk.

79.6   **QUESTIONER** I would like to question about the third-density experience of those just prior to the original extension of the First Distortion to the sub-Logoi to create the split of polarity. Can you describe in general the differences between the third-density experience of these mind/body/spirit complexes and the ones who have evolved upon this planet in this experience that we experience now?

RA I am Ra. This material has been previously covered.[1] Please query for specific interest.

79.7   **QUESTIONER** Specifically, in the experience where only the service-to-others polarity in third density evolved for continued evolution into the higher densities, was the veil that is drawn with respect to knowledge of previous incarnations, etc., in effect for those entities?

RA I am Ra. No.

79.8   **QUESTIONER** Was the reincarnational process like the one that we experience here in which the third-density body is entered and exited for numerous times during the cycle?

RA I am Ra. This is correct.

79.9   **QUESTIONER** Is it possible to give a time of incarnation with respect to our years, and would you do so if it is?

RA I am Ra. The optimal incarnative period is somewhere close to a

---

[1] Previously covered in the discussion starting at 78.20.

measure you call a millennium. This is, as you may say, a constant regardless of other factors of the third-density experience.

79.10 **QUESTIONER** Then prior to the first extension of the First Distortion, the veil, or loss of awareness, did not occur. Then from this I will make the assumption that this veil, or loss of remembering consciously that which occurred before the incarnation, was the primary tool for extending the First Distortion. Is this correct?

RA I am Ra. Your correctness is limited. This was the first tool.

79.11 **QUESTIONER** Then from that statement I assume that the Logos, contemplating a mechanism to become what it was not, first devised the tool of separating the unconscious from the conscious during what we call physical incarnation to achieve its objective? Is this correct?

RA I am Ra. Yes.

79.12 **QUESTIONER** Then from that statement I also assume that many other tools were conceived and used after the first tool of the so-called veil. Is this correct?

RA I am Ra. There have been refinements.

79.13 **QUESTIONER** The archetypical mind of the Logos prior to this experiment in extension of the First Distortion, then, was what I would consider to be less complex than it is now, possibly containing fewer archetypes. Is this correct?

RA I am Ra. We must ask your patience. We perceive a sudden flare of the distortion known as pain in this instrument's left arm and manual appendage. Please do not touch this instrument. We shall examine the mind complex and attempt to reposition the limb so that the working may continue. Then please repeat the query.

[*Two-minute pause.*]

I am Ra. You may proceed.

79.14 **QUESTIONER** Thank you. Prior to the experiment to extend the First Distortion how many archetypes were there for the creation of the Logos of that time?

RA I am Ra. There were nine.

79.15 **QUESTIONER** Nine archetypes. I will guess that those nine were three of mind, three of body, and three of spirit. Is this correct?

RA I am Ra. This is correct.

79.16 **QUESTIONER** I am going to guess that in the system of the tarot those archetypes would roughly correspond to for the mind: the Magician, the Emperor, and the Chariot. Is this correct?

RA I am Ra. This is incorrect.

79.17 **QUESTIONER** Could you tell me what they correspond to?

RA I am Ra. The body, the mind, and the spirit each contained and functioned under the aegis of the Matrix, the Potentiator, and the Significator. The Significator of the mind, body, and spirit is not identical to the Significator of the mind, body, and spirit complexes.

79.18 **QUESTIONER** I now understand what you meant in the previous session by saying to extend free will the Significator must become a complex. It seems that the Significator has become the complex that is the third, fourth, fifth, sixth, and seventh of the mind, the tenth on of the body, and the seventeenth on of the spirit. Is this correct?

RA I am Ra. This is incorrect.

79.19 **QUESTIONER** Could you tell me what you mean by "the Significator must become a complex?"

RA I am Ra. To be complex is to consist of more than one characteristic element or concept.

79.20 **QUESTIONER** I would like to try and understand the archetypes of the mind of this Logos prior to the extension of the First Distortion. In order to better understand that which we experience now I believe that this is a logical approach.

We have, as you have stated, the Matrix, Potentiator, and the Significator. I understand the Matrix as being that which is the conscious, what we call the conscious mind, but since it is also that from which the mind is made, I am at a loss to fully understand these three terms, especially with respect to the time before there a division between conscious and unconscious.

I think it is important to get a good understanding of these three things. Could you expand even more upon the Matrix of the Mind, the Potentiator, and the Significator, how they differ, and what their relationships are, please?

RA I am Ra. The Matrix of Mind is that from which all comes. It is unmoving yet is the activator in potentiation of all mind activity. The Potentiator of the Mind is that great resource which may be seen as the sea into which the consciousness dips ever deeper and more thoroughly in order to create, ideate, and become more self-conscious.

The Significator of each mind, body, and spirit may be seen as a simple and unified concept.

The Matrix of the Body may be seen to be a reflection in opposites of the mind; that is, unrestricted motion. The Potentiator of the Body then is that which, being informed, regulates activity.

The Matrix of the Spirit is difficult to characterize since the nature of spirit is less motile. The energies and movements of the spirit are, by far, the most profound, yet, having more close association with time/space, do not have the characteristics of dynamic motion. Thusly one may see the Matrix as the deepest darkness and the Potentiator of Spirit as the most sudden awakening, illuminating, and generative influence.

This is the description of Archetypes One through Nine before the onset of influence of the co-Creator or sub-Logos' realization of free will.

79.21 QUESTIONER The first change made then for this extension of free will was to make the information or make the communication between the Matrix and Potentiator of the Mind relatively unavailable, one to the other, during the incarnation. Is this correct?

RA I am Ra. We would perhaps rather term the condition as relatively more mystery-filled than relatively unavailable.

79.22 QUESTIONER Well, the idea then was to create some type of veil between Matrix and Potentiator. Is this correct?

RA I am Ra. This is correct.

79.23 QUESTIONER This veil then occurs between what we now call the conscious and the unconscious mind. Is this correct?

RA I am Ra. This is correct.

79.24 **QUESTIONER** It was probably the design of the Logos, by doing this, to allow the conscious mind greater freedom under the First Distortion by partitioning, you might say, the individualized portions of this from the Potentiator, or unconscious, which had a greater communication with the total mind, therefore allowing for, you might say, the birth of uneducated, to use a poor term, portions of consciousness. Is this correct?

RA I am Ra. This is roughly correct.

79.25 **QUESTIONER** Could you de-roughen it, elucidate a bit on that?

RA I am Ra. There is intervening material before we may do so.

79.26 **QUESTIONER** OK. Now, was then this simple experiment carried out and the product of this experiment observed before greater complexity was attempted?

RA I am Ra. As we have said, there have been a great number of successive experiments.

79.27 **QUESTIONER** I was just wondering—since this seems to be the crux of the experiment, this seems to be the large breaking point between no extension of the First Distortion and the extension of the First Distortion—what the result of this original experiment was with respect to that which was created from it. What was the result of that?

RA I am Ra. This is previously covered material.[2] The result of these experiments has been a more vivid, varied, and intense experience of Creator by Creator.

79.28 **QUESTIONER** Well, I was aware of that. I probably didn't state the question correctly. It's a very difficult question to state. I don't know if it's worth attempting to continue with, but what I meant was when this very first experiment with the veiling process occurred, did it result in service-to-self polarization with the first experiment?

RA I am Ra. The early, if we may use this term, Logoi produced service-to-self and service-to-others mind/body/spirit complexes immediately.

---

2 Previously covered in the discussion starting at 78.24.

The harvestability of these entities was not so immediate, and thus refinements of the archetypes began apace.

79.29 **QUESTIONER** Now we are getting to what I was trying to determine. Then at this point were there still only nine archetypes, and the veil had just been drawn between the Matrix and Potentiator?

RA I am Ra. There were nine archetypes and many shadows.

79.30 **QUESTIONER** By shadows do you mean what I might refer to as the birthing of small archetypical biases?

RA I am Ra. Rather, we would describe these shadows as the inchoate thoughts of helpful structures not yet fully conceived.[3]

79.31 **QUESTIONER** Then at this point— Would the Choice exist at this point, the creation of the first service-to-self polarity? Is there a choice at that point, or is it a non-choice?

RA I am Ra. Implicit in the veiling, or separation of two archetypes, is the concept of choice. The refinements to this concept took many experiences.

79.32 **QUESTIONER** I'm sorry that I have much difficulty in asking these questions, but we're on material that I find somewhat difficult.

I find it interesting that the very first experiment of veiling Matrix from the Potentiator and vice-versa created service-to-self polarity. This seems to be a very important philosophical point in the development of the creation and possibly the beginning of a system of what we would call magic not envisioned previously.

Let me ask this question. Prior to the extension of First Distortion was the magical potential of the higher densities as great as it is now when the greatest potential was achieved in consciousness for each density? This is difficult to ask. What I am saying is at the end of fourth density, prior to the extension of free will, was the magical potential, what we call magic, as great, or the ability, or the effect as great as it is now at the end of fourth density?

---

[3] In this context, *inchoate* can be defined as "just begun to form" or "rudimentary."

RA I am Ra. As you understand, if we may use this misnomer, magic, the magical potential in third and fourth density was then far greater than after the change. However, there was far, far less desire or will to use this potential.

79.33 QUESTIONER Now, let me be sure I understand you: prior to the change and the extension of free will—let's take specifically the end-of-fourth-density magical potential for the condition when there was only service-to-others polarization—magical ability or potential was much greater at the end of fourth density than at the end of fourth density immediately after the split of polarization and the extension of free will. Is that correct?

RA I am Ra. Magical ability is the ability to consciously use the so-called unconscious. Therefore, there was maximal ability prior to the innovation of sub-Logoi's free will.

79.34 QUESTIONER OK. At the present time we are experiencing the effects of a more complex, or greater number of archetypes, and I have guessed that the ones we are experiencing now for the mind work as follows: We have the Magician and High Priestess which correspond to the Matrix and Potentiator, which have the veil drawn between them, which is the primary creator of the extension of the First Distortion. Is that correct?

RA I am Ra. We are unable to answer this query without intervening material.

79.35 QUESTIONER OK. Sorry about that.

The next archetype, the Empress, is the Catalyst of the Mind, that which acts upon the conscious mind to change it. The fourth being the Emperor, which is the Experience of the Mind, which is that material stored in the unconscious which creates its continuing bias. Am I correct with those statements?

RA I am Ra. Though far too rigid in your statements, you perceive correct relationships. There is a great deal of dynamic interrelationship in these first four archetypes.

79.36 QUESTIONER Would the Hierophant then be somewhat of a governor or sorter of these effects so as to create the proper assimilation by the unconscious of that which comes through the conscious?

RA I am Ra. Although thoughtful, the supposition is incorrect in its heart.

79.37 **QUESTIONER** What would be the Hierophant?

RA I am Ra. The Hierophant is the Significator of the Body[4] complex, its very nature.

We may note that the characteristics of which you speak do have bearing upon the Significator of the Mind complex but are not the heart. The heart of the mind complex is that dynamic entity which absorbs, seeks, and attempts to learn.

79.38 **QUESTIONER** Then is the Hierophant the link, you might say, between the mind and the body?

RA I am Ra. There is a strong relationship between the Significators of the mind, the body, and the spirit. Your statement is too broad.

79.39 **QUESTIONER** Let me skip over the Hierophant for a minute because I'm really not understanding that at all, and just ask you if the Lovers represent the merging of the conscious and the unconscious, or a communication between conscious and unconscious?

RA I am Ra. Again, without being at all unperceptive, you miss the heart of this particular archetype which may be more properly called the Transformation of the Mind.

79.40 **QUESTIONER** Transformation of the mind into what?

RA I am Ra. As you observe Archetype Six you may see the student of the mysteries being transformed by the need to choose betwixt the light and the dark in mind.

79.41 **QUESTIONER** Would the Conqueror, or Chariot, then, represent the culmination of the action of the first six archetypes into a conquering of the mental processes, even possibly removing the veil?

RA I am Ra. This is most perceptive. The Archetype Seven is one difficult

---

4 Ra refers to the Hierophant as the Significator of the Body complex. The Hierophant is actually the Significator of the Mind complex. Ra corrects this error in 80.0.

to enunciate. We may call it the Path, the Way, or the Great Way of the Mind. Its foundation is a reflection and substantial summary of Archetypes One through Six.

One may also see the Way of the Mind as showing the kingdom or fruits of appropriate travel through the mind in that the mind continues to move as majestically through the material it conceives of as a chariot drawn by royal lions or steeds.

At this time we would suggest one more full query, for this instrument is experiencing some distortions towards pain.

79.42   **QUESTIONER** Then I will just ask for the one of the archetypes which I am least understanding at this point, if I can use that word at all. I am still very much in the dark, so to speak, with respect to the Hierophant and precisely what it is. Could you give me some other indication of what that is, please?

RA I am Ra. You have been most interested in the Significator which must needs become complex. The Hierophant is the original archetype of mind which has been made complex through the subtle movements of the conscious and unconscious.[5] The complexities of mind were evolved rather than the simple melding of experience from Potentiator to Matrix.

The mind itself became an actor possessed of free will and, more especially, will. As the Significator of the mind, the Hierophant has the will to know, but what shall it do with its knowledge, and for what reasons does it seek? The potential[s] of a complex significator are manifold.

Are there any brief queries at this working?

79.43   **QUESTIONER** Only is there anything that we can do to make the instrument more comfortable or improve the contact?

RA I am Ra. All is well. For some small portion of your future the instrument would be well advised to wear upon the hands those aids to comfort which it has neglected to use. There has been some trauma to both hands and arms and, therefore, we have had to somewhat abbreviate this working.

---

5   In this context, *subtile* can be defined as "fine or delicate."

79.44 **QUESTIONER** Thank you.

RA I am Ra. You are conscientious, my friends. We leave you in the love and in the light of the One Infinite Creator. Go forth, therefore, rejoicing in the power and the peace of the One Glorious Infinite Creator. Adonai.

SESSION 80

80.0 **RA** I am Ra. We greet you in the love and in the light of the One Infinite Creator.

Before we initiate this working we would wish to correct an error which we have found in previous material. That archetype, Five, which you have called the Hierophant, is the Significator of the Mind complex.

This instrument is prey to sudden flares towards the distortion known as pain. We are aware of your conscientious attempts to aid the instrument but know of no other modality available to the support group other than the provision of water therapy upon the erect spinal portion of the physical body complex, which we have previously mentioned.

This instrument's distortions of body do not ever rule out, shall we say, such flares during these periods of increased distortion of the body complex. Our contact may become momentarily garbled. Therefore, we request that any information which seems garbled be questioned as we wish this contact to remain as undistorted as the limitations of language, mentality, and sensibility allow.

We communicate now.

80.1 **QUESTIONER** Thank you. Could you please give me the condition of the instrument?

RA I am Ra. This instrument is experiencing mild fluctuations of the physical energy complex which are causing sudden changes from physical energy deficit to some slight physical energy. This is due to many, what you may call, prayers and affirmations offered to and by the instrument— offset by continual greetings whenever it is feasible by the fifth-density entity of whom you are aware.

In other respects, the instrument is in the previously stated condition.

80.2 **QUESTIONER** I had to leave the room for a forgotten item after we performed the banishing ritual. Did this have a deleterious effect on the ritual or the working?

RA I am Ra. Were it the only working the lapse would have been critical. There is enough residual energy of a protective nature in this place of working that this lapse, though quite unrecommended, does not represent a threat to the protection which the ritual of which you spoke offers.

80.3   QUESTIONER Has our fifth-density visitor been less able to affect the instrument during our more recent workings?

RA I am Ra. We shall answer in two parts.

Firstly, during the workings themselves the entity has been bated to a great extent.

Secondly, in the general experiential circumstance of your space/time experience, this fifth-density entity is able to greet this entity with the same effectiveness upon the physical body complex as always since the inception of its contact with your group. This is due to the several physical-complex distortions of the instrument.

However, the instrument has become more mentally and spiritually able to greet this entity with love, thereby reducing the element of fear which is an element the entity counts as a great weapon in the attempt to cause cessation, in any degree, of the Ra contact.

80.4   QUESTIONER What is the reason for the fact that the entity is able to act through physical distortions that are already present as opposed to being unable to act on an entity who's had no physical distortions at all?

RA I am Ra. The key to this query is the term "distortion." Any distortion—be it physical, mental, or spiritual in complex nature—may be accentuated by the suggestion of one able to work magically; that is, to cause changes in consciousness.

This entity has many physical distortions. Each in the group has various mental distortions. Their nature varies. The less balanced the distortion by self-knowledge, the more adeptly the entity may accentuate such a distortion in order to mitigate against the smooth functioning and harmony of the group.

80.5   QUESTIONER As Ra well knows, the information that we accumulate here will be illuminating to but a very minor percentage of those who populate this planet presently simply because there are very, very few people who can understand it. However, it seems that our fifth-density visitor is, shall we say, dead set against this communication.

Can you tell me why this is so important to him since it is of such a limited effect, I would guess, upon the harvest of this planet? Since it seems to me that those who will understand this information will quite possibly already be within the limits of harvestability.

RA I am Ra. Purity does not end with the harvest of third density. The fidelity of Ra towards the attempt to remove distortions is total. This constitutes an acceptance of responsibility for service to others which is of relative purity.

The instrument through which we speak and its support group have a similar fidelity and, disregarding any inconvenience to self, desire to serve others.

Due to the nature of the group the queries made to us by the group have led rapidly into somewhat abstruse regions of commentary. This content does not mitigate against the underlying purity of the contact. Such purity is as a light. Such an intensity of light attracts attention.

80.6 QUESTIONER What would our fifth-density visitor hope to gain for himself if he were to be successful in terminating this contact?

RA I am Ra. As we have previously stated, the entity hopes to gain a portion of that light; that is, the mind/body/spirit complex of the instrument. Barring this, the entity intends to put out the light.

80.7 QUESTIONER I understand this up to a point—that point is if the entity were successful in either of these attempts, of what value would this be to him? Would it increase his ability? Would it increase his polarity? By what mechanism would it do whatever it does?

RA I am Ra. Having attempted for some of your space/time with no long-lasting result to do these things, the entity may be asking this question of itself.

The gain for triumph is an increase in negative polarity to the entity in that it has removed a source of radiance and, thereby, offered to this space/time the opportunity of darkness where there once was light. In the event that it succeeded in enslaving the mind/body/spirit complex of the instrument it would have enslaved a fairly powerful entity, thus adding to its power.

80.8 **QUESTIONER** I am sorry for my lack of penetration of these mechanisms, and I apologize for some rather stupid questions, but I think we have here a point that is somewhat central to what we are presently attempting to understand. So even though my next questions may be almost unacceptably stupid, I will attempt to try to understand what this power that our visitor seeks is and how he uses it. For it seems to me that this is central to the mind and the evolution of it in which we are involved.

As this entity that is our visitor increases his power through these works, what is the power that he increases? Can you describe it?

RA I am Ra. The power of which you speak is a spiritual power. The powers of the mind, as such, do not encompass such works as these.

You may, with some fruitfulness, consider the possibilities of moonlight. You are aware that we have described the Matrix of the Spirit as a night. The moonlight, then, offers either a true picture seen in shadow, or chimera and falsity. The power of falsity is deep, as is the power to discern truth from shadow. The shadow of hidden things is an infinite depth in which is stored the power of the One Infinite Creator.

The adept, then, is working with the power of hidden things illuminated by that which can be false or true. To embrace falsity, to know it, to seek it, and to use it gives a power that is most great. This is the nature of the power of your visitor and may shed some light upon the power of one who seeks in order to serve others as well, for the missteps in the night are oh! so easy.

80.9 **QUESTIONER** Are you saying, then, that this power is of the spirit and not of the mind or the body?

RA I am Ra. The work of the adept is based upon previous work with the mind and the body, else work with the spirit would not be possible on a dependable basis. With this comment we may assert the correctness of your assumption.

80.10 **QUESTIONER** Now, the fifteenth archetype, which is the Matrix of the Spirit, has been called the Devil. Can you tell me why that is so?

RA I am Ra. We do not wish to be facile in such a central query, but we may note that the nature of the spirit is so infinitely subtle that the fructifying influence of light upon the great darkness of the spirit is very often not as apparent as the darkness itself.

The progress chosen by many adepts becomes a confused path as each adept attempts to use the Catalyst of the Spirit. Few there are which are successful in grasping the light of the sun. By far, the majority of adepts remain groping in the moonlight and, as we have said, this light can deceive as well as uncover hidden mystery.

Therefore, the melody, shall we say, of this Matrix often seems to be of a negative and evil, as you would call it, nature.

It is also to be noted that an adept is one which has freed itself more and more from the constraints of the thoughts, opinions, and bonds of other-selves. Whether this is done for service to others or service to self, it is a necessary part of the awakening of the adept. This freedom is seen by those not free as what you would call evil or black. The magic is recognized; the nature is often not.

80.11 QUESTIONER Could I say, then, that implicit in the process of becoming adept is the possible partial polarization towards service to self because simply the adept becomes disassociated with many of his kind or like in the particular density which he inhabits?

RA I am Ra. This is likely to occur. The apparent happening is disassociation: whether the truth is service to self and thus true disassociation from other-selves, or service to others and thus true association with the heart of all other-selves and disassociation only from the illusory husks which prevent the adept from correctly perceiving the self and other-self as one.

80.12 QUESTIONER Then you say that this effect of disassociation on the service-to-others adept is a stumbling block or slowing process in reaching that goal which he aspires to? Is this correct?

RA I am Ra. This is incorrect. This disassociation from the miasma of illusion and misrepresentation of each and every distortion is a quite necessary portion of an adept's path. It may be seen by others to be unfortunate.

80.13 **QUESTIONER** Then, is this, from the point of view or with respect to the fifteenth archetype, somewhat of an excursion into the Matrix of the Spirit in this process? Does that make any sense?

RA I am Ra. The excursion of which you speak and the process of disassociation is most usually linked with that archetype you call Hope—which we would prefer to call Faith. This archetype is the Catalyst of the Spirit and, because of the illuminations of the Potentiator of the Spirit, will begin to cause these changes in the adept's viewpoint.

80.14 **QUESTIONER** I didn't intend to get too far ahead of my questioning process here. The either positively or negatively polarized adept, then, is building a potential to draw directly on the spirit for power. Is this correct?

RA I am Ra. It would be more proper to say that the adept is calling directly through the spirit to the universe for its power, for the spirit is a shuttle.

80.15 **QUESTIONER** Now, the obvious only significant difference, I believe, between the positive and negative adept in using this shuttle is the way they had polarized. Is there a relationship between the archetypes of the spirit and whether the polarization is either positive or negative? Is, for instance, the positive calling through the sixteenth and the [*chuckles*] negative calling through the fifteenth archetype? I am very confused on these points, and I imagine that question is poor or meaningless. Can you answer that?

RA I am Ra. It is a challenge to answer such a query, for there is some confusion in its construction. However, we shall attempt to speak upon the subject.

The adept, whether positive or negative, has the same Matrix. The Potentiator is also identical.

Due to the Catalyst of each adept, the adept may begin to pick and choose that into which it shall look further.

The Experience of the Spirit, that which you have called the Moon, is then, by far, the more manifest of influences upon the polarity of the adept.

Even the most unhappy of experiences, shall we say, which seem to occur in the Catalyst of the adept, seen from the viewpoint of the spirit, may, with the discrimination possible in shadow, be worked with until light equaling the light of brightest noon descends upon the adept and positive or service-to-others illumination has occurred. The service-to-self adept will satisfy itself with the shadows and, grasping the light of day, will toss back the head in grim laughter, preferring the darkness.

80.16 QUESTIONER I guess that the nineteenth archetype of the spirit would be the Significator of the Spirit. Is that correct?

RA I am Ra. This is correct.

80.17 QUESTIONER How would you describe the Significator of the Spirit?

RA I am Ra. In answer to the previous query we set about doing just this. The Significator of the Spirit is that living entity which either radiates or absorbs the love and the light of the One Infinite Creator: radiates it to others or absorbs it for the self.

80.18 QUESTIONER Then would this process of radiation or absorption, since we have what I would call a flux or flux rate, be the measure of the power of the adept?

RA I am Ra. This may be seen to be a reasonably adequate statement.

80.19 QUESTIONER Then for the twentieth archetype I'm guessing that this is the Transformation of the Spirit, possibly analogous to the sixth-density merging of the paths. Is this in any way correct?

RA I am Ra. No.

80.20 QUESTIONER Sorry about that. Can you tell me what the twentieth archetype would be?

RA I am Ra. That which you call the Sarcophagus in your system may be seen to be the material world, if you will. This material world is transformed by the spirit into that which is infinite and eternal.

The infinity of the spirit is an even greater realization than the infinity of consciousness, for consciousness which has been disciplined by will and faith is that consciousness which may contact intelligent infinity directly.

There are many things which fall away in the many, many steps of adepthood. We, of Ra, still walk these steps and praise the One Infinite Creator at each transformation.

80.21 **QUESTIONER** Then I would guess that the twenty-first archetype would represent the contact with intelligent infinity. Is that correct?

RA I am Ra. This is correct, although one may also see the reflection of this contact (as well) as the contact with intelligent energy, which is the Universe, or, as you have called it somewhat provincially, the World.

80.22 **QUESTIONER** Then by this contact also with intelligent energy can you give me an example of what this would be for both: for the contact with intelligent infinity and intelligent energy? Could you give me an example of what type of experience this would result in, if that's at all possible?

RA I am Ra. This shall be the last query of this working of full length.

We have discussed the possibilities of contact with intelligent energy,[1] for this energy is the energy of the Logos, and thus it is the energy which heals, builds, removes, destroys, and transforms all other-selves as well as the self.

The contact with intelligent infinity is most likely to produce an unspeakable joy in the entity experiencing such contact.

If you wish to query in more detail upon this subject, we invite you to do so in another working. Is there a brief query before we close this working?

80.23 **QUESTIONER** Is there anything that we can do to improve the contact or to make the instrument more comfortable?

RA I am Ra. The alignments are most conscientious. We are appreciative. The entity which serves as instrument is somewhat distorted towards that condition you call stiffness of the dorsal regions. Manipulation would be helpful.

I am Ra. I leave you, my friends, glorying in the light and the love of the One Infinite Creator. Go forth, therefore, rejoicing in the power and in the peace of the One Infinite Creator. Adonai.

---

[1] Discussed in 58.23 and 61.13.

SESSION 81

MARCH 22, 1982

81.0   **RA** I am Ra. I greet you in the love and in the light of the One Infinite Creator. We communicate now.

81.1   **QUESTIONER** Could you first please tell me the condition of the instrument?

RA I am Ra. The physical complex energy is in deficit at this particular space/time nexus due to prolonged psychic accentuation of pre-existing distortions. The remainder of the energy complex levels are as previously stated.

81.2   **QUESTIONER** Is this the reason for the instrument's feeling of uninterrupted weariness?

RA I am Ra. There are portions of your space/time in which this may be said to be symptomatic of the psychic greeting reaction. However, the continual weariness is not due to psychic greeting but is, rather, an inevitable consequence of this contact.

81.3   **QUESTIONER** Why is this an inevitable consequence? What is the mechanism of contact creating weariness?

RA I am Ra. The mechanism creating weariness is that connection betwixt the density wherein this instrument's mind/body/spirit complex is safely kept during these workings, and the altogether variant density in which the instrument's physical body complex resides at this space/time. As the instrument takes on more of the coloration of the resting density, the third-density experience seems more heavy and wearisome.

This was accepted by the instrument, as it desired to be of service. Therefore, we accept also this effect about which nothing of which we are aware may be done.

81.4   **QUESTIONER** Is the effect a function of the number of sessions, and has it reached a peak level, or will it continue to increase in effect?

RA I am Ra. This wearying effect will continue but should not be confused with the physical energy levels having only to do with the, as you would call it, daily round of experience.

In this sphere those things which are known already to aid this instrument will continue to be of aid. You will, however, notice the gradual increase in transparency, shall we say, of the vibrations of the instrument.

81.5   **QUESTIONER** I didn't understand what you meant by that last statement. Would you explain?

RA I am Ra. Weariness of the time/space nature may be seen to be that reaction of transparent or pure vibrations with impure, confused, or opaque environs.

81.6   **QUESTIONER** Is there any of this effect upon the other two of us in this group?

RA I am Ra. This is quite correct.

81.7   **QUESTIONER** Then we would also experience the uninterrupted wearying effect as a consequence of the contact. Is this correct?

RA I am Ra. The instrument, by the very nature of the contact, bears the brunt of this effect.

Each of the support group, by offering the love and the light of the One Infinite Creator in unqualified support in these workings, and in energy transfers for the purpose of these workings, experiences between 10 and 15 percent, roughly, of this effect. It is cumulative and identical in the continual nature of its manifestation.

81.8   **QUESTIONER** What could be the result of this continued wearying effect after a long period?

RA I am Ra. You ask a general query with infinite answers. We shall over-generalize in order to attempt to reply.

One group might be tempted and thus lose the very contact which caused the difficulty. So the story would end.

Another group might be strong at first but not faithful in the face of difficulty. Thus the story would end.

Another group might choose the path of martyrdom in its completeness and use the instrument until its physical body complex failed from the harsh toll demanded when all energy was gone.

This particular group, at this particular nexus, is attempting to conserve the vital energy of the instrument. It is attempting to balance love of service and wisdom of service, and it is faithful to the service in the face of difficulty. Temptation has not yet ended this group's story.

We may not know the future, but the probability of this situation continuing over a relatively substantial period of your space/time is large. The significant factor is the will of the instrument and of the group to serve. That is the only cause for balancing the slowly increasing weariness which will continue to distort your perceptions. Without this will the contact might be possible but finally seem too much of an effort.

81.9   **QUESTIONER** The instrument would like to know why she has a feeling of increased vital energy?

RA I am Ra. We leave this answer to the instrument.

81.10   **QUESTIONER** She would like to know if she has an increased sensitivity to foods?

RA I am Ra. This instrument has an increased sensitivity to all stimuli. It is well that it use prudence.

81.11   **QUESTIONER** Going back to the previous session, picking up on the tenth archetype, which is the Catalyst of the Body or the Wheel of Fortune, which represents interaction with other-selves. Is this a correct statement?

RA I am Ra. This may be seen to be a roughly correct statement in that each catalyst is dealing with the nature of those experiences entering the energy web and vibratory perceptions of the mind/body/spirit complex.

The most carefully noted addition would be that the outside stimulus of the Wheel of Fortune is that which offers both positive and negative experience.

81.12   **QUESTIONER** The eleventh archetype, the Experience of the Body, represents the catalyst that has been processed by the mind/body/spirit complex and is called the Enchantress because it produces further seed for growth. Is this correct?

RA I am Ra. This is correct.

81.13   **QUESTIONER** We have already discussed the Significator, so I will skip to number thirteen. Transformation of Body is called Death, for with death the body is transformed to a higher-vibration body for additional learning. Is this correct?

RA I am Ra. This is correct and may be seen to be additionally correct in that each moment, and certainly each diurnal period of the bodily incarnation, offers death and rebirth to one which is attempting to use the catalyst which is offered it.

81.14 **QUESTIONER** And finally, the fourteenth, the Way of the Body, is called the Alchemist because there is an infinity of time for the various bodies to operate within to learn the lessons necessary for evolution. Is this correct?

RA I am Ra. This is less than completely correct as the Great Way of the Body must be seen, as are all the archetypes of the body, to be a mirror image of the thrust of the activity of the mind.

The body is the creature of the mind and is the instrument of manifestation for the fruits of mind and spirit. Therefore, you may see the body as providing the athanor through which the alchemist manifests gold.[1]

81.15 **QUESTIONER** I have guessed that a way that I could enter into a better comprehension of the development experience that is central to our work is to compare what we experience now, after the veil was dropped, with what was experienced prior to that time, starting possibly as far back as the beginning of this octave of experience, to see how we got into the condition we're in now. If this is agreeable, I would like to retreat to the very beginning of this octave of experience to investigate the conditions of mind, body, and spirit as they evolved in this octave. Is this satisfactory, acceptable?

RA I am Ra. The direction of questions is your provenance.

81.16 **QUESTIONER** Ra states that it has knowledge of only this octave, but it seems that Ra has complete knowledge of this octave. Can you tell me why this is?

---

[1] In this context, *athanor* can be defined as "an oven/a fire; a digesting furnance, formerly used in alchemy, so constructed as to maintain a uniform and constant heat."

RA I am Ra. Firstly, we do not have complete knowledge of this octave. There are portions of the seventh density which, although described to us by our teachers, remain mysterious. Secondly, we have experienced a great deal of the available refining catalyst of this octave, and our teachers have worked with us most carefully that we may be one with all, that, in turn, our eventual returning to the great allness of creation shall be complete.

81.17 QUESTIONER Then Ra has knowledge from the first beginnings of this octave through its present experience as, what I might call, direct or experiential knowledge through communication with those space/times and time/spaces, but has not yet evolved to or penetrated the seventh level. Is this a roughly correct statement?

RA I am Ra. Yes.

81.18 QUESTIONER Why does Ra not have any knowledge of that which was prior to the beginning of this octave?

RA I am Ra. Let us compare octaves to islands. It may be that the inhabitants of an island are not alone upon a planetary sphere, but if an ocean-going vehicle in which one may survive has not been invented, true knowledge of other islands is possible only if an entity comes among the islanders and says, "I am from elsewhere." This is a rough analogy. However, we have evidence of this sort, both of previous creation and creation to be, as we in the stream of space/time and time/space view these apparently non-simultaneous events.

81.19 QUESTIONER Well, we presently find ourselves in the Milky Way Galaxy of some 200 or so million— correction, 200 or so billion— stars, and there are millions and millions of these large galaxies spread out through what we call space. To Ra's knowledge, I assume, the number of these galaxies is infinite? Is this correct?

RA I am Ra. This is precisely correct and is a significant point.

81.20 QUESTIONER The point being that we have unity. Is that correct?

RA I am Ra. You are perceptive.

81.21 QUESTIONER Then what portion of these galaxies is Ra aware of? Has Ra experienced consciousness in many other of these galaxies?

RA I am Ra. No.

81.22 **QUESTIONER** Does Ra have any experience, or knowledge of, or travel to, in one form or another, any of these other galaxies?

RA I am Ra. Yes.

81.23 **QUESTIONER** Just . . . it's unimportant, but just roughly how many other of these galaxies has Ra, shall we say, traveled to?

RA I am Ra. We have opened our hearts in radiation of love to the entire creation. Approximately 90 percent of the creation is, at some level, aware of the sending and able to reply. All of the infinite Logoi are one in the consciousness of love. This is the type of contact which we enjoy rather than travel.

81.24 **QUESTIONER** So that I can just get a little idea of what I am talking about, what are the limits of Ra's travel in the sense of directly experiencing or seeing the activities of various places? Is it solely within this galaxy, and if so, how much of this galaxy? Or does it include some other galaxies?

RA I am Ra. Although it would be possible for us to move at will throughout the creation within this Logos—that is to say, the Milky Way Galaxy, so-called—we have moved where we were called to service; these locations being, shall we say, local and including Alpha Centauri, planets of your solar system which you call the Sun, Cepheus, and Zeta Reticuli. To these sub-Logoi we have come, having been called.

81.25 **QUESTIONER** Was the call in each instance from the third-density beings, or was this call from additional or other densities?

RA I am Ra. In general, the latter supposition is correct. In the particular case of the Sun sub-Logos, third density is the density of calling.

81.26 **QUESTIONER** Ra then has not moved at any time into one of the other major galaxies. Is this correct?

RA I am Ra. This is correct.

81.27 **QUESTIONER** Does Ra have knowledge of, say, any other major galaxy or the consciousness or anything in that galaxy?

RA I am Ra. We assume you are speaking of the possibility of knowledge of other major galaxies. There are wanderers from other major galaxies drawn to the specific needs of a single call. There are those among our social memory complex which have become wanderers in other major galaxies.

Thus there has been knowledge of other major galaxies, for to one whose personality, or mind/body/spirit complex, has been crystallized the universe is one place, and there is no bar upon travel.

However, our interpretation of your query was a query concerning the social memory complex traveling to another major galaxy. We have not done this, nor do we contemplate it, for we can reach in love with our hearts.

81.28   **QUESTIONER** Thank you. In this line of questioning I am trying to establish a basis for understanding the foundation for not only the experience that we have now but how the experience was formed and, and how it is related to all the rest of the experience through the portion of the octave as we understand it. I am assuming, then, that all of these galaxies, millions . . . infinite number of galaxies which we can just begin to become aware of with our telescopes, they are all of the same octave. Is this correct?

RA I am Ra. This is correct.

81.29   **QUESTIONER** I was wondering if, in that some of the wanderers from Ra going to the other major galaxies (that is, leaving this system of 200 plus billion stars of lenticular shape and going to another cluster of billions of stars and finding their way to some planetary situation there), would any of these wanderers encounter the dual polarity that we have here, both the service-to-self and the service-to-others polarity?

RA I am Ra. This is correct.

81.30   **QUESTIONER** Now, you stated earlier that toward the center of this galaxy, I believe—in what, to use a poor term, you could call the older portion— you would find no service-to-self polarization, but that this was a, what you might call, a later experience. Am I correct in assuming that this is true of the other galaxies with which wanderers from Ra have experience? That at the center of these galaxies only the service-to-others polarity existed, and the experiment started farther out toward the rim of the galaxy?

RA I am Ra. Various Logoi and sub-Logoi had various methods of arriving at the discovery of the efficiency of free will in intensifying the experience of the Creator by the Creator. However, in each case this has been a pattern.

81.31 **QUESTIONER** You mean then that the pattern is that the service-to-self polarization appeared farther out from the center of the galactic spiral?

RA I am Ra. This is correct.

81.32 **QUESTIONER** From this I will assume that at the beginning of the octave we had the core, with many galactic spirals forming—and I know this is incorrect in the sense of timelessness—but as the spiral formed then I am assuming that, in this particular octave, the experiment then must have started somewhat roughly, simultaneously in many, many of the budding, or building, galactic systems by the experiment of the veiling in extending the free will. Am I in any way correct with this assumption?

RA I am Ra. You are precisely correct.

This instrument is unusually fragile at this space/time, and has used much of the transferred energy. We would invite one more full query for this working.

81.33 **QUESTIONER** Actually, I don't have much more on this except to make the assumption that there must have been some type of communication throughout the octave so that when the first experiment became effective, the knowledge of this then spread rapidly through the octave and was picked up by other budding galactic spirals, you might say. Is this correct?

RA I am Ra. This is correct. To be aware of the nature of this communication is to be aware of the nature of the Logos. Much of what you call creation has never separated from the one Logos of this octave and resides within the One Infinite Creator. Communication in such an environment is the communication of cells of the body. That which is learned by one is known to all. The sub-Logoi, then, have been in the position of refining the discoveries of what might be called the earlier sub-Logoi.

May we ask if we may answer any brief queries at this working?

81.34 **QUESTIONER** Only if there is anything we can do to make the instrument more comfortable or improve the contact?

RA I am Ra. It is difficult to determine the energy levels of the instrument and support group. Of this we are aware. It is, however, recommended that every attempt be made to enter each working with the most desirable configurations of energy possible.

All is well, my friends. You are conscientious, and the alignments are well.

I am Ra. I leave you in the love and the light of the One Infinite Creator. Go forth, therefore, rejoicing in the power and in the peace of the Infinite Creator. Adonai.

Session 82

82.0 **RA** I am Ra. I greet you, my friends, in the love and in the light of the One Infinite Creator. We communicate now.

82.1 **QUESTIONER** Could you first please give me the condition of the instrument?

RA I am Ra. It is as previously stated.

82.2 **QUESTIONER** Is there anything at all that we could do that we are not doing to—besides eliminating the contact—to increase the physical energy of the instrument?

RA I am Ra. There is the possibility/probability that the whirling of the water with spine erect would alter, somewhat, the distortion towards what you call pain which this entity experiences in the dorsal region on a continuous level. This, in turn, could aid in the distortion towards increase of physical energy to some extent.

82.3 **QUESTIONER** Jim has a personal question which is not to be published.[1] He asks, "It seems that my balancing work has shifted from more peripheral concerns such as patience/impatience, to learning to open myself in unconditional love, to accepting my self as whole and perfect, and then to accepting my self as the Creator. If this is a normal progression of focus for balancing, wouldn't it be more efficient, once this is discovered, for a person to work on the acceptance of self as Creator rather than work

---

[1] Jim writes: "Don asked this question for me, and I don't remember why he prefaced the question to Ra by saying that it would not be published. Because Ra answered the question with that understanding, we did not publish this question in the original publication. But Carla and I changed our minds when it came time to publish Book V many years later. It is clear to me that the information in this question and answer could be very helpful to seekers of truth. I know that both Don and Ra would want the product of their efforts to be offered as a service to others as long as there was no possible infringement of free will or any other side issue."

peripherally on the secondary and tertiary results of not accepting the self?"

RA I am Ra. The term efficiency has misleading connotations. In the context of doing work in the disciplines of the personality, in order to be of more full efficiency in the central acceptance of the self, it is first quite necessary to know the distortions of the self which the entity is accepting. Each thought and action needs must then be scrutinized for the precise foundation of the distortions of any reactions. This process shall lead to the more central task of acceptance. However, the architrave must be in place before the structure is builded.

82.4   **QUESTIONER** Thank you. I would like to consider the condition at a time, or position, you might say—if time is a bad word—just prior to the beginning of this octave of experience. I am assuming that, just prior to the beginning of this octave, intelligent infinity had created and already experienced one or more previous octaves. Is this correct?

RA I am Ra. You assume correctly. However, the phrase would more informatively read, infinite intelligence had experienced previous octaves.

82.5   **QUESTIONER** Does Ra have any knowledge of the number of previous octaves; and if so, how many?

RA I am Ra. As far as we are aware we are in an infinite creation. There is no counting.

82.6   **QUESTIONER** That's what I thought you might say. Am I correct in assuming that at the beginning of this octave, out of what I would call a void of space, the seeds of an infinite number of galactic systems such as the Milky Way Galaxy appeared and grew in spiral fashion simultaneously?

RA I am Ra. There are duple areas of potential confusion. Firstly, let us say that the basic concept is reasonably well-stated.

Now we address the confusion. The nature of true simultaneity is such that, indeed, all is simultaneous. However, in your modes of perception you would perhaps more properly view the seeding of the creation as that of growth from the center or core outward.

The second confusion lies in the term, "void." We would substitute the noun, "plenum."[2]

82.7 **QUESTIONER** Then, if I were observing the beginning of the octave at that time through a telescope, say from this position, would I see the center of many, many galaxies appearing and each of them then spreading outward in a spiral condition over what we would consider billions of years? But the spirals spreading outward in approximately what we would consider the same rate, so that all these galaxies began as the first speck of light at the same time and then spread out in roughly the same rate of spreading? Is this correct?

RA I am Ra. The query has confusing elements. There is a center to infinity. From this center all spreads. Therefore, there are centers to the creation, to the galaxies, to star systems, to planetary systems, and to consciousness. In each case you may see growth from the center outward. Thus, you may see your query as being over-general in concept.

82.8 **QUESTIONER** Considering only our Milky Way Galaxy: At its beginnings, I will assume that the first . . . was the first occurrence that we could find presently with our physical apparatus . . . was the first occurrence the appearance of a star of the nature of our sun?

RA I am Ra. In the case of the galactic systems the first manifestation of the Logos is a cluster of central systems which generate the outward swirling energies producing, in their turn, further energy centers for the Logos, or what you would call stars.

82.9 **QUESTIONER** Are these central original creations a cluster of what we call stars, then?

RA I am Ra. This is correct. However, the closer to the, shall we say, beginning of the manifestation of the Logos the star is, the more it partakes in the One Original Thought.

82.10 **QUESTIONER** Why does this partaking in the Original Thought have a gradient radially outward? That's the way I understand your statement.

---

[2] In this context, *plenum* can be defined as "a space which is filled [as opposed to empty]."

RA I am Ra. This is the plan of the One Infinite Creator. The One Original Thought is the harvest of all previous, if you would use this term, experience of the Creator by the Creator.

As It decides to know Itself, It generates Itself into that plenum, full of the glory and the power of the One Infinite Creator, which is manifested to your perceptions as space or outer space. Each generation of this knowing begets a knowing which has the capacity, through free will, to choose methods of knowing Itself.

Therefore, gradually, step by step, the Creator becomes that which may know Itself, and the portions of the Creator partake less purely in the power of the original word or thought. This is for the purpose of refinement of the One Original Thought. The Creator does not properly create as much as It experiences Itself.

82.11 QUESTIONER What was the form, condition, or experience of the first division of consciousness that occurred at the beginning of this octave, at the beginning of this galactic experience?

RA I am Ra. We touch upon previous material.[3] The harvest of the previous octave was the Creator of Love manifested in mind, body, and spirit. This form of the Creator experiencing Itself may, perhaps, be seen to be the first division.

82.12 QUESTIONER I was interested in specifically how this very first division showed up in this octave. I was interested to know if it made the transition through first, second, third, fourth, fifth, etc., densities?

I would like to take the first mind/body/spirit complexes and trace their experience from the very start to the present so that I would better understand the condition that we are in now by comparing it with this original growth. Could you please tell me precisely how this came about as to the formation, possibly, of the planets and the growth through the densities, if that is the way it happened, please?

RA I am Ra. Your queries seem more confused than your basic mental distortions in this area. Let us speak in general, and perhaps you may find

---

[3] Originally discussed in 78.10.

a less confused and more simple method of eliciting information in this area.

A very great deal of creation was manifested without the use of the concepts involved in consciousness, as you know it. The creation itself is a form of consciousness which is unified—the Logos being the one great heart of creation.

The process of evolution through this period, which may be seen to be timeless, is most valuable to take into consideration, for it is against the background of this essential unity of the fabric of creation that we find the ultimate development of the Logoi which chose to use that portion of the harvested consciousness of the Creator to move forward with the process of knowledge of self.

As it had been found to be efficient to use the various densities, which are fixed in each octave, in order to create conditions in which self-conscious sub-Logoi could exist, this was carried out throughout the growing flower-strewn field, as your simile suggests, of the One Infinite Creation.

The first beings of mind, body, and spirit were not complex. The experience of mind/body/spirits at the beginning of this octave of experience was singular. There was no third-density forgetting. There was no veil. The lessons of third density are predestined by the very nature of the vibratory rates experienced during this particular density, and by the nature of the quantum jump to the vibratory experiences of fourth density.

82.13 **QUESTIONER** Am I correct, then, in assuming that the first mind/body/spirit experiences, as this galaxy progressed in growth, were those that moved through the densities; that is, the process we have discussed coming out of second density. For instance, let us take a particular planet, one of the very early planets formed near the center of the galaxy. I will assume that the planet solidified in first density, that life appeared in second density, and all of the mind/body/spirit complexes of third density progressed out of second density on that planet, and evolved in third density. Is this correct?

RA I am Ra. This is hypothetically correct.

82.14 **QUESTIONER** Did this in fact happen on some of the planets or on a large percentage of the planets near the center of this galaxy in this way?

RA I am Ra. Our knowledge is limited. We know of the beginning but cannot asseverate to the precise experiences of those things occurring before us.[4] You know the nature of historical teaching. At our level of learn/teaching we may expect little distortion. However, we cannot, with surety, say there is no distortion as we speak of specific occurrences of which we were not consciously a part. It is our understanding that your supposition is correct. Thus we so hypothesize.

82.15 QUESTIONER Specifically, I am trying to grasp an understanding first of the process of experience in third density before the veil so that I can have a better understanding of the present process. Now, as I understand it, the mind/body/spirit complexes[5] went through the process of what we call physical incarnation in this density, but there was no forgetting. What was the benefit or purpose of the physical incarnation when there was no forgetting?

RA I am Ra. The purpose of incarnation in third density is to learn the Ways of Love.

82.16 QUESTIONER I guess I didn't state that exactly right. What I mean is, since there was no forgetting, since the mind/body/spirit complexes had the consciousness, in what we call physical incarnation, they knew the same thing that they would know not in the physical incarnation. What was the mechanism of teaching that taught this, the Ways of Love, in the third-density physical prior to the forgetting process?

RA I am Ra. We ask your permission to answer this query in an oblique fashion as we perceive an area in which we might be of aid.

82.17 QUESTIONER Certainly.

RA I am Ra. Your queries seem to be pursuing the possibility/probability that the mechanisms of experience in third density are different if a mind/body/spirit is attempting them rather than a mind/body/spirit complex. The nature of third density is constant. Its ways are to be learned the same now and ever.

---

4 In this context, *asseverate* can be defined as "to affirm or declare positively or earnestly."

5 The Questioner indicates "mind/body/spirit complexes" but is referring to "mind/body/spirits."

Thusly, no matter what form the entity facing these lessons, the lessons and mechanisms are the same. The Creator will learn from Itself. Each entity has unmanifest portions of learning and, most importantly, learning which is involved with other-selves.

82.18 **QUESTIONER** Then prior to the forgetting process, there was no concept of anything but service-to-others polarization. What sort of societies and experiences in third density were created and evolved in this condition?

RA I am Ra. It is our perception that such conditions created the situation of a most pallid experiential nexus in which lessons were garnered with the relative speed of the turtle to the cheetah.

82.19 **QUESTIONER** Did such societies evolve with technologies of a complex nature, or were they quite simple? Can you give me a general idea of the evolvement that would be a function of what we would call intellectual activity?

RA I am Ra. There is infinite diversity in societies under any circumstances. There were many highly technologically advanced societies which grew due to the ease of producing any desired result when one dwells within what might be seen to be a state of constant potential inspiration.

That which even the most highly sophisticated, in your terms, societal structure lacked, given the non-complex nature of its entities, was what you might call will or, to use a more plebeian term, gusto, or élan vital.

82.20 **QUESTIONER** Did the highly technological societies evolve travel through what we call space to other planets or other planetary systems? Did some of them do this?

RA I am Ra. This is correct.

82.21 **QUESTIONER** Then even though, from our point of view, there was great evolutionary experience it was deemed at some point by the evolving Logos that an experiment to create a greater experience was appropriate. Is this correct?

RA I am Ra. This is correct and may benefit from comment. The Logos is aware of the nature of the third-density requirement for what you have called graduation. All the previous, if you would use this term, experiments, although resulting in many experiences, lacked what was considered the crucial ingredient: that is, polarization.

There was little enough tendency for experience to polarize entities that entities repeated, habitually, the third-density cycles many times over. It was desired that the potential for polarization be made more available.

82.22   **QUESTIONER** Then since the only possibility at this particular time, as I see it, was a polarization for service to others, I must assume from what you said that even though all were aware of this service-to-others necessity they were unable to achieve it. What was the configuration of mind of the mind/body/spirit complexes at that time?[6] Were they aware of the necessity for the polarization or unaware of it? And if so, why did they have such a difficult time serving others to the extent necessary for graduation since this was the only polarity possible?

RA I am Ra. Consider, if you will, the tendency of those who are divinely happy, as you call this distortion, to have little urge to alter, or better, their condition. Such is the result of the mind/body/spirit which is not complex.

There is the possibility of love of other-selves and service to other-selves, but there is the overwhelming awareness of the Creator in the self. The connection with the Creator is that of the umbilical cord. The security is total. Therefore, no love is terribly important; no pain terribly frightening; no effort, therefore, is made to serve for love or to benefit from fear.

82.23   **QUESTIONER** It seems that you might make an analogy in our present illusion of those who are born into extreme wealth and security. Is this correct?

RA I am Ra. Within the strict bounds of the simile, you are perceptive.

82.24   **QUESTIONER** We have presently an activity between physical incarnations called healing and review of the incarnation. Was anything of this nature occurring prior to the veil between physical incarnations?

---

6 The Questioner indicates "mind/body/spirit complexes" but is referring to "mind/body/spirits."

RA I am Ra. The inchoate structure of this process was always in place, but where there has been no harm there need be no healing.[7]

This, too, may be seen to have been of concern to Logoi which were aware that, without the need to understand, understanding would forever be left undone. We ask your forgiveness for the use of this misnomer, but your language has a paucity of sound vibration complexes for this general concept.

82.25 **QUESTIONER** I don't grasp too well the condition of incarnation, and time between incarnation, prior to the veil in that I do not understand what was the difference other than the manifestation of the third-density, yellow-ray body. Was there any mental difference upon what we call death? Was there any— I don't see the necessity for what we call a review of the incarnation if the consciousness was uninterrupted. Could you clear that point for me?

RA I am Ra. No portion of the Creator audits the course, to use your experiential terms. Each incarnation is intended to be a course in the Creator knowing Itself.

A review or, shall we say, to continue the metaphor, each test is an integral portion of the process of the Creator knowing Itself. Each incarnation will end with such a test. This is so that the portion of the Creator may assimilate the experiences in yellow-ray, physical third density, may evaluate the biases gained, and may then choose, either by means of automatically provided aid, or by the self, the conditions of the next incarnation.

82.26 **QUESTIONER** Before the veil, during the review of incarnation, were the entities at that time aware that what they were trying to do was sufficiently polarize for graduation?

RA I am Ra. This is correct.

82.27 **QUESTIONER** Then I am assuming this awareness was somehow reduced as they went into the yellow-ray third-density incarnative state, even though there was no veil. Is this correct?

---

[7] In this context, *inchoate* can be defined as "just begun and so not fully formed, or rudimentary."

RA I am Ra. This is distinctly incorrect.

82.28 **QUESTIONER** OK. This is the central important point. Why, then, was it so— You've answered this, but it seems to me that if the polarization was the obvious thing that more effort would have been put forward to polarize. Let me see if I can state this. Before the veil there was an awareness of the need for polarization towards service to others in third density by all entities, whether incarnate in third-density, yellow-ray bodies, or whether in between incarnations.

What was the— I assume, then, that the condition of which we earlier spoke, the one of wealth, you might say, was present through the entire spectrum of experience, whether it be between incarnations, or during incarnation, and the entities just simply could not [*chuckles*] get up the desire or manifest the desire to create this polarization necessary for graduation. Is this correct?

RA I am Ra. You begin to grasp the situation. Let us continue the metaphor of the schooling but consider the scholar as being an entity in your younger years of the schooling process. The entity is fed, clothed, and protected regardless of whether or not the schoolwork is accomplished. Therefore, the entity does not do the homework but rather enjoys playtime, mealtime, and vacation. It is not until there is a reason to wish to excel that most entities will attempt to excel.

82.29 **QUESTIONER** You stated in a much earlier session[8] that it is necessary to polarize anything more than 50% service to self to be harvestable fourth-density positive.[9] Was this condition the same at the time before the veil? The same percentage polarization?

RA I am Ra. This shall be the last full query of this working.

The query is not answered easily, for the concept of service to self did not hold sway previous to what we have been calling the veiling process. The necessity for graduation to fourth density is an ability to use, welcome,

---

8   Stated in 17.31.

9   This statement is phrased incorrectly. Properly, an entity would need to polarize more than 50% service to *others* (or *less* than 50% service to self) to be harvestable fourth-density positive. It seems Ra grasped the intent of Don's question without correcting the mistake.

and enjoy a certain intensity of the white light of the One Infinite Creator. In your own terms, at your space/time nexus, this ability may be measured by your previously stated percentages of service.

Prior to the veiling process the measurement would be that of an entity walking up a set of your stairs, each of which was imbued with a certain quality of light. The stair upon which an entity stopped would be either third-density light or fourth-density light. Between the two stairs lies the threshold. To cross that threshold is difficult. There is resistance at the edge, shall we say, of each density.

The faculty of faith or will needs to be understood, nourished, and developed in order to have an entity which seeks past the boundary of third density. Those entities which do not do their homework, be they ever so amiable, shall not cross. It was this situation which faced the Logoi prior to the veiling process being introduced into the experiential continuum of third density.

May we ask if there are any brief queries at this working?

82.30 **QUESTIONER** Is there anything that we can do to improve the contact or make the instrument more comfortable?

RA I am Ra. All parameters are being met. Remain united in love and thanksgiving. We thank you for your conscientiousness as regards the appurtenances.

I am Ra. I leave you in the love and in the light of the One Infinite Glorious Creator. Go forth, therefore, rejoicing merrily in the power and the peace of the One Creator. Adonai.

April 5, 1982

83.0 **RA** I am Ra. I greet you in the love and in the light of the One Infinite Creator. I communicate now.

83.1 **QUESTIONER** Could you first please give me the condition of the instrument?

RA I am Ra. It is as previously stated.

83.2 **QUESTIONER** Could you please tell me why the instrument gains weight now instead of loses it after a session?

RA I am Ra. To assume that the instrument is gaining the weight of the physical bodily complex due to a session or working with Ra is erroneous.

The instrument has no longer any physical material which, to any observable extent, must be used in order for this contact to occur. This is due to the determination of the group that the instrument shall not use the vital energy which would be necessary since the physical energy complex level is in deficit. Since the energy, therefore, for these contacts is a product of energy transfer, the instrument must no longer pay this physical price. Therefore, the instrument is not losing the weight.

However, the weight gain, as it occurs, is the product of two factors. One is the increasing sensitivity of this physical vehicle to all that is placed before it, including that towards which it is distorted in ways you would call allergic. The second factor is the energizing of these difficulties.

It is fortunate for the outlook of this contact and the incarnation of this entity that it is not distorted towards the overeating, as the overloading of this much-distorted physical complex would override even the most fervent affirmations of health/illness, and turn the instrument towards the distortions of illness/health or, in the extreme case, the physical death.

83.3 **QUESTIONER** Thank you. I'm going to ask a rather long, complex question here, and I would request that the answer to each portion of this question be given if there was a significant difference prior to the veil than following the veil so that I can get an idea of how what we experience now is used for better polarization.

Asking if there is any significant difference, and what was the difference, before the veil in the following while incarnate in third density: sleep, dreams, physical pain, mental pain, sex, disease, catalyst programming, random catalyst, relationships, or communication with the higher self or with the mind/body/spirit totality, or any other mind, body, or spirit functions before the veil that would be significant with respect to their difference after the veil?

RA I am Ra. Firstly, let us establish that both before and after the veil the same conditions existed in time/space; that is, the veiling process is a space/time phenomenon.

Secondly, the character of experience was altered drastically by the veiling process. In some cases, such as the dreaming and the contact with the higher self, the experience was quantitatively different due to the fact that the veiling is a primary cause of the value of dreams and is also the single door against which the higher self must stand awaiting entry.

Before veiling, dreams were not for the purpose of using the so-called unconscious to further utilize catalyst but were used to learn/teach from teach/learners within the inner planes, as well as those of outer origin of higher density.

As you deal with each subject of which you spoke you may observe, during the veiling process, not a quantitative change in the experience but a qualitative one.

Let us, as an example, choose your sexual activities of energy transfer. If you have a desire to treat other subjects in detail please query forthwith. In the instance of the sexual activity of those not dwelling within the veiling, each activity was a transfer. There were some transfers of strength. Most were rather attenuated in the strength of the transfer due to the lack of veiling.

In the third density, entities are attempting to learn the Ways of Love. If it can be seen that all are one being it becomes much more difficult for the undisciplined personality to choose one mate and, thereby, initiate itself into a program of service. It is much more likely that the sexual energy will be dissipated more randomly without either great joy or great sorrow depending from these experiences.

Therefore, the green-ray energy transfer, being almost without exception the case in sexual energy transfer prior to veiling, remains weakened and without significant crystallization. The sexual energy transfers and blockages after veiling have been discussed previously.[1]

It may be seen to be a more complex study but one far more efficient in crystallizing those who seek the green-ray energy center.

83.4   **QUESTIONER** Let's take, then, since we are on the subject of sex, the relationship before and after the veil of disease, in this particular case venereal disease. Was this type of disease in existence prior to the veil?

RA I am Ra. There has been that which is called disease, both of this type and others, before and after this great experiment. However, since the venereal disease is in large part a function of the thought-forms of a distorted nature which are associated with sexual energy blockage, the venereal disease is almost entirely the product of mind/body/spirit complexes' interaction after the veiling.

83.5   **QUESTIONER** You mentioned it did exist in a small way prior to the veil. What was the source of its development prior to the veiling process?

RA I am Ra. The source was as random as the nature of disease distortions are, at heart, in general. Each portion of the body complex is in a state of growth at all times. The reversal of this is seen as disease and has the benign function of ending an incarnation at an appropriate space/time nexus. This was the nature of disease, including that which you call venereal.

83.6   **QUESTIONER** I'll make this statement, and you can correct me, then. As I see the nature of the action of disease, specifically before the veil, it seems to me that the Logos had decided upon a program where an individual mind/body/spirit would continue to grow in mind, and the body would be the third-density analog of this mind, and the growth would be continual unless there was a lack of growth or an inability, for some reason, for the mind to continue along the growth patterns.

If this growth decelerated or stopped, then what we call disease would then act in a way so as to eventually terminate this physical experience so

---

[1]   Discussed previously in 26.38, 31.2–5, and 32.2–7.

that a new physical experience could be started to continue the growth process after a review of the entire process had taken place between incarnations. Would you clear up my thinking on that, please?

RA I am Ra. Your thinking is sufficiently clear on this subject.

83.7 QUESTIONER One thing I don't understand is why, if there was no veil, that the review of incarnation after the incarnation would help the process, since it seems to me that the entity should already be aware of what was happening. Possibly this has to do with the nature of space/time and time/space. Could you clear that up, please?

RA I am Ra. It is true that the nature of time/space is such that a lifetime may be seen whole as a book or record, the pages studied, riffled through, and re-read. However, the value of review is that of the testing as opposed to the studying. At the testing, when the test is true, the distillations of all study are made clear.

During the process of study (which you may call the incarnation), regardless of an entity's awareness of the process taking place, the material is diffused, and over-attention is almost inevitably placed upon detail.

The testing upon the cessation of the incarnative state is not that testing which involves the correct memorization of many details. This testing is, rather, the observing of self by self, often with aid, as we have said. In this observation one sees the sum of all the detailed study: that being an attitude, or complex of attitudes, which bias the consciousness of the mind/body/spirit.

83.8 QUESTIONER I just thought of an analogy while you were saying that, in that I fly an airplane, and I have testing in a simulator, but this is not too much of a test since I know we're bolted to the ground and can't get hurt. However, when we're actually flying and making the approach, landing etc., in the airplane, even though it's the same, it is . . . (I guess a poor analogy with respect to what was happening prior to the veil).

I know all of the conditions in both cases, and yet I cannot get too interested in the simulator work because I know that it is bolted to the ground. I see this as the entities prior to the veil knowing they were [chuckles] bolted to the creation, so to speak, or part of it. Is this a reasonable analogy?

RA I am Ra. This is quite reasonable, although it does not bear upon the function of the review of incarnation but rather bears upon the experiential differences before and after veiling.

83.9 **QUESTIONER** Now before the veil an entity would be aware that he was experiencing a disease. As an example, would you give me, if you are aware of a case, of a disease an entity might experience prior to the veil and how he would react to this and think about it, and what effect it would have on him in a complete sense? Would you, could you give me an example, please?

RA I am Ra. Inasmuch as the universe is composed of an infinite array of entities, there is also an infinity of response to stimulus. If you will observe your peoples you will discover greatly variant responses to the same distortion towards disease. Consequently, we cannot answer your query with any hope of making any true statements since the over-generalizations required are too capacious.[2]

83.10 **QUESTIONER** Was there any uniformity or like functions of societies or social organizations prior to the veil?

RA I am Ra. The third density is, by its very fiber, a societal one. There are societies wherever there are entities conscious of the self, and conscious of other-selves, and possessed with intelligence adequate to process information indicating the benefits of communal blending of energies. The structures of society before as after veiling were various.

However, the societies before veiling did not depend, in any case, upon the intentional enslavement of some for the benefit of others, this not being seen to be a possibility when all are seen as one. There was, however, the requisite amount of disharmony to produce various experiments in what you may call governmental or societal structures.

83.11 **QUESTIONER** In our present illusion we have undoubtedly lost sight of techniques of enslavement that are used since we are so far departed from the pre-veil experience. I am sure that many with service-to-others orientation are using techniques of enslavement—even though they are not aware these are techniques of enslavement—simply because they have

---

2   In this context, *capacious* can be defined as "ample; large; containing much."

been evolved over so long a period of time, and we are so deep into the illusion. Is this not correct?

RA I am Ra. This is incorrect.

83.12 QUESTIONER Then you say that there are no cases where those who are service-to-others oriented are using, in any way, techniques of enslavement that have grown as a result of the evolution of our social structures? Is this what you mean?

RA I am Ra. It was our understanding that your query concerned conditions before the veiling. There was no unconscious slavery, as you call this condition, at that period. At the present space/time the condition of well-meant and unintentional slavery are so numerous that it beggars our ability to enumerate them.

83.13 QUESTIONER Then for a service-to-others oriented entity at this time, meditation upon the nature of these little-expected forms of slavery might be productive in polarization, I would think. Am I correct?

RA I am Ra. You are quite correct.

83.14 QUESTIONER I would say that a very high percentage of the laws and restrictions within what we call our legal system are of a nature of enslavement of which I just spoke. Would you agree with this?

RA I am Ra. It is a necessary balance to the intention of law, which is to protect, that the result would encompass an equal distortion towards imprisonment. Therefore, we may say that your supposition is correct.

This is not to denigrate those who, in green- and blue-ray energies, sought to free a peaceable people from the bonds of chaos but only to point out the inevitable consequences of codification of response which does not recognize the uniqueness of each and every situation within your experience.

83.15 QUESTIONER Is the veil supposed to be what I would call semi-permeable?

RA I am Ra. The veil is indeed so.

83.16 QUESTIONER What techniques and methods of penetration of the veil were planned, and are there any others that have occurred other than those planned?

ra I am Ra. There were none planned by the first great experiment. As all experiments, this rested upon the nakedness of hypothesis. The outcome was unknown.

It was discovered, experientially and empirically, that there were as many ways to penetrate the veil as the imagination of mind/body/spirit complexes could provide. The desire of mind/body/spirit complexes to know that which was unknown drew to them the dreaming and the gradual opening to the seeker of all of the balancing mechanisms leading to adepthood and communication with teach/learners which could pierce this veil.

The various unmanifested activities of the self were found to be productive, in some degree, of penetration of the veil. In general we may say that by far the most vivid and even extravagant opportunities for the piercing of the veil are a result of the interaction of polarized entities.

83.17 QUESTIONER Could you expand on what you mean by that interaction of polarized entities in piercing the veil?

ra I am Ra. We shall state two items of note.

The first is the extreme potential for polarization in the relationship of two polarized entities which have embarked upon the service-to-others path or, in some few cases, the service-to-self path.

Secondly, we would note that effect which we have learned to call the doubling effect. Those of like mind which together seek shall far more surely find.

83.18 QUESTIONER Specifically, by what process in the first case, when two polarized entities would attempt to penetrate the veil, whether they be positively or negatively polarized—specifically by what technique would they penetrate the veil?

ra I am Ra. The penetration of the veil may be seen to begin to have its roots in the gestation of green-ray activity, that all-compassionate love which demands no return. If this path is followed the higher energy centers shall be activated and crystallized until the adept is born. Within the adept is the potential for dismantling the veil to a greater or lesser extent that all may be seen again as one. The other-self is primary catalyst in this particular path to the piercing of the veil, if you would call it that.

83.19 **QUESTIONER** What was the mechanism of the very first veiling process? I don't know if you can answer that. Would you try to, though, answer that?

RA I am Ra. The mechanism of the veiling between the conscious and unconscious portions of the mind was a declaration that the mind was complex. This, in turn, caused the body and the spirit to become complex.

83.20 **QUESTIONER** Would you give me an example of a complex activity of the body that we have now and how it was not complex prior to the veil?

RA I am Ra. Prior to the great experiment a mind/body/spirit was capable of controlling the pressure of blood in the vein, the beating of the organ you call the heart, the intensity of the sensation known to you as pain, and all the functions now understood to be involuntary or unconscious.

83.21 **QUESTIONER** When the veiling process originally took place, then, it seems that the Logos must have had a list, you might say, of those functions that would become unconscious and those that would remain consciously controlled. I am assuming that if this occurred there was good reason for these divisions. Am I any way correct on this?

RA I am Ra. No.

83.22 **QUESTIONER** Would you correct me, please?

RA I am Ra. There were many experiments whereby various of the functions, or distortions, of the body complex were veiled and others not. A large number of these experiments resulted in nonviable body complexes, or those only marginally viable. For instance, it is not a survival-oriented mechanism for the nerve receptors to blank out, unconsciously, any distortions towards pain.

83.23 **QUESTIONER** Now before the veil the mind could blank out pain. I assume then that the function of the pain at that time was to signal the body to assume a different configuration so that the source of the pain would leave, but then the pain could be eliminated mentally. Is that correct, and was there another function for pain prior to the veiling?

RA I am Ra. Your assumption is correct. The function of pain at that time was as the warning of the fire alarm to those not smelling the smoke.

83.24 **QUESTIONER** Then let's say that an entity at that time burned its hand due to carelessness. It would immediately remove its hand from the burning object and then, in order to not feel the pain any more, would mentally cut the pain off until healing had taken place. Is this correct?

RA I am Ra. This is correct.

83.25 **QUESTIONER** We would look at this in our present illusion as the elimination of a certain amount of catalyst that would produce an acceleration in our evolution. Is this correct?

RA I am Ra. The attitude towards pain varies from mind/body/spirit complex to mind/body/spirit complex. Your verbalization of attitude towards the distortion known as pain is one productive of helpful distortions as regards the process of evolution.

83.26 **QUESTIONER** What I was trying to indicate was that the plan of the Logos in veiling the conscious from the unconscious in such a way that the pain could not so easily be controlled would have created a system of catalyst that was not previously usable. Is this generally correct?

RA I am Ra. Yes.

83.27 **QUESTIONER** Now, in some cases it seems that this use of catalyst is almost in a runaway condition for some entities; that they are experiencing much more pain than they can make good use of as far as catalytic nature would be concerned. Could you comment on our present condition in the illusion with respect to that particular subject?

RA I am Ra. This shall be the last query of this working of a full length.

You may see, in some cases, an entity which, either by pre-incarnative choice or by constant reprogramming while in incarnation, has developed an esurient program of catalyst.[3] Such an entity is quite desirous of using the catalyst and has determined, to its own satisfaction, that what you may call the large board needs to be applied to the forehead in order to obtain the attention of the self.

In these cases it may indeed seem a great waste of the catalyst of pain; and a distortion towards feeling the tragedy of so much pain may be

---

[3] In this context, *esurient* can be defined as "hungry" or "greedy."

experienced by the other-self. However, it is well to hope that the other-self is grasping that which it has gone to some trouble to offer itself; that is, the catalyst which it desires to use for the purpose of evolution.

May we ask if there are any brief queries at this time?

83.28 **QUESTIONER** I noticed you started this session with "I communicate now." You usually use "We communicate now." Is there any significance or difference with respect to that? And then is there anything that we can do to make the instrument more comfortable or improve the contact?

RA I am Ra. We am Ra. You may see the grammatical difficulties of your linguistic structure in dealing with a social memory complex. There is no distinction between the first person singular and plural in your language when pertaining to Ra.

We offer the following, not to infringe upon your free will, but because this instrument has specifically requested information as to its maintenance, and the support group does so at this querying. We may suggest that the instrument has two areas of potential distortion, both of which may be aided in the bodily sense by the ingestion of those things which seem to the instrument to be desirable.

We do not suggest any hard and fast rulings of diet, although we may suggest the virtue of the liquids. The instrument has an increasing ability to sense that which will aid its bodily complex. It is being aided by affirmations and also by the light which is the food of the density of resting.

We may ask the support group to monitor the instrument, as always, so that in the case of the desire for the more complex proteins that which is the least distorted might be offered to the bodily complex which is, indeed, at this time potentially capable of greatly increased distortion.

I am Ra. We thank you, my friends, for your continued conscientiousness in the fulfilling of your manifestation of desire to serve others. You are conscientious. The appurtenances are quite well aligned.

I am Ra. I leave you, my friends, in the love and in the light of the One Infinite Creator. Go forth, therefore, rejoicing merrily in the power and in the peace of the One Infinite Creator. Adonai.

SESSION 84

APRIL 14, 1982

84.0 **RA** I am Ra. I greet you, my friends, in the love and in the light of the One Infinite Creator. We communicate now.

84.1 **QUESTIONER** Could you first please give me the condition of the instrument?

RA I am Ra. The physical complex energy level of the instrument is in sizeable deficit. The vital energies are well.

84.2 **QUESTIONER** In the last session you mentioned "least distorted complex protein" and that the body complex of the instrument was capable of greatly increased distortion. Would you define the protein of which you spoke? And we would like to know: increased distortion in which direction, towards health or ill-health?

RA I am Ra. We were, in the cautionary statement about complex protein, referring to the distortions of the animal protein which has been slaughtered and preservatives added in order to maintain the acceptability to your peoples of this non-living, physical material. It is well to attempt to find those items which are fresh and of the best quality possible in order to avoid increasing this particular entity's distortions which may be loosely termed allergic.

We were speaking of the distortion towards disease which is potential at this space/time.

84.3 **QUESTIONER** What disease in particular were you speaking of, and what would be its cause?

RA I am Ra. One disease, as you call this distortion, is that of the arthritis and the lupus erythematosus. The cause of this complex of distortions is, at base, pre-incarnative. We refrain from determining the other distortion potential at this space/time due to our desire to maintain the free will of this group. Affirmations may yet cause this difficulty to resolve itself.

Therefore, we simply encouraged the general care with the diet with the instructions about allergy, as you call this quite complex distortion of the mind and body complexes.

84.4 **QUESTIONER** The instrument asked the following question: "Ra has implied that the instrument is on a path of martyrdom, but since all die are we not all martyr to something? When, if ever, does martyrdom partake of wisdom?"

RA I am Ra. This is a thoughtful query. Let us use as exemplar the one known as Jehoshua. This entity incarnated with the plan of martyrdom. There is no wisdom in this plan, but rather understanding and compassion extended to its fullest perfection.

The one known as Jehoshua would have been less-than-fully understanding of its course had it chosen to follow its will at any space/time during its teachings. Several times, as you call this measure, this entity had the possibility of moving towards the martyr's place which was, for that martyr, Jerusalem. Yet in meditation this entity stated, time and again, "It is not yet the hour."

The entity could also have, when the hour came, walked another path. Its incarnation would then have been prolonged but the path for which it incarnated somewhat confused. Thusly, one may observe the greatest amount of understanding, of which this entity was indeed capable, taking place as the entity in meditation felt, and knew, that the hour had come for that to be fulfilled which was its incarnation.

It is indeed so that all mind/body/spirit complexes shall die to the third-density illusion; that is, that each yellow-ray physical-complex body shall cease to be viable. It is a misnomer to, for this reason alone, call each mind/body/spirit complex a martyr, for this term is reserved for those who lay down their lives for the service they may provide to others.

We may encourage meditation upon the functions of the will.

84.5 **QUESTIONER** Can you make any suggestions about the instrument's feet, or how they got in the bad shape they are in? And would alternating the shoes help?

RA I am Ra. The distortion referred to above, that is, the complex of juvenile rheumatoid arthritis and lupus erythematosus, acts in such a way as to cause various portions of the body complex to become distorted in the way in which the instrument's pedal appendages are now distorted.

We may suggest care in resumption of the exercise, but determination as well. The alternation of footwear shall prove efficacious. The undergarment for the feet, which you call the anklet, should be of a softer and finer material than is now being used and should, if possible, conform more to the outline of those appendages upon which it is placed. This should provide a more efficient aid to the cushioning of these appendages.

We may further suggest that the same immersion in the waters which is helpful to the general distortion is, in general, helpful to this specific distortion as well. However, the injury which has been sustained in the metatarsal region of the right pedal appendage should further be treated for some period of your space/time by the prudent application of the ice to the arch of the right foot for brief periods followed always by immersion in the warm water.

84.6 **QUESTIONER** Thank you. The instrument asks if the restricted, unpublishable healing information that was given during the first book be included in Book IV[1] since readers who have gotten that far will be dedicated somewhat?

RA I am Ra. This publication of material shall, in time, shall we say, be appropriate. There is intervening material.

84.7 **QUESTIONER** Thank you. I'm sure that we are getting into an area of problem with the First Distortion here, and also with a difficulty in a bit of transient material here, but I have two questions from people that I'll ask, although I consider especially the first one to be of no lasting value. Andrija Puharich asks about coming physical changes, specifically this summer. Is there anything that we could relay to him about that?

RA I am Ra. We may confirm the good intention of the source of this entity's puzzles and suggest that it is a grand choice that each may make to, by desire, collect the details of the day or, by desire, to seek the keys to unknowing.

---

[1] The original transcripts from the cassette recordings were published in four books under the title, *The Law of One.* (A fifth book containing fragments omitted from Books I–IV, along with accompanying commentary from Carla and Jim, was published years later in 1998.) See "The Relistening Report" in Volume 1 for information about how the new transcripts were produced and consequently this book, *The Ra Contact,* published.

84.8 **QUESTIONER** I'm interested . . . I can't help but be interested in the fact that he had reported being taken on board craft. Could you tell me something about that?[2]

RA I am Ra. The nature of contact is such that—in order for the deep portion of the trunk of the tree of mind affected to be able to accept the contact—some symbology which may rise to the conscious mind is necessary as a framework for the explanation of the fruits of the contact. In such cases the entity's own expectations fashion the tale which shall be most acceptable to that entity; and in the dream state, or a trance state in which visions may be produced, this seeming memory is fed into the higher levels of the so-called subconscious and the lower levels of the conscious. From this point the story may surface as any memory and cause the instrument to function without losing balance or sanity.

84.9 **QUESTIONER** Thank you. Going back to the previous session, it was stated that each sexual activity was a transfer before the veil. I am assuming from that that you mean that there was a transfer of energy for each sexual activity before the veil which indicates to me that a transfer doesn't take place every time. Taking the case before the veil, would you trace the flow of energy that is transferred and tell me if that was the planned activity or a planned transfer by the designing Logos?

RA I am Ra. The path of energy transfer before the veiling during the sexual intercourse was that of the two entities possessed of green-ray capability. The awareness of all as Creator is that which opens the green energy center. Thusly there was no possibility of blockage due to the sure knowledge of each by each that each was the Creator. The transfers were weak due to the ease with which such transfers could take place between any two polarized entities during sexual intercourse.

84.10 **QUESTIONER** What I was getting at more precisely was: is the path of energy transfer— When we close an electrical circuit, it's easy to follow the path of energy. It goes along the conductor. I am trying to determine whether this transfer is between the heart chakras of each entity. I am trying to trace the physical flow of the energy to try to get an idea of

---

[2] This question refers to material that Ra asked not be published. See Book V notes to this session.

blockages after the veil. I may be off on a wrong track here. If I'm wrong, we'll just drop it. Can you tell me something about that?

RA I am Ra. In such a drawing or schematic representation of the circuitry of two mind/body/spirits, or mind/body/spirit complexes, in sexual or other energy transfer, the circuit opens always at the red or base center and moves as possible through the intervening energy centers. If baffled, it will stop at orange. If not, it shall proceed to yellow. If still unbaffled, it shall proceed to green.

It is well to remember in the case of the mind/body/spirit that the chakras, or energy centers, could well be functioning without crystallization.

84.11 QUESTIONER In other words, they would be functioning, but it would be equivalent in electrical circuitry to having a high resistance, shall we say. Although the circuit would be complete, red through green, the total quantity of energy transferred would be less. Is this correct?

RA I am Ra. We might most closely associate your query with the concept of voltage. The uncrystallized, lower centers cannot deliver the higher voltage. The crystallized centers may become quite remarkable in the high voltage characteristics of the energy transfer as it reaches green ray. And indeed, as green ray is crystallized, this also applies to the higher energy centers until such energy transfers become an honestation for the Creator.[3]

84.12 QUESTIONER Would you please correct me on this statement, then? I'm guessing that what happens is that, when a transfer takes place, the energy is that light energy that comes in through the feet of the entity, and starts the— The voltage or potential difference starts with the red energy center and, in the case of the green-ray transfer, terminates at the green energy center and then must leap or flow from the green energy center of one entity to the green of the other, and then something happens to it. Could you clear up my thinking on that?

RA I am Ra. Yes.

84.13 QUESTIONER Would you please do that?

---

[3] In this context, *honestation* can be defined as "adornment or grace."

RA I am Ra. The energy transfer occurs in one releasing of the potential difference. This does not leap between green and green energy centers but is the sharing of the energies of each from red ray upwards. In this context it may be seen to be at its most efficient when both entities have orgasm simultaneously.

However, it functions as transfer if either has the orgasm. And, indeed, in the case of the physically expressed love between a mated pair which does not have the conclusion you call orgasm, there is nonetheless a considerable amount of energy transferred due to the potential difference which has been raised, as long as both entities are aware of this potential and release its strength to each other by desire of the will in a mental or mind complex dedication. You may see this practice as being used to generate energy transfers in some of your practices of what you may call other than Christian religious-distortion systems of the Law of One.

84.14 QUESTIONER Would you give me an example of that last statement?

RA I am Ra. We preface this example with the reminder that each system is quite distorted and its teachings always half-lost. However, one such system is that called the tantric yoga.

84.15 QUESTIONER Considering individual A and individual B, if individual A experiences the orgasm is the energy, then, transferred to individual B in a greater amount? Is that correct?

RA I am Ra. Your query is incomplete. Please restate.

84.16 QUESTIONER What I am trying to determine is the direction of energy transfer as a function of orgasm. Which entity gets the transferred energy? I know it's a dumb question, but I want to be sure I have it cleared up.

RA I am Ra. If both entities are well polarized and vibrating in green-ray love, any orgasm shall offer equal energy to both.

84.17 QUESTIONER I see. Before the veil can you describe any other physical difference that we haven't talked about yet with respect to the sexual energy transfers or relationships or anything prior to veiling?

RA I am Ra. Perhaps the most critical difference of the veiling, before and after, was that before the mind, body, and spirit were veiled, entities were aware that each energy transfer—and, indeed, very nearly all that proceeds from any intercourse, social or sexual, between two entities—has its character and substance in time/space rather than space/time.

The energies transferred during the sexual activity are not, properly speaking, of space/time. There is a great component of what you may call metaphysical energy transferred. Indeed, the body complex as a whole is greatly misunderstood due to the post-veiling assumption that the physical manifestation called the body is subject only to physical stimuli. This is emphatically not so.

84.18   **QUESTIONER** After the veil, in our particular case now, we have, in the circuitry of which we were speaking, what you'd call a blockage that first occurs in orange ray. Could you describe what occurs with this first blockage and what its effects are on each of the entities, assuming that one blocks, and the other does not, or if both are blocked?

RA I am Ra. This material has been covered previously.[4] If both entities are blocked, both will have an increased hunger for the same activity, seeking to unblock the baffled flow of energy.

If one entity is blocked and the other vibrates in love, the entity baffled will hunger still but have a tendency to attempt to continue the procedure of sating the increasing hunger with the one vibrating green ray due to an impression that this entity might prove helpful in this endeavor.

The green-ray active individual shall polarize slightly in the direction of service to others but have only the energy with which it began.

84.19   **QUESTIONER** I didn't mean to cover previously covered material. I was trying to work into a better understanding of what we're talking about, with background of the veiling process, and what I was actually attempting to do was to discover something new in asking the question, so please if I ask any questions in the future that have already been covered don't bother to repeat the material.

I am just searching the same area for the possibility of greater enlightenment with respect to the particular area, since it seems to be one of the major areas of experience in our present condition of veiling that produces a very large amount of catalyst. And I am trying to understand,

---

4   Previously covered in 26.38 and 32.2.

to use a poor term, how this veiling process created a greater experience, and how this experience evolved, shall I say. The questions are very difficult at times to ask.

It occurs to me that many statues or drawings of the one known as Lucifer, or the Devil, is shown with an erection. Is this a function of this orange-ray blockage? And was this, shall we say, known by, in some minimal way, you might say, by those who devised these statues and drawings etc.?

RA I am Ra. There is, of course, much other distortion involved in a discussion of any mythic archetypical form. However, we may answer in the affirmative and note that you are perceptive.

84.20 QUESTIONER Then, with respect to the green, blue, and indigo transfers of energy: How would the mechanism for these transfers differ in making them possible or setting the groundwork for them than the orange ray?

I know this is very difficult to ask, and I may not be making any sense, but what I am trying to do is get to an understanding of the foundation for transfers in each of the rays, and the preparations for the transfers, you might say, or the fundamental requirements and biases and potentials for these transfers. Could you expand on that for me please? I am sorry for the poor question.

RA I am Ra. We would take a moment to state in reply to a previous comment that we shall answer each query, whether or not it has been previously covered, for not to do so would be to baffle the flow of quite another transfer of energy.

To respond to your query we firstly wish to agree with your supposition that the subject you now query upon is a large one, for in it lies an entire system of opening the gateway to intelligent infinity. You may see that some information is necessarily shrouded in mystery by our desire to preserve the free will of the adept.

The great key to blue, indigo, and finally that great capital of the column of sexual energy transfer, violet energy transfers, is the metaphysical bond or distortion which has the name among your peoples of unconditional love.

In the blue-ray energy transfer the quality of this love is refined in the fire of honest communication and clarity; this, shall we say, normally—

meaning in general—takes a substantial portion of your space/time to accomplish, although there are instances of matings so well refined in previous incarnations and so well remembered that the blue ray may be penetrated at once.

This energy transfer is of great benefit to the seeker in that all communication from this seeker is thereby refined, and the eyes of honesty and clarity look upon a new world. Such is the nature of blue-ray energy, and such is one mechanism of potentiating and crystallizing it.

As we approach indigo-ray transfer we find ourselves in a shadowland where we cannot give you information straight out or plain, for this is seen by us to be an infringement.

We cannot speak at all of violet-ray transfer as we do not, again, desire to break the Law of Confusion.

We may say that these jewels, though dearly bought, are beyond price for the seeker; and might suggest that just as each awareness is arrived at through a process of analysis, synthesis, and inspiration, so should the seeker approach its mate and evaluate each experience, seeking the jewel.

84.21 **QUESTIONER** Is there any way to tell which ray the transfer was for an individual after the experience? Is there any way for the individual to tell in which particular ray the transfer occurred?

RA I am Ra. There is only a subjective yardstick or measure of such. If the energies have flowed so that love is made whole, green-ray transfer has taken place.

If, by the same entities' exchange, greater ease in communication and greater sight has been experienced, the energy has been refined to the blue-ray energy center.

If the polarized entities, by this same energy transfer experience, find that the faculties of will and faith have been stimulated, not for a brief while but for a great duration of what you call time, you may perceive the indigo-ray transfer.

We may not speak of the violet-ray transfer except to note that it is an opening to the gateway of intelligent infinity. Indeed, the indigo-ray transfer is also this, but, shall we say, the veil has not yet been lifted.

84.22 **QUESTIONER** Before the veil, were there— Let me put it this way: Did the Logos, or did most Logoi plan before the veil to create a system of random sexual activity, or specific pairing of entities for periods of time, or did they have an objective in this respect?

RA I am Ra. This shall be the last full query of this working.

The harvest from the previous creation was that which included the male and female mind/body/spirit. It was the intention of the original Logoi that entities mate with one another in any fashion which caused a greater polarization. It was determined, after observation of the process of many Logoi, that polarization increased manyfold if the mating were not indiscriminate. Consequent Logoi thusly preserved a bias towards the mated relationship which is more characteristic of more disciplined personalities and of what you may call higher densities. The free will of each entity, however, was always paramount, and a bias only could be offered.

May we ask if there may be any brief queries before we leave this instrument?

84.23 **QUESTIONER** Is there anything we can do to make the instrument more comfortable or improve the contact?

RA I am Ra. We would ask that each of the support group be especially vigilant in the, what you would call, immediate future due to this instrument's unbidden but serious potential for increased distortion towards illness/health.

You are most conscientious. We thank you, my friends, and leave you in the glorious light and love of the One Infinite Creator. Go forth, therefore, rejoicing in the power and in the peace of the One Infinite Creator. Adonai.

SESSION 85

APRIL 26, 1982

85.0 **RA** I am Ra. We communicate now.

[*There is a 40-second pause here.*]

85.1 **QUESTIONER** Could you first give me the condition of the instrument?

RA I am Ra. We ask your permission to preface this answer by the inclusion of the greeting which we use.

85.2 **QUESTIONER** That's agreeable.

RA I am Ra. We greet you in the love and in the light of the One Infinite Creator. We were having some difficulty with the channel of energy influx due to pain flare, as you call this distortion of the physical body complex of this instrument. Therefore, it was necessary to speak as briefly as possible until we had safely transferred the mind/body/spirit complex of this instrument. We beg your kind indulgence for our discourtesy. It was appropriate.

The condition of this instrument is as follows: The necessity for extreme vigilance is less due to the somewhat lessened physical complex energy deficit. The potential for distortion remains, and continued watchfulness over the ingestion of helpful foodstuffs continues to be recommended. Although the instrument is experiencing more than the, shall we say, normal (for this mind/body/spirit complex) distortion towards pain at this space/time nexus, the basic condition is less distorted. The vital energies are as previously stated.

We commend the vigilance and care of this group.

85.3 **QUESTIONER** What is the current situation with respect to our fifth-density, service-to-self polarized companion, shall I say?

RA I am Ra. Your companion has never been more closely associated with you than at the present nexus. You may see a kind of crisis occurring upon the so-called magical level at this particular space/time nexus.

85.4 **QUESTIONER** What is the nature of this crisis?

RA I am Ra. The nature of this crisis is the determination of the relative polarity of your companion and yourselves. You are in the position of being in the third-density illusion and consequently having the conscious collective magical ability of the neophyte, whereas your companion is most adept. However, the faculties of will and faith and the calling to the light have been used by this group to the exclusion of any significant depolarization from the service-to-others path.

If your companion can possibly depolarize this group it must do so, and that quickly, for in this unsuccessful attempt at exploring the wisdom of separation it is encountering some depolarization. This shall continue. Therefore, the efforts of your companion are pronounced at this space/time and time/space nexus.

85.5 **QUESTIONER** I am totally aware of the lack of necessity or even rational need for naming of entities or things. I was wondering if this particular entity had a name, just so that we could increase our efficiency of communicating with respect to him. Does he have a name?

RA I am Ra. Yes.

85.6 **QUESTIONER** Would it be magically bad for us to know that name, or would it make no difference?

RA I am Ra. It would make a difference.

85.7 **QUESTIONER** What would the difference be?

RA I am Ra. If one wishes to have power over an entity it is an aid to know that entity's name. If one wishes no power over an entity but wishes to collect that entity into the very heart of one's own being, it is well to forget the naming. Both processes are magically viable. Each is polarized in a specific way. It is your choice.

85.8 **QUESTIONER** I am assuming that it would be a problem for the instrument if she were to meditate without the hand pressure from the other-self at this time because of the continued greeting. Is this correct?

RA I am Ra. This is correct if the instrument wishes to remain free from this potential separation of mind/body/spirit complex from the third density it now experiences.

85.9 **QUESTIONER** I am assuming that if for no other reason, since our fifth-density companion has been monitoring our communications with Ra, it has been made aware of the veiling process of which we have been speaking.

And it seems to me that, from an intellectual point of view, that conscious knowledge and acceptance of the fact that this veiling process was used for the purpose for which it was used, that it would be difficult to maintain high negative polarization once it was intellectually, consciously accepted that this veiling process did in fact occur the way that you have described. Could you clear up my thinking on that point?

RA I am Ra. We are unsure as to our success in realigning your modes of mentation. We may, however, comment.

The polarization process, as it enters fourth density, is one which occurs with full knowledge of the veiling process which has taken place in third density. This veiling process is that which is a portion of the third-density experience. The knowledge and memory of the outcome of this, and all portions of the third-density experience, informs the higher-density polarized entity.

It, however, does not influence the choice which has been made and which is the basis for further work past third density in polarization. Those which have chosen the service-to-others[1] path have simply used the veiling process in order to potentiate that which is not. This is an entirely acceptable method of self-knowledge of and by the Creator.

85.10 **QUESTIONER** You just stated that those who are on the service-to-others path use the veiling process to potentiate that which is not. I believe I am correct in repeating what you said. Is that correct?

RA I am Ra. Yes. [2]

85.11 **QUESTIONER** Then the service-to-others path have potentiated that which is not. Could you expand that a little bit so I can understand it better?

RA I am Ra. If you see the energy centers in their various colors completing the spectrum you may see that the service-to-others[3] choice is

---

[1] This should be service-to-self. Don and Ra corrected the error in 85.13.

[2] As previous footnote indicates, in 85.13 Ra corrected the error, conveying they intended to say "service to self."

[3] Corrected to "service to self" in 85.13.

one which denies the very center of the spectrum—that being universal love.

Therefore, all that is built upon the penetration of the light of harvestable quality by such entities is based upon an omission. This omission shall manifest in fourth density as the love of self; that is, the fullest expression of the orange and yellow energy centers which then are used to potentiate communication and adepthood.

When fifth-density refinement has been achieved, that which is not is carried further, the wisdom density being explored by entities which have no compassion, no universal love. They experience that which they wish by free choice, being of the earnest opinion that green-ray energy is folly.

That which is not may be seen as a self-imposed darkness in which harmony is turned into an eternal disharmony. However, that which is not cannot endure throughout the octave of third density,[4] and, as darkness eventually calls the light, so does that which is not eventually call that which is.

85.12 **QUESTIONER** I believe that there were salient errors in the communication we just completed because of transmission difficulties. Are you aware of these errors?

RA I am Ra. We are unaware of errors although this instrument is experiencing flares of pain, as you call this distortion. We welcome and encourage your perceptions in correcting any errors in transmission.

85.13 **QUESTIONER** I think simply that the statement was made that we were speaking of the service-to-others path. Would you check that, please?

RA I am Ra. May we ask that you be apprised of our intention to have spoken of the service-to-self path as the path of that which is not.

85.14 **QUESTIONER** I am just interested in the problem here that we sometimes have with transmission since the word "others" was used three times in

---

4   Though unknown, there is the potential that "octave of third density" is an uncorrected error. While each density could be considered its own octave, the journey of polarity is not confined to the boundaries of third density alone, but transpires in the larger octave of seven densities, beginning in third and concluding in early sixth.

the transmission rather than the word "self." And could you give me an idea of the problem of communication that we had there that creates that type of an anomaly which, if I didn't catch, could create a rather large discrepancy in communication?

RA I am Ra. Firstly, we may note the clumsiness of language and our unfamiliarity with it in our native, shall we say, experience. Secondly, we may point out that once we have miscalled or misnumbered an event or thing, that referent is quite likely to be reused for some transmission time, as you call this measurement, due to our original error having gone undetected by ourselves.

85.15 **QUESTIONER** Thank you. Do you have use of all of the words in the English language and, for that matter, all of the words in all languages that are spoken upon this planet at this time?

RA I am Ra. No.

85.16 **QUESTIONER** I have a question here from Jim. It states: "I believe that one of my primary pre-incarnative choices was to open my green-ray energy center for healing purposes. As I see my compassion developing, is it more appropriate to balance this compassion with wisdom in my healing exercises or to allow the compassion to develop as much as possible without being balanced?"

RA I am Ra. This query borders upon that type of question to which answers are unavailable due to the free-will prohibitions upon information from teach/learners.

To the student of the balancing process we may suggest that the most stringent honesty be applied. As compassion is perceived it is suggested that, in balancing, this perception be analyzed. It may take many, many essays into compassion before true universal love is the product of the attempted opening and crystallization of this all-important springboard energy center.

Thus the student may discover many other components to what may seem to be all-embracing love. Each of these components may be balanced and accepted as part of the self, and as transitional material, as the entity's seat of learn/teaching moves ever more fairly into the green ray.

When it is perceived that universal love has been achieved, the next balancing may or may not be wisdom. If the adept is balancing manifestations it is indeed appropriate to balance universal love and wisdom. If the balancing is of mind or spirit there are many subtleties to which the adept may give careful consideration. Love and wisdom, like love and light, are not black and white, shall we say, but faces of the same coin, if you will. Therefore, it is not in all cases that balancing consists of a movement from compassion to wisdom.

We may suggest at all times the constant remembrance of the density from which each adept desires to move. This density learns the lessons of love. In the case of wanderers there are half-forgotten overlays of other lessons and other densities.

We shall leave these considerations with the questioner and invite observations which we shall then be most happy to respond to in what may seem to be a more effectual manner.

[There is a 30-second pause here.]

85.17 **QUESTIONER** What changes of functions, or control, or understanding, etc., of the mind/body/spirits were most effective in producing the evolution desired due to the veiling process?

RA I am Ra. We are having difficulty retaining clear channel through this instrument. It has a safe margin of transferred energy but is experiencing pain flares. May we ask that you repeat the query as we have a better channel now.

85.18 **QUESTIONER** After the veiling process certain veiled functions or activities must have been paramount in creating evolution in desired polarized directions. I was just wondering which of these had the greatest effect on polarization?

RA I am Ra. The most effectual veiling was that of the mind.

85.19 **QUESTIONER** I would like to carry that on to find out what specific functions of the mind were most effectual, and the three or four most effective changes brought about to create the polarization.

RA I am Ra. This is an interesting query. The primary veiling was of such significance that it may be seen to be analogous to the mantling of the earth over all the jewels within the earth's crust; whereas previously all facets of the Creator were consciously known. After the veiling, almost no facets of the Creator were known to the mind. Almost all was buried beneath the veil.

If one were to attempt to list those functions of mind most significant in that they might be of aid in polarization, one would need to begin with the faculty of visioning, envisioning, or far-seeing. Without the veil the mind was not caught in your illusory time. With the veil, space/time is the only obvious possibility for experience.

Also upon the list of significant veiled functions of the mind would be that of dreaming. The so-called dreaming contains a great deal which, if made available to the conscious mind and used, shall aid it in polarization to a great extent.

The third function of the mind which is significant and which has been veiled is that of the knowing of the body. The knowledge of and control over the body, having been lost to a great extent in the veiling process, is thusly lost from the experience of the seeker. Its knowledge before the veiling is of small use. Its knowledge after the veiling, and in the face of what is now a dense illusion of separation of body complex from mind complex, is quite significant.

Perhaps the most important and significant function that occurred due to the veiling of the mind from itself is not in itself a function of mind but rather is a product of the potential created by this veiling. This is the faculty of will or pure desire.

We may ask for brief queries at this time. Although there is energy remaining for this working we are reluctant to continue this contact, experiencing continual variations due to pain flares, as you call this distortion. Although we are unaware of any misgiven material, we are aware that there have been several points during which our channel was less-than-optimal. This instrument is most faithful, but we do not wish to misuse this instrument. Please query as you will.

85.20   QUESTIONER Well, I will just ask in closing: is an individualized portion or entity of Ra inhabiting the instrument's body for the purpose of communication? And then is there anything that we can do to improve the contact or make the instrument more comfortable?

RA I am Ra. We of Ra communicate through narrow-band channel through the violet-ray energy center. We are not, as you would say, physically indwelling in this instrument; rather, the mind/body/spirit complex of this instrument rests with us.

You are diligent and conscientious. The alignments are excellent. We leave you rejoicing in the power and in the peace of the One Infinite Creator. Go forth, then, my friends, rejoicing in the power and in the peace of the infinite love and the ineffable light of the One Creator. I am Ra. Adonai.

86.0   RA I am Ra. I greet you in the love and in the light of the One Infinite Creator. We communicate now.

86.1   QUESTIONER Could you first please give me the condition of the instrument?

RA I am Ra. The instrument's distortion towards physical energy complex deficit has slightly increased since the last asking. The vital energy levels have had significant calls upon them and are somewhat less than the last asking also.

86.2   QUESTIONER What was the nature of these significant calls on the vital energy?

RA I am Ra. There are those entities which entertain the thought-distortion towards this entity that it shall remove, for the other-selves, all distortions for the other-self. This entity has recently been in close contact with a larger than normal number of entities with these thought-complex distortions. This entity is of the distortion to provide whatever service is possible and is not consciously aware of the inroads made upon the vital energies.

86.3   QUESTIONER Am I correct in assuming that you're speaking of incarnate third-density entities that were creating the condition of use of the vital energy?

RA I am Ra. Yes.

86.4   QUESTIONER What's the present situation with our fifth-density service-to-self polarized companion?

RA I am Ra. The period which you may call crisis remains.

86.5   QUESTIONER Can you tell me anything of the nature of this crisis?

RA I am Ra. The polarity of your companion is approaching the critical point at which the entity shall choose either to retreat for the nonce and leave any greetings to fourth-density minions, or lose polarity. The only other potential is that in some way this group might lose polarity in which case your companion could continue its form of greeting.

86.6   **QUESTIONER** In the last session you had mentioned the properties precipitating from the veiling of the mind, the first being visioning, envisioning, or far-seeing. Would you explain the meaning of that?

RA I am Ra. Your language is not overstrewn with non-emotional terms for the functional qualities of what is now termed the unconscious mind. The nature of mind is something which we have requested that you ponder. However, it is, shall we say, clear enough to the casual observer that we may share some thoughts with you without infringing upon your free learn/teaching experiences.

The nature of the unconscious is of the nature of concept rather than word. Consequently, before the veiling the use of the deeper mind was that of the use of unspoken concept. You may consider the emotive and connotative aspects of a melody. One could call out, in some stylized fashion, the terms for the notes of the melody. One could say, "a quarter note A, a quarter note A, a quarter note A, whole note F." This bears little resemblance to the beginning of the melody of one of your composers' most influential melodies, that known to you as a symbol of victory.

This is the nature of the deeper mind. There are only stylized methods with which to discuss its functions. Thusly our descriptions of this portion of the mind, as well as the same portions of body and spirit, were given terms such as "far-seeing," indicating that the nature of penetration of the veiled portion of the mind may be likened unto the journey too rich and exotic to contemplate adequate describing thereof.

86.7   **QUESTIONER** You stated that dreaming, if made available to the conscious mind, will aid greatly in polarization. Would you define dreaming, or tell us what it is and how it aids in polarization?

RA I am Ra. Dreaming is an activity of communication through the veil of the unconscious mind and the conscious mind. The nature of this activity is wholly dependent upon the situation regarding the energy center blockages, activations, and crystallizations of a given mind/body/spirit complex.

In one who is blocked at two of the three lower energy centers dreaming will be of value in the polarization process in that there will be a repetition of those portions of recent catalyst as well as deeper-held blockages, thereby giving the waking mind clues as to the nature of these blockages, and hints as to possible changes in perception which may lead to the unblocking.

This type of dreaming, or communication through the veiled portions of the mind, occurs also with those mind/body/spirit complexes (which are functioning with far less blockage and enjoying the green-ray activation or higher activation) at those times at which the mind/body/spirit complex experiences catalyst, momentarily reblocking or baffling or otherwise distorting the flow of energy influx.

Therefore, in all cases it is useful to a mind/body/spirit complex to ponder the content and emotive resonance of dreams.

For those whose green-ray energy centers have been activated—as well as for those whose green-ray energy centers are offered an unusual unblockage due to extreme catalyst, such as what is termed the physical death of the self, or one which is beloved occurring in what you may call your near future—dreaming takes on another activity. This is what may loosely be termed precognition, or a knowing which is prior to that which shall occur in physical manifestation in your yellow-ray third-density space/time. This property of the mind depends upon its placement, to a great extent, in time/space so that the terms of present and future and past have no meaning. This will, if made proper use of by the mind/body/spirit complex, enable this entity to enter more fully into the all-compassionate love of each and every circumstance, including those circumstances against which an entity may have a strong distortion towards what you may call unhappiness.[1]

As a mind/body/spirit complex consciously chooses the path of the adept and, with each energy center balanced to a minimal degree, begins to open the indigo-ray energy center, the so-called dreaming becomes the most efficient tool for polarization; for if it is known by the adept that work may be done in consciousness while the so-called conscious mind rests, this adept may call upon those which guide it, those presences which surround it, and, most of all, the magical personality (which is the

---

[1] Originally transmitted without the word "complex," Ra and Don corrected the error in session 87.

higher self in space/time analog) as it moves into the sleeping mode of consciousness.[2] With these affirmations attended to, the activity of dreaming reaches that potential of learn/teaching which is most helpful to increasing the distortions of the adept towards its chosen polarity.

There are other possibilities of the dreaming not so closely aligned with the increase in polarity which we do not cover at this particular space/time.

86.8 **QUESTIONER** How is the dream designed or programmed? Is this done by the higher self, or who is responsible for this?

RA I am Ra. In all cases the mind/body/spirit complex makes what use it can of the faculty of the dreaming. It, itself, is responsible for this activity.

86.9 **QUESTIONER** Then you are saying that the subconscious is responsible for what I would call design or scriptwriting for the dream. Is this correct?

RA I am Ra. This is correct.

86.10 **QUESTIONER** Is the memory that the individual has upon waking from the dream usually reasonably accurate? Is the dream easily remembered?

RA I am Ra. You must realize that we are over-generalizing in order to answer your queries as there are several sorts of dreams. However, in general, it may be noted that it is only for a trained and disciplined observer to have reasonably good recall of the dreaming. This faculty may be learned by virtue of a discipline of the recording immediately upon awakening of each and every detail which can be recalled. This training sharpens one's ability to recall the dream. The most common perception of a mind/body/spirit complex of its dreams is muddied, muddled, and quickly lost.

86.11 **QUESTIONER** In that remembering dreams, you are saying that the individual can find specific clues to current energy center blockages and may, thereby, reduce or eliminate those blockages. Is this correct?

RA I am Ra. This is so.

---

[2] Same as previous footnote.

86.12 **QUESTIONER** Is there any other function of dreaming that is of value in the evolutionary process?

RA I am Ra. Although there are many which are of some value we would choose two to note, since these two, though not of value in polarization, may be of value in a more generalized sense.

The activity of dreaming is an activity in which there is made a finely wrought and excellently fashioned bridge from conscious to unconscious. In this state the various distortions which have occurred in the energy web of the body complex, due to the mis-precision[3] with which energy influxes have been received, are healed. With the proper amount of dreaming comes the healing of these distortions. Continued lack of this possibility can cause seriously distorted mind/body/spirit complexes.

The other function of the dreaming which is of aid is that type of dream which is visionary and which prophets and mystics have experienced from days of old. Their visions come through the roots of mind and speak to a hungry world. Thus the dream is of service without being of a personally polarizing nature. However, in that mystic or prophet [who] desires to serve, such service will increase the entity's polarity.

86.13 **QUESTIONER** There is a portion of sleep that has been called R.E.M. Is this the state of dreaming?

RA I am Ra. This is correct.

86.14 **QUESTIONER** It was noticed that this occurs in small units during the night with gaps in between. Is there any particular reason for this?

RA I am Ra. Yes.

86.15 **QUESTIONER** If it is of any value to know that, would you tell me why the dreaming process works like that?

RA I am Ra. The portions of the dreaming process which are helpful for polarization and also for the vision of the mystic take place in time/space and, consequently, use the bridge from metaphysical to physical for what

---

3 Though not a word in the English language, Ra did say "mis-precision" (the hyphen is an educated guess). The term makes contextual sense, but there is a small chance that Ra intended to say "misprision," a term they used in 64.6.

seems to be a brief period of your space/time. The time/space equivalent is far greater.

The bridge remains, however, and traduces each distortion of mind, body, and spirit as it has received the distortions of energy influxes so that healing may take place. This healing process does not occur with the incidence of rapid eye movement but, rather, occurs largely in the space/time portion of the mind/body/spirit complex using the bridge to time/space for the process of healing to be enabled.

86.16 **QUESTIONER** You mentioned loss of knowledge and control over the body as being a factor that was helpful in the evolutionary process due to veiling. Could you enumerate the important losses of knowledge and control over the body?

RA I am Ra. This query contains some portions which would be more helpfully answered were some intervening material requested.

86.17 **QUESTIONER** I'm at a loss to know what to request. Can you [*chuckles*] give me an idea of what area of intervening material I should work on?

RA I am Ra. No. However, we shall be happy to answer the original query if it is still desired if you first perceive that there is information lacking.

86.18 **QUESTIONER** Perhaps I can question it slightly differently here. I might ask why loss of knowledge and control over the body was helpful?

RA I am Ra. The knowledge of the potentials of the physical vehicle before the veiling offered the mind/body/spirit a free range of choices with regard to activities and manifestations of the body but offered little in the way of the development of polarity.[4] When the knowledge of these

---

[4] The sentence as Ra communicated it read, "The loss to the conscious mind of the knowledge of the potentials of the physical vehicle before the veiling offered the mind/body/spirit complex a free range of choices with regard to activities and manifestations of the body, but offered little in the way of the development of polarity."

The phrase "The loss to the conscious mind of" has been removed from the beginning of the answer because Ra appears to have started speaking about post-veil conditions ("loss to the conscious mind") but then changed their focus to pre-veil ("potentials of the physical vehicle before veiling") without realizing it.

potentials and functions of the physical vehicle is shrouded from the conscious mind complex, the mind/body/spirit complex is often nearly without knowledge of how to best manifest its beingness.

However, this state of lack of knowledge offers an opportunity for a desire to grow within the mind complex. This desire is that which seeks to know the possibilities of the body complex. The ramifications of each possibility and the eventual biases thusly built have within them a force which can only be generated by such desire or will to know.

86.19 **QUESTIONER** Perhaps you could give examples of use of the body prior to veiling and after veiling in the same aspect so that we could understand the change in knowledge and control over the body more clearly. Could you do this, please?

RA I am Ra. We could.

86.20 **QUESTIONER** Will you do this?

RA I am Ra. Yes. Let us deal with the sexual energy transfer. Before the veiling such a transfer was always possible due to there being no shadow upon the grasp of the nature of the body and its relationship to other mind/body/spirits in this particular manifestation. Before the veiling process there was a near total lack of the use of this sexual energy transfer beyond green ray.

This also was due to the same unshadowed knowledge each had of each. There was, in third density then, little purpose to be seen in the more intensive relationships of mind, body, and spirits[5] which you may call those of the mating process, since each other-self was seen to be the Creator, and no other-self seemed to be more the Creator than another.

After the veiling process it became infinitely more difficult to achieve green-ray energy transfer due to the great areas of mystery and unknowing concerning the body complex and its manifestations.

Ra also originally said "mind/body/spirit complex" here. Ra and Don corrected the error in session 87 to remove "complex."

[5] In this and the previous two instances in the preceding paragraph, Ra originally said, "body complex," "mind/body/spirit complexes," and "mind, body, and spirit complexes." In each instance "complex" was removed per the Ra and Don's error correction in session 87.

However, also due to the great shadowing of the manifestations of the body from the conscious mind complex, when such energy transfer was experienced it was likelier to provide catalyst which caused a bonding of self with other-self in a properly polarized configuration.

From this point it was far more likely that higher energy transfers would be sought by this mated pair of mind/body/spirit complexes, thus allowing the Creator to know Itself with great beauty, solemnity, and wonder. Intelligent infinity having been reached by this sacramental use of this function of the body, each mind/body/spirit complex of the mated pair gained greatly in polarization and in ability to serve.

86.21 **QUESTIONER** Did any of the other aspects of loss of knowledge or control over the body approach, to any degree in efficiency, what you've just described?

RA I am Ra. Each function of the body complex has some potential after the veiling to provide helpful catalyst. We did choose the example of sexual energy transfer due to its central place in the functionary capabilities of the body complex made more useful by means of the veiling process.

This instrument grows somewhat low in energy. We would prefer to retain the maximal portion of reserved energy for which this instrument has given permission. We would, therefore, ask for one more full query at this working.

86.22 **QUESTIONER** I will assume that the veiling of the sexual aspect was of great efficiency because it is an aspect that has to do totally with a relationship with another self. It would seem to me that the bodily veilings having to do with other-self interaction would be most efficient, and those only related to the self be lower in efficiency in producing either positive or negative polarization. Am I correct in this assumption?

RA I am Ra. You are correct to a great extent. Perhaps the most notable exception is the attitude, of one already strongly polarized negatively, towards the appearance of the body complex. There are those entities upon the negative path which take great care in the preservation of the distortion your peoples perceive as fairness/ugliness. This fairness of form is, of course, then used in order to manipulate other-selves.

May we ask if there are any brief queries?

86.23 **QUESTIONER** Is there anything that we can do to make the instrument more comfortable or improve the contact?

RA I am Ra. We are pleased that this instrument was more conscientious in preparing itself for contact by means of the careful mental vibrations which you call prayer. This enabled the channel to be free from the distortions which the contact fell prey to during the last working.

We would suggest to the support group some continued care in the regulating of the physical activities of the instrument. However, at this nexus it is well to encourage those activities which feed the vital energies, as this instrument lives in this space/time present almost completely due to the careful adherence to the preservation of those mental and spiritual energies which make up the vital energy complex of this entity. Each is conscientious. The alignments are good.

We would caution the support group as to the physical alignment of the appurtenance known as the censer. There has been some slight difficulty due to variation in the pattern of the effluvium of this incense.

I am Ra. I leave you rejoicing in the power and in the peace of the One Infinite Creator. Go forth, then, rejoicing in the love and in the light of the One Creator. Adonai.

87.0 **RA** I am Ra. I greet you in the love and in the light of the One Infinite Creator. I communicate now.

87.1 **QUESTIONER** First, please give me the condition of the instrument.

RA I am Ra. The distortions of the physical complex are unchanged. The vital energy levels are greatly enhanced.

87.2 **QUESTIONER** Thank you. In considering what was mentioned in the last session about the censer, I have thought about the fact that the position of the origin of the smoke changes approximately six inches horizontally. Would it be better to have a censer in a single, horizontal smoking position?

RA I am Ra. This alteration would be an helpful one given that the censer is virgin.

87.3 **QUESTIONER** What would be the optimum geometrical arrangement of censer, chalice, and candle with respect to Bible and table and the positions we now have them in?

RA I am Ra. Both chalice and candle occupy the optimal configuration with respect to the book most closely aligned with the Law of One in the distortion complexes of this instrument. It is optimal to have the censer to the rear of this book and centered at the spine of its open configuration.

87.4 **QUESTIONER** Would a position directly between the chalice and the candle be optimum, then, for the censer?

RA I am Ra. This is not an exact measurement since both chalice and candle are irregularly shaped. However, speaking roughly, this is correct.

87.5 **QUESTIONER** Thank you. What is the present situation with respect to our fifth-density negative companion?

RA I am Ra. This entity has withdrawn for a period of restoration of its polarity.

87.6   **QUESTIONER** Would you expand upon the concept of the acquisition of polarity by this particular entity, and its use, specifically, of this polarity other than with the simple, obvious need for sixth-density harvest, if this is possible, please?

RA I am Ra. We would. The nature of the densities above your own is that a purpose may be said to be shared by both positive and negative polarities. This purpose is the acquisition of the ability to welcome more and more the less and less distorted love/light and light/love of the One Infinite Creator.

Upon the negative path the wisdom density is one in which power over others has been refined until it is approaching absolute power. Any force such as the force your group and those of Ra offer which cannot be controlled by the power of such a negative fifth-density mind/body/spirit complex then depolarizes the entity which has not controlled other-selves.

It is not within your conscious selves to stand against such refined power, but rather it has been through the harmony, the mutual love, and the honest calling for aid from the forces of light which have given you the shield and buckler.

87.7   **QUESTIONER** What is the environmental situation of this particular fifth-density negative entity and how does he work with fourth-density negative in order to establish power and control? And what is his particular philosophy with respect to himself as Creator and his use of the First Distortion and the extension of this use of the First Distortion to the fourth-density negative? I hope that this isn't too complex a question.

RA I am Ra. The environment of your companion is that of the rock, the cave, the place of barrenness, for this is the density of wisdom. That which is needed may be thought and received. To this entity very little is necessary upon the physical, if you will, or space/time complex of distortions.

Such an entity spends its consciousness within the realms of time/space in an attempt to learn the Ways of Wisdom through the utmost use of the powers and resources of the self. Since the self is the Creator, the wisdom density provides many informative and fascinating experiences for the negatively polarized entity.

In some respects one may see a more lucid early attachment to wisdom from those of negative polarity, as the nexus of positions of consciousness upon which wisdom is laid is simpler.

The relationship of such an entity to fourth-density negative entities is one of the more powerful and the less powerful. The negative path posits slavery of the less powerful as a means of learning the desire to serve the self to the extent that the will is brought to bear. It is in this way that polarity is increased in the negative sense. Thus fourth-density entities are willing slaves of such a fifth-density entity, there being no doubt whatsoever of the relative power of each.

87.8   **QUESTIONER** A reflection of this could be seen in our density in many of those leaders that instigate war and have followers who support, in total conviction that the direction of conquest is correct. Is this correct?

RA I am Ra. Any organization which demands obedience without question upon the basis of relative power is functioning according to the above-described plan.

87.9   **QUESTIONER** One point that I am not clear on is the understanding and use of the First Distortion by fifth- and fourth-density negative entities in manipulating third-density entities. I would like to know how the First Distortion affects the attempts to carry out the conquest of third-density entities, and the attempt to add them, through or under the premise of the First Distortion, to their social memory complexes. Would you expand that, please?

RA I am Ra. This latter plan is not one of which fourth-density negative social memory complexes are capable. The fourth-density habit is that of offering temptations and of energizing pre-existing distortions. Fourth-density entities lack the subtlety and magical practice which the fifth-density experience offers.

87.10   **QUESTIONER** It seems, though, that in the case of many UFO contacts that have occurred on this planet, that there must be some knowledge and use of the First Distortion, in that the fourth-density entities have carefully remained aloof and anonymous, you might say, for the most part, so that no proof in a concrete way of their existence is too obvious. How are they oriented with respect to this type of contact?

RA I am Ra. We misperceived your query, thinking it was directed towards this particular type of contact. The nature of the fourth-density's observance of the Free Will Distortion while pursuing the seeding of the third-density thought patterns is material which has already been covered.[1] That which can be offered of the negatively oriented information is offered. It is altered to the extent that the entity receiving such negative information is of positive orientation. Thus many such contacts are of a mixed nature.

87.11 **QUESTIONER** I'm sorry for getting confused on the question here and not asking it correctly. There is a philosophical point of central importance to me that I am trying to clear up here. It has to do with the fact that fourth-density negative seems to be aware of the First Distortion, and they are in a nonveiled condition. And they seem to use this knowledge of the First Distortion to maintain the situation that they maintain in their contacts with this planet.

I am trying to extract their ability to understand the mechanism of the First Distortion and the consequences of the veiling process and still remain in a mental configuration of separation on the negative path. I hope that I have made myself clear there. I have had a hard time asking this question.

RA I am Ra. The answer may still not satisfy the questioner. We ask that you pursue it until you are satisfied. The fourth-density negative entity has made the choice available to each at third-density harvest. It is aware of the full array of possible methods of viewing the universe of the One Creator, and it is convinced that the ignoring and non-use of the green-ray energy center will be the method most efficient in providing harvestability of fourth density. Its operations among those of third density which have not yet made this choice are designed to offer to each the opportunity to consider the self-serving polarity and its possible attractiveness.

87.12 **QUESTIONER** It seems to me that this is a service-to-others action in offering the possibility of the self-serving path. What is the relative effect of polarization of this? I don't understand that point.

---

[1] Previously covered in 11.18, 12.15, 16.2–7, 26.34, 62.20, 67.7, and 68.16.

RA I am Ra. In your armed bands a large group marauds and pillages successfully. The success of the privates is claimed by the corporals, the success of corporals by sergeants, then lieutenants, captains, majors, and finally the commanding general. Each successful temptation, each successful harvestable entity is a strengthener of the power and polarity of the fourth-density social memory complex which has had this success.

87.13 **QUESTIONER** If one mind/body/spirit complex is harvested from third density into a fourth-density social memory complex, does the total power of the social memory complex, before the absorption of this single entity, double when this entity is absorbed?

RA I am Ra. No.

87.14 **QUESTIONER** The Law of Doubling does not work in this way. How much does the power of the social memory complex increase relatively when this single entity is harvested and absorbed into it?

RA I am Ra. If one entity in the social memory complex is responsible for this addition to its being, that mind/body/spirit complex will absorb, in linear fashion, the power contained in the, shall we say, recruit. If a sub-group is responsible, the power is then this sub-group's. Only very rarely is the social memory complex of negative polarity capable of acting totally as one being. The loss of polarity due to this difficulty, to which we have previously referred as a kind of spiritual entropy, is quite large.[2]

87.15 **QUESTIONER** Then assuming that a single negatively polarized entity is responsible for the recruiting of a harvested third-density entity and adds this polarity to his negative polarity and power, what type of ability or what type of benefit is this, and how is it used by the entity?

RA I am Ra. The so-called pecking order is immediately challenged, and the entity with increased power exercises that power to control more other-selves and to advance within the social memory complex structure.

87.16 **QUESTIONER** How is this power measured? How is it obvious that this entity has gained this additional power?

RA I am Ra. In some cases there is a kind of battle. This is a battle of

---

[2] Previously discussed in 7.15 and 36.15.

wills, and the weapons consist of the light that can be formed by each contender. In most cases where the shift of power has been obvious it simply is acknowledged, and those seeing benefit from associating with this newly more-powerful entity aid it in rising within the structure.

87.17   **QUESTIONER** Thank you. We noticed the possibility of a confusion between the term "mind/body/spirit" and "mind/body/spirit complex" in the last session. Were there a couple of misuses of those terms, shifting one for the other?

RA I am Ra. There was an error in transmission. The use of the term "mind/body/spirit" should refer to those entities dwelling in third density prior to the veiling process, the term "mind/body/spirit complex" referring to those entities dwelling in third density after the veiling process. We also discover a failure on our part to supply the term "complex" when speaking of body after the veiling. Please correct these errors.[3]

Also, we ask that you keep a vigilant watch over these transmissions for any errors, and question without fail as it is our intention to provide as undistorted a series of sound vibration complexes as is possible.

This entity, though far better cleared of distortions towards the pain flares when prepared by those mental vibration complexes you call prayer, is still liable to fluctuation due to its pre-incarnative body-complex distortions and the energizing of them by those of negative polarity.

87.18   **QUESTIONER** Thank you. We will make the corrections. In the last session you made the statement that before veiling, sexual energy transfer was always possible. I would like to know what you meant by "it was always possible" and why it was not always possible after the veiling, just to clear up that point?

RA I am Ra. We believe that we grasp your query and will use the analogy in your culture of the battery which lights the flashlight bulb. Two working batteries placed in series always offer the potential of the bulb's illumination. After the veiling, to continue this gross analogy, the two batteries being placed not in series would then offer no possible

---

3   The text was corrected before printing and now reads as it should. Footnotes were added to each instance of correction.

illumination of the bulb. Many mind/body/spirit complexes after the veiling have, through blockages, done the equivalent of reversing the battery.

87.19 **QUESTIONER** What was the primary source of the blockages that caused the battery reversal analogy?

RA I am Ra. Please query more specifically as to the mind/body/spirits or mind/body/spirit complexes about which you request information.

87.20 **QUESTIONER** Before the veil there was knowledge of the bulb-lighting technique, shall we say. After the veil some experiments created a bulb lighting; some resulted in no bulb lighting. Other than the fact that information was not available on methods of lighting the bulb, was there some root cause of the experiments that resulted in no bulb lighting?

RA I am Ra. This is correct.

87.21 **QUESTIONER** What was this root cause?

RA I am Ra. The root cause of blockage is the lack of the ability to see the other-self as the Creator, or to phrase this differently, the lack of love.

87.22 **QUESTIONER** OK. In our particular illusion, the sexual potential, it seems, for the male peaks somewhere prior to age twenty and the female some ten years later. What is the cause of this difference in peaking sexual energy, I will say?

RA I am Ra. We must make clear distinction between the yellow-ray, third-density, chemical bodily complex, and the body complex which is a portion of the mind/body/spirit complex. The male, as you call this polarity, has an extremely active yellow-ray desire at the space/time in its incarnation when its sperm is the most viable and full of the life-giving spermata. Thusly the red ray seeks to reproduce most thickly at the time when this body is most able to fulfill the red-ray requirements.

The yellow-ray, chemical body complex of the female, as you call this polarity, must needs have a continued and increasing desire for the sexual intercourse, for it can only conceive once in one fifteen to eighteen month period, given that it carries the conceived body complex, bears it, and suckles it. This is draining to the physical body of yellow ray. To compensate for this the desire increases so that the yellow-ray body is predisposed to continue in sexual congress, thus fulfilling its red-ray requirement to reproduce as thickly as possible.

The more, shall we say, integral sexuality or polarity of the body complex, which is a portion of the mind/body/spirit complex, does not concern itself with these yellow-ray manifestations but, rather, follows the ways of the seeking of energy transfer and the furthering of aid and service to others or to the self.

87.23 **QUESTIONER** In addition, why is the ratio of male to female orgasms so heavily loaded on the side of the male?

RA I am Ra. We refer now to the yellow-ray, physical body or, if you will, body complex (at this level the distinction is unimportant). The male orgasm which motivates the sperm forward to meet its ovum is essential for the completion of the red-ray desire to propagate the species. The female orgasm is unnecessary. Again, as mind/body/spirit complexes begin to use the sexual energy transfer to learn, to serve, and to glorify the One Infinite Creator, the function of the female orgasm becomes more clear.

87.24 **QUESTIONER** What was this ratio before the veil?

RA I am Ra. The ratio of male to female orgasms before the veil was closer to one-to-one by a great deal as the metaphysical value of the female orgasm was clear and without shadow.

87.25 **QUESTIONER** Is it meaningful to give this ratio in early fourth density, and if so, would you do that?

RA I am Ra. In many ways it is quite meaningless to speak of orgasm of male and female in higher densities as the character and nature of orgasm becomes more and more naturally a function of the mind/body/spirit complex as an unit.

It may be said that the veil in fourth density is lifted and the choice has been made. In positive polarities true sharing is almost universal. In negative polarities true blockage so that the conqueror obtains orgasm, the conquered almost never, is almost universal.

In each case you may see the function of the sexual portion of experience as being a most efficient means of polarization.

87.26 **QUESTIONER** In our illusion we have physical definitions for possible transfers of energy. We label them as the conversion of potential to kinetic or kinetic to heat and examine this with respect to its increasing entropy. When we speak of sexual energy transfers and other more basic forms of energy I am always at a loss to properly use, you might say, the terms since I am not understanding, and probably can't understand, the basic form of energy that we speak of.

However, I intuit that this is the energy of pure vibration; that is, at the basic level of our illusion, that vibration between the space and time portion of the space/time continuum and yet somehow is transferred into our illusion in a more basic form than that. Could you expand on this area for me, please?

RA I am Ra. Yes.

87.27 **QUESTIONER** Would you do that?

RA I am Ra. You are correct in assuming that the energy of which we speak in discussing sexual energy transfers is a form of vibratory bridge between space/time and time/space. Although this distinction is not apart from that which follows, that which follows may shed light upon that basic statement:

Due to the veiling process the energy transferred from male to female is different than that transferred from female to male. Due to the polarity difference of the mind/body/spirit complexes of male and female, the male stores physical energy; the female, mental and mental/emotional energy. When third-density sexual energy transfer is completed the male will have offered the discharge of physical energy. The female is, thereby, refreshed, having far less physical vitality. At the same time, if you will use this term, the female discharges the efflux of its stored mental and mental/emotional energy, thereby offering inspiration, healing, and blessing to the male which by nature is less vital in this area.

At this time may we ask for one more full query.

87.28 **QUESTIONER** Why is the male and the female nature different?

RA I am Ra. When the veiling process was accomplished, to the male polarity was attracted the Matrix of the Mind and to the female, the

Potentiator of the Mind; to the male the Potentiator of the Body, to the female the Matrix of the Body.

May we ask if there are any brief queries before we close this working?

87.29 **QUESTIONER** Is there anything we can do to make the instrument more comfortable or improve the contact?

RA I am Ra. We shall find the suggested readjustment of the censer helpful. The alignments are good. You have been conscientious, my friends. We leave you now in the love and in the light of the One Infinite Creator. Go forth, therefore, rejoicing merrily in the power and in the ineffable peace of the One Infinite Creator. Adonai.

SESSION 88

88.0   **RA** I am Ra. I greet you in the love and in the light of the One Infinite Creator. We communicate now.

88.1   **QUESTIONER** Could you first please give me the condition of the instrument?

RA I am Ra. The physical complex energy deficit is considerable at this space/time. There has been also a significant loss of the vital energies. However, these energies are still well within the distortion you may call strength.

88.2   **QUESTIONER** Of all of the things that you have mentioned before for replenishing these energies, at this particular space/time which would be most appropriate for the replenishing of both of these energies?

RA I am Ra. As you note, there are many factors which contribute to the aiding of the strength distortions and the amelioration of distortions towards weakness in this instrument. We suggest to each that those many things which have been learned be conscientiously applied.

We would single out one physical distortion for discussion. The fourth-density negative minions which visit your group at this time are energizing a somewhat severe complex of imbalances in the manual appendages of this instrument and, to a lesser extent, those distortions of the thoracic region. We suggest care be taken to refrain from any unnecessary use of these appendages.

As this instrument will not appreciate this suggestion we suggest the appropriate discussion.

88.3   **QUESTIONER** I assume from this that our fifth-density negative companion is still on R and R. Is this correct?

RA I am Ra. Your fifth-density companion is not accompanying you at this time. However, it is not resting.

88.4   **QUESTIONER** Is the censer we have provided all right? They do go out prior to the end of the session. Would it be better if it did not go out prior to the end of the session?

RA I am Ra. The new configuration of the censer is quite helpful to the more subtle patterns of energy surrounding these workings. It would be helpful to have a continuously burning amount of cense. However, the difficulty is in providing this without overpowering this enclosure with the amount of effluvium and physical product of combustion. Having to choose betwixt allowing the censer to finish its burning and having an overabundance of the smoke, we would suggest the former as being more helpful.

88.5 **QUESTIONER** The instrument has mentioned what she refers to as bleed-through or being aware, during these sessions sometimes, of the communication. Would you comment on this?

RA I am Ra. We have the mind/body/spirit complex of the instrument with us. As this entity begins to awaken from the metaphorical crib of experiencing light and activity in our density, it is beginning to be aware of the movement of thought. It does not grasp these thoughts any more than your third-density infant may grasp the first words it perceives.

The experience should be expected to continue, and is an appropriate outgrowth of the nature of these workings and of the method by which this instrument has made itself available to our words.

88.6 **QUESTIONER** The instrument mentioned a recurrence of the need for going to the bathroom prior to this session. Is this because of the low vital energy?

RA I am Ra. It is part of the cause of the lowered vital energy level. This entity has been sustaining a level of the distortion you call pain which few among your peoples experience without significant draining of the energies. Indeed, the stability of the entity is notable. However, the entity has thusly become drained and, further, has felt other distortions such as those for a variety of experiences accentuated, for this is one means of balancing the inward-looking experience of the physical pain.

Due to concern for this entity such activities have been discouraged. This has further drained the entity.

The will to be of service to the Creator through the means of offering itself as instrument in these workings, therefore, was given an opportunity for the testing of resolve. This entity used some vital energy to fuel and replenish the will. No physical energy has been used by the instrument, but the vital energies were tapped so that this entity might have the opportunity to once again consciously choose to serve the One Infinite Creator.

88.7 **QUESTIONER** Is the small crystal that the instrument uses upon her during the session of any benefit or detriment?

RA I am Ra. This crystal is beneficial as long as he who has charged it is functioning in a positively oriented manner.

88.8 **QUESTIONER** Who charged the crystal?

RA I am Ra. This crystal was charged for use by this instrument by the one known as Neil.

88.9 **QUESTIONER** It would be an abridgment of the First Distortion to tell us whether he is still functioning in a positive manner, would it not?

RA I am Ra. We perceive you have replied to your own query.

88.10 **QUESTIONER** Our publisher requests pictures for the book, *The Law of One*, that is going to press at this time.[1] Would you comment on the advisability, benefit or detriment, magical or otherwise, of us using pictures of this particular setup, the instrument, and the appurtenances in the book?

RA I am Ra. The practical advisability of such a project is completely a product of your discrimination. There are magical considerations.

Firstly, if pictures be taken of a working, the visual image must needs be that which is; that is, it is well for you to photograph only an actual working and no sham nor substitution of any material. There shall be no distortions which this group can avoid any more than we would wish distortions in our words.

Secondly, it is inadvisable to photograph the instrument or any portion of the working room while the instrument is in trance. This is a narrow-band contact, and we wish to keep electrical and electromagnetic energies constant when their presence is necessary, and not present at all otherwise.

---

[1] See footnote on 84.6 for information regarding the original books.

88.11 QUESTIONER From what you. . . I'm sorry. Go ahead. If you meant to continue, continue. If not, I'll ask a question.

RA I am Ra. We wished to state, thirdly, that once the instrument is aware that the picture-taking will be performed, that during the entire picture-taking, whether before or after the working, the instrument be required to continuously respond to speech, thus assuring that no trance is imminent.

88.12 QUESTIONER From what you have told me, then, I have planned the following: We will, after a session is complete and the instrument has been awakened, before moving the instrument, have the instrument continually talk to us while I take pictures of the configuration the instrument is in at this time. In addition to this, I will take some other pictures of the instrument in the other room, and probably ourselves, too, just for additional pictures of us as requested by the publisher. Is this the optimal or one of the optimal fillings of this requirement?

RA I am Ra. Yes. We ask that any photographs tell the truth, that they be dated and shine with a clarity so that there is no shadow of any but genuine expression which may be offered to those which seek truth.

We come as humble messengers of the Law of One, desiring to decrease distortions. We ask that you, who have been our friends, work with any considerations such as above discussed, not with the thought of quickly removing an unimportant detail, but, as in all ways, regard such as another opportunity to, as the adept must, be yourselves and offer that which is in and with you without pretense of any kind.

88.13 QUESTIONER Thank you. I would like to ask you, as to the initial production of the tarot, where this concept was first formed, and where the tarot was first recorded, where did this . . . the very first concept?

RA I am Ra. The concept of the tarot originated within the planetary influence you call Venus.

88.14 QUESTIONER Was the concept given to . . . let me ask . . . you say it originated there . . . was this concept devised for a training tool for those inhabiting Venus at that time, or was it devised by those of Venus as a training tool for those of Earth?

RA I am Ra. The tarot was devised by the third-density population of Venus a great measure of your space/time in your past.

As we have noted, the third-density experience of those of Venus dealt far more deeply and harmoniously with what you would call relationships with other-selves, sexual energy transfer work, and philosophical or metaphysical research. The product of many, many generations of work upon what we conceived to be the archetypical mind produced the tarot which was used by our peoples as a training aid in developing the magical personality.

88.15   QUESTIONER I'll make a guess that those of Venus third density who were the initial ones to partially penetrate the veil gleaned information as to the nature of the archetypical mind and the veiling process, and from this designed the tarot as a method of teaching others. Is this correct?

RA   I am Ra. It is so.

88.16   QUESTIONER I will also assume, which may not be correct, that the present list that I have of the twenty-two names of the tarot cards are not in exact agreement with Ra's original generation of the tarot. Could you describe the original tarot, first telling me if there were twenty-two archetypes? That must have been the same. And if they were the same as the list that I have read you in a previous session, or if there were differences?

RA   I am Ra. As we have stated previously,[2] each archetype is a concept complex and may be viewed not only by individuals but by those of the same racial and planetary influences in unique ways. Therefore, it is not informative to reconstruct the rather minor differences in descriptive terms between the tarot used by us, and that used by those of Egypt and the spiritual descendants of those first students of this system of study.

The one great breakthrough which was made after our work in third density was done was the proper emphasis given to the Arcanum Number Twenty-Two which we have called The Choice. In our own experience we were aware that such an unifying archetype existed but did not give that archetype the proper complex of concepts in order to most efficaciously use that archetype in order to promote our evolution.

88.17   QUESTIONER I will make this statement as to my understanding of some

---

[2]   Stated previously in 67.30, 77.12–13, and 77.23.

of the archetypes and let you correct this statement. It seems to me that the Significator of Mind, Body, and Spirit are acted upon in each of these by the Catalyst. This produces Experience which then leads to the Transformation and produces the Great Way. This is the same process for mind, the body, and spirit. The archetypes are just repeated but act in a different way as catalyst because of the differences of mind, body, and spirit.

They produce a different type of Experience for each because of the differences in the three. The Transformation is slightly different. The Great Way is somewhat different, but the archetypes are all basically doing the same thing. They are just acting on three different portions of the mind/body/spirit complex so that we can condense the entire archetypical mind into a way of saying that, in making the Significator a complex, basically we have provided a way for Catalyst to create Transformation more efficiently. Would you correct my statement, please?

RA I am Ra. In your statement, correctness is so plaited up with tendrils of the most fundamental misunderstanding that correction of your statement is difficult. We shall make comments and from these comments request that you allow a possible realignment of conceptualization to occur.

The archetypical mind is a great and fundamental portion of the mind complex, one of its most basic elements and one of the richest sources of information for the seeker of the One Infinite Creator. To attempt to condense the archetypes is to make an erroneous attempt. Each archetype is a significant *ding an sich*, or thing in itself, with its own complex of concepts.

While it is informative to survey the relationships of one archetype to another, it can be said that this line of inquiry is secondary to the discovery of the purest gestalt or vision or melody which each archetype signifies to both the intellectual and intuitive mind.

The Significators of Mind, Body, and Spirit complexes are complex in and of themselves; and the archetypes of Catalyst, Experience, Transformation, and the Great Way are most fruitfully viewed as independent complexes which have their own melodies with which they may inform the mind of its nature.

We ask that you consider that the archetypical mind informs those thoughts which then may have bearing upon the mind, the body, or the spirit. The archetypes do not have a direct linkage to body or spirit. All must be drawn up through the higher levels of the subconscious mind to the conscious mind, and thence they may flee whither they have been bidden to go. When used in a controlled way they are most helpful.

Rather than continue beyond the boundaries of your prior statement we would appreciate the opportunity for your re-questioning at this time so that we may answer you more precisely.

88.18 **QUESTIONER** I will ask the following questions to clear up . . . possibly . . . only . . . the method of teaching these concepts which may give me important clues to understanding the concepts themselves. Did Ra use cards similar to the tarot cards for the training purpose in third density?

RA I am Ra. No.

88.19 **QUESTIONER** What did Ra use in third density?

RA I am Ra. You are aware in your attempts at magical visualization of the mental configuration of sometimes rather complex visualizations. These are mental and drawn with the mind. Another example well-known in your culture is the visualization, in your Mass (of the distortion of the love of the One Infinite Creator called Christianity) wherein a small portion of your foodstuffs is seen to be a mentally configured but entirely real man, the man known to you as Jehoshua or, as you call this entity now, Jesus. It was by this method of sustained visualization over a period of training that we worked with these concepts.

These concepts were occasionally drawn. However, the concept of one visualization per card was not thought of by us.

88.20 **QUESTIONER** Well, how did the teacher relay information to the student with respect to visualization?

RA I am Ra. The process was cabalistic; that is, of the oral tradition of mouth to ear.

88.21 **QUESTIONER** Then when Ra attempted to teach the Egyptians the concept of the tarot, was the same process used or a different one?

RA I am Ra. The same process was used. However, those which were teach/learners after us first drew these images to the best of their ability within the place of initiation and later began the use of what you call cards bearing these visualizations' representations.

88.22 QUESTIONER Were the Court Arcana and the Minor Arcana a portion of Ra's teachings, or was this something that came along later?

RA I am Ra. Those cards of which you speak were the product of the influence of those of Chaldea and Sumer.

88.23 QUESTIONER You mentioned earlier that the tarot was a method of divination. Would you explain that?

RA I am Ra. We must first divorce the tarot as a method of divination from this Major Arcana as representative of twenty-two archetypes of the archetypical mind.

The value of that which you call astrology is significant when used by those initiated entities which understand, if you will pardon the misnomer, the sometimes intricate considerations of the Law of Confusion. As each planetary influence enters the energy web of your sphere, those upon the sphere are moved much as the moon which moves about your sphere moves the waters upon your deeps.

Your own nature is water in that you as mind/body/spirit complexes are easily impressed and moved. Indeed, this is the very fiber and nature of your journey and vigil in this density: to not only be moved but to instruct yourself as to the preferred manner of your movement in mind, body, and spirit.

Therefore, as each entity enters the planetary energy web each entity experiences two major planetary influxes: that of the conception—which has to do with the physical, yellow-ray manifestation of the incarnation— and that of the moment you call birth when the breath is first drawn into the body complex of chemical yellow ray.

Thus those who know the stars and their configurations and influences are able to see a rather broadly drawn map of the country through which an entity has traveled, is traveling, or may be expected to travel, be it upon the physical, the mental, or the spiritual level. Such an entity will have developed abilities of the initiate which are normally known among your peoples as psychic or paranormal.

When the archetypes are shuffled into the mix of astrologically oriented cards which form the so-called Court Arcana and Minor Arcana, these archetypes become magnetized to the psychic impressions of the one working with the cards, and thusly become instruments of a linkage between the practitioner of the astrological determinations and divinations and the one requesting information.

Oft times such archetypical representations will appear in such a manner as to have seemingly interesting results, meaningful in configuration to the questioner. In and of themselves the Major Arcana have no rightful place in divination, but rather are tools for the further knowledge of the self by the self for the purpose of entering a more profoundly, acutely realized present moment.

88.24 **QUESTIONER** Ra must have had a, shall we say, lesson plan or course of training for the twenty-two archetypes to be given either to those of third density of Ra or, later on, to those in Egypt. Would you describe this scenario for the training course?

RA I am Ra. This shall be the last full query of this working.

We find it more nearly appropriate to discuss our plans in acquainting initiates upon your own planet with this particular version of the archetypes of the archetypical mind. Our first stage was the presentation of the images, one after the other, in the following order:

- one, eight, fifteen;
- two, nine, sixteen;
- three, ten, seventeen;
- four, eleven, eighteen;
- five, twelve, nineteen;
- six, thirteen, twenty;
- seven, fourteen, twenty-one;
- twenty-two.

In this way the fundamental relationships between mind, body, and spirit could begin to be discovered; for as one sees, for instance, the Matrix of the Mind in comparison to the Matrices of Body and Spirit, one may draw certain tentative conclusions.

When at length the student had mastered these visualizations and had considered each of the seven classifications of archetype (looking at the relationships between mind, body, and spirit) we then suggested consideration of archetypes in pairs:

- one and two;
- three and four;
- five;
- six and seven.

You may continue in this form for the body and spirit archetypes.

You will note that the consideration of the Significator was left unpaired, for the Significator shall be paired with Archetype Twenty-Two.

At the end of this line of inquiry the student was beginning to grasp more and more deeply the qualities and resonances of each archetype. At this point, using various other aids to spiritual evolution, we encouraged the initiate to learn to become each archetype and, most importantly, to know, as best as possible within your illusion, when the adoption of the archetype's persona would be spiritually or metaphysically helpful.

As you can see, much work was done creatively by each initiate. We have no dogma to offer. Each perceives that which is needful and helpful to the self.

May we ask if there are any brief queries before we leave this working?

88.25 **QUESTIONER** Is there anything that we can do to improve the contact or make the instrument more comfortable?

RA I am Ra. We again ward you concerning the distortions of the instrument's hands. The fourth-density influence upon them could be inconvenient in that, if allowed to proceed without abatement, what you call your surgery shall be almost immediately necessary.

The alignments are good. You have been fastidious.

We leave you, my friends, in the love and in the light of the One Infinite Creator. Go forth, therefore, rejoicing merrily in the power and in the glorious peace of the One Infinite Creator. Adonai.

SESSION 89

89.0 **RA** I am Ra. I greet you in the love and in the light of the One Infinite Creator. We communicate now.

89.1 **QUESTIONER** Could you first please give me the condition of the instrument?

RA I am Ra. It is as previously stated.

89.2 **QUESTIONER** I have two questions of a personal nature. First, during the last intensive meditation the instrument experienced very strong conditioning from an entity which did not identify itself and which did not leave when she asked it to. Will you tell us what was occurring then?

RA I am Ra. We find the instrument to have been given the opportunity to become a channel for a previously known friend. This entity was not able to answer the questioning of spirits in the name of Christ, as is this instrument's distortion of the means of differentiating betwixt those of positive and those of negative orientation. Therefore, after some resistance, the entity found the need to take its leave.

89.3 **QUESTIONER** Was this particular entity the fifth-density visitor that we have had quite often previously?

RA I am Ra. This is correct.

89.4 **QUESTIONER** Is he back with us at this time?

RA I am Ra. No. The attempt to speak was due to the vigilant eye of the minions of this entity which noted what one may call a surge of natural telepathic ability upon the part of the instrument. This ability is cyclical, of the eighteen diurnal period cycle, as we have mentioned aforetimes.[1] Thusly, this entity determined to attempt another means of access to the instrument by free will.

89.5 **QUESTIONER** Was this what I might refer to as an increase of ability to

---

[1] Mentioned aforetimes in 61.3 and 64.10.

receive telepathically over a broader range of basic frequencies so as to include not only the Confederation but this particular entity?

RA I am Ra. This is incorrect. The high point of the cycle sharpens the ability to pick up the signal but does not change the basic nature of the carrier wave. Shall we say, there is greater power in the receiving antenna.

89.6 **QUESTIONER** This question may be meaningless, but would a fifth-density entity of the Confederation who was positively polarized transmit on the same frequency as our negatively polarized fifth-density companion?

RA I am Ra. This is correct and is the reason that the questioning of all contacts is welcomed by the Confederation of Planets in the Service of the Infinite Creator.

89.7 **QUESTIONER** Question two: Jim has also felt very strong conditioning which was unbidden while channeling Latwii recently and in his personal meditations. Would you also tell us what occurred in these cases?

RA I am Ra. The entity which has been your companion has a vibratory frequency—but a small amount lesser—than that of the social memory complex known as Latwii. Also, Latwii is the primary comforter of the Confederation for entities seeking at the vibratory complex level of the one known as Jim.

Therefore, this same companion has been attempting the contact of this instrument also. Although this instrument would have great difficulty in distinguishing the actual contact due to the lack of experience of your companion at this type of service, nevertheless, it is well that this instrument also choose some manner of the challenging of contacts.

89.8 **QUESTIONER** How many of our years ago was Ra's third density ended?

RA I am Ra. The calculations necessary for establishing this point are difficult since so much of what you call time is taken up before and after third density, as you see the progress of time from your vantage point. We may say, in general, that the time of our enjoyment of the choice-making was approximately 2.6 million of your sun-years in your past. However— we correct this instrument. Your term is billion, 2.6 billion of your years in your past. However, this time, as you call it, is not meaningful, for our intervening space/time has been experienced in a manner quite unlike your third-density experience of space/time.

89.9 **QUESTIONER** It appears that the end of Ra's third density coincided with the beginning of this planet's second density. Is that correct?

RA I am Ra. This is roughly correct.

89.10 **QUESTIONER** Did the planet Venus become a fourth-density planet at that time?

RA I am Ra. This is so.

89.11 **QUESTIONER** Did it later, then, become a fifth-density planet?

RA I am Ra. It later became a fourth/fifth-density planet; then, later a fifth-density planet for a large measure of your time. Both fourth- and fifth-density experiences were possible upon the planetary influence of what you call Venus.

89.12 **QUESTIONER** What is its density at present?

RA I am Ra. Its core vibrational frequency is sixth density. However we, as a social memory complex, had elected to leave that influence. Therefore, the beings inhabiting this planetary influence at this space/time are fifth-density entities. The planet may be considered a fifth/sixth-density planet.

89.13 **QUESTIONER** What was your reason for leaving?

RA I am Ra. We wished to be of service.

89.14 **QUESTIONER** I have here a deck of twenty-two tarot cards which have been copied, according to information we have, from the walls of, I would suspect, the large pyramid at Giza. If necessary we can duplicate these cards in the book that we are preparing. I would ask Ra if these cards represent an exact replica of that which is in the Great Pyramid?

RA I am Ra. The resemblance is substantial.

89.15 **QUESTIONER** In other words, you might say that these were better than, say, 95% correct as far as representing what is on the walls of the Great Pyramid?

RA I am Ra. Yes.

89.16 QUESTIONER The way I understand this, then: Ra gave these archetypical concepts to the priests of Egypt who then drew them upon the walls of one of the chambers of the Great Pyramid. What was the technique of transmission of this information to the priests? At this time was Ra walking the surface among the Egyptians, or was this done through some form of channeling?

RA I am Ra. This was done partially through old teachings and partially through visions.

89.17 QUESTIONER Then at this particular time Ra had long since vacated the planet as far as walking among the Egyptians. Is this correct?

RA I am Ra. Yes.

89.18 QUESTIONER I would like to question Ra on each of these cards in order to better understand the archetypes. Is this agreeable?

RA I am Ra. As we have previously stated,[2] these archetypical concept complexes are a tool for learn/teaching. Thusly, if we were to offer information that were not a response to observations of the student we would be infringing upon the free will of the learn/teacher by being teach/learner and learn/teacher at once.

89.19 QUESTIONER In that case I'll ask you: you stated that Ra used the tarot to develop the magical personality. Was this done by the system of learning to become, in mind, the essence of each archetype, and in this way develop the magical personality?

RA I am Ra. This is incorrect. The clothing one's self within the archetype is an advanced practice of the adept which has long studied this archetypical system.

The concept complexes which together are intended to represent the architecture of a significant and rich portion of the mind are intended to be studied as individual concept complexes—as Matrix, Potentiator, etc.—in viewing mind/body/spirit connections; and in pairs with some concentration upon the polarity of the male and the female.

---

[2] Previously stated in 88.14–15.

If these are studied there comes the moment when the deep threnodies and joyful ditties of the deep mind can successfully be brought forward to intensify, articulate, and heighten some aspect of the magical personality.[3]

89.20 **QUESTIONER** You stated that each archetype is a concept complex. Would you please define what you mean by that statement?

RA I am Ra. Upon the face of it such a definition is without merit, being circular. A concept complex is a complex of concepts just as a molecule is a complex structure made up of more than one type of energy nexus or atom. Each atom within a molecule is its unique identity and, by some means, can be removed from the molecule. The molecule of water can, by chemical means, be caused to separate into hydrogen and oxygen. Separately they cannot be construed to equal water. When formed in the molecular structure which exemplifies water the two are irrefragably water.[4]

Just in this way each archetype has within it several root atoms of organizational being. Separately the overall structure of the complex cannot be seen. Together, the concept complex is irrefragably one thing.

However, just as it is most useful in grasping the potentials in your physical systems of the constituting nature of water, so in grasping the nature of an archetype it is useful to have a sense of its component concepts.

89.21 **QUESTIONER** In Archetype Number One, represented by tarot card number one, the Matrix of the Mind seems to me to have four basic parts to the complex. Looking at the card we have, first and most obvious, the Magician as a part, and what seems to be an approaching star. A stork or similar bird seems to be in a cage. On top of the cage we have something that is very difficult to discern. Am I in any way correct in this analysis?

RA I am Ra. You are competent at viewing pictures. You have not yet grasped the nature of the Matrix of the Mind as fully as is reliably possible upon contemplation. We would note that the representations drawn by

---

[3] In this context, *threnody* can be defined as "a poem, speech, or song of lamentation."

[4] In this context, *irrefragably* can be defined as "indisputably."

priests were somewhat distorted by acquaintance with and dependence upon the astrologically based teachings of the Chaldees.

89.22   **QUESTIONER** When Ra originally trained or taught the Egyptians about the tarot, did Ra act as teach/learners to a degree that Ra became learn/teachers?

RA I am Ra. This distortion we were spared.

89.23   **QUESTIONER** Then could you tell me what information you gave to the Egyptian priest, or Egyptian, who first was contacted or taught with respect to the first archetype? Is that possible for you to do within the limits of the First Distortion?

RA I am Ra. It is possible. Our first step, as we have said, was to present the descriptions in verbal form of three images: one, eight, fifteen; then the questions were asked: "What do you feel that a bird might represent?" "What do you feel that a wand might represent?" "What do you feel that the male represents?" and so forth until those studying were working upon a system whereby the images used became evocative of a system of concepts. This is slow work when done for the first time.

We may note, with sympathy, that you undoubtedly feel choked by the opposite difficulty, that of a great mass of observation upon this system, all of which has some merit as each student will experience the archetypical mind and its structure in an unique way useful to that student. We suggest that one or more of this group do that which we have suggested in order that we may, without infringement, offer observations on this interesting subject which may be of further aid to those inquiring in this area.

We would note at this time that the instrument is having almost continuous pain flares. Therefore, we ask that each of the support group be especially aware of any misinformation in order that we may correct any distortions of information the soonest possible.

89.24   **QUESTIONER** Now as I understand it, what you suggest as far as the tarot goes is to study the writings that we have available and from those formulate questions. Is this correct?

RA I am Ra. No.

89.25 **QUESTIONER** Sorry, I didn't understand exactly what you meant with respect to that. Would it be appropriate then for me to answer the questions with respect to what I think is the meaning of the three items that you spoke of for Card One and then Card Eight, etc.? Is this what you meant?

RA I am Ra. This is very close to our meaning. It was our intention to suggest that one or more of you go through the plan of study which we have suggested.

The queries having to do with the archetypes as found in the tarot, after this point, may take the form of observing what seem to be the characteristics of each archetype; relationships between mind, body, and spiritual archetypes of the same ranking, such as Matrix; or archetypes as seen in relationship to polarity, especially when observed in the pairings.

Any observations made by a student which has fulfilled these considerations will receive our comments in return. Our great avoidance of interpreting, for the first time, for the learn/teacher various elements of a picture upon a piece of pasteboard is involved both with the Law of Confusion and with the difficulties of the distortions of the pictures upon the pasteboard. Therefore, we may suggest a conscientious review of that which we have already given concerning this subject as opposed to the major reliance being either upon any rendition of the archetype pictures, or any system which has been arranged as a means of studying these pictures.

89.26 **QUESTIONER** All right, we'll attempt to do that. Ra stated that a major breakthrough was made when proper emphasis was put on Arcanum Twenty-Two. This didn't happen until after Ra had completed third density. I assume from this that Ra, being polarized positively, probably had some of the same difficulty that occurred prior to the veil in that the negative polarity was not appreciated. That's a guess. Is this correct?

RA I am Ra. In one way it is precisely correct. Our harvest was overwhelmingly positive, and our appreciation of those which were negative was relatively uninformed.

However, we were intending to suggest that (in the use of the system known to you as the tarot for advancing the spiritual evolution of the self) a proper understanding, if we may use this misnomer, of Archetype Twenty-Two is greatly helpful in sharpening the basic view of the

Significator of Mind, Body, and Spirit; and, further, throws into starker relief the Transformation and Great Way of Mind, Body, and Spirit complexes.

89.27 **QUESTIONER** Were some of Ra's population negatively harvested at the end of Ra's third density?

RA I am Ra. We had no negative harvest as such, although there had been two entities which had harvested themselves during the third density in the negative or service-to-self path. There were, however, those upon the planetary surface during third density whose vibratory patterns were in the negative range but were not harvestable.

89.28 **QUESTIONER** What was Ra's average total population incarnate on Venus in third density, the number?

RA I am Ra. We were a small population which dwelt upon what you would consider difficult conditions. Our harvest was approximately 6 million 500 thousand mind/body/spirit complexes. There were approximately 32 million mind/body/spirit complexes repeating third density elsewhere.

89.29 **QUESTIONER** What was the attitude just prior to harvest of those harvestable entities of Ra with respect to those who were obviously unharvestable?

RA I am Ra. Those of us which had the gift of polarity felt deep compassion for those who seemed to dwell in darkness. This description is most apt as ours was a harshly bright planet in the physical sense.

There was every attempt made to reach out with whatever seemed to be needed. However, those upon the positive path have the comfort of companions, and we of Ra spent a great deal of our attention upon the possibilities of achieving spiritual or metaphysical adepthood, or work in indigo ray, through the means of relationships with other-selves. Consequently, the compassion for those in darkness was balanced by the appreciation of the light.

89.30 **QUESTIONER** Would Ra's attitude toward the same unharvestable entities be different at this nexus than at the time of harvest of third density?

RA I am Ra. Not substantially. To those who wish to sleep we could only offer those comforts designed for the sleeping. Service is only possible to the extent it is requested. We were ready to serve in whatever way we could. This still seems satisfactory as a means of dealing with other-selves in third density. It is our feeling that to be each entity which one attempts to serve is to simplify the grasp of what service is necessary or possible.

89.31   QUESTIONER   What techniques did the two negatively harvested entities use for negative polarization on such a positively polarized planet?

RA   I am Ra. The technique of control over others and domination unto the physical death was used in both cases. Upon a planetary influence much unused to slaughter these entities were able to polarize by this means. Upon your third-density environment at the time of your experiencing, such entities would merely be considered, shall we say, ruthless despots which waged the holy war.

89.32   QUESTIONER   Did these two entities evolve from the second density of the planet Venus along with the rest of the population of Venus that became Ra, from second density to third?

RA   I am Ra. No.

89.33   QUESTIONER   What was the origin of the two entities of which you speak?

RA   I am Ra. These entities were wanderers from early positive fifth density.

89.34   QUESTIONER   And yet, though they had already evolved through a positive fourth density they, shall we say, flipped polarity in the reincarnating in third density. Is this correct?

RA   I am Ra. This is correct.

89.35   QUESTIONER   What was the catalyst for their change?

RA   I am Ra. In our peoples there was what may be considered, from the viewpoint of wisdom, an overabundance of love. These entities looked at those still in darkness and saw that those of a neutral or somewhat negative viewpoint found such harmony, shall we say, sickening. The wanderers felt that a more wisdom-oriented way of seeking love could be more appealing to those in darkness.

First one entity began its work. Quickly the second found the first. These entities had agreed to serve together, and so they did, glorifying the One

Creator, but not as they intended. About them were soon gathered those who found it easy to believe that a series of specific knowledges and wisdoms would advance one towards the Creator.

The end of this was the graduation into fourth-density negative of the wanderers, which had much power of personality, and some small deepening of the negatively polarized element of those not polarizing positively. There was no negative harvest as such.

89.36 **QUESTIONER** What was the reason for the wandering of these two wanderers, and were they male and female?

RA I am Ra. All wanderers come to be of assistance in serving the Creator, each in its own way. The wanderers of which we have been speaking were indeed incarnated male and female as this is by far the most efficient system of partnership.

89.37 **QUESTIONER** As a wild guess, one of these entities wouldn't be the one who has been our companion here for some time in our sessions, would it?

RA I am Ra. No.

89.38 **QUESTIONER** Then from what you say I am guessing that these wanderers returned or wandered to Ra's third density to possibly seed greater wisdom into what they saw as an overabundance of compassion in the Ra culture. Is this correct?

RA I am Ra. This is incorrect in the sense that before incarnation it was the desire of the wanderers only to aid in service to others. The query has correctness when seen from the viewpoint of the wanderers within that incarnation.

89.39 **QUESTIONER** I just can't understand why they would think that a planet that was doing as well as Ra was doing, as far as I can tell, would need wanderers in order to help with a harvest. Was this at an early point in Ra's third density?

RA I am Ra. It was in the second cycle of 25,000 years. We had a harvest of six out of thirty, to speak roughly, millions of mind/body/spirit complexes, less than 20%. Wanderers are always drawn to whatever percentage has not yet polarized and come when there is a call. There was a call from those which were not positively polarized as such but which sought to be positively polarized and sought wisdom, feeling the compassion of other-selves upon Venus as complacent or pitying towards other-selves.

89.40 **QUESTIONER** What was the attitude of these two entities after they graduated into fourth-density negative and, the veil being removed, they realized that they had switched polarities?

RA I am Ra. They were disconcerted.

89.41 **QUESTIONER** Then did they continue striving to polarize negatively for a fifth-density negative harvest, or did they do something else?

RA I am Ra. They worked with the fourth-density negative for some period until, within this framework, the previously learned patterns of the self had been recaptured and the polarity was, with great effort, reversed. There was a great deal of fourth-density positive work then to be retraced.

89.42 **QUESTIONER** How is Ra aware of this information? By what means does Ra know the precise orientation of these two entities in fourth-density negative, etc.?

RA I am Ra. These entities joined Ra in fourth-density positive for a portion of the cycle which we experienced.

89.43 **QUESTIONER** I assume, then, that they came in late. Is this correct?

RA I am Ra. Yes.

89.44 **QUESTIONER** I didn't mean to get so far off the track of my original direction of questioning, but I think some of these excursions are very enlightening and will help in understanding of the basic mechanisms that we are so interested in in evolution.

Ra stated that archetypes are helpful when used in a controlled way. Would you give me an example of what you mean by using an archetype in a controlled way?

RA I am Ra. We speak with some regret in stating that this shall be our last query of length. There is substantial energy left, but this instrument has distortions that rapidly approach the limit of our ability to maintain secure contact.

The controlled use of the archetype is that which is done within the self for the polarization of the self—and to the benefit of the self, if negatively polarized, or others, if positively polarized—upon the most subtle of levels.

Keep in mind at all times that the archetypical mind is a portion of the deep mind and informs thought processes. When the archetype is translated without regard for magical propriety into the manifested daily actions of an individual, the greatest distortions may take place, and great infringement upon the free will of others is possible.

This is more nearly acceptable to one negatively polarized. However, the more carefully polarized of negative mind/body/spirits[5] will also prefer to work with a finely tuned instrument.

May we ask if there are any brief queries before we leave this working?

89.45 **QUESTIONER** I'll just make the statement that I perceive that a negative polarity harvest is possible with less negativity in the environment like Ra's environment than in the environment such as we have at present and ask if that is correct, and then is there anything that we can do to improve the contact or the comfort of the instrument?

RA I am Ra. Firstly, the requirements of harvest are set. It is, however, easier to serve the self completely or nearly so if there is little resistance.

In the matter of the nurturing of the instrument we suggest further manipulation of the dorsal side and appendages of this instrument and the whirling of the waters, if possible. The alignments are conscientious. We ask for your vigilance in alignments and preparations. All is well, my friends.

I am Ra. I leave you in the love and in the light of the One Infinite Creator. Go forth, then, rejoicing in the power and in the peace of the One Infinite Creator. Adonai.

---

5 Should be mind/body/spirit complexes, presumably.

SESSION 90

90.0   **RA** I am Ra. I greet you in the love and in the light of the One Infinite Creator. We communicate now.

90.1   **QUESTIONER** First, please give me the condition of the instrument.

   RA I am Ra. The physical complex energy deficit is somewhat increased by continued distortions towards pain. The vital energy levels are as previously stated, having fluctuated slightly between askings.

90.2   **QUESTIONER** Could you tell me the situation with respect to our fourth- and fifth-density companions at this time?

   RA I am Ra. The fourth-density league of companions accompanies your group. The fifth-density friend, at this space/time nexus, works within its own density exclusively.

90.3   **QUESTIONER** By what means do these particular fourth-density entities get from their origin to our position?

   RA I am Ra. The mechanism of calling has been previously explored.[1] When a distortion which may be negatively connotated is effected, this calling occurs.

   In addition, the light of which we have spoken, emanating from attempts to be of service to others in a fairly clear and lucid sense, is another type of calling in that it represents that which requires balance by temptation.

   Thirdly, there have been certain avenues into the mind/body/spirit complexes of this group which have been made available by your fifth-density friend.

90.4   **QUESTIONER** Actually, the question I intended was how do they get here? By what means of moving?

   RA I am Ra. In the mechanism of the calling, the movement is as you

---

[1]   Explored previously in many places, including 6.23, 7.1–8, 10.13, 24.8, 68.16, 72.7–8, 73.3–4, 73.8, 74.12–13, 80.5, and 87.9.

would expect; that is, the entities are within your planetary influence and are, having come through the quarantine web, free to answer such calling.

The temptations are offered by those negative entities of what you would call your inner planes. These, shall we say, dark angels have been impressed by the service-to-self path offered by those which have come through quarantine from days of old. And these entities, much like your angelic presences of the positive nature, are ready to move in thought within the inner planes of this planetary influence working from time/space to space/time.

The mechanism of the fifth-density entity is from density to density and is magical in nature. The fourth density, of itself, is not capable of building the highway into the energy web. However, it is capable of using that which has been left intact. These entities are, again, the Orion entities of fourth density.

90.5   **QUESTIONER** You stated previously that fifth-density entities bear a resemblance to those of us in third density on planet Earth, but fourth density does not. Could you describe the fourth-density entities, and tell me why they do not resemble us?

RA I am Ra. The description must be bated under the Law of Confusion. The cause for a variety of so-called physical vehicles is the remaining variety of heritages from second-density physical vehicular forms. The process of what you call physical evolution continues to hold sway into fourth density. Only when the Ways of Wisdom have begun to refine the power of what you may loosely call thought is the form of the physical complex manifestation more nearly under the direction of the consciousness.

90.6   **QUESTIONER** Well, if the population of this planet presently looks similar to the fifth-density entities, I was wondering why this is? If I understand you correctly, the process of evolution would normally be the third density resembling that from which it evolved in second density, and then refining in fourth, and then again in fifth becoming what the population of this planet looks like in third. Why is this planet— It seems to me that this planet is ahead of itself in the way the mind/body/spirit complex, or body complex of that, looks. What is the reason for this?

RA I am Ra. Your query is based upon a misconception. Do you wish us to comment, or do you wish to re-question?

90.7 **QUESTIONER** Please comment on my misconception if that is possible.

RA I am Ra. In fifth density the manifestation of the physical complex is more and more under the control of the conscious mind complex. Therefore, the fifth-density entity may dissolve one manifestation and create another. Consequently, the choice of a fifth-density entity or complex of entities wishing to communicate with your peoples would choose to resemble your peoples' physical-complex, chemical, yellow-ray vehicles.

90.8 **QUESTIONER** I see. Very roughly, if you were to move a third-density entity from some other planet to this planet, roughly what percentage of all of those within the knowledge of Ra would look enough like those entities of Earth so that they would go unnoticed in a crowd?

RA I am Ra. Perhaps five percent.

90.9 **QUESTIONER** Then there is an extreme variation in the form of the physical vehicle in third density in the universe. I assume this is also true of fourth density. Is this correct?

RA I am Ra. This is so. We remind you that it is a great theoretical distance between demanding that the creatures of an infinite creation be unnoticeably similar to oneself and observing those signs which may be called human which denote the third-density characteristics of self-consciousness: the grouping into pairs, societal groups, and races; and the further characteristic means of using self-consciousness to refine and search for the meaning of the milieu.

90.10 **QUESTIONER** Well, within Ra's knowledge of third-density physical forms, what percentage would be similar enough to this planet's physical form that we would assume the entity to be human even though they were a bit different? This would have to be very rough because of my definition being very rough.

RA I am Ra. This percentage is still small, perhaps thirteen to fifteen percent due to the capabilities of various second-density life forms to carry out each necessary function for third-density work. Thusly to be observed would be behavior indicating self-consciousness and purposeful interaction with a sentient ambiance about the entity, rather than those characteristics which familiarly connote to your peoples the humanity of your third-density form.

90.11 **QUESTIONER** Now my line of questioning . . . I am trying to link to the creation of various Logos and their original use of a system of archetypes in their creation, and I apologize for possibly a lack of efficiency in doing this, but I find this somewhat difficult. Now, for this particular Logos in the beginning, prior to its creation of first density, did the archetypical system which it had chosen for its creations include the forms that would evolve, and in particular third-density human form, or was this related to the archetypical concept at all?

RA I am Ra. The choice of form is prior to the formation of the archetypical mind. As the Logos creates Its plan for evolution, then the chosen form is invested.

90.12 **QUESTIONER** Was there a reason for choosing the forms that have evolved upon this planet, and if so, what was it?

RA I am Ra. We are not entirely sure why our Logos and several neighboring Logoi of approximately the same space/time of flowering chose the bipedal, erect form of the second-density apes to invest. It has been our supposition—which we share with you as long as you are aware that this is mere opinion—that our Logos was interested in, shall we say, further intensifying the veiling process by offering to the third-density form the near complete probability for the development of speech taking complete precedence over concept communication or telepathy.

We also have the supposition that the so-called opposable thumb was looked upon as an excellent means of intensifying the veiling process so that, rather than rediscovering the powers of the mind, the third-density entity would, by the form of its physical manifestation, be drawn to the making, holding, and using of physical tools.

90.13 **QUESTIONER** I will guess that the system of archetypes then was devised to further extend these particular principles. Is this correct?

RA I am Ra. The phrasing is faulty. However, it is correct that the images of the archetypical mind are the children of the third-density physical manifestations of form of the Logos which has created the particular evolutionary opportunity.

90.14 **QUESTIONER** Now, as I understand it the archetypes are the biases of a very fundamental nature that, under free will, generate the experiences of each entity. Is this correct?

RA I am Ra. The archetypical mind is part of that mind which informs all experience. Please recall the definition of the archetypical mind as the repository of those refinements to the cosmic, or all-mind, made by this particular Logos and peculiar only to this Logos.

Thus it may be seen as one of the roots of mind, not the deepest but certainly the most informative in some ways. The other root of mind to be recalled is that racial or planetary mind which also informs the conceptualizations of each entity to some degree.

90.15 **QUESTIONER** At what point in the evolutionary process does the archetypical mind first have effect upon the entity?

RA I am Ra. At the point at which an entity, either by accident or design, reflects an archetype, the archetypical mind resonates. Thusly random activation of the archetypical resonances begins almost immediately in third-density experience. The disciplined use of this tool of evolution comes far later in this process.

90.16 **QUESTIONER** What was the ultimate objective of this Logos in designing the archetypical mind as It did?

RA I am Ra. Each Logos desires to create a more eloquent expression of experience of the Creator by the Creator. The archetypical mind is intended to heighten this ability to express the Creator in patterns more like the fanned peacock's tail: each facet of the Creator vivid, upright, and shining with articulated beauty.

90.17 **QUESTIONER** Is Ra familiar with the archetypical mind of some other Logos that is not the same as the one we experience?

RA I am Ra. There are entities of Ra which have served as far wanderers to those of another Logos. The experience has been one which staggers the intellectual and intuitive capacities, for each Logos sets up an experiment enough at variance from all others that the subtleties of the archetypical mind of another Logos are most murky to the resonating mind, body, and spirit complexes of this Logos.

90.18 **QUESTIONER** There seems to have been created by this Logos (to me anyway) a large percentage of entities whose distortion was toward warfare, in that we had the Maldek and the Mars experience and now Earth. It seems that Venus was the exception to what we could almost call the rule of warfare. Is this correct? And was this envisioned and planned into the construction of the archetypical mind—possibly not with respect particularly to warfare as we have experienced it but to the extreme action to polarization in consciousness?

RA I am Ra. It is correct that the Logos designed Its experiment to attempt to achieve the greatest possible opportunities for polarization in third density. It is incorrect that warfare of the types specific to your experiences was planned by the Logos. This form of expression of hostility is an interesting result which is apparently concomitant with the tool-making ability. The choice of the Logos to use the life-form with the grasping thumb is the decision to which this type of warfare may be traced.

90.19 **QUESTIONER** Then did our Logos hope to see generated a positive and negative harvest from each density up to the sixth, starting with the third, as being the most efficient form of generating experience known to It at the time of Its construction of this system of evolution?

RA I am Ra. Yes.

90.20 **QUESTIONER** Then built into the basis for the archetypes is, possibly, the mechanism for creating the polarization in consciousness for service to others and service to self. Is this, in fact, true?

RA I am Ra. Yes. You will notice the many inborn biases which hint to the possibility of one path's being more efficient than the other. This was the design of the Logos.

90.21 **QUESTIONER** Then what you are saying is that once the path is recognized, either the positive or the negative polarized entity can find hints along his path as to the efficiency of that path. Is this correct?

RA I am Ra. That which you say is correct upon its own merits but is not a repetition of our statement. Our suggestion was that within the experiential nexus of each entity, within its second-density environment and within the roots of mind, there were placed biases indicating to the watchful eye the more efficient of the two paths. Let us say, for want of a more precise adjective, that this Logos has a bias towards kindness.

90.22 **QUESTIONER** Then you say that the more efficient of the two paths was suggested in a subliminal way to second density to be the service-to-others path. Am I correct?

RA I am Ra. We did not state which was the more efficient path. However, you are correct in your assumption, as you are aware from having examined each path in some detail in previous querying.

90.23 **QUESTIONER** Would this be the reason for the greater positive harvests? I suspect that it isn't, but would there be Logoi that have greater negative percentage harvests because of this type of biasing?

RA I am Ra. No. There have been Logoi with greater percentages of negative harvests. However, the biasing mechanisms cannot change the requirements for achieving harvestability either in the positive or in the negative sense.

There are Logoi which have offered a neutral background against which to polarize. This Logos chose not to do so but instead to allow more of the love and light of the Infinite Creator to be both inwardly and outwardly visible and available to the sensations and conceptualizations of mind/body/spirits[2] undergoing Its care in experimenting.

90.24 **QUESTIONER** Were there any other circumstances, biases, consequences, or plans set up by the Logos other than those we have discussed for the evolution of Its parts through the densities?

RA I am Ra. Yes.

90.25 **QUESTIONER** What were these?

RA I am Ra. One more; that is, the permeability of the densities so that there may be communication from density to density and from plane to plane or sub-density to sub-density.

90.26 **QUESTIONER** Then as I see the plan for the evolution by this Logos: it was planned to create as vivid an experience as possible, but also one which was somewhat informed with respect to the Infinite Creator and able to accelerate progress as a function of will because of the permeabilities of

---

[2] Should be mind/body/spirit complexes, presumably.

densities. Have I covered accurately the general plan of this Logos with respect to Its evolution?

RA I am Ra. Excepting the actions of the unmanifested self and the actions of self with other-self, you have been reasonably thorough.

90.27 QUESTIONER Then, is the major mechanism forming the ways and very essence of the experience that we presently experience here the archetypical mind and the archetypes?

RA I am Ra. These resources are a part of that which you refer to.

90.28 QUESTIONER What I am really asking is what percentage part, roughly, are these responsible for?

RA I am Ra. We ask once again that you consider that the archetypical mind is a part of the deep mind. There are several portions to this mind. The mind may serve as a resource. To call the archetypical mind the foundation of experience is to oversimplify the activities of the mind/body/spirit complex. To work with your query as to percentages is, therefore, enough misleading in any form of direct answer that we would ask that you re-question.

90.29 QUESTIONER That's OK. I don't think that was that good a question anyway.

Now, when Ra initially planned for helping the Egyptians with their evolution, what was the most, or the primary concept—and also secondary and tertiary, if you can name those—that Ra wished to impart to the Egyptians? In other words, what was Ra's training plan or schedule for making the Egyptians aware of what was necessary for their evolution?

RA I am Ra. We came to your peoples to enunciate the Law of One. We wished to impress upon those who wished to learn of unity that in unity all paradoxes are resolved; all that is broken is healed; all that is forgotten is brought to light.

We had no teaching plan, as you have called it, in that our intention when we walked among your peoples was to manifest that which was requested by those learn/teachers to which we had come.

We are aware that this particular line of querying—that is, the nature and architecture of the archetypical mind—has caused the questioner to attempt, to its own mind unsuccessfully, to determine the relative importance of these concepts. We cannot learn/teach for any, nor would we take this opportunity from the questioner. However, we shall comment.

The adept has already worked much, not only within the red, orange, yellow, and green energy centers, but already in the opening of blue and indigo. Up through this point the archetypes function as the great base or plinth of a builded structure or statue, keeping the mind complex viable, level, and available as a resource whenever it may be evoked.

There is a point at which the adept takes up its work. This is the point at which a clear and conscious consideration of the archetypical mind is useful.

90.30 **QUESTIONER** I have an observation on Archetype One made by Jim and request comment by Ra. I will read it. "The Matrix of the Mind is the conscious mind and is sustained by the power of the spirit, symbolized by the star, which flows to it through the subconscious mind. It contains the will which is symbolized by the scepter of power in the Magician's hand. All of creation is made through the power of the will directed by the conscious mind of the Magician, and the bird in the cage represents the illusion in which the self seems trapped. The Magician represents maleness or the radiance of being manifested as the creation through which each entity moves."

RA I am Ra. As this instrument is becoming somewhat weary we shall not begin this considerable discussion. We would request that this series of observations be repeated at the outset of the next working. We would suggest that each concept be discussed separately or, if appropriate, a pair of concepts be related one to the other within the concept complex. This is slow work but shall make the eventual building of the concept complexes more smoothly accomplished.

Were we to have answered the observations as read by you at this space/time, as much space/time would have been given to the untangling of various concepts as to the building up of what were very thoughtful perceptions.

May we ask if there are any brief queries at this time?

90.31 **QUESTIONER** Is there anything that we can do to make the instrument more comfortable or improve the contact?

RA I am Ra. It is well that the appliances for the arms were placed upon the instrument. We ask that continued vigilance be accorded these distortions which are, if anything, more distorted towards dis-ease than at our previous cautionary statement.

All is well, my friends. You are conscientious and faithful in your alignments. We appreciate your fastidiousness.

I am Ra. I leave you now, rejoicing merrily in the love and the light of the One Infinite Creator. Go forth, then, rejoicing in the power and in the peace of the One Infinite Creator. Adonai.

Session 91

JUNE 26, 1982

91.0 **RA** I am Ra. I greet you in the love and in the light of the One Infinite Creator. We communicate now.

91.1 **QUESTIONER** Could you first please give me the condition of the instrument?

RA I am Ra. It is as previously stated.

91.2 **QUESTIONER** I have listed the different minds and would like to know if they are applied in this particular aspect: first, we have the cosmic mind which is, I would think, the same for all sub-Logoi like our sun. Is this correct?

RA I am Ra. This is correct.

91.3 **QUESTIONER** The sub-Logos such as our sun, then, in creating Its own particular evolution of experience, refines the cosmic mind or, shall we say, articulates it by Its own additional bias or biases. Is this a correct observation?

RA I am Ra. It is a correct observation with the one exception that concerns the use of the term "addition," which suggests the concept of that which is more than the all-mind. Instead, the archetypical mind is a refinement of the all-mind in a pattern peculiar to the sub-Logos' choosing.

91.4 **QUESTIONER** Then the very next refinement that occurs as the cosmic mind is refined is what we call the archetypical mind. Is this correct?

RA I am Ra. Yes.

91.5 **QUESTIONER** This then creates, I would assume, the planetary or racial mind. Is this correct?

RA I am Ra. No.

91.6 **QUESTIONER** What is the origin of the planetary or racial mind?

RA I am Ra. This racial or planetary mind is, for this Logos, a repository of biases remembered by the mind/body/spirit complexes which have enjoyed the experience of this planetary influence.

91.7 **QUESTIONER** Now, some entities on this planet evolved through second density into third, and some were transferred from other planets to re-cycle in third density here. Did the ones who were transferred here to re-cycle in third density add to the planetary or racial mind?

RA I am Ra. Not only did each race add to the planetary mind, but also each race possesses a racial mind. Thus we made this distinction in discussing this portion of mind.

This portion of mind is formed in the series of seemingly non-simultaneous experiences which are chosen in freedom of will by the mind/body/spirit complexes of the planetary influence. Therefore, although this Akashic, planetary, or racial mind is, indeed, a root of mind, it may be seen in sharp differentiation from the deeper roots of mind which are not a function of altering memory, if you will.

We must ask your patience at this time. This channel has become somewhat unclear due to the movement of the cover which touches this instrument. We ask that the opening sentences be repeated and the breath expelled.

[*The microphones attached to the cover upon the instrument were pulled slightly as a rug was being placed over a noisy tape recorder. The Circle of One was walked; breath was expelled two feet above the instrument's head from her right to her left; and the Circle of One was walked again as requested.*]

I am Ra. We communicate now.

91.8 **QUESTIONER** Were we successful in re-establishing clear contact?

RA I am Ra. There was the misstep which then needed to be re-repeated. This was done. The communication is once again clear. We enjoyed the humorous aspects of the necessary repetitions.

91.9 **QUESTIONER** What occurred when the microphone cords were slightly moved?

RA I am Ra. The link between the instrument's mind/body/spirit complex and its yellow-ray, chemical, physical vehicle was jarred. This caused some maladjustment of the organ you call the lungs, and, if the repair had not been done, would have resulted in a distorted physical complex condition of this portion of the instrument's physical vehicle.

91.10 **QUESTIONER** What kind of distortion?

RA I am Ra. The degree of distortion would depend upon the amount of neglect. The ultimate penalty, shall we say, for the disturbing of the physical vehicle is the death, in this case by what you would call the congestive heart failure. As the support group was prompt, there should be little or no distortion experienced by the instrument.

91.11 **QUESTIONER** Why does such a very minor effect like the slight movement of the microphone cord result in this situation? Not mechanically or chemically, but philosophically, if you can answer this question?

RA I am Ra. We can only answer mechanically as there is no philosophy to the reflexes of physical vehicular function.

There is what you might call the silver cord reflex; that is, when the mind/body/spirit complex dwells without the environs of the physical shell and the physical shell is disturbed, the physical shell will reflexively call back the absent enlivener; that is, the mind/body/spirit complex which is connected with what may be metaphysically seen as what some of your philosophers have called the silver cord.

If this is done suddenly the mind/body/spirit complex will attempt entry into the energy web of the physical vehicle without due care, and the effect is as if one were to stretch one of your elastic bands and let it shrink rapidly. The resulting snap would strike hard at the anchored portion of the elastic band.

The process through which you as a group go in recalling this instrument could be likened unto taking this elastic and gently lessening its degree of tension until it was without perceptible stretch.

91.12 **QUESTIONER** To get back to what we were talking about: would then possibly the different races that inhabit this planet be from different planets in our local vicinity, or the planets of nearby Logoi that have evolved through their second-density experiences, to create the large number of different races that we experience on this planet? Is this correct?

RA I am Ra. There are correctnesses to your supposition. However, not all races and sub-races are of various planetary origins. We suggest that in looking at planetary origins one observes not the pigmentation of the integument but the biases concerning interactions with other-selves and definitions regarding the nature of the self.

91.13 QUESTIONER How many different planets have supplied the individuals that now inhabit this planet in this third density?

RA I am Ra. This is perceived by us to be unimportant information, but harmless. There are three major planetary influences upon your planetary sphere besides those of your own second-density derivation, and thirteen minor planetary groups in addition to the above.

91.14 QUESTIONER Thank you. One more question before we start on the specific questions with respect to archetypes. Do all Logoi evolving after the veil have twenty-two archetypes?

RA I am Ra. No.

91.15 QUESTIONER Is it common for Logoi to have twenty-two archetypes, or is this relatively unique with respect to our Logos?

RA I am Ra. The system of sevens is the most articulated system yet discovered by any experiment by any Logos in our octave.

91.16 QUESTIONER What is the largest number of archetypes, to Ra's knowledge, used by a Logos?

RA I am Ra. The sevens plus The Choice is the greatest number which has been used, by our knowledge, by Logoi. It is the result of many, many previous experiments in articulation of the One Creator.

91.17 QUESTIONER I assume, then, that twenty-two is the greatest number of archetypes. I'll also ask what is the minimum number presently in use by any Logos, to Ra's knowledge?

RA I am Ra. The fewest are the two systems of five which are completing the cycles or densities of experience.

You must grasp the idea that the archetypes were not developed at once but step by step, and not in order as you know the order at this space/time, but in various orders. Therefore, the two systems of fives were using two separate ways of viewing the archetypical nature of all experience. Each, of course, used the Matrix, the Potentiator, and the Significator, for this is the harvest with which our creation began.

One way or system of experimentation had added to these the Catalyst and the Experience. Another system, if you will, had added Catalyst and Transformation. In one case the methods whereby experience was processed was further aided, but the fruits of experience less aided. In the second case, the opposite may be seen to be the case.

91.18   QUESTIONER Thank you. We have some observations on the archetypes as follows. First, the Matrix of the Mind is depicted in the Egyptian tarot by a male, and this we take as creative energy intelligently directed. Would Ra comment on this?

RA I am Ra. This is an extremely thoughtful perception seeing as it does the male not specifically as biological male but as a male principle.

You will note that there are very definite sexual biases in the images. They are intended to function both as information as to which biological entity or energy will attract which archetype, but also as a more general view which sees polarity as a key to the archetypical mind of third density.

91.19   QUESTIONER Secondly, we have the wand which has been seen as the power of will. Would Ra comment?

RA I am Ra. The concept of will is indeed pouring forth from each facet of the image of the Matrix of the Mind. The wand, as the will, however, is, shall we say, an astrological derivative of the out-reaching hand forming the, shall we say, magical gesture.

The excellent portion of the image—which may be seen distinctly as separate from the concept of the wand—is that sphere which indicates the spiritual nature of the object of the will of one wishing to do magical acts within the manifestation of your density.

91.20   QUESTIONER The hand downward has been seen as seeking from within, not outwardly active dominance over the material world. Would Ra comment?

RA I am Ra. Look again, O student. Does the hand reach within? Nay. Without potentiation the conscious mind has no inwardness. That hand, O student, reaches towards that which, outside its unpotentiated influence, is locked from it.

91.21   QUESTIONER The square cage may represent the material illusion, an unmagical shape. Would Ra comment?

RA I am Ra. The square, wherever seen, is the symbol of the third-density illusion and may be seen either as unmagical or, in the proper configuration, as having been manifested within; that is, the material world given life.

91.22   QUESTIONER The dark area around the square would then be the darkness of the subconscious mind. Would Ra comment?

RA I am Ra. There is no further thing to say to the perceptive student.

91.23   QUESTIONER The checkered portion would represent polarity?

RA I am Ra. This also is satisfactory.

91.24   QUESTIONER The bird is a messenger that the hand is reaching down to unlock. Can Ra comment on that?

RA I am Ra. The wingèd visions or images in this system are to be noted not so much for their distinct kind as for the position of the wings. All birds are, indeed, intended to suggest flight, and messages, and movement, and in some cases, protection.

The folded wing in this image is intended to suggest that just as the Matrix figure, the Magician, cannot act without reaching its wingèd spirit, so neither can the spirit fly lest it be released into conscious manifestation and fructified thereby.

91.25   QUESTIONER The star could represent the potentiating force of the subconscious mind. Is this correct?

RA I am Ra. This particular part of this image is best seen in astrological terms. We would comment at this space/time that Ra did not include the astrological portions of these images in the system of images designed to evoke the archetypical leitmotifs.[1]

---

[1]   In this context, *leitmotif* can be defined as "a recurring theme or element in a musical or literary composition, or any other expressive work, which often serves as a guiding or central element within the work."

91.26 **QUESTIONER** Are there any other additions to Card Number One, other than the star, that are of other than the basic archetypical aspects?

RA I am Ra. There are details of each image seen through the cultural eye of the time of inscription. This is to be expected. Therefore, when viewing the, shall we say, Egyptian costumes and systems of mythology used in the images, it is far better to penetrate to the heart of the costumes' significance or the creatures' significance rather than clinging to a culture which is not your own.

In each entity the image will resonate slightly differently. Therefore, there is the desire upon Ra's part to allow for the creative envisioning of each archetype using general guidelines rather than specific and limiting definitions.

91.27 **QUESTIONER** The cup may represent the mixture of positive and negative passions. Would Ra comment, please?

RA I am Ra. The otic portions of this instrument's physical vehicle did not perceive a significant portion of your query. Please re-query.

91.28 **QUESTIONER** There is apparently a cup which we have as containing a mixture of positive and negative influences. However, I personally doubt this. Would Ra comment, please?

RA I am Ra. Doubt not the polarity, O student, but release the cup from its stricture. It is indeed a distortion of the original image.

91.29 **QUESTIONER** What was the original image?

RA I am Ra. The original image had the checkering as the suggestion of polarity.

91.30 **QUESTIONER** Then was this a representation of the waiting polarity to be tasted by the Matrix of the Mind?

RA I am Ra. This is exquisitely perceptive.

91.31 **QUESTIONER** I have listed here the sword as struggle. I am not sure that I even can call anything in this diagram a sword. Would Ra comment on that?

RA I am Ra. Doubt not the struggle, O student, but release the sword from its stricture. Observe the struggle of a caged bird to fly.

91.32   **QUESTIONER** I have listed the coin as work accomplished. I am also in doubt about the existence of the coin in this diagram. Would Ra comment?

RA I am Ra. Again, doubt not that which the coin is called to represent, for does not the Magus strive to achieve through the manifested world? Yet release the coin from its stricture.

91.33   **QUESTIONER** And finally, the Magician represents the conscious mind. Is this correct?

RA I am Ra. We ask the student to consider the concept of the unfed conscious mind, the mind without any resource but consciousness. Do not confuse the unfed conscious mind with that mass of complexities which you as students experience, as you have so many, many times dipped already into the processes of potentiation, catalyst, experience, and transformation.

91.34   **QUESTIONER** Are these all of the components, then, of this first archetype?

RA I am Ra. These are all you, the student, sees. Thusly the complement is complete for you. Each student may see some other nuance.

We, as we have said, did not offer these images with boundaries, but only as guidelines intending to aid the adept and to establish the architecture of the deep or archetypical portion of the deep mind.

91.35   **QUESTIONER** How is a knowledge of the facets of the archetypical mind used by the individual to accelerate his evolution?

RA I am Ra. We shall offer an example based upon this first explored archetype or concept complex.

The conscious mind of the adept may be full to bursting of the most abstruse and unmanageable of ideas, so that further ideation becomes impossible, and work in blue ray or indigo is blocked through over-activation. It is then that the adept would call upon the new mind, untouched and virgin, and dwell within the archetype of the new and unblemished mind without bias, without polarity, full of the magic of the Logos.

91.36   **QUESTIONER** Then you are saying that (if I am correct in understanding what you have just said) that the conscious mind may be filled with an almost infinite number of concepts, but there is a set of basic concepts which are what I would call important simply because they are the foundations for the evolution of consciousness, and will, if carefully applied, accelerate the evolution of consciousness. Whereas the vast array of concepts, ideas, experiences that we meet in our daily lives may have little or no bearing upon the evolution of consciousness except in a very indirect way. In other words, what we are attempting to do here is find the great motivators of evolution and utilize them to move through our evolutionary track. Is this correct?

RA I am Ra. Not entirely. The archetypes are not the foundation for spiritual evolution but rather are the tool for grasping in an undistorted manner the nature of this evolution.

91.37 **QUESTIONER** So for an individual who wishes to consciously augment his own evolution, an ability to recognize and utilize the archetypes would be beneficial in sorting out that which he wished to seek and that which he found—and that which would be found then as not as efficient a seeking tool. Would this be a good statement?

RA I am Ra. This is a fairly adequate statement. The term "efficient" might also fruitfully be replaced by the term "undistorted." The archetypical mind, when penetrated lucidly, is a blueprint of the builded structure of all energy expenditures and all seeking, without distortion. This, as a resource within the deep mind, is of great potential aid to the adept.

We would ask for one more query at this space/time as this instrument is experiencing continuous surges of the distortion you call pain, and we wish to take our leave of the working while the instrument still possesses a sufficient amount of transferred energy to ease the transition to the waking state, if you would call it that.

91.38 **QUESTIONER** Since we are at the end of the Matrix of the Mind I will just ask if there is anything we can do to improve the contact or make the instrument more comfortable?

RA I am Ra. Each is most conscientious. The instrument might be somewhat more comfortable with the addition of the swirling of the waters with spine erect. All other things which can be performed for the instrument's benefit are most diligently done.

We commend the continual fidelity of the group to the ideals of harmony and thanksgiving. This shall be your great protection. All is well, my friends. The appurtenances and alignments are excellent.

I am Ra. I leave you glorying in the love and in the light of the One Infinite Creator. Go forth, then, rejoicing in the power and the peace of the One Infinite Creator. Adonai.

SESSION 92

92.0   **RA** I am Ra. I greet you in the love and in the light of the One Infinite Creator. We communicate now.

92.1   **QUESTIONER** Could you first please give me the condition of the instrument?

RA I am Ra. The condition of this instrument is slightly more distorted towards weakness in each respect since the previous asking.

92.2   **QUESTIONER** Is there a specific cause for this, and could you tell us what it is if so?

RA I am Ra. The effective cause of the increased physical distortions have to do with the press of continued substantial levels of the distortion you call pain. Various vehicular distortions, other than the specifically arthritic, have been accentuated by psychic greeting, and the combined effect has been deleterious.

The continued slight but noticeable losses of the vital energies is due to the necessity for the instrument to call upon this resource in order to clear the, shall we say, way for a carefully purified service-to-others working. The use of the will in the absence of physical and, in this particular case, mental and mental/emotional energies requires vital energies.

92.3   **QUESTIONER** We have been attempting to figure out how to provide the instrument with the swirling water, which we hope to do very soon. Is there any other thing that we can do to improve this situation?

RA I am Ra. Continue in peace and harmony. Already the support group does much. There is the need for the instrument to choose the manner of its beingness. It has the distortion, as we have noted, towards the martyrdom. This can be evaluated and choices made only by the entity.

92.4   **QUESTIONER** What is the present situation with the fifth-density negative visitor we have [*inaudible*]?

RA I am Ra. It is with this group.

92.5   **QUESTIONER** What prompted its return?

RA I am Ra. The promptings were duple. There was the recovery of much negative polarity upon the part of your friend of fifth density and, at the same approximate nexus, a temporary lessening of the positive harmony of this group.

92.6 **QUESTIONER** Is there anything that we can do about the instrument's stomach problem or constipation?

RA I am Ra. The healing modes of which each is capable are already in use.

92.7 **QUESTIONER** In the last session we discussed the first tarot card of the Egyptian type. Are there any distortions in the cards that we have (which we will publish in the book if possible) that Ra did not originally intend, with the exception of the star, which we know is a distortion? Or any additions that Ra did intend in this particular tarot?

RA I am Ra. The distortions remaining after the removal of astrological material are those having to do with the mythos of the culture to which Ra offered this teach/learning tool. This is why we have suggested approaching the images looking for the heart of the image rather than being involved overmuch by the costumes and creatures of a culture not familiar to your present incarnation. We have no wish to add to an already distorted group of images, feeling that, although distortion is inevitable, there is the least amount which can be procured in the present arrangement.

92.8 **QUESTIONER** Then you are saying that the cards that we have here are the best available cards in our present illusion at this date?

RA I am Ra. Your statement is correct in that we consider the so-called Egyptian tarot the most undistorted version of the images which Ra offered. This is not to intimate that other systems may not, in their own way, form an helpful architecture for the adept's consideration of the archetypical mind.

92.9 **QUESTIONER** I would like to attempt an analogy of the first archetype in that when a baby is first born and enters this density of experience, I am assuming, then, that the Matrix is new and undistorted, veiled from the Potentiator and ready for that which is to be experienced: the incarnation. Is this correct?

RA I am Ra. Yes.

92.10 QUESTIONER I will read several statements here and ask for Ra's comment on the statement.

First: Until an entity becomes consciously aware of the evolutionary process, the Logos, or intelligent energy, creates the potentials for an entity to gain the experience necessary for polarization. Would Ra comment on that?

RA I am Ra. This is so.

92.11 QUESTIONER Then, this occurs because the Potentiator of the Mind is directly connected, through the roots of the tree of mind, to the archetypical mind and to the Logos which created it, and because the veil between the Matrix and Potentiator of the Mind allows for the development of the will. Would Ra comment?

RA I am Ra. Some untangling may be needed. As the mind/body/spirit complex which has not yet reached the point of the conscious awareness of the process of evolution prepares for incarnation it has programmed for it a less-than-complete, that is to say, a partially randomized system of learnings. The amount of randomness of potential catalyst is proportional to the newness of the mind/body/spirit complex to third density.

This, then, becomes a portion of that which you may call a potential for incarnational experience. This is, indeed, carried within that portion of the mind which is of the deep mind, the architecture of which may be envisioned as being represented by that concept complex known as the Potentiator.

It is not in the archetypical mind of an entity that the potential for incarnational experience resides, but in the mind/body/spirit complex's insertion, shall we say, into the energy web of the physical vehicle and the chosen planetary environment. However, to more deeply articulate this portion of the mind/body/spirit complex's beingness, this archetype, the Potentiator of the Mind, may be evoked with profit to the student of its own evolution.

92.12 QUESTIONER Then are you saying that the source of pre-incarnative programmed catalyst is the Potentiator of Mind?

RA I am Ra. No. We are suggesting that the Potentiator of the Mind is an archetype which may aid the adept in grasping the nature of this pre-incarnative and continuingly incarnative series of choices.

92.13 **QUESTIONER** Thank you. Third: Just as Free Will taps intelligent infinity, which yields intelligent energy, which then focuses and creates the densities of this octave of experience, the Potentiator of Mind utilizes its connection with intelligent energy and taps or potentiates the Matrix of the Mind, which yields Catalyst of the Mind. Is this correct?

RA I am Ra. This is thoughtful but confused. The Matrix of the Mind is that which reaches—just as the kinetic phase of intelligent infinity, through free will, reaches for the Logos (or, in the case of the mind/body/spirit complex, the sub-sub-Logos, which is the free-will-potentiated beingness of the mind/body/spirit complex)—to intelligent infinity, Love, and all that follows from that Logos; to the Matrix or, shall we say, the conscious, waiting self of each entity, the Love or the sub-sub-Logos spinning through free will all those things which may enrich the experience of the Creator by the Creator.[1]

It is indeed so that the biases of the potentials of a mind/body/spirit complex cause the catalyst of this entity to be unique and to form a coherent pattern that resembles the dance, full of movement, forming a many-figured tapestry of motion.

92.14 **QUESTIONER** Fourth: When the Catalyst of the Mind is processed by the entity the Experience of the Mind results. Is this correct?

RA I am Ra. There are subtle misdirections in this simple statement having to do with the overriding qualities of the Significator. It is so that catalyst yields experience. However, through free will and the faculty of imperfect memory, catalyst is most often only partially used, and the experience thus correspondingly skewed.

92.15 **QUESTIONER** The dynamic process between the Matrix, Potentiator, Catalyst, and Experience of the Mind forms the nature of the mind or the Significator of the Mind. Is this correct?

---

1 Much debate has been waged on the question of how to punctuate this tangle of a reply. This particular punctuation is one among other possible subjective interpretations of what Ra intended to say.

RA I am Ra. As our previous response suggests, the Significator of the Mind is both actor and acted upon. With this exception the statement is largely correct.

92.16 QUESTIONER As the entity becomes consciously aware of this process it programs this activity itself before the incarnation. Is this correct?

RA I am Ra. This is correct. Please keep in mind that we are discussing, not the archetypical mind which is a resource available equally to each but unevenly used, but that to which it speaks: the incarnational experiential process of each mind/body/spirit complex.

We wish to make this distinction clear, for it is not the archetypes which live the incarnation, but the conscious mind/body/spirit complex—which may, indeed, live the incarnation without recourse to the quest for articulation of the processes of potentiation, experience, and transformation.

92.17 QUESTIONER Thank you. Then finally: As each energy center becomes activated and balanced the Transformation of the Mind is called upon more and more frequently. When all of the energy centers are activated and balanced to a minimal degree, contact with intelligent infinity occurs; the veil is removed; and the Great Way of the Mind is called upon. Is this correct?

RA I am Ra. No. This is a quite eloquent look at some relationships within the archetypical mind. However, it must be seen once again that the archetypical mind does not equal the acting incarnational mind/body/spirit complex's progression or evolution.

Due to the first misperception we hesitate to speak to the second consideration but shall attempt clarity. While studying the archetypical mind we may suggest that the student look at the Great Way of the Mind not as that which is attained after contact with intelligent infinity, but rather as that portion of the archetypical mind which denotes and configures the particular framework within which the Mind, the Body, or the Spirit archetypes move.

92.18 QUESTIONER Turning, then, to my analogy—or shall we say, example—of the newborn infant with the undistorted Matrix, this newborn infant has its subconscious veiled from the Matrix. The second archetype, the Potentiator of Mind, is going to act at some time through—I won't say through the veil, I don't think that is a very good way of stating it—but the Potentiator of Mind will act to create a condition, and I will use an example of the infant touching a hot object. The hot object we could take as random catalyst. The infant can either leave its hand on the hot object or rapidly remove it. My question is: is the Potentiator of Mind involved at all in this experience and, if so, how?

RA I am Ra. The Potentiator of Mind and of Body are both involved in the questing of the infant for new experience. The mind/body/spirit complex which is an infant has one highly developed portion which may be best studied by viewing the Significators of Mind and Body.

You notice we do not include the spirit. That portion of a mind/body/spirit complex is not reliably developed in each and every mind/body/spirit complex. Thusly the infant's significant self, which is the harvest of biases of all previous incarnational experiences, offers to this infant biases with which to meet new experience.

However, the portion of the infant which may be articulated by the Matrix of the Mind is indeed unfed by experience, and has the bias of reaching for this experience through free will just as intelligent energy, in the kinetic phase, through free will, creates the Logos.

This sub-sub-Logos then (or that portion of the mind/body/spirit complex which may be articulated by consideration of the Potentiators of Mind and Body), through free will, chooses to make alterations in its experiential continuum.

The results of these experiments in novelty are then recorded in the portion of the mind and body articulated by the Matrices thereof.

92.19 QUESTIONER Are all activities that the entity has, as it experiences things from the state of infancy, a function of the Potentiator of Mind?

RA I am Ra. Firstly, although the functions of the mind are indeed paramount over those of the body—the body being the creature of the mind—certainly not all actions of a mind/body/spirit complex could be seen to be due to the potentiating qualities of the mind complex alone, as the body and in some cases the spirit also potentiates action.

Secondly, as a mind/body/spirit complex becomes aware of the process of spiritual evolution, more and more of the activities of the mind and body which precipitate activity are caused by those portions of the mind/body/spirit complex which are articulated by the archetypes of Transformation.

92.20 **QUESTIONER** The Matrix of the Mind is depicted seemingly as male on the card and the Potentiator as female. Could Ra state why this is and how this affects these two archetypes?

RA I am Ra. Firstly, as we have said, the Matrix of the Mind is attracted to the biological male and the Potentiator of the Mind to the biological female. Thusly in energy transfer the female is able to potentiate that which may be within the conscious mind of the male so that it may feel enspirited.

In a more general sense, that which reaches may be seen as a male principle; that which awaits the reaching may be seen as a female principle.

The richness of the male and female system of polarity is interesting, and we would not comment further but suggest consideration by the student.

92.21 **QUESTIONER** Card #2, the Potentiator of the Mind: we see a female sitting on a rectangular block. She is veiled and between two pillars which seem to be identically covered with drawings, but one much darker than the other. I am assuming that the veil represents the veil between the conscious and subconscious or Matrix and Potentiator. Is this correct?

RA I am Ra. This is quite correct.

92.22 **QUESTIONER** I am assuming that she sits between the different colored columns, one on her left, one on her right (the dark one is on her left), to indicate at this position an equal opportunity, you might say, for potentiation of the mind to be of the negative or positive paths. Would Ra comment on this?

RA I am Ra. Although this is correct it is not as perceptive as the notice that the Priestess, as this figure has been called, sits within a structure in which polarity, symbolized as you correctly noted by the light and dark pillars, is an integral and necessary part.

The unfed mind has no polarity just as intelligent infinity has none. The nature of the sub-sub-sub-Logos which offers the third-density experience is one of polarity, not by choice but by careful design.

We perceive an unclear statement. The polarity of Potentiator is there not for the Matrix to choose. It is there for the Matrix to accept as given.

92.23   **QUESTIONER** In other words, this particular illusion has polarity as its foundation which might be represented by the structural significance of these columns. Is this correct?

RA I am Ra. This is correct.

92.24   **QUESTIONER** It seems to me that the drawings on each of these columns are identical, but that the left-hand column, that is the one on the Priestess's left, has been shaded much darker indicating that the events or the experiences may be identical in the incarnation, but may be approached and viewed and utilized with either polarity as the bias. Is this in any way correct?

RA I am Ra. This is correct. You will note also, from the symbol denoting spirit in manifestation upon each pillar, that the One Infinite Creator is no respecter of polarity but offers Itself in full to all.

92.25   **QUESTIONER** There seems to be a book on the Priestess's lap which is half hidden by the robe or material that covers her right shoulder. It would seem that this indicates that knowledge is available if the veil is lifted, but is not only hidden by the veil, but hidden partially by her very garment which she must somehow move to become aware of the knowledge which she has available. Is this correct?

RA I am Ra. In that the conceit of the volume was not originated by Ra we ask that you release the volume from its strictured form. Your perceptions are quite correct.

The very nature of the feminine principle of mind which, in Ra's suggestion, was related specifically to what may be termed sanctified sexuality is, itself, without addition, the book which neither the feminine nor the male principle may use until the male principle has reached and penetrated, in a symbolically sexual fashion, the inner secrets of this feminine principle.

All robes, in this case indicating the outer garments of custom, shield these principles. Thusly there is great dynamic tension, if you will, betwixt the Matrix and the Potentiator of the Mind.

92.26 **QUESTIONER** Are there any other parts of this picture that were not given by Ra?

RA I am Ra. The astrological symbols offered are not given by Ra.

92.27 **QUESTIONER** The fact that the Priestess sits atop the rectangular box indicates to me the Potentiator of the Mind has dominance or is above and over the material illusion. Is this in any way correct?

RA I am Ra. Let us say, rather, that this figure is immanent, near at hand, shall we say, within all manifestation. The opportunities for the reaching to the Potentiator are numerous. However, of itself the Potentiator does not enter manifestation.

92.28 **QUESTIONER** Would the half moon on the crown represent the receptivity of the subconscious mind?

RA I am Ra. This symbol is not given by Ra, but it is not distasteful, for within your own culture the moon represents the feminine, the sun the masculine. Thusly we accept this portion as a portion of the image, for it seems without significant distortion.

92.29 **QUESTIONER** Was the symbol on the front of the Priestess' shirt given by Ra?

RA I am Ra. The crux ansata is the correct symbol. The addition and slight distortion of this symbol thereby is astrological and may be released from its stricture.

92.30 **QUESTIONER** Would this crux ansata then be indicating a sign of life or spirit enlivening matter?

RA I am Ra. This is quite correct. Moreover, it illuminates a concept which is a portion of the archetype which has to do with the continuation of the consciousness which is being potentiated in incarnation, beyond incarnation.

92.31 **QUESTIONER** Were the grapes depicted upon the cloth covering the shoulder of the Priestess of Ra's communication?

RA I am Ra. Yes.

92.32 **QUESTIONER** We have taken those as indicating the fertility of the subconscious mind. Is this correct?

RA I am Ra. This is correct, O student, but note ye the function of the mantle. There is great protection given by the very character of potentiation. To bear fruit is a protected activity.

92.33 **QUESTIONER** The protection here seems to be depicted as being on the right-hand side but not the left. Would this indicate greater protection for the positive path than the negative?

RA I am Ra. You perceive correctly an inborn bias offering to the seeing eye and listing ear information concerning the choice of the more efficient polarity.

We would at this time, as you may call it, suggest one more full query.

92.34 **QUESTIONER** I will just, then, attempt an example of the Potentiator of Mind acting. Would, as the infant gains time in incarnation, it experience the Potentiator offering both positive and negative potential acts (or thoughts, shall I say) for the Matrix to experience, which then begin to accumulate in the Matrix, and color it one way or the other in polarity depending upon its continuing choice of that polarity offered by the Potentiator? Is this in any way correct?

RA I am Ra. Firstly, again may we distinguish between the archetypical mind and the process of incarnational experience of the mind/body/spirit complex.

Secondly, each potentiation which has been reached for by the Matrix is recorded by the Matrix but experienced by the Significator.

The experience of the Significator of this potentiated activity is, of course, dependent upon the acuity of its processes of Catalyst and Experience.

May we ask if there are briefer queries before we leave this instrument?

92.35 **QUESTIONER** Is there anything that we can do to make the instrument more comfortable or improve the contact?

RA I am Ra. The support group is functioning well.

The instrument, itself, might ponder some earlier words and consider their implications. We say this because the continued calling upon vital energies, if allowed to proceed to the end of the vital energy, will end this contact. There is not the need for continued calling upon these energies.

The instrument must find the key to this riddle or face a growing loss of this particular service at this particular space/time nexus.

All is well. The alignments are exemplary.

I am Ra. I leave you, my friends, in the love and the light of the One Infinite Creator. Go forth, then, rejoicing in the power and in the peace of the One Infinite Creator. Adonai.

SESSION 93

93.0   **RA** I am Ra. I greet you in the love and in the light of the One Infinite Creator. We communicate now.

93.1   **QUESTIONER** Could you first please give me the condition of the instrument?

RA I am Ra. The physical-complex distortions of this instrument far more closely approach what you might call the zero mark; that is, the instrument, while having no native physical energy, is not nearly so far in physical-energy deficit-distortions. The vital-energy distortions are somewhat strengthened since the last asking.

93.2   **QUESTIONER** What is the position and condition of our fifth-density negatively oriented visitor?

RA I am Ra. This entity is with this group but in a quiescent state due to some bafflement as to the appropriate method for enlarging upon its chosen task.

93.3   **QUESTIONER** Thank you. The foundation of our present illusion we have stated previously to be the concept of polarity. I would ask that, since we have defined the two polarities as service to others and service to self, is there a more complete or eloquent or enlightening definition? Or any more information that we don't have at this time on the two ends of the poles that would give us a better insight into the nature of polarity itself?

RA I am Ra. It is unlikely that there is a more pithy or eloquent description of the polarities of third density than "service to others" and "service to self" due to the nature of the mind/body/spirit complex's distortions towards perceiving concepts relating to philosophy in terms of ethics or activity. However, we might consider the polarities using slightly variant terms. In this way a possible enrichment of insight might be achieved for some.

One might consider the polarities with the literal nature enjoyed by the physical polarity of the magnet. The negative and positive, with their electrical characteristics, may be seen to be just as in the physical sense.

It is to be noted in this context that it is quite impossible to judge the polarity of an act or an entity, just as it is impossible to judge the relative goodness of the negative and positive poles of the magnet.

Another method of viewing polarities might involve the concept of radiation/absorption. That which is positive is radiant; that which is negative is absorbent.

93.4   QUESTIONER Now, if I understand correctly, prior to the veiling process the electrical polarities, the polarities of radiation and absorption, all existed in some part of the creation, but the service-to-others/service-to-self polarity that we're familiar with had not evolved and only showed up after the veiling process as an addition to the list of possible polarities, you might say, that could be made in the creation. Is this correct?

RA I am Ra. No.

93.5   QUESTIONER Would you correct me on that?

RA I am Ra. The description of polarity as service to self and service to others, from the beginning of our creation, dwelt within the architecture of the primal Logos. Before the veiling process the impact of actions taken by mind/body/spirits upon their consciousnesses was not palpable to a significant enough degree to allow the expression of this polarity to be significantly useful. Over the period of what you would call time this expression of polarity did, indeed, work to alter the biases of mind/body/spirits so that they might eventually be harvested. The veiling process made the polarity far more effective.

93.6   QUESTIONER I might make the analogy, then, in that when a polarization in the atmosphere occurs to create thunderstorms, lightning, and much activity, this more vivid experience could be likened to the polarization in consciousness which creates the more vivid experience. Would this be appropriate?

RA I am Ra. There is a shallowness to this analogy in that one entity's attention might be focused upon a storm for the duration of the storm. However, the storm-producing conditions are not constant, whereas the polarizing conditions are constant. Given this disclaimer, we may agree with your analogy.

93.7   **QUESTIONER** With the third tarot card we come to the first addition of archetypes after the veiling process, as I understand it. And I am assuming that this third archetype is, shall I say, loaded in a way so as to create, if possible, polarization, since that seems to be one of the primary objectives of this particular Logos in the evolutionary process. Am I in any way correct on this?

RA I am Ra. Before we reply to your query we ask your patience as we must needs examine the mind complex of this instrument in order that we might attempt to move the left manual appendage of the instrument. If we are not able to effect some relief from pain we shall take our leave. Please have patience while we do that which is appropriate.

[*Thirty-second pause.*]

I am Ra. There will continue to be pain flares. However, the critical portion of the intense pain has been alleviated by repositioning.

Your supposition is correct.

93.8   **QUESTIONER** There seems to be no large hint of polarity in this drawing except for the possible coloration of the many cups in the wheel. Part of them are colored black, and part of the cup is white. Would this indicate that each experience has within it a possible negative or positive use of that experience that is randomly generated by this seeming wheel of fortune?

RA I am Ra. Your supposition is thoughtful. However, it is based upon an addition to the concept complex which is astrological in origin. Therefore, we request that you retain the concept of polarity, but release the cups from their strictured form. The element you deal with is not in motion in its original form, but is, indeed, the abiding sun which, from the spirit, shines in protection over all catalyst available from the beginning of complexity to the discerning mind/body/spirit complex.

Indeed you may, rather, find polarity expressed, firstly, by the many opportunities offered in the material illusion which is imaged by the not-white and not-dark square upon which the entity of the image is seated; secondly, upon the position of that seated entity. It does not meet opportunity straight on but glances off to one side or another.

In the image you will note a suggestion that the offering of the illusion will often seem to suggest the opportunities lying upon the left-hand path or, as you might refer to it more simply, the service-to-self path. This is a portion of the nature of the Catalyst of the Mind.

93.9 **QUESTIONER** The feet of the entity seem to be on an unstable platform that is dark to the rear and light to the front. I am guessing that possibly this indicates that the entity standing on this could sway in either direction, toward the left or the right-hand path. Is this in any way correct?

RA I am Ra. This is most perceptive.

93.10 **QUESTIONER** The bird, I am guessing, might be a messenger, the two paths depicted by the position of the wings, bringing catalyst which could be used to polarize on either path. Is this in any way correct?

RA I am Ra. It is a correct perception that the position of the wingèd creature is significant. The more correct perception of this entity and its significance is the realization that the mind/body/spirit complex is, having made contact with its potentiated self, now beginning its flight towards that great Logos which is that which is sought by the adept.

Further, the nature of the wingèd creature is echoed both by the female holding it and the symbol of the female upon which the figure's feet rest; that is, the nature of catalyst is overwhelmingly of an unconsciousness, coming from that which is not of the mind and which has no connection with the intellect, as you call it, which precedes or is concomitant with catalytic action.

All uses of catalyst by the mind are those consciously applied to catalyst. Without conscious intent the use of catalyst is never processed through mentation, ideation, and imagination.

93.11 **QUESTIONER** I would like, if possible, an example of the activity we call Catalyst of the Mind in a particular individual undergoing this process. Could Ra give an example of that?

RA I am Ra. All that assaults your senses is catalyst. We, in speaking to this support group through this instrument, offer catalyst. The configurations of each in the group of body offer catalyst through comfort/discomfort. In fact all that is unprocessed that has come before the notice of a mind/body/spirit complex is catalyst.

93.12 **QUESTIONER** Then presently we receive catalyst of the mind as we are aware of Ra's communication, and we receive catalyst of the body as our body senses all of the inputs to the body, as I understand it. But could Ra then describe catalyst of the spirit, and are we at this time receiving that catalyst also? And if not, could Ra give an example of that?

RA I am Ra. Catalyst being processed by the body is catalyst for the body. Catalyst being processed by the mind is catalyst for the mind. Catalyst being processed by the spirit is catalyst for the spirit. An individual mind/body/spirit complex may use any catalyst which comes before its notice—be it through the body and its senses, or through mentation, or through any other more highly developed source—and use this catalyst in its unique way to form an experience unique to it, with its biases.

93.13 **QUESTIONER** Would I be correct in saying that the archetype for the Catalyst of the Mind is the Logos's model for its most efficient plan for the activity or use or action of the catalyst of the mind?

RA I am Ra. Yes.

93.14 **QUESTIONER** Then the adept, in becoming familiar with the Logos's archetype in each case, would then be able to most efficiently use the Logos's plan for evolution. Is this correct?

RA I am Ra. In the archetypical mind one has the resource of not specifically a plan for evolution, but rather a blueprint or architecture of the nature of evolution. This may seem to be a small distinction, but it has significance in perceiving more clearly the use of this resource of the deep mind.

93.15 **QUESTIONER** Then Ra presented the images which we know now as the tarot so that the Egyptian adepts of the time could accelerate their personal evolution. Is this correct, and was there any other reason for the presentation of these images by Ra?

RA I am Ra. You are correct.

93.16 **QUESTIONER** Are there any other uses at all of value of these images or tarot cards than the one I just stated?

RA I am Ra. To the student, the tarot images offer a resource for learn/teaching the processes of evolution. To any other entity these images are pictures and no more.

93.17 **QUESTIONER** I was specifically thinking of the fact that Ra, in an earlier session, spoke of the tarot as a system of divination. Could you tell me what you meant by that?

RA I am Ra. Due to the influence of the Chaldees, the system of archetypical images was incorporated by the priests of that period into a system of astrologically based study, learning, and divination. This was not a purpose for which Ra developed the tarot.

93.18 **QUESTIONER** The third card also shows the wand (I am assuming it is) in the right hand; the ball at the top being the round magical shape. Am I in any way correct in guessing that Catalyst of the Mind suggests possible eventual use of the magic depicted by this wand?

RA I am Ra. The wand is astrological in its origin and as an image may be released from its stricture. The sphere of spiritual power is an indication, indeed, that each opportunity is pregnant with the most extravagant magical possibilities for the far-seeing adept.

93.19 **QUESTIONER** Would the fact that the clothing of the entity is transparent indicate the semi-permeability of the veil for the mental catalytic process?

RA I am Ra. We again must pause.

[*Fifteen-second pause.*]

I am Ra. We continue under somewhat less-than-optimal conditions. However, due to the nature of this instrument's opening to us, our pathway is quite clear, and we shall continue. Due to pain flares we must ask that you repeat your last query.

93.20 **QUESTIONER** I was just wondering if the transparency of the garment on the third card indicates the semi-permeable nature of the veil between conscious and subconscious?

RA I am Ra. This is a thoughtful perception and cannot be said to be incorrect. However, the intended suggestion, in general, is an echo of our earlier suggestion that the nature of catalyst is that of the unconscious; that is, outward catalyst comes through the veil.

All that you perceive seems to be consciously perceived. This is not the correct supposition. All that you perceive is perceived as catalyst unconsciously. By the, shall we say, time that the mind begins its appreciation of catalyst, that catalyst has been filtered through the veil, and in some cases much is veiled in the most apparently clear perception.

93.21 QUESTIONER I'm at a loss to know the significance of the serpents that adorn the head of the entity on this drawing. Are they of Ra, and, if so, what do they signify?

RA I am Ra. They are cultural in nature. In the culture to which these images were given the serpent was the symbol of wisdom. Indeed, to the general user of these images perhaps the most accurate connotation of this portion of the concept complexes might be the realization that the serpent is that which is powerful magically.

In the positive sense this means that the serpent will appear at the indigo-ray site upon the body of the image figures. When a negative connotation is intended one may find the serpent at the solar plexus center.

93.22 QUESTIONER Is there any significance to the serpent? Is there any polarity to the serpent as we experience it in this illusion?

RA I am Ra. We assume that you question the serpent as used in these images rather than the second-density life form which is a portion of your experience. There is a significance to the serpent form in a culture which coexists with your own but which is not your own; that is, the serpent as symbol of that which some call the kundalini, and which we have discussed in previous material.[1]

93.23 QUESTIONER Is there any other aspect of this third card that Ra could comment on at this time?

RA I am Ra. There may be said to be many aspects which another student might note and ponder in this image. However, it is the nature of teach/learning to avoid trespass into the realms of learn/teaching for the student. We are quite agreed to comment upon all observations that the student may make. We cannot speak further than this for any student.

We would add that it is expected that each student shall naturally have an unique experience of perception dealing with each image. Therefore, it is not expected that the questioner ask comprehensively for all students. It is, rather, expected and accepted that the questioner will ask a moiety of

---

[1] Previously covered in 49.5–6.

questions which build up a series of concepts concerning each archetype which then offer to each succeeding student the opportunity for more informed study of the archetypical mind.[2]

May we ask for one more query at this time. We are pleased to report that this instrument has remembered to request the reserving of some transferred energy to make more comfortable the transition back to the waking state. Therefore, we find that there is sufficient energy for one more query.

93.24 **QUESTIONER** I am assuming that you mean one full question, and I'll make that question: I'd like to know the significance of the shape of the crux ansata, and if that's too much of an answer I will just ask if there is anything we can do to make the instrument more comfortable or improve the contact?

RA I am Ra. There are mathematical ratios within this image which may yield informative insights to one fond of riddles. We shall not untangle the riddle.

We may indicate that the crux ansata is a part of the concept complexes of the archetypical mind: the circle indicating the magic of the spirit; the cross indicating that nature of manifestation which may only be valued by the losing. Thus the crux ansata is intended to be seen as an image of the eternal in and through manifestation, and beyond manifestation, through the sacrifice and transformation of that which is manifest.

The support group functions well. The swirling waters experienced by the instrument since our previous working have substantially aided the instrument in its lessening of the distortion of pain.

All is well. The alignments are well guarded.

We leave you, my friends, in the love and the light of the Infinite One. Go forth, therefore, rejoicing in the power and in the peace of the One Infinite and Glorious Creator. Adonai.

---

[2] In this context, *moiety* can be defined as "part or portion, especially a lesser share."

SESSION 94

AUGUST 26, 1982

94.0 **RA** I am Ra. I greet you in the love and in the light of the One Infinite Creator. I communicate now.

94.1 **QUESTIONER** Could you first please give me the condition of the instrument?

RA I am Ra. There is some small increase in physical energy deficit. It is not substantial. All else is as at the previous asking.

94.2 **QUESTIONER** I have questions here from the instrument. One: "Is our fifth-density friend responsible for the instrument's extreme distortion towards pain during and just after sessions?"

RA I am Ra. Yes.

94.3 **QUESTIONER** Is there anything that we can do that we are not doing to remedy this situation so that the instrument does not experience this pain or as much of it?

RA I am Ra. There is little that can be done due to a complex of pre-existing distortions. The distortions are triple in the source:

There is the, shall we say, less-than-adequate work of your chirurgeons which allows for various distortions in the left wrist area.[1]

There is the distortion called systemic lupus erythematosus which causes the musculature of the lower left and right arms to allow for distortions in the normal, shall we say, configuration of both.

Lastly, there is the nerve damage, more especially to the left, but in both appendages from the thoracic outlet.

In the course of the waking behavior the instrument can respond to the various signals which ring the tocsin of pain, thus alerting the mind complex, which in turn moves the physical complex in many and subtle configurations which relieve the various distortions. Your friend greets

---

[1] In this context, *chirurgeon* is simply an archaic alternative for the word "surgeon."

these distortions, as has been stated before, immediately prior to the beginning of the working.[2]

However, during the working the instrument is not with its yellow-ray chemical vehicle, and thusly the many small movements which could most effectively aid in the decrease of these distortions is not possible. Ra must carefully examine the mental configurations of the mind complex in order to make even the grossest manipulation. It is not our skill to use a yellow-ray vehicle.

The weight of the cover has some deleterious effect upon these distortions in some cases, and thus we mentioned that there was a small thing which could be done; that is, the framing of that which lifted the coverlet from the body slightly. In order to compensate for loss of warmth the wearing of material warming the manual appendages would then be indicated.

94.4　QUESTIONER I immediately think of the instrument wearing long underwear under the robe that it now wears and an extremely light, white cover. Would this be satisfactory?

RA I am Ra. Due to this instrument's lack of radiant physical energy the heavier cover is suggested.

94.5　QUESTIONER In your statement, near the beginning of it, you said "less-than-adequate work of your," and there was a word that I didn't understand at all. Are you familiar with the word that I am trying to understand?

RA I am Ra. No.

94.6　QUESTIONER We'll have to wait until we transcribe the material then. I assume that our fifth-density negative friend doesn't cause the distortion all the time simply because he wishes to emphasize the fact that the instrument is going to be distorted only if she attempts one of these service-to-others workings, therefore attempting to stifle the working. Is this correct?

RA I am Ra. This is partially correct. The incorrect portion is this: The entity of which you speak has found its puissance less than adequate to

---

[2] In this context, *tocsin* can be defined as meaning "alarm or warning signal."

mount a continuous assault upon this instrument's physical vehicle and has, shall we say, chosen the more effective of the space/time nexi of this instrument's experience for its service. [3]

94.7   **QUESTIONER** Could you tell me why I have felt so extremely tired on several recent occasions?

RA I am Ra. This has been covered in previous material. [4]

The contact which you now experience costs a certain amount of the energy which each of the group brought into manifestation in the present incarnation. Although the brunt of this cost falls upon the instrument, it is caparisoned by pre-incarnative design with the light and gladsome armor of faith and will to a far more conscious extent than most mind/body/spirit complexes are able to enjoy without much training and initiation. [5]

Those of the support group also offer the essence of will and faith in service to others, supporting the instrument as it releases itself completely in the service of the One Creator. Therefore, each of the support group also experiences a weariness of the spirit which is indistinguishable from physical energy deficit, except that if each experiments with this weariness, each shall discover the physical energy in its usual distortion.

94.8   **QUESTIONER** Thank you. I really didn't mean to go over previous material. I should have phrased my question more carefully so that . . . that is what I expected. I was trying to get confirmation of the fact that I suspected that. I will be more careful in questioning from now on.

From the instrument we have the question: "While vacationing I uncovered a lot about myself not consciously known before. It seems to me that I coast on the spiritual gifts given at birth and never have spent any time getting to know my human self which seems to be a child, immature and irrational. Is this so?"

---

3   In this context, *puissance* can be defined as "the power to accomplish or achieve; potency."

4   Previously covered in 81.2–8.

5   In this context, *caparisoned* can be defined as "outfitted with an ornamental covering or clothing."

RA I am Ra. This is partially correct.

94.9 **QUESTIONER** Then she says: "If this is so, this seems to be part of the riddle about the manner of beingness that Ra spoke of. I fear if I do not work successfully on my human distortions I shall be responsible for losing the contact. Yet also Ra suggests the over-dedication to any outcome is unwise. Could Ra comment on these thoughts?"

RA I am Ra. We comment in general, first upon the query about the contact which indicates, once again, that the instrument views the mind/body/spirit complex with jaundiced eye.

Each mind/body/spirit complex that is seeking shall almost certainly have the immature and irrational behaviors. It is also the case that this entity—as well as almost all seekers—has done substantial work within the framework of the incarnative experience and has, indeed, developed maturity and rationality. That this instrument should fail to see that which has been accomplished and see only that which remains to be accomplished may well be noted. Indeed, any seeker discovering in itself this complex of mental and mental/emotional distortions shall ponder the possible non-efficacy of judgment.

As we approach the second portion of the query we view the possibility of infringement upon free will. However, we believe we may make reply within the boundaries of the Law of Confusion.

This particular instrument was not trained, nor did it study, nor worked it at any discipline in order to contact Ra. We were able, as we have said many times, to contact this group using this instrument because of the purity of this instrument's dedication to the service of the One Infinite Creator, and also because of the great amount of harmony and acceptance enjoyed each by each within the group; this situation making it possible for the support group to function without significant distortion.

We are humble messengers. How can any thought be taken by an instrument as to the will of the Creator?

We thank this group that we may speak through it, but the future is mazed. We cannot know whether our geste may, after one final working, be complete.[6]

---

[6] In this context, *geste* may be defined as "a tale of adventure" or "a deed or exploit."

Can the instrument, then, think for a moment that it shall cease in the service of the One Infinite Creator? We ask the instrument to ponder these queries and observations.

94.10 **QUESTIONER** From the previous session the statement was made that much is veiled to the most apparently clear observation. Would Ra expand on what was meant by that statement? I assume that this means the veiling of all of that that is outside the limits of what we call our physical perception having to do with the spectrum of light, etc., but I also intuit there is more than that veiled. Would Ra expand on that concept?

RA I am Ra. You are perceptive in your supposition. Indeed, we meant not any suggestions that the physical apparatus of your current illusion were limited as part of the veiling process. Your physical limits are as they are.

However, because of the unique biases of each mind/body/spirit complex, there are sometimes quite simple instances of distortion when there is no apparent cause for such distortion. Let us use the example of the virile and immature male who meets and speaks clearly with a young female whose physical form has the appropriate configuration to cause, for this male entity, the activation of the red-ray sexual arousal.

The words spoken may be upon a simple subject such as naming, information as to the occupation, and various other common interchanges of sound vibratory complex. The male entity, however, is using almost all the available consciousness it possesses in registering the desirability of the female. Such may also be true of the female.

Thusly an entire exchange of information may be meaningless because the actual catalyst is of the body. This is unconsciously controlled and is not a conscious decision. This example is simplistic.

94.11 **QUESTIONER** I have drawn a small diagram in which I simply show an arrow which represents catalyst penetrating a line at right angles to the arrow, which is the veil, and then depositing in one of two repositories: one which I would call on the right-hand path, one on the left-hand path. And I have labeled these two repositories for the catalytic action as it's filtered through the veil "the Experience." Would this be a very rough analogy of the way the catalyst is filtered through the veil to become experience?

RA I am Ra. Again, you are partially correct. The deeper biases of a mind/body/spirit complex pilot the catalyst around the many isles of positivity and negativity as expressed in the archipelago of the deeper mind. However, the analogy is incorrect in that it does not take into account the further polarization which most certainly is available to the conscious mind after it has perceived the partially polarized catalyst from the deeper mind.

94.12   QUESTIONER It seems to me that the Experience of the Mind would act in such a way as to change the nature of the veil so that catalyst would be filtered so as to be more acceptable in the bias that is increasingly chosen by the entity. For instance, if the entity had chosen the right-hand path, the Experience of the Mind would change the permeability of the veil to accept more and more positive catalyst, and also the other would be true for accepting more negative if the left-hand path were the one that was repeatedly chosen. Is this correct?

RA I am Ra. This is not only correct but there is a further ramification. As the entity increases in experience it shall, more and more, choose positive interpretations of catalyst if it is upon the service-to-others path, and negative interpretations of catalyst if its experience has been along the service-to-self path.

94.13   QUESTIONER Then the mechanism designed by the Logos, of the action of catalyst resulting in experience, was planned to be self-accelerating in that it would create this process of, shall I say, variable permeability that was of the function of the chosen path. Is this an adequate statement?

RA I am Ra. There is no variable permeability involved in the concepts we have just discussed. Except for this, you are quite correct.

94.14   QUESTIONER I can understand, to use a poor term again, the necessity for an archetype for Catalyst, or a model for Catalyst of the Mind, but what is the reason for having a blueprint or model for Experience of the Mind other than this simple model of the dual repository for the negative and positive catalyst? It would seem to me that the First Distortion of Free Will would be better served if no model for experience were made. I'm somewhat confused on this. Could you clear it up?

RA I am Ra. Your question is certainly interesting and your confusion hopefully productive. We cannot learn/teach for the student. We shall simply note, as we have previously,[7] the attraction of various archetypes to male and to female. We suggest that this line of consideration may prove productive.

94.15 QUESTIONER In the fourth archetype the card shows a male whose body faces forward. I assume this indicates that the Experience of the Mind will reach for catalyst. However, the face is to the left, indicating to me that, in reaching for catalyst, negative catalyst will be more apparent in its power and effect than the positive. Would Ra comment on this?

RA I am Ra. The archetype of Experience of the Mind reaches not, O student, but with firm authority grasps what it is given. The remainder of your remarks are perceptive.

94.16 QUESTIONER Experience is seated on the square of the material illusion which is colored much darker than in Card Number Three. However, there is a cat inside this. I am guessing that as experience is gained the second-density nature of the illusion is understood, and the negative and positive aspects are separated. Would Ra comment on this?

RA I am Ra. This interpretation varies markedly from Ra's intention. We direct the attention to the cultural meaning of the great cat which guards. What, O student, does it guard? And with what oriflamme does it lighten that darkness of manifestation?[8]

The polarities are, indeed, present; the separation nonexistent except through the sifting which is the result of cumulative experience. Other impressions were intended by this configuration of the seated image with its milk-white leg and its pointed foot.

94.17 QUESTIONER What was the last word that Ra communicated? I didn't quite hear it.

RA I am Ra. We spoke the sound vibration complex, foot. Due to some pain flares we are at times less than secure in the speaking. However, the way is open, and conditions remain good for this working. Please continue to query if there is any difficulty in transmission.

---

7   Noted previously in 87.28, 91.18, and 92.20.

8   In this context, *oriflamme* can be defined as "inspiring principle, ideal, or symbol."

94.18 **QUESTIONER** In Card Three the feet of the female entity are upon the unstable platform, signifying dual polarity by its color. In Card Four, one foot pointed indicates that if the male entity stands on the toe it would be carefully balanced. The other foot is pointed to the left. Would Ra comment on my observation that if the entity stands on this foot it will be very, very carefully balanced?

RA I am Ra. This is an important perception, for it is a key to not only this concept complex but to others as well.

You may see the T-square which at times riven as is one foot from secure fundament by the nature of experience, yet still—by this same nature of experience—is carefully, precisely, and architecturally placed in the foundation of this concept complex, and, indeed, in the archetypical mind complex.[9]

Experience[10] has the nature of more effectively and poignantly expressing the architecture of experience, both the fragility of structure and the surety of structure.

94.19 **QUESTIONER** It would seem to me that from the configuration of this male entity in Card Four—who looks to the left, and the right foot is pointed to the left—that this card would indicate that you must be in a defensive position with respect to the left-hand path, with no need to concern yourself about protection with respect to the right-hand path. Would Ra comment on that?

RA I am Ra. Again, this is not the suggestion we wished to offer by constructing this image. However, the perception cannot be said to be incorrect.

94.20 **QUESTIONER** The magical shape is on the right edge of the card indicating to me that the spiritual significance is on the right edge of the card, indicating to me that the spiritual experience would be the right-hand path. Could Ra comment on that?

RA I am Ra. Yes. The figure is expressing the nature of experience by having its attention caught by what may be termed the left-hand catalyst.

---

9 In this context, *riven* can be defined as "to tear apart; to rend".

10 Card Number Four, Experience of the Mind.

Meanwhile, the power, the magic, is available upon the right-hand path.

The nature of experience is such that the attention shall be constantly given varieties of experience. Those that are presumed to be negative, or interpreted as negative, may seem in abundance. It is a great challenge to take catalyst and devise the magical, positive experience. That which is magical in the negative experience is much longer coming, shall we say, in the third density.

94.21 **QUESTIONER** Now, both the third and fourth archetypes, as I see it, work together for the sole purpose of creating the polarity in the most efficient manner possible. Is this correct?

RA I am Ra. This cannot be said to be incorrect. We suggest contemplation of this thought complex.

94.22 **QUESTIONER** Then prior to the veiling process, that which we call catalyst after the veiling was not catalyst simply because it was not efficiently creating polarity; because this loading process, you might say, that I have diagrammed of catalyst passing through the veil and becoming polarized experience was not in effect; because the viewing of what we call catalyst by the entity was seen much more clearly as simply an experience of the One Creator and not something that was a function of other mind/body/spirit complexes. Would Ra comment on that statement?

RA I am Ra. The concepts discussed seem without significant distortion.

94.23 **QUESTIONER** Thank you. Then we're expecting, in Card Number Four, to see the result of catalytic action and, therefore, a greater definition between the dark and the light areas. In this card we notice that it is more definitely darkly colored in some areas and more white in others, in a general sense, than Card Number Three, indicating to me that the separation along the two biases has occurred, and should occur, to follow the blueprint for experience. Could Ra comment on that?

RA I am Ra. You are perceptive, O student.

94.24 **QUESTIONER** The bird in Card Three seems to be now internalized in the center of the entity in Card Four in that it has changed from the— The flight then has achieved its objective and become a part of, a central part of, the experience. Could Ra comment on that?

RA I am Ra. This perception is correct, O student, but what shall the student find the bird to signify?

94.25 **QUESTIONER** I would guess that the bird signifies that a communication that comes as catalyst signified in Card Three is accepted by the female and used becomes a portion of the experience. I'm not sure of that at all. Am I in any way correct?

RA I am Ra. That bears little of sense.

94.26 **QUESTIONER** I'll have to work on that.

Then I am guessing that the crossed legs of the entity in Card Four have a meaning similar to the cross of the crux ansata. Is this correct?

RA I am Ra. This is correct. The cross formed by the living limbs of the image signifies that which is the nature of mind/body/spirit complexes in manifestation within your illusion. There is no experience which is not purchased by effort of some kind—no act of service to self or others which does not bear a price to the entity manifesting, commensurate with its purity.

All things in manifestation may be seen in one way or another to be offering themselves in order that transformations may take place upon the level appropriate to the action.

94.27 **QUESTIONER** The bird is within a circle on the front of the entity in Card Four. Would that have the same significance as the circular part of the crux ansata?

RA I am Ra. It is a specialized form of this meaningful shape. It is specialized in great part due to the nature of the crossed legs of manifestation which we have previously discussed.[11]

94.28 **QUESTIONER** The entity of Card Four wears a strangely shaped skirt. Is there a significance to the shape of this skirt?

RA I am Ra. Yes.

94.29 **QUESTIONER** The skirt is extended toward the left hand but is somewhat

---

[11] Previously discussed in the preceding answer as well as 94.18.

shorter toward the right. There is a black bag hanging from the belt of the entity on the left side. It seems to me that this black bag has a meaning of the acquiring of material possessions of wealth as a part of the left-hand path. Would Ra comment on that?

RA I am Ra. Although this meaning was not intended by Ra as part of this complex of concepts, we find the interpretation quite acceptable.

[*Thirty-second pause.*]

I am Ra. As we observe a lull in the questioning we shall take this opportunity to say that the level of transferred energy dwindles rapidly, and we would offer the opportunity for one more full question at this working if it is desired.

94.30 **QUESTIONER** I would just state that this card, being male, would indicate that as experience is gained the mind becomes the motivator or that which reaches or "does" more than the simple experiencer prior to the catalytic action. That is, there is a greater tendency for the mind to direct the mind/body/spirit complex.

And other than that I would just ask if there is anything that we can do to make the instrument more comfortable or improve the contact?

RA I am Ra. In the context of your penultimate query we would suggest that you ponder again the shape of the garment which the image wears. Such habiliment is not natural.[12] The shape is significant and is so along the lines of your query.

The support group cares well for the instrument. We would ask that care be taken as the instrument has been offered the gift of a distortion towards extreme cold by the fifth-density friend which greets you.

Although you may be less than pleased with the accoutrements, may we say that all was as carefully prepared as each was able. More than that none can do. Therefore, we thank each for the careful alignments. All is well.

---

12 In this context, *habiliment* can be defined as "clothing, especially clothing suited for one's status or occupation."

We leave you, my friends, in the love and in the light of the One Glorious Infinite Creator. Go forth, then, rejoicing in the power and in the peace of the One. Adonai.

Session 95

SEPTEMBER 2, 1982

95.0 **RA** I am Ra. I greet you, my friends, in the love and in the light of the One Infinite Creator. We communicate now.

95.1 **QUESTIONER** Could you first please give me the condition of the instrument?

RA I am Ra. It is as previously stated.

95.2 **QUESTIONER** Thank you. What is the situation with respect to our fifth-density negative associate?

RA I am Ra. The aforenamed entity has chosen various means to further its service, and though each is effective in itself, does not lead to the lessening of the dedication to service for others or the valuing of harmonious interaction. Therefore, the entity, though not as quiet as it has been, is somewhat depolarized on balance.

95.3 **QUESTIONER** There seems to be an extremely high probability that we will move from this position to another residence. If we should move from this residence and cease using this room for workings with Ra, is there a magically appropriate ritual for closing the use of this place of working? Or is there anything that we should do with respect to leaving this particular place?

RA I am Ra. It would be appropriate to remove from this room and, to a lesser extent, from the dwelling, the charging of what you might call the distortion towards sanctity. To remove this charge it is valuable either to write upon your paper your own working, or to use existing rituals, for the deconsecration of a sacred place such as one of your churches.

95.4 **QUESTIONER** Thank you. The new room that we choose will of course be carefully cleaned and marred surfaces made well. We shall also use the Banishing Ritual of the Lesser Pentagram prior to a working. Is there anything else that Ra could suggest? And I would also know if there is anything in particular that Ra might suggest with respect to the particular place that has been chosen for the new location.

RA I am Ra. We scan the recent memory configurations of the questioner.

Firstly, there has been some less-than-harmonious interaction within this dwelling. The dynamics of this interaction were potent enough to attract a lesser thought-form. Therefore, we suggest the salting and ritual cleansing by blessed water of all windows and doorways which offer adit into the domicile or any out-buildings thereof.[1]

Further, we suggest the hanging of the cut garlic clove in the portion of the room which has accommodated those whose enjoyment has turned into a darker emotion centering upon the area we find you call the wet bar, also the room intended for the sleeping which is found near the kitchen area.

The appropriate words used to bid farewell to those of the lower astral shall be used in connection with the hanging of the garlic cloves for the period of approximately 36 of your hours. We believe that this is equivalent to two of your night periods and one of your lit periods. This should cleanse the house as you find it to the extent that it is neutral in its vibrations.

We suggest that you then request of this living entity that it now be welcoming and absorbent for the vibrations of harmony, love, and thanksgiving which this group shall then, as the incarnational experience proceeds, offer to the domicile.[2]

95.5 **QUESTIONER** I am assuming that we would prepare the blessed water the same as we prepare the water for the instrument to drink after a session, and then would wipe the windows and doors with this water . . . probably have to be done in a bucket. And I would like to know if this is correct, and what was meant by salting of the windows and doors?

RA I am Ra. Firstly, you may bless the water yourselves or may request so-called holy water from any blessed place; that is, blessed by intention.

---

[1] In this context, *adit* can be defined as "entrance."

[2] To read a consolidated set of instructions for using salt or garlic to cleanse the metaphysical environment, see the Resource Series.

Secondly, the water shall be carefully shaken from the fingers along the sills of all windows and doors as they have been opened.

Thirdly, prior to the sprinkling of this cleansing, blessing sacrament of water, the salt shall be trailed along these sills in a line and, again, allowed to exist in this configuration for 36 to 48 hours.

Then the virgin broom may ritually sweep the salt out of each window and doorway, sweeping with each stroke the less fortunate of the vibrations within the dwelling which might find coexistence with your group difficult.

95.6   **QUESTIONER** I assume you mean that we should put the salt on the outer doors only and not the inner doors of the house. Is that correct?

RA I am Ra. This is correct.

We cannot express the nature of salt and water and garlic with clarity enough to inform you as to the efficacy with which salt absorbs vibrations which have been requested to move into salt when salt has been given water. We cannot express the full magical nature of your water, nor can we express the likeness and attractiveness of the garlic cut to lower astral forms. The attractiveness is negative, and no service-to-self astral form will accept coexistence with the cut garlic.

Therefore, we offer these suggestions. We also request, carefully, that the broom be clean and that the garlic be burned. The virginity of the broom is most efficacious.

95.7   **QUESTIONER** Let me see if I have the scenario correctly. I'll repeat my version of it. We would hang garlic, fresh-cut garlic, in the area of the wet bar and the area of the bedroom that is adjacent to the kitchen area. We would salt all window sills, and all outer wall door sills, and then sprinkle blessed water from our fingers on all of the salted areas. We would then say appropriate words to bid farewell to lower astrals. Those words I am not sure of. Would Ra comment on the scenario that I've just stated?

RA I am Ra. Your grasp of our suggestions is good. We note that the salt be poured in the straight line with no gaps. There are various ritual words of blessing and farewell to entities such as you are removing. We might suggest the following:

When the salt is laid you may repeat: "We praise the One Creator which gave to salt the ability to enable those friends, to which we wish to bid farewell, to find a new home."

As the water is sprinkled you may say: "We give thanks to the One Creator for the gift of water. Over it the Creator moves Its hand and stirs Its will to be done."

The hanging of the cut garlic may be accompanied by the words: "We praise the One Creator for the gift of garlic, and bless its ability to offer to those friends to whom we wish to bid farewell the arrow which points their way of egress."

When the sweeping is done you may say: "We praise the One Creator and give thanksgiving for the spiritual cleanliness of this dwelling place."

As the garlic is burned you may say: "We give thanks to the One Creator for the gift of spiritual cleanliness in our dwelling place, and seal the departure of all those who have left by this exit, by the consuming of this substance."

95.8   **QUESTIONER** Is any place more appropriate than another to hang the garlic in the rooms; for instance, over the windows or anything like that? I know it is supposed to be hung in the area of the bar, but I meant in the bedroom. Is there any more appropriate place than another?

RA I am Ra. The windows and the doorways are most appropriate and, in addition, we suggest the salting and sprinkling of any door which may lead elsewhere than out of the dwelling in order to afford to the entities the understanding that they are not desired elsewhere within the dwelling.

95.9   **QUESTIONER** Okay, I understand that the garlic is to be used at the bar area and in the bedroom that is close to the kitchen and has an exit onto the carport. If I am correct, then, those are the only two places to use the garlic: the bar and that room with the exit to the carport. That's correct, isn't it?

RA I am Ra. This is correct.

95.10   **QUESTIONER** We would like to pick the most appropriate room for sanctifying for the Ra contact. And we will not use that bedroom even though we've cleansed it. I would imagine it would be better not to use it.

I'm not sure. But is there any room that would be most appropriate that Ra could name?

RA I am Ra. When you have finished with your work the dwelling shall be as a virgin dwelling in the magical sense. You may choose that portion of the dwelling that seems appropriate, and once having chosen it, you may then commence with the same sort of preparation of the place with which you have been familiar here in this dwelling place.

95.11 **QUESTIONER** I am assuming that the newly chosen place meets parameters for best contact on the exterior of the house, and would ask Ra at this time if there is any suggestions with respect to the exterior of the house?

RA I am Ra. The dwelling seems surrounded with the trees and fields of your countryside. This is acceptable.

We suggest the general principle of preparing each part of your environment, as it best suits each in the group, with the beauty which each may feel to be appropriate. There is much of blessing in the gardening and the care of surroundings, for when this is accomplished in love of the creation the second-density flowers, plants, and small animals are aware of this service and return it.

95.12 **QUESTIONER** On one end of the house there are four stalls that have been occupied by horses. Would it be appropriate or necessary to modify in any way the condition of that area even though it is outside the living area of the house?

RA I am Ra. There has been no undesirable negative energy stored in this area. Therefore, it is acceptable if physically cleaned.

95.13 **QUESTIONER** Is there any other comment in closing this questioning area upon the new location that Ra could make other than the comments already made on the new location or any part of it?

RA I am Ra. We are gratified that this query was offered to us, for there has been a concentration of negative thought patterns at a distance north to 10° of north, approximately 45 of what you call yards, extending therefrom to all four directions in a rectangular but irregular shape.

We ask that the garlic be strung approximately 60-70 feet beyond the far verge of this area which is approximately 57 yards from the dwelling on a bearing north to 10° off north. We suggest that the garlic be hung in the funnel so that the energies are drawn into the south, small end of the funnel, and traduced northward and away from the dwelling. The procedure of the hanging will be one for testing your ingenuity, but there are several ways to suspend the substance, and it is well to do so.

95.14 **QUESTIONER** I envision a cardboard funnel approximately three feet in length, and then a smaller cardboard funnel of the same configuration inside that funnel; garlic placed between the two cardboard surfaces so the garlic is actually a funnel of garlic itself, and then held in place by the two cardboard cones: the smaller end of the cone being toward the house, the open or larger end being away from the house.

I also would like to be sure that I accurately know the position that we're talking about by taking a specific point on the house, such as the front door (the door with the little roof extending over it at the front of the house), and taking a direction from that. I suspect the direction is up toward the road that leads out of the property, and an exact measurement from the front doorknob to the center of the area of negativity of which we speak would be helpful. Would Ra comment on what I have just said?

RA I am Ra. We were working from the other side of the dwelling. However, the exact distance is not important due to the generalized nature of the astral leavings. The heading would be approximately 10° east of north to 5° east of north. This is not a heading in which absolute fastidiousness needs be paramount. The yardage is approximately as given.

As to the hanging of the garlic, it must be able to be blown by the wind. Therefore, the structure which was envisioned is less than optimal. We might suggest the stringing between two placed posts on either side of the funnel of the strung cloves.

95.15 **QUESTIONER** In order to make this funnel of garlic cloves, would a wire framework such as chicken wire which has a small inch-square mesh, or something like that shaped into a cone, with the garlic attached to it all around it, and with the small end toward the house, and the open end away from it, strung between two poles. Would that be appropriate, or must the wind blow it more than that?

RA I am Ra. That is appropriate. You see in this case the center of the negativity is as described, but there will be a general cleansing of the dwelling and its acreage by this means.

One action you might take in order to improve the efficacy of the cleansing of the environment is the walking of the perimeter with the opened clove in hand, swinging the clove. No words need be said unless each wishes to silently or verbally speak those words given for garlic previously.

95.16 **QUESTIONER** Is there any other thing that we can do to prepare this new place for the parameters of beingness and communication with Ra in our own living or dwelling conditions that would be appropriate that Ra could mention at this time?

RA I am Ra. There are no more specific suggestions for the specific location you contemplate.

In general, the cleanliness is most helpful. The removal from the mind complex of those thoughts not of harmony is most helpful. And those practices which increase faith and will that the Spirit may do Its work are most helpful.[3]

95.17 **QUESTIONER** After the suggestions are accomplished with respect to cleansing of the property, does Ra anticipate that our contact with Ra will be as efficient with respect to the location parameters in that particular place as they are in this particular place?

RA I am Ra. All places in which this group dwells in love and thanksgiving are acceptable to us.

95.18 **QUESTIONER** Thank you. A question has been asked which I'll ask at this time. In processing the catalyst of dreams is there a universal language of

---

3   Jim writes: "It is my personal supposition that Ra anomalously departs here from their consistent use of the term spirit as the 'spirit complex' and instead uses the term in the more colloquial sense of the 'Spirit of God,' or the One Creator. In 95.7, Ra provided us words to use in conjunction with salt, water, and garlic to help cleanse our dwelling. In each instance the One Creator is mentioned as being part of this cleansing activity, so it seems quite reasonable to me that Ra is referring to the same Creator in this question. We had done our part as mind/body/spirit complexes, and now the Spirit/Creator would do Its part. Thus I feel that 'Spirit' and 'Its' ought to be capitalized."

the unconscious mind which may be used to interpret the meaning of dreams? Or does each entity have a unique language of its unconscious mind which it may use to interpret the meaning of dreams?

RA I am Ra. There is what might be called a partial vocabulary of the dreams due to the common heritage of all mind/body/spirit complexes. Due to each entity's unique incarnational experiences there is an overlay which grows to be a larger and larger proportion of the dream vocabulary as the entity gains experience.

95.19 QUESTIONER Thank you. In the last session you made a statement about the immature male meeting the female with respect to what occurred because of the veil: that the information exchange was quite different. Would you give an example of the information exchange prior to the veil for this same case, please?

RA I am Ra. Given this same case—that is, the random red-ray sexual arousal being activated in both male and female—the communication would far more likely have been to the subject of the satisfying of that red-ray, sexual impulse. When this had occurred other information such as the naming could be offered with clear perception.

It is to be noted that the catalyst which may be processed by the pre-veil experience is insignificant compared to the catalyst offered to the thoroughly bemused male and female after the veil. The confusion which this situation, simplistic though it is, offers is representative of the efficiency of the enlargement of the catalytic processes occurring after the veiling.

95.20 QUESTIONER For the condition of the meeting after the veiling process, either entity will choose as a function of its previous biases (or, shall I say, will choose as a function of Card Four, the Experience) the way in which it will approach or handle the situation with respect to polarity, therefore producing, most probably, more catalyst for itself along the chosen path of polarization. Would Ra comment on that statement?

RA I am Ra. This statement is correct.

95.21 QUESTIONER In Card Four in the last session we spoke of the shape of the skirt, and it has occurred to us that the skirt of the entity representing the archetype of Experience is extended to the left to indicate that other-selves would not be able to get close to this entity if it had chosen the left-hand path. There would be a greater separation between it and other-selves. Whereas if it had chosen the right-hand path there would be much less of a separation. Would Ra comment on that observation?

RA I am Ra. The student is perceptive.

95.22 **QUESTIONER** And it seems that the square upon which the entity sits, which is almost totally black, is a representation of the material illusion, and the white cat is guarding the right-hand path which is now separated in experience from the left. Would Ra comment on that observation?

RA I am Ra. O student, your sight almost sees that which was intended. However, the polarities need no guardians. What, then, O student, needs the guard?

95.23 **QUESTIONER** What I meant to say was that the entity is guarded along the right-hand path (once it is chosen) from effects of the material illusion that are of a negative polarity. Would Ra comment on that?

RA I am Ra. This is an accurate perception of our intent, O student. We may note that the great cat guards in direct proportion to the purity of the manifestations of intention and the purity of inner work done along this path.

95.24 **QUESTIONER** From that statement I interpret the following meaning: That if the Experience of the Mind has sufficiently chosen the right-hand path—as total purity is approached in choosing of the right-hand path—then total imperviousness from the effect of the left-hand catalyst is also approached. Is this correct?

RA I am Ra. This is exquisitely perceptive. The seeker which has purely chosen the service-to-others path shall certainly not have a variant apparent incarnational experience. There is no outward shelter in your illusion from the gusts, flurries, and blizzards of quick and cruel catalyst.

However, to the pure, all that is encountered speaks of the love and the light of the One Infinite Creator. The cruelest blow is seen with an ambiance of challenges offered and opportunities to come. Thusly, the great pitch of light is held high above such an one so that all interpretation may be seen to be protected by light.

95.25 **QUESTIONER** I have often wondered about the action of random and programmed catalyst with respect to the entity with the very strong positive or negative polarization. Would one or either be free to a great extent from random catalyst occurring such as great natural catastrophes, or warfare, or something like that that generates a lot of random catalyst in the physical vicinity of a highly polarized entity? Does this great cat, then, have effect on such random catalyst upon the right-hand path?

RA I am Ra. In two circumstances this is so:

Firstly, if there has been the pre-incarnative choice that, for instance, one shall not take life in the service of the cultural group, events shall fall in a protective manner.

Secondly, if any entity is able to dwell completely in unity, the only harm that may occur to it is the changing of the outward physical, yellow-ray vehicle into the more light-filled mind/body/spirit complex's vehicle by the process of death. All other suffering and pain is as nothing to one such as this.

We may note that this perfect configuration of the mind, body, and spirit complexes while within the third-density vehicle is extraordinarily rare.

95.26 QUESTIONER Am I to understand, then, that there is no protection at all if the Experience of the Mind has become negative and the negative path is traveled? All random catalyst may affect the negatively polarized individual as a function of the statistical nature of the random catalyst. Is this correct?

RA I am Ra. This is correct. You may note some of those of your peoples which, at this space/time nexus, seek places of survival. This is due to the lack of protection when service to self is invoked.

95.27 QUESTIONER The possibility of the legs of the entity of Card Four being at approximate right angles was linked with the tesseract[4]—mentioned in a much earlier session by Ra[5]—as the direction of transformation from space/time into time/space, and I was thinking that possibly it was also linked with the crux ansata. Am I in any way correct with this observation?

---

[4] In this context, *tesseract* can be defined as "the fourth-dimensional analog to a cube." A tesseract is to a cube as a cube is to a square.

[5] Mentioned in 52.10.

RA I am Ra. This shall be the last query of this working as transferred energy wanes.

The observation of the right angles and their transformational meaning is most perceptive, O student. Each of the images leading to the Transformations of Mind, Body, and Spirit—and ultimately to the great transformative Choice—has the increasing intensity of increasing articulation of concept; that is to say, each image in which you find this angle may increasingly be seen to be a more and more stridently calling voice of opportunity to use each resource—be it Experience as you now observe, or further images—for the grand work of the adept which builds towards transformation using the spirit's bountiful shuttle to intelligent infinity.

Please ask any brief queries at this space/time.

95.28 **QUESTIONER** Is there anything that we can do to make the instrument more comfortable or improve the contact?

RA I am Ra. We observe some small worsening of the distortions of the dorsal side. This is due to the nature of the beginning use of the swirling waters. The difficulties are physically accentuated as the swirling waters begin to aid the musculature surrounding the nexi of distortions. We encourage the swirling waters and note that complete immersion in them is somewhat more efficacious than the technique now used.

We ask that the support group attempt to aid the instrument in remembering to preserve the physical energies and not expend them upon movements associated with the packing, as you call this activity, and the movement between geographical locations upon your sphere.

The alignments are excellent. All is well.

We leave you glorying in the love and in the light of the One Infinite Creator. Go forth, therefore, rejoicing in the mighty peace of the One Infinite Creator. Adonai.

SESSION 96

96.0 RA I am Ra. I greet you in the love and in the light of the One Infinite Creator. We communicate now.

96.1 QUESTIONER Could you first please give me the condition of the instrument?

RA I am Ra. The physical energy deficit is significantly greater than the last asking. There has been substantive lessening also of the vital energies, although the perquisite degree of energy for mental/emotional distortions of normalcy are yet available.

96.2 QUESTIONER Could you tell me the cause of the lessening of the physical and vital energies?

RA I am Ra. We found the need of examining the mental configurations of the instrument before framing an answer due to our reluctance to infringe upon its free will. Those concepts relating to the spiritual contemplation of personal catalyst have been appreciated by the entity, so we may proceed.

This entity has an habitual attitude which is singular; that is, when there is some necessity for action the entity is accustomed to analyzing the catalyst in terms of service and determining a course. There was a most unusual variation in this configuration of attitude when this instrument beheld the dwelling which is to be inhabited by this group.

The instrument perceived those elementals and beings of astral character of which we have spoken. The instrument desired to be of service by achieving the domicile in question but found its instincts reacting to the unwelcome presences. The division of mind configuration was increased by the continuing catalyst of lack of control. Had this entity been able to physically begin cleansing the dwelling, the, shall we say, opening would not have occurred.

Although this entity attempted clear communication upon this matter, and although each in the support group did likewise, the amount of blue-ray work necessary to uncover and grasp the nature of the catalyst was not effected. Therefore, there was an opening quite rare for this mind/body/spirit complex, and into this opening the one which greets you moved and performed what may be considered to be the most potent of its purely magical manifestations to this present nexus, as you know time.

It is well that this instrument is not distorted towards what you may call hysteria, for the potential of this working was such that had the instrument allowed fear to become greater than the will to persevere when it could not breathe, each attempt at respiration would have been even more nearly impossible until the suffocation occurred, which was desired by the one which greets you in its own way. Thus the entity would have passed from this incarnation.

96.3   **QUESTIONER** Does this threat, shall I say, still exist, and if so is there something we can do to alleviate it?

RA I am Ra. This threat no longer exists, if you wish to phrase this greeting in this manner. The communication which was effected by the scribe and then by the questioner did close the opening and enable the instrument to begin assimilating the catalyst it had received.

96.4   **QUESTIONER** The instrument asks, since this has to do with that house, is the house capable of being transformed by the painting and cleaning? We are able to undertake . . . that is, we don't plan to put down all new carpets. Are the carpets that are there now acceptable?

I want to either bring this particular house up to acceptable limits— You say it will be neutral after we do the salting. I have only a concern with the conditions for our work here. The physical location isn't that important. In fact I don't consider this important at all. If the house is not capable of being brought up to good conditions that will afford us no problems of the type we've experienced then I may select a different one. It's not that important. Would Ra comment on this?

RA I am Ra. It is, of course, the preference of this group which is the only consideration in the situation for contact with Ra.

The domicile in question has already been offered a small amount of blessing by this group through its presence, and, as we have previously stated, each of your days spent in love, harmony, and thanksgiving will continue transforming the dwelling.

It is correct, as we have previously stated, that physical cleanliness is most important. Therefore, the efforts shall be made to most thoroughly cleanse the dwelling. In this regard it is to be noted that neither in the dwelling as a whole wherein you now reside or in the chamber of this working is there an absence of your dust, earth, and other detritus which is *in toto* called dirt.

If the intention is to clean, as much as is physically possible, the location, the requirements for physical cleanliness are fulfilled. It is only when a lower astral entity has, shall we say, placed portions of itself in the so-called dirt that care should be taken to remove the sentient being. These instructions we have given.[1]

May we note that just as each entity strives in each moment to become more nearly one with the Creator but falls short, just so is physical spotlessness striven for but not achieved. In each case the purity of intention and thoroughness of manifestation are appreciated. The variance between the attempt and the goal is never noted and may be considered unimportant.

96.5   **QUESTIONER** The sequence of events that I am considering, which may be easily changed, is first the painting, then the cleaning, then the moving in of the furniture, then the salting and use of garlic. Is this sequence as good as any other sequence, or would a different sequence be better for those events?

RA I am Ra. Any sequence which results in the cleansings is acceptable. It is to be noted that the thresholds are not to be crossed during the cleansing. Since such stricture upon use of the limen may affect your considerations we make note of this.[2]

96.6   **QUESTIONER** Was the unusual sound on the instrument's tape recorder that occurred while she was trying to record her singing a greeting from our fifth-density negative associate?

RA I am Ra. No. Rather it was a greeting from a malfunctioning electronic machine.

---

[1] Given in 95.4–8 and 95.13–15.

[2] In this context, *limen* can be defined as "threshold."

96.7 **QUESTIONER** There was no catalyst for the machine to malfunction from any of the negative entities then. Is that right? I mean, it just was a function only of the random malfunction of the machine. Am I correct?

RA I am Ra. No.

96.8 **QUESTIONER** What was the origin of this malfunction?

RA I am Ra. There are two difficulties with the machine. Firstly, this instrument has a strong effect upon electromagnetic and electronic machines and instruments, and likely, if continued use of these is desired, should request that another handle the machines.

Also, there was some difficulty from physical interference due to the material you call tape catching upon adjoining, what you would call, buttons when the "play" button, as you call it, is depressed.

96.9 **QUESTIONER** How is Ra able to know all of this information? This is a somewhat unimportant question, but it is just amazing to me that Ra is able to know all of these trivial things. What do you do, move in time/space and inspect the problem or what?

RA I am Ra. Your former supposition is correct, your latter unintelligible to us.

96.10 **QUESTIONER** You mean you move in time/space and inspect the situation to determine the problem. Is that correct?

RA I am Ra. This is so.

96.11 **QUESTIONER** Sorry to ask the unimportant question. I was thinking of the future readers, and that they would be totally mystified as to how much . . .

Was there a significance with respect to the hawk that landed the other day just outside of the kitchen window?

RA I am Ra. This is correct. We may note that we find it interesting that queries offered to us are often already known. We assume that our confirmation is appreciated.

96.12 **QUESTIONER** This seems to be connected with the concept of the birds being messengers in the tarot, and this is a demonstration of this concept in the tarot, and I was wondering about the mechanics, you might say, of this type of a message. I assume the hawk was a messenger. And I assume that as I thought of the possible meaning of this with respect to our activities I was, in the state of free will, getting a message through the appearance of this very unusual bird—unusual, I say, in that it came so close. I would be very interested to know the origin of the message. (Of course, the origin is the One Creator.) The mechanics of this are very mystifying to me. Would Ra comment on this, please?

RA I am Ra. No.

96.13 **QUESTIONER** I was afraid that you would say that. Am I correct in assuming that this is the same type of communication as depicted in Card Number Three in the Catalyst of the Mind?

RA I am Ra. We may not comment due to the Law of Confusion. There is an acceptable degree of confirmation of items known, but when the recognized subjective sigil is waived and the message not clear, then it is that we must remain silent.[3]

96.14 **QUESTIONER** Would Ra comment on the technique of blessing the water we will use to sprinkle on the salt? I assume we just sprinkle the water directly off of our fingertips onto the line of salt. And also how much, in general, should be sprinkled on the salt? How wet we should get it? This is trivial, but I'd like to get it right.

RA I am Ra. The blessing of the water may be that one we have previously given, or it may be that one which is written within the liturgy of this instrument's distortion of the worship of the One Creator, or it may simply be obtained from what you call your Catholic Church in the form of holy water.

The intention of blessing is the notable feature of blessed water. The water may be sprinkled not so that all salt is soaked, but so that a goodly portion has been dampened. This is not a physical working. The substances need to be seen in their ideal state, so that water may be seen to be enabling the salt.

96.15 **QUESTIONER** I planned to re-draw the tarot cards eliminating extraneous

---

[3] In this context, *sigil* may be defined as "a seal or signet; a mark or sign supposed to exercise occult power."

additions by those who came after Ra's initial giving. And I would like quickly to go through those things that I intend to eliminate from each card we've gone over and ask Ra if there is anything else that should be eliminated to make the cards as they were when they were originally drawn before the astrological and other appendages were added.

I would eliminate all of the letters around the edge of the card with the possible exception of the number of the card: one, two, three, etc. That would be the case for all of the cards, I think—the exterior lettering and numbering.

In Card Number One I would eliminate the star at the upper right hand corner and eliminate the wand in the Magician's hand. I understand that the sphere remains, but I am not really sure where it should be. Would Ra comment on that please?

RA I am Ra. Firstly, the elimination of letters is acceptable.

Secondly, the elimination of stars is acceptable in all cases.

Thirdly, the elimination of the wand is appropriate.

Fourthly, the sphere may be seen to be held by the thumb and index and second finger.

Fifthly, we would note that it is not possible to offer what you may call a pure deck, if you would use this term, of tarot due to the fact that when these images were first drawn there was already distortion in various and sundry ways, mostly cultural.

Sixthly, although it is good to view the images without the astrological additions (it is to be noted that the more general positions, phases, and characteristics of each concept complex are those which are significant), the removal of all distortion is unlikely and, to a great extent, unimportant.

96.16 **QUESTIONER** I didn't think we could ever remove all distortion, but some of this is very difficult to interpret because of the quality of the drawing. And as we go through these cards we get a better idea of what some of these things are and how they should be drawn, and I think that we can improve greatly on the quality of the card and also remove some of the extraneous material that is misleading.

On the second card, in addition to removing the letters and stars I assume we should— At the center of the female form here, where something that looks a little like a crux ansata is, we should change that. Is that correct?

RA I am Ra. We perceive an incomplete query. Please re-question.

96.17 **QUESTIONER** I think that I should put a crux ansata in place of this thing that looks a little like a crux ansata on the front of the female. Is that correct?

RA I am Ra. This is correct.

96.18 **QUESTIONER** And as to the thing that she wears on her head—that, I believe, is a bit confusing. What should it be shaped like?

RA I am Ra. We shall allow the student to ponder this point. We note that although it is an astrologically based addition to the concept complex, it is not entirely unacceptable when viewed with a certain feeling. Therefore, we suggest, O student, that you choose whether to remove the crown or to name its meaning in such a way as to enhance the concept complex.

96.19 **QUESTIONER** Would Ra please give me any information possible on the ratios of the dimensions, and the dimensions and shape of the crux ansata as it should be made or drawn?

RA I am Ra. No.

96.20 **QUESTIONER** Card Number Three, we will remove all of the letters, etc., and the stars. And I assume that it would be advisable to remove all these little cups around the outside of the rays representing the sun. Is that correct?

RA I am Ra. Yes.

96.21 **QUESTIONER** In Card Number Four we will remove the letters around the outside and all of the stars, and it seems that again we have a situation of removing the wand and putting the sphere in the hand. Is that correct?

RA I am Ra. Again, this is a matter of choice. Though astrological in nature, this particular scepter has possibilities of relevancy in the originally intended concept complex.

This instrument is experiencing some small lack of that distortion which you call the proper breathing due to the experience of your near past, as you perceive it. Therefore, as this instrument has requested a substantial enough amount of transferred energy to be retained that it might effect a comfortable re-entry, we shall at this time ask for one more query, after noting the following:

We did not complete our statement upon the dimensions of the crux ansata. It is given in many places. There are decisions to be made as to which drawing of this image is the appropriate one. We may, of course, suggest viewing the so-called Great Pyramid if the puzzle is desired. We do not wish to work this puzzle. It was designed in order that in its own time it be deciphered. In general, of course, this image has the meaning previously stated.[4]

96.22 **QUESTIONER** Is there anything that we can do to make the instrument more comfortable or improve the contact?

RA I am Ra. Continue in harmony, communication, praise, and thanksgiving.

We would note that this instrument's distortions would be lessened were it to refrain from the speaking to some extent for a diurnal period, or perhaps two, if the difficulty remains. We would also recommend against the activity such as running which would cause rapid respiration.

This after-effect of the greeting is not necessarily long-lasting. However, as this instrument has some blood vessels in the forward regions of the skull—that is, the integument covering the skull—greatly swollen at this time, and since this instrument has the distortion known as the streptococcal infection, it is best to be full of care for a short period in order that the distortions do not catapult the entity into longer-term after-effects.

All is well. We find the alignments satisfactory.

I am Ra. I leave you in the love and light of the Infinite One. Go forth, therefore, rejoicing in the power and in the peace of the One Infinite Creator. Adonai.

---

4 Previously stated in 92.30 and 93.24.

97.0   RA   I am Ra. I greet you in the love and in the light of the One Infinite Creator. We communicate now.

97.1   QUESTIONER   Could you first please give me the condition of the instrument?

RA   I am Ra. It is as previously stated.

97.2   QUESTIONER   What's the situation with our fifth-density negative friend?

RA   I am Ra. It is as previously stated.

97.3   QUESTIONER   I've been doing some consideration of the appearance of the hawk and have made this analysis of the bird in Card Three:

The bird is a message from the higher self, and the position of the wings in Card Three, one wing pointing toward the female, indicates that it is a message to the female acting as catalyst for the mind. The position of the downward wing indicates that the message is of a negative nature, or of a nature indicating the inappropriateness of certain mental activity or plan. Would Ra comment on that?

RA   I am Ra. No.

97.4   QUESTIONER   Is the reason for this lack of comment the First Distortion?

RA   I am Ra. This is correct.

97.5   QUESTIONER   I have analyzed the hawk that I saw immediately after returning from the house in Atlanta as a message (most probably from my higher self) indicating that the plan of moving was not the best, was not too appropriate since, without the hawk, everything would have continued as planned with no added catalyst. This single catalyst of a remarkable nature then, logically, from my point of view, could only mean that there was a message as to the inappropriateness of the plan for some reason yet to be discovered. Would Ra comment on that?

RA   I am Ra. We tread as close as possible to the Law of Confusion in suggesting that not all wingèd creatures have an archetypical meaning. We might suggest that the noticing of shared subjectively notable phenomena is common when, in another incarnational experience, work significant to the service of increased polarity has been shared.

These subjectively interesting shared phenomena then act as a means of communication, the nature of which cannot be discussed by those outside of the shared incarnational experience without the interference with the free will of each entity involved in the complex of subjectively meaningful events.

97.6   **QUESTIONER** Can Ra please tell us the source of the unusual odor in this room this morning?

RA I am Ra. There are two components to this odor. One is, as has been surmised, the decomposing physical vehicle of one of your second-density Rodentia. The second is an elemental which is attempting to take up residence within the putrefying remains of this small creature.

The cleansing of the room and the burning of the incense has discouraged the elemental. The process of decomposition shall, in a short period of your space/time, remove the less than harmonious sensations provided for the nose.

97.7   **QUESTIONER** I find myself presently in a difficult position of decision, primarily because of the appearance of the aforementioned hawk after our return from Atlanta. The only objective of any value at all is the work that we are doing, which includes not only the contact but communication and dissemination of information to those who might request it.

Since the move was connected with that, and since the hawk was, to me, obviously a function of that process, I am at present in a quandary with respect to the optimal situation since I have not yet decided definitely on the significance of the hawk, or the advantages or efficaciousness of the move, and do not want to create a process which is basically irreversible if it is going to result in a lack of our ability to be of service to those who would seek that which we are able to manifest through our efforts here. Would Ra comment on that situation?

RA I am Ra. The questioner presumes much, and to comment is an infringement upon its free will. We may suggest the pondering of our previous comments regarding the wingèd creatures of which you speak. We repeat that any place of working, properly prepared by this group, is acceptable to Ra. The discrimination of choice is yours.

97.8   **QUESTIONER** Are there any items in the first four cards not of Ra's intention that we could remove to present a less confusing card as we make our new drawings?

RA I am Ra. We find much material in this query which would constitute repetition. May we suggest rephrasing the query?

97.9   **QUESTIONER** Possibly I didn't phrase that the way I meant to, which was: we already have determined the items that should be removed from the first four cards. The question was: have I missed anything that should be removed which were not of Ra's original intention in the last few sessions of determining what should be removed?

RA I am Ra. We shall repeat our opinion that there are several concepts which, in each image, are astrologically based. However, these concepts are not without merit within the concept complex intended by Ra, given the perception by the student of these concepts in an appropriate manner.

We wish not to form that which may be considered by any mind/body/spirit complex to be a complete and infallible series of images. There is a substantial point to be made in this regard. We have been, with the questioner's aid, investigating the concept complexes of the great architecture of the archetypical mind. To more clearly grasp the nature, the process, and the purpose of archetypes, Ra provided a series of concept complexes.

In no way whatsoever should we, as humble messengers of the One Infinite Creator, wish to place before the consideration of any mind/body/spirit complex, which seeks its evolution, the palest tint of the idea that these images are anything but a resource for working in the area of the development of the faith and the will.

To put this into perspective we must gaze, then, at the stunning mystery of the One Infinite Creator. The archetypical mind does not resolve any paradox or bring all into unity. This is not the property of any resource which is of the third density.

Therefore, may we ask the student to look up from inward working and behold the glory, the might, the majesty, the mystery, and the peace of oneness. Let no consideration of bird or beast, darkness or light, shape or shadow keep any which seeks from the central consideration of unity.

We are not messengers of the complex. We bring the message of unity. In this perspective only may we affirm the value to the seeker of adepthood of the grasping, articulating, and use of this resource of the deep mind exemplified by the concept complexes of the archetypes.

97.10 **QUESTIONER** Thank you. Card Number Five, the Significator of the Mind, indicates, firstly, as I see it, simply a male within a rectangularly structured form. This suggests to me that the Significator of the Mind in third density is well-bounded within the illusion, as is also suggested by the fact that the base of the male is a rectangular form showing no ability for movement. Would Ra comment on that?

RA I am Ra. O student, you have grasped the barest essence of the nature of the Significator's complete envelopment within the rectangle. Consider for the self, O student, whether your thoughts can walk. The abilities of the most finely honed mentality shall not be known without the use of the physical vehicle which you call the body. Through the mouth the mind may speak. Through the limbs the mind may effect action.

97.11 **QUESTIONER** The entity looks to the left, indicating that the mind has the tendency to notice more easily the negative catalyst or negative essence of its environment. Would Ra comment on that observation?

RA I am Ra. This is substantially correct.

97.12 **QUESTIONER** There are two small entities at the bottom of the seat, one black and one white. I would first ask Ra: is this drawing correct in the coloring? Is the black one in the proper position with respect to Ra's original drawings?

RA I am Ra. That which you perceive as black was first red. Other than this difference the beings in the concept complex are placed correctly.

97.13 **QUESTIONER** The red coloration is a mystery to me then. We had originally decided that these represented polarization of the mind, either positive or negative, as its significant self would be either significant as one or the other polarity. Would Ra comment on that?

RA I am Ra. The indications of polarity are as presumed by the questioner. The symbolism of old for the left-hand path was the russet coloration.

97.14 **QUESTIONER** Would—

RA We shall pause at this time if the questioner will be patient. There are fairly serious difficulties with the instrument's throat. We shall attempt to ameliorate the situation and suggest the re-walking of the Circle of One.

[*Cough.*]

[*Cough.*]

[*The Circle of One was re-walked and breath expelled two feet above the instrument's head.*]

I am Ra. Please continue.

97.15 **QUESTIONER** What was the nature of the problem? What caused it?

RA I am Ra. The fifth-density entity which greets this instrument affected a previous difficulty distorting the throat and chest area of the instrument. Some fraction of this distortion remained unmentioned by the instrument. It is helpful if the instrument speaks as clearly as possible to the support group of any difficulties that more care may be taken.

However, we find very little distortion left in the chest area of the instrument. However, immediately preceding the working the instrument was offered an extreme activation of what you may call the allergies, and the mucus from the flow which this distortion causes began to cause difficulty to the throat.

At this juncture the previous potential for the tightening of the throat was somewhat activated by reflex of the yellow-ray, chemical body over which we have only gross control.

We would appreciate your reminding us to cause this instrument to cough before or after each query for the remainder of this working. Once conscious, this instrument should have no serious difficulty.

97.16 **QUESTIONER** I was wondering why the dark entity was on the right side of the card as far as the male figure, which is the Significator, is concerned, and the light white entity is on the left. If you could comment on that after making the instrument cough, please?

RA [*Cough.*] The nature of— We pause.

[*Ten second pause.*]

I am Ra. There was a serious pain flare. We may now continue.

The nature of polarity is interesting in that those experiences offered to the Significator as positive frequently become recorded as productive of biases which may be seen to be negative, whereas the fruit of those experiences apparently negative is frequently found to be helpful in the development of the service-to-others bias. As this is perhaps the guiding characteristic of that which the mind processes and records, these symbols of polarity have thusly been placed.

You may note that the hands of the central image indicate the appropriate bias for right- and left-hand working; that is, the right hand gestures in service to others, offering its light outward. The left hand attempts to absorb the power of the spirit and point it for its use alone.

97.17 **QUESTIONER** The eight cartouches at the bottom would possibly signify the energy centers and the evolution through those centers . . . possibility for either the positive or negative polarization because of the white and black coloration of the figures. Would Ra comment on that after making the instrument cough?

RA [*Cough.*] I am Ra. The observations of the student are perceptive. It is informative to continue the study of octaves in association with this concept complex. Many are the octaves of a mind/body/spirit complex's beingness. There is not one that does not profit from being pondered in connection with the considerations of the nature of the development of polarity exemplified by the concept complex of your Card Number Five.

97.18 **QUESTIONER** Do the symbols on the face of each of these little cartouches such as the birds and the other symbols have a meaning in this card that is of value in considering the archetype? Would you answer that after making the instrument cough, please?

RA [*Cough.*] I am Ra. These symbols are letters and words much as your language would receive such an entablature. They are, to a great extent, enculturated by a people not of your generation. Let us, in the rough, suggest that the information written upon these cartouches be understood to be such as the phrase, "And you shall be born again to eternal life."

97.19 **QUESTIONER** Thank you. I thought that the wings at the top of the card might indicate the protection of the spirit over the process of evolution. Would Ra comment on that after having the instrument cough?

RA [*Cough.*] I am Ra. We shall end this session for we are having considerable difficulty in using the sympathetic nervous system in order to aid the instrument in providing sufficient of your air for its respiration. Therefore, we prematurely suggest ending this session.

Is there any brief query before we leave this instrument?

97.20 **QUESTIONER** It's not necessary to answer this if you want to end right now for the instrument's benefit, but is there anything we can do to improve the contact or make the instrument more comfortable?

RA I am Ra. All is well. The support group functions well.

It is suggested that the instrument be encouraged to take steps to recover completely from the distortion towards the aching of the throat and, to a lesser extent, the chest. There is no way in which we or you may remove that working which has been done. It simply must be removed by physical recovery of the normal distortion. This is not easy due to this instrument's tendency towards allergy.

The alignments are being carefully considered.

I am Ra. I leave you, my friends, glorying and rejoicing in the love and the light of the Infinite Creator. Go forth, then, in the great dance, empowered by the peace of the One Infinite Creator. Adonai.

SESSION 98

98.0   RA   I am Ra. I greet you in the love and in the light of the One Infinite Creator. We communicate now.

98.1   QUESTIONER   Could you first please give me the condition of the instrument?

RA   I am Ra. The physical energy deficit has somewhat increased. The vital-energy distortions are somewhat improved.

98.2   QUESTIONER   We eliminated our meditation prior to the session. Would Ra comment on that?

RA   I am Ra. The purpose of preparation for a working is the purification of each entity involved with the working. The removal of a portion of this preparation has a value determined by the purity of each, which takes part in the working, has achieved without that particular aid.

98.3   QUESTIONER   I had just taken a wild guess that it was possibly during that meditation prior to the working that was used by our fifth-density negative friend to create the allergic reactions and other in the instrument. Was I correct on that or incorrect?

RA   I am Ra. This entity greets the instrument as close to the working in your space/time continuum as is practicable. The elimination of that preparation caused the fifth-density entity to greet this instrument at this juncture of decision not to meditate. The greeting does not take what you would call a noticeable amount of your time.

98.4   QUESTIONER   Was the greeting as effective as it would have been if the meditation had been done?

RA   I am Ra. Yes.

98.5   QUESTIONER   I have a question from the instrument. She states: "Could Ra tell us what factors are allowing our fifth-density negative companion to be able to continue greeting the instrument in the throat area as well as with other unusual sensations such as dizziness, smelling of orange blossoms, the feeling of stepping on imaginary creatures? And what can be done to lessen these greetings? And why the greetings occur on walks?"

RA I am Ra. There are various portions of the query. We shall attempt answer to each. We tread close to the Law of Confusion, saved only by the awareness that given lack of information this instrument would, nonetheless, continue to offer its service.

The working of your fifth-density companion, which still affects the instrument, was, as we have stated, a potent working. The totality of those biases which offer to the instrument opportunities for increased vital and physical strength, shall we say, were touched by the working.

The blue-ray difficulties were not entirely at an end after the first asking. Again, this group experienced blockage rare for the group; that is, the blue-ray blockage of unclear communication. By this means the efficacy of the working was reinforced.

The potential of this working is significant. The physical exercising, the sacred music, the varieties of experience, and indeed simple social intercourse are jeopardized by a working which attempts to close the throat and the mouth. It is to be noted that there is also the potential for the loss of this contact.

We suggest that the instrument's allergies create a continuous means whereby the distortion created by the magical working may be continued. As we have stated, it shall be necessary, in order to remove the working, to completely remove the distortion within the throat area caused by this working. The continuous aggravation of allergic reactions makes this challenging.

The orange blossom is the odor which you may associate with the social memory complex of fifth-density positive which is known to you as sound vibration, Latwii. This entity was with the instrument as requested by the instrument. The odor was perceived due to the quite sensitive nature of the instrument due again to its, shall we say, acme in the eighteen-day cycle.

The sensation of stepping upon the small animal and killing it was a greeting from your fifth-density negative companion also made possible by the above circumstance.

As to the removal of the effects of the magical working, we may make two suggestions, one immediate and one general.

Firstly, within the body of knowledge which those healers known among your peoples as medical doctors have is the use of harsh chemical substances which you call medicine. These substances almost invariably cause far more changes than are intended in the mind/body/spirit complex. However, in this instance the steroids or, alternately, the antibiotic family might be useful in the complete removal of the difficulty within which the working is still able to thrive. Of course, the allergies would persist after this course of medicine were ended, but the effects of the working would no longer come into play.

The one you call Jerome might well be of aid in this somewhat unorthodox medical situation.

As allergies are quite misunderstood by your orthodox healers, it would be inappropriate to subject the instrument to the services of your medical doctors which find the amelioration of allergic effects to be connected with the intake of these same toxins in milder form. This, shall we say, treats the symptom. However, the changes offered to the body complex are quite inadvisable.

The allergy may be seen to be the rejection, upon a deep level of the mind complex, of the environment of the mind/body/spirit complex. Thus the allergy may be seen in its pure form as the mental/emotional distortion of the deeper self.

The more general recommendation lies with one which does not wish to be identified. There is a code name "Prayer Wheel." We suggest ten treatments from this healer, and further suggest a clear reading and subsequent following, upon the part of the instrument, of the priorities of allergy, especially to your foodstuffs.

Lastly, the effects of the working become apparent upon the walking when the body complex has begun to exert itself to the point of increased respiration.

Also a contributing factor is the number of your second-density substances to which this instrument is allergic.

98.6   **QUESTIONER** Thank you. The second question is: "Our oldest cat, Gandalf, has a growth near his spine. Is there any factor that makes the surgical removal of this growth less appropriate than the surgical removal of the growth that we had performed a year ago last April? And would the most appropriate actions on our part to aid his recovery be the visualization of light surrounding him during the surgery and the repeating of ritual phrases at periodical intervals while he is at the veterinarians?"

RA I am Ra. No. There is no greater cause for caution than previously. And, yes, the phrases of which you speak shall aid the entity. Although this entity is in body complex old—and, therefore, liable to danger from what you call your anesthetic—its mental, emotional, and spiritual distortions are such that it is strongly motivated to recover that it might once again rejoin the loved one. Keep in mind that this entity is harvestable third density.

98.7 QUESTIONER Would you explain the reason for saying "Keep in mind that this is harvestable third density" and tell me if you have any other specific recommendations with respect to the proposed operation on the growth?

RA I am Ra. We stated this in order to elucidate our use of the term "spirit complex" as applied to what might be considered a second-density entity. The implications are that this entity shall have far more cause to abide and heal that it may seek the presence of the loved ones.

98.8 QUESTIONER Is there any additional recommendation that Ra could make with respect to the proposed operation?

RA I am Ra. No.

98.9 QUESTIONER I was wondering if I was correct in my assumption that the reason for the growths was a state of anger in the cat, Gandalf, because of the introduction of the newer cats into his environment. Was I correct?

RA I am Ra. The original cause of what you call cancer was the distortion caused by this event. The proximate cause of this growth is the nature of the distortion of the body cells which you call cancer.

98.10 QUESTIONER Are there any other cancerous growths at this time within the cat, Gandalf?

RA I am Ra. Yes.

98.11 QUESTIONER Can we alleviate those, and, if so, how and where are they?

RA I am Ra. None can be alleviated at this space/time nexus. One is located within the juncture of the right hip. Another which is very small is near the organ you call the liver. There are also small cell distortions under the, we may call it, arm (to distinguish the upper appendages) on both sides.

98.12 **QUESTIONER** Is there anything that we can do to alleviate these problems—other than surgical—that would have a good effect to help Gandalf alleviate them?

RA I am Ra. Continue in praise and thanksgiving, asking for the removal of these distortions. There are two possible outcomes:

Firstly, the entity shall dwell with you in contentment until its physical vehicle holds it no more due to distortions caused by the cancerous cells.

Secondly, the life path may become that which allows the healing.

We do not infringe upon free will by examining this life path although we may note the preponderance of life paths which use some distortion such as this to leave the physical body, which in this case is the orange-ray body.

98.13 **QUESTIONER** Does the cat, Fairchild, have any of this same type of problem?

RA I am Ra. Not at this space/time nexus.

98.14 **QUESTIONER** Was it necessary for the cat, Gandalf, to be a mind/body/spirit complex harvestable third density to have the anger result in cancer?

RA I am Ra. No.

98.15 **QUESTIONER** Then any mind/body complex can develop cancer as a result of anger. Is this correct?

RA I am Ra. This is correct.

At this time we would break our routine by making an observation. We observe the following coincidence:

Firstly, the congestion of this instrument's throat due to the flow of mucus caused by energized allergic reaction has, at this point, become such that we may safely predict the probability/possibility vortex approaching certainty that within one-half of an hour we shall need to depart from this working.

Secondly, as we noted the above, the sound vibration made by one of your sound vibration recording devices was audible to us. If this group desires it may choose to have sessions which are brought to an ending soon after this sound vibration occurs. This decision would ensure the minimal distortions within the instrument towards the discomfort/comfort within the throat until the effects of the magical working of your fifth-density companion have been removed.

98.16 **QUESTIONER** That is perfectly fine with us. That noise occurs at the forty-five minute time since the tape is forty-five minutes on a side.

I would just ask as a final question then: If the new table that Jim has built for the appurtenances is satisfactory to hold them since it will give us more room to walk around the bed, and if it is better to leave it in its natural condition as it is, or to coat it with linseed oil or varnish or paint?

RA I am Ra. We view this appurtenance. It sings with joy. The pine vibrates in praise. Much investment of this working in wood has been done. It is acceptable. We may suggest it be left either as it is or rubbed with the oil which also is easily magnetized and holds the proffered vibration to a profound extent.

98.17 **QUESTIONER** I was wondering if this would be an appropriate time to end since the tape recorder has clicked some time ago?

RA I am Ra. This is a matter for your discrimination. The instrument remains open to our use although, as we have noted, the physical distortions begin to mount.

98.18 **QUESTIONER** Think we had better close to maintain the instrument's physical energy. And I will ask if there is anything that we can do to improve the contact or make the instrument more comfortable?

RA I am Ra. All is well. We find your concerns appropriate.

We leave you in the love and in the light of the One Infinite Creator. Go forth, therefore, rejoicing in the power and in the peace of the One. Adonai.

SESSION 99

NOVEMBER 18, 1982

99.0   RA   I am Ra. I greet you in the love and in the light of the One Infinite Creator. We communicate now.

99.1   QUESTIONER   Would you please give me the condition of the instrument?

RA   I am Ra. This instrument's physical deficit continues but has the potential for the lessening due to the removal in your probable future of foodstuffs to which the instrument has significant allergy. The vital energy levels are somewhat lessened than the last asking but remain strong. The change in the mental/emotional energy level is towards the distortion of the weakening of this complex.

99.2   QUESTIONER   What are the foodstuffs that are creating the allergic reaction?

RA   I am Ra. That which you call the buttermilk, though appropriately used in the healing work undertaken for the throat and chest areas, is the substance to which the entity has allergy.

99.3   QUESTIONER   The instrument asks if it will be all right to keep the small gold cross on while she is in one of these sessions, or will it cause some distortion that is not advisable?

RA   I am Ra. We scan the mental distortions of the instrument. Although the presence of the metallic substance is in general not recommended, in this instance, as we find those distortions weakening the mental/emotional complex of the instrument due to its empathic distortions, the figure is specifically recommended for use by this instrument. We would request that should any strengthening be done to the chain (as we find intended by this instrument) the strengthening links which symbolize eternity to this instrument be as high in purity, or higher, than the remainder of the device.

In this nexus that which this device represents to this instrument is a much-needed strengthener of the mental/emotional patterns which have been much disrupted from the usual configuration of distortions.

99.4   **QUESTIONER** Is there anything further that needs to be done for or by the instrument to remove the magical working, or any of its after-effects, on her throat area by our fifth-density negative companion?

RA I am Ra. No.

99.5   **QUESTIONER** Finally, of the preliminary questions, one from Jim stating: "For the last three weeks I have often been at the edge of anger and frustration, have had a nearly constant dull pain at my indigo-ray center, and have felt quite drained of energy. Would Ra comment on the source of these experiences and any thoughts or actions that might alleviate it?"

RA I am Ra. As in all distortions, the source is the limit of the viewpoint. We may, without serious infringement, suggest three courses of behavior which shall operate upon the distortion expressed.

Firstly, it would be well for the scribe to engage, if not daily then as nearly so as possible, in a solitary strenuous activity which brings this entity to the true physical weariness. Further, although any activity may suffice, an activity chosen for its intended service to the harmony of the group would be quite efficacious.

The second activity is some of your space/time and time/space taken by the entity, directly or as nearly so as possible to the strenuous activity, for solitary contemplation.

Thirdly, the enthusiastic pursuit of the balancing and silent meditations cannot be deleted from the list of helpful activities for this entity.

We may note that the great forte of the scribe is summed in the inadequate sound vibration complex, power. The flow of power, just as the flow of love or wisdom, is enabled not by the chary conserver of its use, but by the constant user.[1] The physical manifestation of power being either constructive or destructive strenuous activity, the power-filled entity must needs exercise that manifestation.

This entity experiences a distortion in the direction of an excess of stored energy. It is well to know the self and to guard and use those attributes which the self has provided for its learning and its service.

---

[1]   In this context, *chary* can be defined as "cautious or reluctant."

99.6   **QUESTIONER** We now have an additional set of tarot images. We will refer to them as the *Royal Road* images, since that's the name of the book they came from. They are similar to, but in some instances different from, the C.C. Zain images. Which of these two sets are closer to Ra's original intention? And if they are mixed, let me know that.

RA I am Ra. The principle which moves in accordance with the dynamics of teach/learning with most efficiency is constancy. We could explore the archetypical mind using that set of images produced by the one known as Fathman, or we could use those which have been used.

In point of fact, those which are being used have some subtleties which enrich the questioning. As we have said, this set of images is not that which we gave. This is not material. We could use any of a multitude of devised tarot sets. Although this must be at the discretion of the questioner, we suggest the maintaining of one and only one set of distorted images to be used for the querying and note that the images you now use are good.

99.7   **QUESTIONER** The only problem is something that I am sure is quite foreign to Ra's way of thinking which is called "copyright laws." We have been unable to get copyright privileges from the publishers of the cards that we started with, and we'll have to circumnavigate that problem some way or another, which could conceivably cause us to use a different set of images as we go along.

The wings of Card Five, I am guessing, have to do with a protection over the—they're above the Significator of the Mind, and I am guessing they are a symbol of protection. Is this in any way correct?

RA I am Ra. Let us say that you are not incorrect but rather less than correct. The Significator owns a covenant with the spirit which it shall, in some cases, manifest through the thought and action of the adept. If there is protection in a promise, then you have chosen the correct sound vibration, for the outstretched wings of spirit, high above manifestation, yet draw the caged mind onward.

99.8   **QUESTIONER** Thank you. Card Number Six I see as the Transformation of the Mind; the male's crossed arms representing transformation, transformation being possible either toward the left- or the right-hand path; the path being beckoned or led by the female, the Potentiator.

The one on the right having the serpent of wisdom at the brow and being fully clothed; the one on the left having less clothing and indicating that the Matrix or Potentiator would be more concerned and attracted to the physical illusion as the left-hand path is chosen, and more concerned and attracted to the mental as the right-hand path is chosen.

The creature above points an arrow at the left-hand path indicating that if this path is chosen, the chips, shall we say, will fall where they may—the path being unprotected as far as the random activity of catalyst. And the intellectual abilities of the chooser of that path would be the main guardian rather than a designed or built-in protection by the Logos for the right-hand path.

The entity firing the arrow, being what seems to be a second density entity, would indicate that this catalyst could be produced by a lesser-evolved source, you might say.

Would Ra comment on these observations of Card Six, the Transformation of the Mind?

RA I am Ra. We shall speak upon several aspects seriatim.[2] Firstly, let us examine the crossed arms of the male who is to be transformed. What, O student, do you make of the crossing? What see you in this tangle? There is a creative point to be found in this element which was not discussed overmuch by the questioner.

Let us now observe the evaluation of the two females. The observation that to the left-hand path moves the roughly physical and to the right-hand path the mental has a shallow correctness. There are deeper observations to be made concerning the relationship of the great sea of the unconscious mind to the conscious mind which may fruitfully be pursued. Remember, O student, that these images are not literal. They haunt rather than explicate.

Many use the trunk and roots of mind as if that portion of mind were a badly used, prostituted entity. Then this entity gains from this great storehouse that which is rough, prostituted, and without great virtue. Those who turn to the deep mind seeing it in the guise of the maiden go forth to court it. The courtship has nothing of plunder in its semblance

---

[2] In this context, *seriatim* can be defined as "point by point, one after another."

and may be protracted, yet the treasure gained by such careful courtship is great. The right-hand and left-hand transformations of the mind may be seen to differ by the attitude of the conscious mind towards its own resources as well as the resources of other-selves.

We now speak of that genie, or elemental, or mythic figure, culturally determined, which sends the arrow to the left-hand transformation. This arrow is not the arrow which kills but, rather, that which, in its own way, protects. Those who choose separation, that being the quality most indicative of the left-hand path, are protected from other-selves by a strength and sharpness equivalent to the degree of transformation which the mind has experienced in the negative sense.

Those upon the right-hand path have no such protection against other-selves, for upon that path the doughty seeker shall find many mirrors for reflection in each other-self it encounters.

99.9 **QUESTIONER** In the previous session you mentioned the use of the forty-five minute interval of the tape recorder as a signal for ending the session. Is this still the appropriate time?

RA I am Ra. This is, of course, at the discretion of the questioner, for this instrument has some transferred energy and remains open, as it has unfailingly done. However, the fragility of the instrument has been more and more appreciated by us. We, in the initial observations, saw the strength of will and overestimated greatly the recuperative abilities of the physical complex of this entity.

Therefore, we may say that ending a working at approximately this amount of energy expenditure—that is, some point soon following upon the sound vibration of which you speak—would be appropriate; and insofar as we may determine, may well extend the incarnational amount of your space/time which this instrument shall be able to offer to this contact.

99.10 **QUESTIONER** In that case I will just ask one additional short question as we terminate for this session. May I ask if the Logos of this system planned for the mating process as possibly depicted in Card Six—I don't know if this is related—by some type of DNA imprinting as has been studied by our science? Many second-density creatures seem to have some sort of imprinting that creates a lifetime mating relationship, and I was

wondering if this was designed by the Logos for that particular mechanism, and if it was also carried into third density?

RA I am Ra. There are some of your second-density fauna which have instinctually imprinted monogamous mating processes. The third-density physical vehicle which is the basic incarnational tool of manifestation upon your planet arose from entities thusly imprinted, all the aforesaid being designed by the Logos.

The free will of third-density entities is far stronger than the rather mild carryover from second-density DNA encoding, and it is not part of the conscious nature of many of your mind/body/spirit complexes to be monogamous due to the exercise of free will. However, as has been noted there are many signposts in the deep mind indicating to the alert adept the more efficient use of catalyst. As we have said, the Logos of your peoples has a bias towards kindness.

99.11 **QUESTIONER** Thank you. In closing I will just ask if there is anything that we can do to make the instrument more comfortable or improve the contact?

RA I am Ra. We note the relative discomfort of this group at this space/time and offer those previous statements made by Ra as possible aids to the regaining of the extraordinary harmony which this group has the capability of experiencing in a stable manner.

We find the addition of the swirling waters to be helpful. The appurtenances are conscientiously aligned.

We encourage the conscious strengthening of those invisible ribands which fly from the wrists of those who go forward to seek what you may call the Grail.[3] All is well, my friends. We leave you in hopes that each may find true colors to fly in that great metaphysical quest and urge each to urge each other in love, praise, and thanksgiving.

I am Ra. We leave you in the love and light of the One Infinite Creator. Go forth rejoicing in the power and in the peace of the One Glorious Infinite Creator. Adonai.

---

[3] In this context, *riband* can be defined as "a decorative ribbon used in heraldry."

SESSION 100

100.0 **RA** I am Ra. I greet you, my friends, in the love and in the light of the One Infinite Creator. We communicate now.

100.1 **QUESTIONER** Could you first please give me the condition of the instrument?

RA I am Ra. It is as previously stated with the exception of the vital-energy distortion which leans more towards strength/weakness than the last asking.

100.2 **QUESTIONER** Thank you. The instrument asks if there is some problem with the swirling waters since she feels very dizzy after each application. Could Ra comment on that, please?

RA I am Ra. Yes.

100.3 **QUESTIONER** Would Ra please comment?

RA I am Ra. As has been previously noted, the instrument has the propensity for attempting to exceed its limits. If one considers the metaphysical or time/space aspect of an incarnation, this is a fortunate and efficient use of catalyst as the will is constantly being strengthened. And, further, if the limitations are exceeded in the service of others the polarization is also most efficient.

However, we perceive the query to speak to the space/time portion of incarnational experience, and in that framework would again ask the instrument to consider the value of martyrdom. The instrument may examine its range of reactions to the swirling waters. It will discover a correlation between it and other activity.

When the so-called aerobic exercise is pursued, no less than three of your hours, and preferably five of your hours, should pass betwixt it and the swirling waters. When the walking has been accomplished, a period of no less than, we believe, forty of your minutes must needs transpire before the swirling waters, and preferably twice that amount of your space/time.

It is true that some greeting has encouraged the dizziness felt by the instrument. However, its source is largely the determination of the instrument to remain immersed in the swirling waters past the period of space/time it may abide therein without exceeding its physical limits.

100.4 **QUESTIONER** Thank you. I feel obligated to ask the next somewhat transient question because of a request from Colonel Stevens. I also, for my own edification, would like to better understand the effect of the quarantine and First Distortion. Would Ra comment on the purpose of the so-called Pleiades contact in Switzerland with Billy Meier by an entity known as Semjase and others.

RA I am Ra. It is not our practice to judge the value of a contact of metaphysical origin. We cannot confirm the contact referred to by the questioner as pure Confederation contact. However, we might suggest that there is some positive material within the recorded transcript of converse during this contact. As we have spoken previously to the various characteristics of so-called mixed contact,[1] we shall not repeat but note that all communication is of the One Infinite Creator in its infinite distortions.

100.5 **QUESTIONER** Is it all right for Colonel Stevens to receive the information that Ra just gave to us?

RA I am Ra. We find this information to be confirmation of already perceived ideas. Therefore, permission is freely given.

100.6 **QUESTIONER** Thank you. To continue with the tarot, I would like to make the additional observation with respect to Card Six that the male's arms being crossed, if the female to his right pulls on his left hand it would cant, in effect turn him, his entire body, toward the right.[2] And the same is true for the female on the left: pulling on his right hand she will turn his entire body to her side. Which is my interpretation of what's meant by the tangle of the arms—that the transformation occurs by pull which attempts to turn the entity toward the left- or the right-hand path. Would Ra comment on that observation?

RA I am Ra. We shall. The concept of the pull towards mental polarity

---

[1] Previously covered extensively in various passages. See the entry "Mixed Contacts" in the index for a complete list.

[2] In this context, *cant* may be defined as "to put in an oblique position, or tilt."

may well be examined in the light of what the student has already accreted concerning the nature of the conscious, exemplified by the male, and the unconscious, exemplified by the female. Indeed, both the prostituted and the virginal of deep mind invite and await the reaching.

In this image of Transformation of Mind, then, each of the females points the way it would go but is not able to move; nor are the two female entities striving to do so. They are at rest.

The conscious entity holds both and will turn itself one way or the other, or potentially backwards and forwards, rocking first one way, then the other, and not achieving the Transformation. In order for the Transformation of Mind to occur, one principle governing the use of the deep mind must be abandoned.

It is to be noted that the triangular shape formed by the shoulders and crossed elbows of consciousness is a shape to be associated with transformation. Indeed, you may see this shape echoed twice more in the image, each echo having its own riches to add to the impact of this complex of concepts.

100.7 **QUESTIONER** Thank you. We will probably return to this card next session for more of an observation after we study Ra's comments. To conserve and efficiently use the time at this time I will make some notes with respect to Card Seven.

First, the veil between the conscious and the unconscious mind has been removed. The veil is the curtain, I would assume, at the top which is lifted. Even though this veil has been removed perception of intelligent infinity is still distorted according to the seeker's beliefs and means of seeking. Would Ra comment on that?

RA I am Ra. As one observes the veil of the image of the Great Way of Mind it may be helpful to ideate using the framework of environment. The Great Way of Mind, Body, or Spirit is intended to limn the milieu within which the work of mind, body, or spirit shall be placed.[3]

Thusly the veil is shown both somewhat lifted and still present, since the

---

3 In this context, *limn* can be defined as "depict or describe," and *milieu* can be defined as "surroundings" or "the setting in which something happens or develops."

work of mind and its transformation involves progressive lifting of the great veil betwixt conscious and deep minds. The complete success of this attempt is not properly a portion of third-density work and, more especially, third-density mental processes.

100.8 **QUESTIONER** The fact that the veil is raised higher on the right-hand side than on the left indicates to me that the adept choosing the positive polarity will have greater success in penetrating the veil. Would Ra comment?

RA I am Ra. This is a true statement if it is realized that the questioner speaks of potential success. Indeed, your third-density experience is distorted or skewed so that the positive orientation has more aid than the so-called negative.

100.9 **QUESTIONER** It would also seem to me that since Ra stated in the last session the limit of the viewpoint is the source of all distortions, that the very nature of the service-to-self distortions that create the left-hand path are a function of the veil and, therefore, are dependent, you might say, to some degree on at least a partial continued veiling. Does this make any sense?

RA I am Ra. There is the thread of logic in what you suppose.

The polarities are both dependent upon a limited viewpoint. However, the negative polarity depends more heavily upon the illusory separation betwixt the self and all other mind/body/spirit complexes. The positive polarity attempts to see through the illusion to the Creator in each mind/body/spirit complex, but for the greater part is concerned with behaviors and thoughts directed towards other-selves in order to be of service.

This attitude in itself is full of the stuff of your third-density illusion.

100.10 **QUESTIONER** The crown of three stars, we are guessing, indicates mastery and balancing of the mind, body, and spirit. Is this in any way correct?

RA I am Ra. This device is astrological in origin and the interpretation given somewhat confusing. We deal in this image with the environment of mind. It is perhaps appropriate to release the starry crown from its stricture.

100.11 **QUESTIONER** The entities (the small black, or russet, and white entities) have been now changed so that they appear to be sphinxes which we are assuming mean that the catalyst has been mastered.

I am also assuming that they act as the power that moves the chariot depicted here so as this mastery enables the mind in its transformation to become mobile, unlike it was prior to this mastery, locked within the illusion. Would Ra comment on that?

RA I am Ra. Firstly, we ask that the student consider the Great Way not as the culmination of a series of seven activities or functions but as a far more clearly delineated image of the environment within which the mind, body, or spirit shall function. Therefore, the culturally determined creatures called sphinxes do not indicate mastery over catalyst.

The second supposition, that of placing the creatures as the movers of the chariot of mind, has far more virtue. You may connote the concept of time to the image of the sphinx. The mental and mental/emotional complex ripens, and moves, and is transformed in time.

100.12 **QUESTIONER** There is the forty-five minute signal. Does Ra suggest a termination of this session, taking into consideration the instrument's condition and all the other conditions that we have placed on this?

RA I am Ra. Information pertinent to this query has been previously covered.[4] The choice of termination time, as you call it, is solely that of the questioner until the point at which we perceive the instrument beginning to use its vital resources due to the absence of transferred or native physical energy. The instrument remains open, as always.

100.13 **QUESTIONER** In that case I will ask only one more question and that will be having to do with the sword and the scepter. It would seem that the sword would be the power of the negative adept indicating control over other-selves, and the scepter would indicate the power of the positive adept with unity in mind, body, and spirit. However, they seem to be in opposite hands than I would have guessed. Would Ra comment on that?

RA I am Ra. These symbols are astrological in origin. The shapes, therefore, may be released from their stricture.

---

4 Previously covered in 98.15–16 and 99.9.

We may note that there is an overriding spiritual environment and protection for the environment of the mind.

We may further note that the negatively polarized adept will attempt to fashion that covenant for its own use, whereas the positively polarized entity may hold forth that which is exemplified by the astrological sword; that is, light and truth.

100.14 **QUESTIONER** Would there be two more appropriate objects or symbols to have the entity in Card Seven holding in its hands, other than the ones shown?

RA I am Ra. We leave this consideration to you, O student, and shall comment upon any observation which you may make.

100.15 **QUESTIONER** I will save that for next session, and I will ask if there is anything we can do to make the instrument more comfortable or improve the contact?

RA I am Ra. All is well. The appurtenances are most conscientiously placed. We thank this diligent group. There is much greater distortion towards harmony at this asking, and we join you in praise and thanksgiving. This is always the greatest boon to improvement of the contact, for it is the harmony of the group which supports this contact.

I am Ra. I leave you in the love and the light of the One. Go forth, therefore, rejoicing in the power and in the peace of the One Infinite Creator. Adonai.

101.0 **RA** I am Ra. I greet you in the love and in the light of the One Infinite Creator. We communicate now.

101.1 **QUESTIONER** Could you first please give me the condition of the instrument?

RA I am Ra. All energy levels of the instrument are somewhat diminished due to the distortions of physical pain and recent mental/emotional catalyst. However, the energy levels appear to be very liable to be improved in what you call your immediate future.

101.2 **QUESTIONER** Thank you. What has caused the swelling in Jim's body, and what can be done to heal it?

RA I am Ra. For the answer to this query we must begin with the consideration of the serpent, signifying wisdom. This symbol has the value of the ease of viewing the two faces of the one who is wise. Positive wisdom adorns the brow, indicating indigo-ray work. Negative wisdom, by which we intend to signify expressions which effectually separate the self from the other-self, may be symbolized by the poison of the fangs. To use that which a mind/body/spirit complex has gained of wisdom for the uses of separation is to invite the fatal bite of that wisdom's darker side.

The entity has a mental/emotional tendency, which has been lessening in distortion for some of your space/time, towards negative wisdom. The entity being already aware of this causes us not to dwell upon this point but merely to specifically draw the boundaries of the metaphysical background for the energizing of a series of bites from one of your second-density species. In this case the bite was no more than that of one of the arachnids, sometimes called the wood spider.

However, it is possible that were enough work done to test the origin of the pathology of the entity, it is within possibility/probability limits that the testing would show the bite of the cottonmouth rather than the bite of the common wood spider.

The energizing took its place within the lymphatic system of the entity's yellow-ray, physical body. Therefore the working continues. There is increasing strain upon the spleen, the supra-renal glands, the renal complex, and some possibility/probability of difficulty with the liver. Further, the lymphatic difficulties have begun to strain the entity's bronchial system. This is some general information upon what is to be noted as a somewhat efficient working.

The removal of these distortions has several portions:

Firstly, it is well to seek the good offices of the one known as Stuart so that harsh chemical means may be taken to reawaken the histaminic reflexes of the entity and to aid in the removal of edema.

Secondly, we suggest that which has already begun; that is, the request of the one known now to this group as Bob that this entity may focus its aid upon the metaphysical connections with the yellow-ray body.

Thirdly, the entity must take note of its physical vehicle's need for potassium. The ingesting of the fruit of the banana palm is recommended.

Fourthly, the links between the swelling of contumely and the apparent present situation is helpful.[1]

As always the support of the harmonious group is an aid, as is meditation. It is to be noted that this entity requires some discipline in the meditation which the others of the group do not find necessary in the same manner. Therefore, the entity may continue with its forms of meditation knowing that each in the group supports it entirely, although the instinct to share in the discipline is not always present.

Each entity has its ways of viewing and learning from the illusion, and each processes catalyst using unique circuitry. Thus all need not be the same to be equal in will and faith.

101.3 QUESTIONER Thank you. I will make a statement as to the way I see the action, and I would request Ra's comment. I see the present position as the Creator knowing Itself presently using the concept of polarization. We seem to accentuate or to produce catalyst to increase the desired polarization, whether the mechanism be random, through what we call

---

[1] In this context *contumely* may be defined as "arrogance, haughtiness, or insolence."

the higher self, or through the services of an oppositely polarized entity acting upon us with catalyst.

All of these seem to produce the same effect which is more intense polarization in the desired direction once that direction has been definitely chosen. I see catalyst of the second-density insect bite being a function of either, or of any, of the sources of which I have spoken, from random, to augmented through the higher self, or through the oppositely polarized services of those who monitor our activities—all of which have roughly the same ultimate effect. Would Ra comment on my observation?

RA I am Ra. We find your observations unexceptional and, in the large, correct.

101.4 **QUESTIONER** In this particular case, which avenue was the one that produced the catalyst of the bite?

RA I am Ra. The nature of catalyst is such that there is only one source, for the catalyst and experience are further attempts at specificity in dealing with the architecture of the unconscious mind of the self. Therefore, in an incarnational experience the self as Creator, especially the higher self, is the base from which catalyst stands to offer its service to the mind, body, or spirit.

In the sense which we feel you intend, the source was the fifth-density negative friend which had noted the gradual falling away of the inharmonious patterns of the distortion called anger/frustration in the entity. The insect was easily led to an attack, and the physical vehicle, which had long-standing allergies and sensitivities, was also easily led into the mechanisms of the failure of lymphatic function and the greatly diminished ability of the immune system to remove from the yellow-ray body that which distorted it.

101.5 **QUESTIONER** Something occurred to me. I am going to make a guess that my illness over the past week was a function of some action by my higher self to eliminate the possibility of a residence in the proximity of the large number of bees that I observed. Would Ra comment on my statement?

RA I am Ra. We can comment, not upon the questioner's physical distortions but upon the indubitable truth of second-density hive creatures; that is, that a hive mentality as a whole can be influenced by one strong metaphysical impulse. Both the instrument and the scribe have the capacity for great distortions toward nonviability, given such an attack by a great number of the stinging insects.

101.6   **QUESTIONER**   Are the thought-form parameters and other general parameters of the Oakdale Road address in Atlanta such that no cleansing would be necessary, if Ra has this information?

RA   I am Ra. No.

101.7   **QUESTIONER**   Would cleansing of the nature suggested for the other house just south of the airport in Atlanta be advisable for the Oakdale Road address?

RA   I am Ra. We note that any residence, whether previously benign (as is the one of which you speak) or previously of malignant character, needs the basic cleansing of the salt, water, and broom.

The benign nature of the aforementioned domicile is such that the cleansing could be done in two portions: that is, no egress or entrance through any but one opening for one cleansing. Then egress and entrance from all other places while the remaining portal is properly sealed.

The placing of salt may be done at the place which is not being sealed [during] the first of the cleansings, and the salt may be requested to act as seal and yet allow the passage of gentle spirits such as yourselves. We suggest that you speak to this substance and name each entity for which permission is needed in order to pass. Let no person pass without permission being asked of the salt. This is the case in the residence of which you speak.

101.8   **QUESTIONER**   Thank you. Could Ra give information on any way that we could give information to Greta Woodrew as to how to alleviate her present condition of swelling?

RA   I am Ra. We may only suggest that the honor of propinquity to light carries with it the Law of Responsibility.[2] The duty to refrain from contumely, discord, and all things which, when unresolved within, make way for workings lies before the instrument of which you speak. This

---

[2]   In this context, *propinquity* can be defined as "closeness or proximity."

entity may, if it is desired by the scribe, share our comments upon the working of the latter entity.

The entity which is given constant and unremitting approval by those surrounding it suffers from the loss of the mirroring effect of those which reflect truthfully rather than unquestioningly. This is not a suggestion to reinstate judgment but merely a suggestion for all those supporting instruments; that is, support, be harmonious, share in love, joy, and thanksgiving, but find love within truth, for each instrument benefits from this support more than from the total admiration which overcomes discrimination.

101.9   **QUESTIONER**   Thank you. I see that the forty-five minute timer window has passed, so I will ask if there is anything we can do to make the instrument more comfortable or improve the contact?

RA   I am Ra. We find that this instrument has used all the transferred energy and has been speaking using its vital energy reserve. We do suggest using the transferred sexual energy to the total exclusion of vital reserves if possible.

The alignments are as they must be for all to continue well. We are grateful for the conscientiousness of the support group.

I am Ra. I leave this group glorying in the love and in the light of the One Infinite Creator. Go forth rejoicing, therefore, in the power and in the peace of the Creator. Adonai.

SESSION 102

102.0 **RA** I am Ra. I greet you in the love and in the light of the One Infinite Creator. We communicate now.

102.1 **QUESTIONER** Would you first please give me the condition of the instrument?

RA I am Ra. The physical energy deficit of this entity is the most substantial across which we have come. The mental and mental/emotional distortions are near to balance, and the vital energy of the instrument as a whole is distorted towards health, or strength/weakness, due to the will of the instrument.

102.2 **QUESTIONER** Will Ra please tell us what caused the pain and cramping in the instrument's stomach, and what could be done to heal it?

RA In order to observe the cause of physical distortions toward illness one must look to the energy center which is blocked. In this situation, the blockage being yellow-ray, the experience has had the characteristics of that region of the chemical body. The so-called lacuna in the wind-written armor of light and love was closed and not only repaired but much improved.[1]

However, the distortions energized during this momentary lapse from free energy flow are serious and shall be continuing for, in all possibility/probability vortices, some of your space/time, for a predisposition to spasticity in the transverse colon has been energized.

There is also pre-existing weakness in pancreatic function, especially that linked with the hypothalamus. There is also the pre-existing damage to portions of the liver.

These lacks or distortions manifest in that portion of the system directly proceeding from the jejunum. Further, there is some irritation closer to the duodenum which causes the instrument to fail in assimilating foodstuffs. This is an allopathically caused irritation.

---

[1] In this context, *lacuna* can be defined as "an unfilled space or a gap."

The diet is of central import. We can go no further in observing the system of the entity as a full discussion of those distortions towards various weakness/strengths which contribute to the present difficulty begin with the lips and end with the anus.

We may note that the instrument has remained centered upon the Creator at a percentage exceeding ninety. This is the key. Continue in thanksgiving and gratitude for all things.

There are stronger anti-spasmodic drugs which the one not known to this instrument, but known as Arthur, may aid by the offering. The recommendation to do this—being as it is that which does not retain or remove life, and does further remove from the instrument its opportunities for study in this situation—needs must be withheld. We are not in a position to recommend treatment at this space/time beyond the watching of the types of foodstuffs ingested.

102.3 **QUESTIONER** I'm not quite sure I understood everything you said. Can you give me the last name of this Arthur, and where he is located?

RA I am Ra. We can.

102.4 **QUESTIONER** Will you please do that?

RA I am Ra. The entity, sound vibration Arthur, has a surname Schoen, and is of your locality.

102.5 **QUESTIONER** What foods should the instrument eliminate from her diet in order to alleviate these painful attacks?

RA I am Ra. The information gained from the one known as Bob is that which is to be recommended.

Further, all foodstuffs are to be cooked so that those things which are ingested be soft and easily macerated.

There is a complex addiction, due to long-standing eating habits, to your sugars. It is to be recommended that, therefore, this sugar be given in its more concentrated form in your time of late afternoon, as you term it, with the ingestion of the sugared libation approximately one to two of your hours after the evening meal.

It is further suggested that, since this instrument has been using sugars for carbohydrates, that a small amount of carbohydrate, low in sugar, be ingested approximately one to two of your hours before the sleeping period.

102.6 **QUESTIONER** As I understand what you say, the instrument is to have no sugar until late in the afternoon. Is that correct?

RA I am Ra. No.

102.7 **QUESTIONER** I didn't fully understand what you meant about when she should have the sugar. Could you clear that up, please?

RA I am Ra. The concentrated sugar; that is, the dessert, the ice cream, the cookie, should be ingested at that time. Small amounts of the fructose, maple, or raw honey may be ingested periodically, for, as we have said, the chemistry of this yellow-ray body is such that the sugar is being used by blood enzymes as would carbohydrates in a less distorted yellow-ray, physical vehicle.

102.8 **QUESTIONER** I'm sorry that I am so slow at picking up precisely what we're getting at here, but I want to be sure we get this right, so I'll probably ask a few more stupid questions. Was the spasm that caused the extreme pain a spasm of the ileum?

RA I am Ra. Partially. The transverse colon also spasmed, as did the ducts to the liver in its lower portion. There were also muscle spasms from the bronchial coverings down through the pelvis and from shoulder blades to hips. These sympathetic spasms are a symptom of the exhaustion of the entity's physical vehicle.

102.9 **QUESTIONER** Then these spasms, of course, were originally— The opening was made by yellow-ray blockage, but these spasms then are triggered, I am assuming, by the foodstuff which has to do with the ingestion of sugar, as I understand it. Am I correct?

RA I am Ra. You are partially correct.

102.10 **QUESTIONER** Then what else causes the spasm?

RA I am Ra. We speak of two types of cause:

The first or proximate cause was a meal with too much oil and too large a burden of undercooked vegetable material. The sugar of the dessert and the few sips of your coffee mixture also were not helpful.

The second cause—and this shall be stated clearly—is the energizing of any pre-existing condition in order to keep this group from functioning by means of removing the instrument from the ranks of those able to work with those of Ra.

102.11 **QUESTIONER** Now, is there— The two areas then that the instrument can look to for curing this problem . . . I understand that the yellow-ray blockage problem has completely repaired, shall I say. If this is not correct, could you make suggestions on that please?

RA I am Ra. Each entity must, in order to completely unblock yellow ray, love all which are in relationship to it, with hope only of the other-selves' joy, peace, and comfort.

102.12 **QUESTIONER** The second thing that the instrument must do to effect this cure is to be careful of diet which includes all that Ra has just stated and what Bob recommends from his readings.

There seem to be so many different things that could cause this spasm. I was just wondering if there is a general approach to foods. Could Ra recommend, say, those foods the instrument could eat that would have no chance of creating the problem that caused the spasm. Could Ra do that, please?

RA I am Ra. No.

102.13 **QUESTIONER** Is this because of the First Distortion?

RA I am Ra. No.

102.14 **QUESTIONER** Why cannot Ra do that?

RA I am Ra. There are no foods which this instrument can take with total confidence that no spasm shall occur. The spasming portions of the vehicle have become sensitized through great distortions towards that which you call pain.

102.15 **QUESTIONER** Is there a group of foods which is most likely not to cause the spasming condition, or any foods that Ra could mention that are highly probable not to cause spasm?

RA I am Ra. Yes.

102.16 **QUESTIONER** Would Ra please mention which foods are highly probable in not causing any spasming in the instrument's digestive system?

RA I am Ra. The liquids not containing carbonation, the well-cooked vegetable which is most light and soft, the well-cooked grains, the non-fatted meat such as the fish. You may note that some recommended foodstuffs overlap allergies and sensitivities due to the juvenile-rheumatoid-arthritic distortions. Further, although sugar, such as is in your sweetened desserts, represents a potential, we may suggest that it be included at this period for aforementioned reasons.

102.17 **QUESTIONER** Would Ra please estimate the length of time in our time periods for the probability of this problem, if we follow these curative measures, for the probability of this problem to continue in any extreme severity?

RA I am Ra. One of your moon's revolutions has a good possibility/probability vortex of seeing either the worsening of the spastic condition so that surgery becomes indicated, or the bettering of the situation so that the diet continues to be watched but the spasms be removed. The housing of the working is within the infection within the duodenum, the stomach, the jejunum, the ileum, the transverse colon, and portions of the liver. This shall be somewhat difficult to remove and constitutes perhaps the most efficient working to date.

We may suggest, again, that the one known as Bob may be of aid. The one known as Stuart could, if it wished, discover the infection which is only marginally detectable, but may prefer not to do so. In this case it would be well to request physical aid from an allopathic specialist such as that which has been mentioned.

102.18 **QUESTIONER** Do you mean by that Arthur Schoen?

RA I am Ra. That is correct.

102.19 **QUESTIONER** You mentioned the possibility of surgery. What would be the surgery to be done, specifically?

RA I am Ra. The body cannot long bear the extreme acidity which is the environment of such spasms and will develop the holes or ulcerations which then do appear upon the allopathic testings and suggest to the chirurgeon that which is to be excised.

102.20   **QUESTIONER** In other words, the removal of ulcers. Would this be a duodenic ulcer? Would this be the type of operation that you would perform for a duodenic ulcer?

RA I am Ra. If the ulceration occurs, it shall be past the jejunum and most likely include the ileum and upper portions of the transverse colon.

May we ask for one more query of normal length as this entity, though filled with enough transferred energy, has the most fragile framework through which we may channel this and our energies.

102.21   **QUESTIONER** Obviously we would very much like to not get to the point of surgery, and the only other alternative that comes to mind—other than the diet and the instrument's personal mental work—is healing through a healer. And I would like Ra's recommendation with respect to a non-allopathic type healer and any recommendations Ra could make for either Jim or myself to act in that capacity, or anyone else Ra could recommend so that we wouldn't have to go through this surgical operation if it seems to become necessary. And if we could start working on one of these other approaches right away I think it might be highly recommended.

Would Ra comment on that, please?

RA I am Ra. We salute the opening of compassion circuitry in the questioner but note that that which is being experienced by this group is being experienced within an healing atmosphere. The healing hands of each have limited use when the distortion has so many metaphysical layers and mixtures.

Therefore, look not to a healing but to the joy of companionship, for each is strong and has its feet set upon the way. The moon casts its shadows. What shall you see? Link hands and walk towards the sun. In this instance this is the greatest healing. For the physical vehicle we can suggest far less than you had hoped.

102.22   **QUESTIONER** I'll just ask then if there's anything we can do to make the instrument more comfortable or improve the contact?

RA I am Ra. All is well. Find love and thanksgiving together, and each shall support each. The alignments are conscientious.

We are known to you as Ra. We leave you in the love and in the light of the One Infinite Creator. Go forth, then, merry and glad in His power and peace. Adonai.

SESSION 103

103.0 **RA** I am Ra. I greet you in the love and in the light of the One Infinite Creator. We communicate now.

103.1 **QUESTIONER** Could you first please give me the condition of the instrument?

RA I am Ra. The physical distortions of the instrument remain serious.

Further, the vital energies of this mind/body/spirit complex are much diminished, although acceptable for the needs of this working. This is to be noted as the lowest, or most distorted, vital reading of this all-important energy.

The mental and mental/emotional distortions are as last seen.

We find the will of the instrument, having been unwisely used, to have encouraged the distortions of vital energy. It is well that the instrument ponder this.

103.2 **QUESTIONER** What is the situation with respect, and condition with respect, to the physical problems with the digestive portions of the body that the instrument had previously?

RA The yellow-ray— We must correct ourselves. I am Ra. Please expel breath across this instrument's chest area.

[*This was done as directed.*]

103.3 **RA** I am Ra. The channel is now satisfactory. We find the yellow-ray, chemical body of the instrument to be exhausted but to be attempting the improvement by action such as exercise and diet.

We may state that the infection has not completely left the body complex, although it is far less virulent.

103.4 **QUESTIONER** The instrument asks the question why she lost her joy in the recent past? Would Ra comment, please?

RA I am Ra. The instrument made a free-will decision not to address the physical catalyst causing great pain by means of the allopathically prescribed chemical compound, which the instrument was sure would be efficacious due to its reliance upon the suggestions of Ra.

Thus the catalyst was given in a more complete form. The outer service to others became nearly impossible, causing the entity to experience, once again, the choice of the martyr; that is, to put value in a fatal action and die, or to put value on consciousness of the creation and of the One Creator and, thereby, live. The instrument, through will, chose the latter path.

However, the mind and mental/emotional distortions did not give the support to this decision necessary to maintain a state of unity which this entity normally experiences and has experienced since its incarnation's beginnings.

Since this catalyst has been accepted, the work begun to remove distortions blocking the indigo ray might well be continued apace.

103.5 **QUESTIONER** Could Ra recommend work appropriate for removing indigo-ray blockage?

RA I am Ra. We cannot recommend for the general situation, for in each case the distortional vortex is unique. In this particular nexus, the more appropriate working is in the mental and mental/emotional powers of analysis and observation. When the strongest and least distorted complex is set in support, then the less strong portions of the complex shall be strengthened.

This entity has long worked with this catalyst. However, this is the first occasion wherein the drugs to dull the pain that sharpens the catalyst have been refused.

103.6 **QUESTIONER** What is the present situation with respect to our fifth-density, service-to-self oriented companion?

RA I am Ra. This entity has, for some period of your space/time, been at rest. However, it has been alerted to the workings taking place and is soon to be your companion once again.

103.7 **QUESTIONER** Can Ra recommend anything that the instrument can do, or that we can do, to improve any of the energies of the instrument?

RA I am Ra. This is previously covered material. We have outlined the path the instrument may take in thought.

103.8 **QUESTIONER** I didn't mean to cover previously covered material. I meant to add any of this to specifically focus on at this time, the best possible thing that we or the instrument could do to improve these energies, the salient activity.

RA I am Ra. Before responding we ask your vigilance during pain flares as the channel is acceptable but is being distorted periodically by the severe physical distortions of the yellow-ray, chemical body of the instrument.

Those salient items for the support group are praise and thanksgiving in harmony. These the group has accomplished with such a degree of acceptability that we cavil not at the harmony of the group.[1]

As to the instrument, the journey from worth-in-action to worth-*in-esse* is arduous.[2] The entity has denied itself in order to be free from that which it calls addiction.[3] This sort of martyrdom—and here we speak of the small but symbolically great sacrifice of the clothing—causes the entity to frame a selfhood in poorness which feeds unworthiness, unless the poverty is seen to be true richness.

In other words, good works for the wrong reasons cause confusion and distortion. We encourage the instrument to value itself and to see that its true requirements are valued by the self. We suggest contemplation of true richness of being.

103.9 **QUESTIONER** Is there anything else that either we or the instrument can do that would specifically work on the vital energy to increase it—of the instrument?

RA I am Ra. We have come up against the full stop of free will.

---

1 In this context, *cavil* can be defined as "to make petty or unnecessary objections."

2 Likewise, *in esse* can be defined as "in being," or, as Carla defined it years later: "*in esse* is Latin for: in and of yourself; just because you are, you're worthwhile."

3 Carla had made a New Year's resolution to give up buying clothes for herself for one year.

103.10 **QUESTIONER** In that case I have a few questions on Card Seven in order to finish off our first run-through of the archetypes of the mind. There is a T with two right angles above it on the chest of the entity in Card Seven. We have guessed that the lower T has to do with the possibility of choosing either path in the transformation, and the upper two angles representing the Great Way of the left- or the right-hand path in a mental transformation that makes the change from space/time into time/space, you might say.

This is difficult to express. Is there anything correct [*chuckles*] in this guess?

RA I am Ra. Yes.

103.11 **QUESTIONER** Would Ra comment on that?

RA I am Ra. The use of the tau and the architect's square is, indeed, intended to suggest the proximity of the space/time of the Great Way's environment to time/space.[4] We find this observation most perceptive.

The entire mood, shall we say, of the Great Way is, indeed, dependent upon its notable difference from the Significator. The Significator is the significant self, to a great extent but not entirely, influenced by the lowering of the veil.

The Great Way of the Mind, the Body, or the Spirit draws the environment which has been the new architecture caused by the veiling process and, thusly, dipped in the great, limitless current of time/space.

103.12 **QUESTIONER** I am guessing that the wheels on this chariot indicate the ability of the mind to be able now to move in time/space. Is this correct?

RA I am Ra. We cannot say that the observation is totally incorrect, for there is as much work in time/space as the individual who evokes this complex of concepts has assimilated.

---

4   *Tau* is the 19th letter of the Greek alphabet (τ), and in this context refers to the "tau cross," a shape which is similar to a capitalized "T". Also in heraldry, a type of cross called a "tau cross."

However, it would be more appropriate to draw the attention to the fact that although the chariot is wheeled, it is not harnessed to that which draws it by a physical or visible harness. What then, O student, links and harnesses the chariot's power of movement to the chariot?

103.13 QUESTIONER I'll have to think about that one. Unless— I'll come back to that.

We were thinking of replacing the sword in the right hand with the magical sphere and a downward scepter in the left hand (similar to Card Five, the Significator) as more appropriate for this card. Would Ra comment on that, please?

RA I am Ra. This is quite acceptable, especially if the sphere may be imaged as spherical and effulgent.

103.14 QUESTIONER The bent left leg of the two sphinxes indicates a transformation that occurs on the left that doesn't on the right, possibly an inability in that position to move. Does this have any merit?

RA I am Ra. The observation has merit in that it may serve as the obverse of the connotation intended.

The position is intended to show two items, one of which is the dual possibilities of the time-full characters there drawn. The resting is possible in time, as is the progress. If a mixture is attempted, the upright, moving leg will be greatly hampered by the leg that is bent.

The other meaning has to do with the same right angle, with its architectural squareness, as the device upon the breast of the actor.

Time/space is close in this concept complex, brought close due to the veiling process and its efficaciousness in producing actors who wish to use the resources of the mind in order to evolve.

103.15 QUESTIONER I am assuming that the skirt is skewed to the left for the same reason that it is in Card Number Four, indicating the distance service-to-self polarized entities keep from others. And I am also assuming that the face is turned to the left for the same reason that it is in Card Number Five, because of the nature of catalyst. Is this roughly correct?

RA I am Ra. Please expel breath over the breast of the instrument from right to left.

[*This was done as directed.*]

I am Ra. That is well.

Your previous supposition is, indeed, roughly correct.

We might also note that we, in forming the original images for your peoples, were using the cultural commonplaces of artistic expression of those in Egypt. The face is drawn to the side most often, as are the feet turned. We made use of this and, thus, wish to soften the significance of the side-long look. In no case thus far in these deliberations, however, has any misinterpretation or unsuitable interpretation been drawn.

103.16 **QUESTIONER** Our appropriate time for working right now, I believe, is close to a close, and I would like to ask . . . that is, the two times we had to expel breath . . . what is the problem, or what is— Why in this session do we have to do that, when we didn't in most others?

RA I am Ra. This instrument is unaware of the method used to contact Ra. However, its desire was particularly strong at the outset of this working for this working to transpire. Thus it inadvertently was somewhat premature in its leaving of the yellow-ray, physical body.

In this state the object was dropped upon the instrument which you call the tie-pin microphone. The unexpected contact caused injury of the chest muscles, and we would advise some care depending from this working to avoid stress so that this injury may heal.

There is a metaphysical component to this injury and, therefore, we wished to be quite sure that all portions of the environment were cleansed. Since this place of working has not its usual level of protection, we used your breath to so cleanse the environment which was at risk.

103.17 **QUESTIONER** Is the reason for the lack of usual level of protection the fact that it has been a considerable time since we have worked in here?

RA I am Ra. No.

103.18 **QUESTIONER** What is the reason?

RA I am Ra. The lack of regular repetition of the so-called Banishing Ritual is the lack of which we spoke.

103.19 **QUESTIONER** From this I assume that it would be most appropriate to daily perform the Banishing Ritual in this room. Is this correct?

RA I am Ra. That is acceptable.

103.20 **QUESTIONER** I don't want to overtire the instrument. We're running close to time. I will just ask if there is anything we can do to improve the contact or make the instrument more comfortable, or if there is anything else that Ra could state at this time that would aid us?

RA I am Ra. We find the alignments quite fastidiously observed. You are conscientious. Continue in support, one for the other, and find the praise and thanksgiving that harmony produces. Rest your cares and be merry.

I am Ra. I leave you glorying in the love and in the light of the One Infinite Creator. Go forth, therefore, rejoicing in the power and in the peace of the One Infinite Creator. Adonai.

104.0 **RA** I am Ra. We greet you in the love and in the light of the One Infinite Creator. We communicate now.

104.1 **QUESTIONER** Could you first please give me the condition of the instrument?

RA I am Ra. The readings are somewhat less distorted towards physical bankruptcy and vital [energy] loss than at the previous asking. There is still considerable bias in these readings.

104.2 **QUESTIONER** The instrument would like to know what's the optimum amount of aerobics, walking, and whirlpool exercises for the best condition at this time?

RA I am Ra. We shall answer in two ways:

Firstly, to speak to the general case, which pertains to this instrument in varying degree, each form of exercise is well accomplished approximately three to four times per your week. The amount of exercise, all quantified as one sum, is approximately one hour per diurnal period.

We now answer in a second way, distorted in this response to the duple conditions of yellow-ray, physical difficulty and mind-complex distortion. The swirling waters then must needs be viewed as being appropriate four to five of your times per week. The walking and the exercising, as much as is desired by the entity. The total of all these should in no case exceed ninety minutes per diurnal period.

The yellow-ray, physical body has been experiencing that which is called lupoid changes in much tissue of muscle and some of the organs as well. The exercise regains the wasting physical muscular strength. In some ways the walking is the more appropriate exercise due to the proximity of the entity to second-density creatures, particularly your trees.

However, the habitation you enjoy does not offer such opportunity, and instead offers the proximity to creations of mind/body/spirit complexes. This does not feed the mental/emotional needs of this entity although it produces the same physical result. The exercise fulfills more of the mental/emotional need due to the entity's fondness for rhythmic expressions of the body such as those found in athletic endeavors derivative of the artifact system which is known among your peoples as the dance.[1]

We suggest the support group encourage any exercise except that which exceeds the time limit, which is already far beyond the physical limitations of this body complex.

It is the way of distortion that in order to balance a distortion one must accentuate it. Thusly, the over-wearing of the body may, if correctly motivated, produce a lack of deficit, at which juncture the lesser exercise limitations should be put into practice.

104.3 **QUESTIONER** The instrument has determined that the unwise use of her will is its use without the joy and faith components and constitutes martyrdom. Would Ra comment on that, please?

RA I am Ra. We are pleased that the entity has pondered that which has been given. We would comment as follows:

It is salubrious for the instrument to have knowledge which is less distorted towards martyrdom and which is rich in promise.[2] The entity which is strong to think shall either be strong to act or that which it has shall be removed. Thus manifestation of knowledge is an area to be examined by the instrument.

We would further note that balancing—which, in this entity's case, is best accomplished in analysis and manifestation seated with the contemplation of silence—may be strengthened by manifested silence and lack of routine activity. We may go no further than this recommendation of regularized leisure, and desire that the entity discover the fundamental truths of these distortions as it will.

104.4 **QUESTIONER** Is there anything further that we can do to help the instrument's stomach and back spasming problem?

RA I am Ra. The greatest aid is already being given to the fullest. The encouragement of the instrument to refrain from the oil-fried nature of foodstuffs in its intake is helpful. Cheerful harmony is helpful.

---

[1] What Ra took 26 words to say was that Carla loved to dance.

[2] In this context, *salubrious* can be defined as "favorable to health or well-being."

The spasms must subside as a function of the entity's indigo-ray work and, to some extent, the recommendations made in response to a previous query.

The definitive refraining from over-stepping the already swollen boundaries of physical limitation is recommended. The infection remains, and the symptoms are now far less medicable, the entity having chosen the catalyst.

104.5 **QUESTIONER** Can you tell us what is wrong with our cat Gandalf's eyes?

RA I am Ra. The one known as Gandalf nears the end of its incarnation. Its eyesight dims, and the aqueous membrane becomes tough. This is not a comfortable circumstance, but is one which causes the entity no true discomfort.

104.6 **QUESTIONER** Is there anything that we can do to alleviate this situation?

RA I am Ra. There is a course of therapy which would aid the situation. However, we do not recommend it as the condition is more benign than the treatment.

104.7 **QUESTIONER** I don't understand. Could you explain what you meant?

RA I am Ra. A doctor of the allopathic tradition would give you the drops for the eyes. The cat would find the experience of being confined while the drops were given more distorted than the discomfort it now feels but is able to largely ignore.

104.8 **QUESTIONER** Can the cat see at all?

RA I am Ra. Yes.

104.9 **QUESTIONER** Well, does it seem that the cat will lose all of its vision in the near future, or is the cat very near death?

RA I am Ra. The one known as Gandalf will not lose eyesight, or life, on most possibility/probability vortices for three of your seasons, approximately.

104.10 **QUESTIONER** I feel very bad about the condition of the cat and really would like to help it. Can Ra suggest anything that we can do to help out Gandalf?

RA I am Ra. Yes.

104.11 QUESTIONER What would that be?

RA I am Ra. Firstly, we would suggest that possibility/probability vortices include those in which the entity known as Gandalf has a lengthier incarnation.

Secondly, we would suggest that this entity goes to a graduation if it desires. Otherwise, it may choose to reincarnate to be with those companions it has loved.

Thirdly, the entity known to you as Betty has the means of making the entity more distorted towards comfort/discomfort.

104.12 QUESTIONER Do you want to tell me who you mean by Betty? I'm not sure who that is. And what Betty would do?

RA I am Ra. The one known as Carla has this information.

104.13 QUESTIONER Well, I was concerned about the possibility of moving. If we did move this would make it very difficult for Gandalf to find his way around a new place if he can't see. Does he see enough to be able to find his way around a new environment?

RA I am Ra. The vision is less than adequate but is nearly accommodated by a keen sense of smell and of hearing. The companions and the furnishings being familiar, a new milieu would be reasonably expected to be satisfactorily acceptable within a short period of your space/time.

104.14 QUESTIONER Could we administer the drops you spoke of that would help his eyesight so that he wouldn't find the . . . so that he wouldn't be confined? Is there any way that we could do that?

RA I am Ra. It is unlikely.

104.15 QUESTIONER There's nothing that we can do to— Is there any other possibility of using any techniques to help his eyesight?

RA I am Ra. No.

104.16 QUESTIONER Is this loss of eyesight— What is the metaphysical reason for the loss of the eyesight? What brought it about?

RA I am Ra. In this case the metaphysical component is tiny. This is the condign catalyst of old age.[3]

104.17 **QUESTIONER** Would the drops that you spoke of that would aid the eyesight . . . how much would they aid the eyesight if they were to be administered?

RA I am Ra. Over a period of applications the eyesight would improve somewhat, perhaps 20, perhaps 30%. The eye region would feel less tight. Balanced against this is rapidly increasing stiffness of motion so that the holding in a still position is necessarily quite uncomfortable.

104.18 **QUESTIONER** Then Ra thinks that the benefit derived from the drops would not be worth the cat's discomfort. This would probably— Is there any way that the cat could be given anesthetic and drops put in the eyes so that the cat was not aware of getting the drops?

RA I am Ra. The harm done by putting the allopathic anesthetic into the body complex of this harvestable entity far overshadows the stillness accruing therefrom which would allow administration of medicaments.

104.19 **QUESTIONER** I'm sorry to belabor this subject so much, but I was really hoping to come up with some way of helping Gandalf. I assume, then, that Ra has suggested that we just leave things as they are.

How many applications of drops would be necessary to get some help for the eyes, roughly?

RA Approximately 40 to 60.

104.20 **QUESTIONER** Forty to six— What, each day, once a day, or something like that?

RA I am Ra. Please expel breath over this instrument's breast.

[*This was done as directed.*]

104.21 **QUESTIONER** Is that satisfactory?

RA I am Ra. Yes.

---

3 In this context, *condign* can be defined as "appropriate or worthy."

104.22 **QUESTIONER** I had asked if the drops should be administered once per diurnal period. Is that correct?

RA I am Ra. This depends upon the allopathic physician from whom you receive them.

104.23 **QUESTIONER** What is the name of the drops?

RA I am Ra. We have a difficulty. Therefore, we shall refrain from answering this query.

104.24 **QUESTIONER** I am sorry to belabor this point. I am very concerned about the cat, and I understand that Ra recommend we don't use it. I just . . . use the drops, and we won't. I just wanted to know what it was we weren't doing that would help the eyesight. I apologize for belaboring this point.

I'll close just by asking Ra if you have any further recommendation that you could make with respect to this animal . . . this cat?

RA I am Ra. Rejoice in its companionship.

104.25 **QUESTIONER** [Sigh.] When we got our introduction back from our publisher to the book which was originally called *The Law Of One*,[4] in the introduction Carla had been speaking of reincarnation, and there was a sentence added. It said: "For although originally part of Jesus' teachings, they were censored from all subsequent editions by the Empress." Would Ra please comment on the source of that being placed in our introduction?

RA I am Ra. This follows the way of subjectively interesting happenings, conditions, circumstances, or coincidences.

We would suggest one more full query at this time.

104.26 **QUESTIONER** Prior to the veiling process there was, I am assuming, no archetypical plan for the evolutionary process. It was totally left up to the free will of the mind/body/spirits to evolve in any way that they desired. Is this correct?

RA I am Ra. No.

---

4 See footnote on 84.6 for information regarding the original books.

I am Ra. We leave you in appreciation of the circumstances of the great illusion in which you now choose to play the pipe and timbrel and move in rhythm. We are also players upon a stage. The stage changes. The acts ring down. The lights come up once again. And throughout the grand illusion, and the following, and the following, there is the undergirding majesty of the One Infinite Creator. All is well. Nothing is lost. Go forth rejoicing in the love and the light, the peace and the power of the One Infinite Creator.

I am Ra. Adonai.

SESSION 105

105.0 **RA** I am Ra. I greet you, my friends, in the love and in the light of the One Infinite Creator. We communicate now.

105.1 **QUESTIONER** Could you first please give me the condition of the instrument?

RA I am Ra. The vital energies of this instrument are in a much more biased state than the previous asking, with the faculties of will and faith having regained their prominent place in this entity's existence and balance. The physical deficit continues.

105.2 **QUESTIONER** Sorry that we have to ask so many maintenance questions. We seem to be in a confused condition now with respect to our abilities to continue in the direction we wish to with questioning on the archetypical mind.

I feel it necessary to ask what the cause of the symmetrical welts on the instrument's back is, and is there anything further that we can do to heal the instrument of any conditions, including these welts or their cause?

RA I am Ra. The welting is a symptom of that which has been a prolonged psychic greeting. The opportunity for this entity to experience massive allergic reaction from streptococcal and staphylococcal viruses[1] has been offered in hopes that this entity would wish to leave the incarnation. The previous occurrence of this state of the mind complex occurring upon, in your time-numbering system, the ninth month, the twelfth day, of your present planetary solar revolution caught your fifth-density companion unprepared. The entity is now prepared.

There have been two instances wherein this entity could have started the reaction since the first opportunity was missed:

Firstly, the opportunity to separate self from other-self in connection with the choosing of an house.

Secondly, the possible vision of self separated from other-self in regard to

---

[1] These are actually bacteria.

the dissolving of mundane bonds concerning the leaving of this dwelling.

Both opportunities were met by this entity with a refusal to separate self from other-self, with further work also upon the indigo-ray level concerning the avoidance of martyrdom while maintaining unity in love.

Thusly, this instrument has had its immunal defenses breached and its lymphatic system involved in the invasion of these viri. You may see some merit in a purging of the instrument's yellow-ray, chemical body in order to more quickly aid the weakened body complex in its attempt to remove these substances. Techniques include therapeutic enemas or colonics, the sauna once or twice in a day, and the use of vigorous rubbing of the integument for the period of approximately seven of your diurnal periods.

We speak not of diet, not because it might not aid, but because this entity ingests small quantities of any substance and is already avoiding certain substances, notably fresh milk and oil.

105.3 **QUESTIONER** Is there any particular place the integument should be vigorously rubbed?

RA I am Ra. No.

105.4 **QUESTIONER** Could you please tell me what caused Jim's kidney problem to return, and what could be done to heal it?

RA I am Ra. The entity, Jim, determined that it would cleanse itself and thus would spend time/space and space/time in pursuit and contemplation of perfection. The dedication to this working was intensified until the mind/body/spirit complex rang in harmony with this intention.

The entity did not grasp the literal way in which metaphysical intentions are translated by the body complex of one working in utter unity of purpose. The entity began the period of prayer, fasting, penitence, and rejoicing.

The body complex, which was not yet fully recovered from the nephrotic syndrome, began to systematically cleanse each organ, sending all the detritus that was not perfect through kidneys which were not given enough liquid to dilute the toxins being released. The toxins stayed with the body complex and reactivated a purely physical illness. There is no metaphysical portion in this relapse.

The healing is taking place in manifestation of an affirmation of body complex health which, barring untoward circumstance, shall be completely efficacious.

105.5 **QUESTIONER** Is there any consideration of the appropriateness of the house at Lake Lanier, which we intend to move to, or special preparation other than that planned advisable?

RA I am Ra. We believe you have queried obliquely. Please re-query.

105.6 **QUESTIONER** We planned to cleanse the property at the Lake Lanier location using the techniques prescribed by Ra in earlier sessions having to do with salt for 36 hours, etc. I would like to know if this is sufficient, or if there is any salient problem with respect to moving to that house that Ra could advise upon at this time, please.

RA I am Ra. The cleansing of the dwelling of which you speak need be only three nights and two days. This dwelling is benign. The techniques are acceptable.

We find three areas in which the use of garlic as previously described would be beneficial:

Firstly, the bunk bed room, below the top sleeping pallet.

Secondly, the exterior of the dwelling facing the road, and centering about the small rocks, approximately two-thirds of the length of the dwelling from the driveway side.

Thirdly, there is the matter of the boathouse. We suggest weekly cleansings of that area with garlic, the cut onion, and the walking of a light-filled perimeter. The garlic and onion, renewed weekly, should remain permanently hung, suspended from string or wire between workings.

105.7 **QUESTIONER** Just so I don't make a mistake in interpreting your directions with respect to the second area outside the house, could you give me a distance and magnetic compass heading from, say, the exact center of the dwelling to that position?

RA I am Ra. We may only be approximate but would suggest a distance of 37 feet, a magnetic heading of 84 to 92 degrees.

105.8 **QUESTIONER** I know it's unimportant for our purposes, but from a philosophical point of view I don't want to do anything to upset the Law of Confusion, so don't feel that it is necessary to answer this, but I was wondering what the condition was that created the necessity for such continual cleansing of the boathouse?

RA I am Ra. The intent is to create a perimeter within which the apiary denizens will not find it necessary to sting and, indeed, will not find it promising to inhabit.

105.9 **QUESTIONER** Are you speaking of bees or wasps or creatures of that type?

RA I am Ra. That is so.

105.10 **QUESTIONER** Are Jim's plans and ritual for deconsecrating this dwelling sufficient, or should something be added or changed?

RA I am Ra. No change is necessary. The points necessary to be included in consecration or deconsecration of a place are covered. We may suggest that each second-density, woody plant which you have invested during your tenancy within this dwelling be thanked and blessed.

105.11 **QUESTIONER** Is there any other suggestion that Ra could make with respect to any part of this move that is planned? And will we have any problems at all in contacting Ra in the new dwelling, and if so, would Ra tell us about those, and what we could do to alleviate any problems in contacting Ra in the new [*location*]?

RA I am Ra. We weigh this answer carefully, for it comes close to abrogation of free will, but find the proximity acceptable due to this instrument's determination to be of service to the One Infinite Creator regardless of personal circumstance.

Any physical aid upon the part of the instrument in the packing and unpacking will activate those allergic reactions lying dormant, for the most part, at this time. This entity is allergic to those items which are unavoidable in transitions within your third-density illusion—that is, dust, mildew, etc. The one known as Bob will be of aid in this regard. The scribe should take care also to imbibe a doubled quantity of liquids in order that any allergically caused toxins may be flushed from the body complex.

There is no difficulty in resuming contact through this tuned instrument with the social memory complex, Ra, in the chosen dwelling, or, indeed, in any place whatsoever once physical and metaphysical cleansing has been accomplished.

105.12 **QUESTIONER** I have come to the conclusion that the meaning of the hawk that we had about a year ago when we started to move the first time had to do with the non-benign nature, in the metaphysical sense, of the house which I had picked for the move. If it isn't a problem with the Law of Confusion I think that it'd be philosophically interesting to know if I am correct with respect to that.

RA I am Ra. What bird comes to affirm for Ra? What bird would be chosen to warn? We ask the questioner to ponder these queries.

105.13 **QUESTIONER** We have been, you might say, experimentally determining a lot of things about the body—the next portion of the tarot—and have been experiencing some of the feedback effects, I might say, between the mind and the body. I sense, from everything that we have done so far with respect to these effects, that the great value of the third-density, yellow-ray body at this time is as a device that feeds back catalyst to a mind to create the polarization.

I would say that this is the major value of the third-density body here, and would ask Ra if initially when the mind/body/spirit (not the mind/body/spirit complex, but the mind/body/spirit) was designed for third-density experience, if this was the major use of the yellow-ray body? And if not, what was the purpose of the yellow-ray body?

RA I am Ra. The description which began your query is suitable for the function of the mind/body/spirit or the mind/body/spirit complex. The position in creation of physical manifestation changed not one whit when the veil of forgetting was dropped.

105.14 **QUESTIONER** Then the yellow-ray body, from the very beginning, was designed as what Ra has called an athanor for the mind: a device, you might say, to accelerate the evolution of the mind. Is this correct?

RA I am Ra. It is perhaps more accurate to note that the yellow-ray, physical vehicle is a necessity without which the mind/body/spirit complex cannot pursue evolution at any pace.

105.15 **QUESTIONER** Then you are saying that the evolution of that portion of the individual that is not yellow-ray is not possible without the clothing, at intervals, in the yellow-ray body. Is this correct?

RA I am Ra. No.

105.16 **QUESTIONER** Would you clear up my thinking on that? I didn't quite understand your statement.

RA I am Ra. Each mind/body/spirit, or mind/body/spirit complex, has an existence simultaneous with that of creation. It is not dependent upon any physical vehicle. However, in order to evolve, change, learn, and manifest the Creator, the physical vehicles appropriate to each density are necessary. Your query implied that physical vehicles accelerated growth. The more accurate description is that they permit growth.

105.17 **QUESTIONER** Now, as an example I would like to take the distortion of a disease or bodily malfunction prior to the veil and compare it to that after the veil. Let us assume that the conditions that Jim, for instance, experienced with respect to his kidney malfunction had been an experience that occurred prior to the veil. Would this experience have occurred prior to the veil? Would it have been different? And if so, how?

RA I am Ra. The anger of separation is impossible without the veil. The lack of awareness of the body's need for liquid is unlikely without the veil. The decision to contemplate perfection in discipline is quite improbable without the veil.

105.18 **QUESTIONER** Now, I would like to, then, examine a sample, shall we say, bodily distortion prior to the veil and how it would affect the mind. Could Ra give an example of that, please?

RA I am Ra. This general area has been covered.[2] We shall recapitulate here.

The patterns of illness, disease, and death are a benignant demesne within the plan of incarnational experience.[3] As such, some healing would occur

---

[2] Previously covered in 83.3–5, 83.20, and 105.17.

[3] In this context, *demesne* can be defined as "territory over which authority is exercised." It is an archaic synonym of the present-day "domain."

by decision of mind/body/spirits, and incarnations were experienced with the normal ending of illness to death, accepted as such since, without the veil, it is clear that the mind/body/spirit continues. Thusly, the experiences, both good and bad, or joyful and sad, of the mind/body/spirit before veiling would be pale, without vibrancy or the keen edge of interest that such brings in the post-veiling mind/body/spirit complex.

105.19 **QUESTIONER** At the end of an incarnation, before veiling, did the entity appear physically to have aged, say like entities at the normal end of incarnation in our present illusion— Did they . . . were they wrinkled and old, did they . . . did the Significator look like that?

RA I am Ra. The Significator of Mind, Body, or Spirit is a portion of the archetypical mind and looks as each envisions such to appear. The body of a mind/body/spirit before veiling showed all the signs of aging which acquaint you now with the process leading to the removal from third-density incarnation of the mind/body/spirit complex. It is well to recall that the difference betwixt mind/body/spirits and mind/body/spirit complexes is a forgetting within the deeper mind. Physical appearances and surface and instinctual activities are much the same.

105.20 **QUESTIONER** Then I was wondering the root reason for the change in appearance that we see as the aging process? I am trying to uncover a basic philosophical premise here that I may be shooting in the dark at and not questioning on correctly, but I am trying to get at the reason behind the design of this change in appearance when it seems to me that it was just as possible for the mind/body/spirit, or mind/body/spirit complex, just to simply look the same throughout an incarnation. Could Ra explain the reason for this change?

RA I am Ra. When the discipline of the personality has led the mind/body/spirit complex into the fifth, and especially the sixth, level of study, it is no longer necessary to build destruction of the physical vehicle into its design, for the spirit complex is so experienced as a shuttle that it is aware when the appropriate degree of intensity of learning and increment of lesson has been achieved.

Within third density, not to build into the physical vehicle its ending would be counterproductive to the mind/body/spirit complexes therein residing; for within the illusion it seems more lovely to be within the illusion than to drop the garment which has carried the mind/body/spirit complex and move on.

105.21 QUESTIONER I see, then, that it is, shall we say, when an individual reaches a very old age, then it becomes apparent to him in third density that he's worn out. Therefore, he's not attached to this vehicle as firmly, with a desire to stay in it, as he would be with a good-looking, well-functioning one.

Now, after the veil, the body is definitely an athanor for the mind. Prior to the veiling, did the body serve as an athanor for the mind at all?

RA I am Ra. Yes.

You may ask one more full query.

105.22 QUESTIONER I believe that I should ask at this time . . . is there anything that we can do to make the instrument more comfortable or improve the contact? (Since last session I wasn't able to get that in, and I think it's important.)

RA I am Ra. We find the weariness of the group well-balanced by its harmony. That weariness shall continue in any future circumstance during your incarnations. Therefore look you to your love and thanksgiving for each other, and join always in fellowship, correcting each broken strand of that affection with patience, comfort, and quietness.

We find all meticulously observed in the alignments and give you these words only as reminder. All that can be done for the instrument seems done with an whole heart, and the instrument itself is working in the indigo ray with perseverance.

We have previously mentioned some temporary measures for the instrument. If these are adopted, additional liquids shall be imbibed by the instrument and by the questioner, whose bond with the instrument is such that each difficulty for one is the same, in sympathy, for the other.

I am Ra. I leave you rejoicing merrily in the love and the light, the power and the peace of the One Infinite Creator. Adonai.

SESSION 106

106.0 **RA** I am Ra. I greet you in the love and in the light of the One Infinite Creator. We communicate now.

106.1 **QUESTIONER** Could you first please give me the condition of the instrument?

RA I am Ra. The parameters of this instrument are marginal, both physically and mental/emotionally. The vital energy of this entity is biased towards strength/weakness.

106.2 **QUESTIONER** By "marginal," do you mean that— Well, let me put it this way. What would the instrument do to make the marginal condition much better?

RA I am Ra. The instrument is proceeding through a portion of the incarnational experience during which the potential for mortal distortion of the left renal system is great. Less important, but adding to the marginality of distortion towards viability, are severe allergic reactions and the energizing of this and other distortions towards weakness/strength. The mental/emotional complex is engaged in what may best be termed inappropriate compassion.

106.3 **QUESTIONER** Would Ra please recommend the steps we should take to alleviate or reverse the conditions of which you just spoke?

RA I am Ra. We can do this. The renal distortions are subject to affirmations. The entity, at present, beginning what may be called initiation, is releasing toxins, and therefore larger amounts of liquid to aid in the dilution of these toxins is helpful. The allergies are already being largely controlled by affirmation and the near-constant aid of the healer known as Bob. Further aid may be achieved by the relocation of dwelling and future vigilance against humidity exceeding the healthful amount in the atmosphere breathed.

The mental/emotional distortions are somewhat less easily lessened. However, the questioner and instrument together shall find it possible to do such a working.

106.4 **QUESTIONER** How serious and critical is this renal problem? Is drinking liquids (I assume water is the best) the only thing we can do for that, or is there something else?

RA I am Ra. Note the interrelationship of mind and body complexes. This is one example of such interweaving of the design of catalyst and experience. The period of renal delicacy is serious, but only potentially. Should the instrument desire to leave this incarnational experience, the natural and non-energized opportunity to do so has been in-built—just as the period during which the same entity did, in fact, leave the incarnational experience and then return by choice was inlaid.[1]

However, the desire to leave and be no more a portion of this particular experiential nexus can and has been energized. This is a point for the instrument to ponder, and an appropriate point for the support group to be watchful in regards to care for the instrument. So are mind and body plaited up as the tresses of hair of a maiden.

The nature of this entity is gay and sociable so that it is fed by those things we have mentioned previously: the varieties of experience with other-selves and other locations and events being helpful, as well as the experience of worship and the singing, especially of sacred music.

---

[1] Jim writes: "First mentioned in 63.2–3, Ra was referring to a near-death experience that Carla had when she was 13 years old. Carla was a child prodigy with many unique talents. Her parents decided that the best way to develop her gifts was never to compliment her but only offer constructive criticism. All of her life Carla wanted nothing more than to be of service. But because she was constantly getting this critical feedback from her parents, she felt by the age of 13 that she was a failure who couldn't offer service to anyone. So she prayed to die.

Six months later her kidneys failed. At the hospital she was expected to die, and to the perception of the staff, she did. At that moment, Carla no longer perceived herself in the hospital bed. She found herself in a beautiful meadow surrounded by woods. Finally free of pain, she rejoiced. But a voice spoke to her, informing her that it was not her time to go. She was given a choice of dividing her lessons into another lifetime or continuing with her current one. She decided to return to complete her lessons and finish her journey.

Immediately she was back in her pain-filled body in the hospital surrounded by doctors and nurses working feverishly to bring her back to life. From then forward she continued with a sense that she was of service and that she had work to do, a mission, even, to fulfill."

This entity chose to enter a worshipful situation with a martyr's role when first in this geographical location. Therefore, the feeding by worship has taken place only partially. Similarly the musical activities, though enjoyable and therefore of a feeding nature, have not included the aspect of praise to the Creator.

The instrument is in a state of relative hunger for those spiritual homes which it gave up when it felt a call to martyrdom and turned from the planned worship at the location you call the Cathedral of St. Philip. This, too, shall be healed gradually due to the proposed alteration in location of this group.

106.5   **QUESTIONER**   Then, as I understand it, the best thing for us to do is advise the instrument to drink much more liquid. And I would imagine the spring water would be best. And we will, of course, move. We could move her out of here immediately, tomorrow, say, if necessary. Would this be considerably better than waiting two to three weeks for the allergies and everything else?

RA   I am Ra. Such decisions are a matter for free-will choice. Be aware of the strength of the group harmony.

106.6   **QUESTIONER**   Is there anything with respect to the present spiritual, or metaphysical condition, or physical condition of this [*house address*] that we're contemplating that Ra could tell us about that would be deleterious to the instrument's health?

RA   I am Ra. We may speak to this subject only to note that there are mechanical electrical devices which control humidity. The basement level is one location, the nature of which is much like that which you have experienced at the basement level of your previous domicile. Less humid conditions would remove the opportunity for the growth of those spores to which the instrument has sensitivity. The upper portions of the domicile are, almost in every case, at acceptable levels of humidity.

106.7   **QUESTIONER**   How about the metaphysical quality of the house? Could Ra appraise that please?

RA   I am Ra. This location is greatly distorted. We find an acceptable description of this location's quality to elude us without recourse to hackneyed words. Forgive our limitations of expression. The domicile and

its rear aspect, especially, is blessèd, and angelic presences have been invoked for some of your time past.

106.8 **QUESTIONER** I'm not sure that I understand what Ra means by that. I'm not sure that I understand whether the place is metaphysically extremely good or extremely negative. Could Ra clear that up please?

RA I am Ra. We intended to stress the metaphysical excellence of the proposed location. The emblements of such preparation may well be appreciated by this group.

106.9 **QUESTIONER** Would the cleansing by salt and water, then, be necessary for this property? Or would it be recommended, shall I say?

RA I am Ra. There is the recommended metaphysical cleansing as in any relocation. No matter how fine the instrument, the tuning still is recommended between each concert or working.

106.10 **QUESTIONER** OK. And if the instrument stays out of the basement, do you think the humidity and physical conditions would be good for the instrument then? Is that correct?

RA I am Ra. No.

106.11 **QUESTIONER** The humidity... we must do something about the humidity in the whole house then to make it good for the instrument. Is that correct?

RA I am Ra. Yes.

106.12 **QUESTIONER** I'm going to come back to a couple of points here, but I have to get in a question here about myself. It'd seem to be critical at this point. Can Ra tell me what is physically wrong with me, and what's causing it, and what I could do to alleviate it?

RA I am Ra. The questioner is one also in the midst of further initiation. During this space/time the possibility for mental/emotional distortion approaching that which causes the entity to become dysfunctional is markèd.

Further, the yellow-ray, chemical vehicle of the questioner is aging and has more difficulty in the absorption of needed minerals, such as iron and other substances such as papain, potassium, and calcium.

At the same time the body of yellow ray begins to have more difficulty eliminating trace elements such as aluminum. The energizing effect has occurred in the colon of the questioner, and the distortions in that area are increasingly substantial. Lastly, there is a small area of infection in the mouth of the questioner which needs attention.

106.13 **QUESTIONER** Could Ra recommend what I should do to improve my state of health?

RA I am Ra. We tread most close to the Law of Confusion in this instance but feel the appropriateness of speaking due to potentially fatal results to the instrument. We pause to give the questioner and the scribe a few moments of space/time to aid us by stepping away from those distortions which cause us to invoke the Law of Confusion. This would be helpful.

[*A few moments pause.*]

I am Ra. We appreciate your attempts. Even confusion on your behalves is helpful.

The questioner has, in the recent past, allowed a complete transfer of mental/emotional pain from the questioner to the instrument. The key to this deleterious working was when the instrument said words to the effect of the meaning that it would be the questioner and be the strong one; the questioner could be as the instrument, small and foolish. The questioner, in full ignorance of the firm intent of the instrument, and not grasping the possibility of any such energy transfer, agreed.

These two entities have been as one for a timeless period and have manifested this in your space/time. Thusly, the deleterious working occurred. By agreement in care and caution it may be undone.

We urge the attention to thanksgiving and harmony on the part of the questioner.

We may affirm the previous recommendation, in general, of the skills and the purity of intention of the one known as Bob, and may note the sympathetic illness which has occurred due to the instrument's sensitivities.

Lastly, we may note that, to the one known as Peter, several aspects of the distortions experienced by the questioner, the instrument, and the scribe may be quite apparent and rather simply traduced to lesser distortions.

106.14 **QUESTIONER** What is Peter's last name? I am not familiar with who he is.

RA I am Ra. The name by which this entity chooses to be known is Inman.

106.15 **QUESTIONER** Would Ra recommend— Let me put it this way: Would Ra think that surgery in my case would be of any help?

RA I am Ra. We assume you speak of the colonic indisposition and its potential aid by your chirurgeons. Is this correct?

106.16 **QUESTIONER** Yes.

RA Again, I am Ra. Please blow across the face and heart of the instrument.

[*This was done as directed.*]

I am Ra. We shall continue. The atmosphere has been meticulously prepared. However, there are those elements which cause difficulty to the instrument: the neurasthenia of the right side of the face being added to other arthritically energized pain flares.

Such an operation would be of aid in the event that the entity chose this physical cleansing as an event which collaborated with changes in the mental, mental/emotional, and physical orientations of the entity. Without the latter choice, the distortion would recur.

106.17 **QUESTIONER** Now, summarizing what we can do for the instrument: through praise and thanksgiving and harmony we can . . . Is that all that we can do, other than advising her to drink a considerable amount of liquid, and moving her into a better atmosphere? Am I correct on that?

RA I am Ra. We examine the statement and find two items missing, one important relative to the other. The chief addition is the grasping of the entity's nature. The less important is, for little it may seem to be, perhaps helpful; that is, the entity absorbs much medication and finds it useful to feed itself when these substances are ingested. The substitution of substances such as fruit juice for the cookie is recommended, and, further, the ingestion of substances containing sucrose which are not liquid is not recommended within four of your hours before the sleeping period.

106.18 **QUESTIONER** My experience with dehumidifiers indicates to me that it will probably be impossible to lower the humidity in that house much with a dehumidifier, although we can try that. And probably if we do move in there, we'll have to move out very shortly.

Is there anything further that need be done to complete the healing of Jim's kidney problem?

RA I am Ra. If it be realized that the condition shall linger in potential for some months after the surcease of all medication, then care will be taken, and all will continue well.

We may note that, for the purposes you intend, the location, [*address*], whether humid or arid, is uncharacteristically well-suited. The aggravated present distortions of the instrument having abated due to lack of acute catalyst, the condition of the location about which the assumption was made is extremely beneficial.

106.19 **QUESTIONER** Then the effect of the . . . you were saying the effect of the humidity . . . we will try to get it as low as possible, but you are saying the effect of the humidity is a relatively minor consideration when all the other beneficial factors are taken in with respect to the Louisville address? Is this correct?

RA I am Ra. Yes.

106.20 **QUESTIONER** I am quite concerned about the instrument's health at this point and must ask if there is anything I failed to consider with respect to the health of the instrument? Anything at all that we could do for her to improve her condition other than that which has already been recommended?

RA I am Ra. All is most whole-heartedly oriented for support here. Perceive the group as here: a location in time/space. Within this true home, keep the light touch. Laugh together, and find joy in and with each other. All else is most fully accomplished or planned for accomplishment.

106.21 **QUESTIONER** Is it as efficacious to cleanse the house with salt and water after we move in as it is to do it prior to . . . we move in?

RA I am Ra. In this case it is not an urgent metaphysical concern as timing would be in a less benign and happy atmosphere. One notes the relative simplicity of accomplishing such prior to occupancy. This is unimportant except as regards the catalyst with which you wish to deal.

106.22 **QUESTIONER** Can you tell me what the instrument's difficulty was with her last whirlpool?

RA I am Ra. The instrument took on the mental/emotional nature and distortion complex of the questioner as we have previously noted. The instrument has been taking the swirling waters at temperatures which are too hot and at rates of vibration which, when compounded by the heat of the swirling waters, bring about the state of light shock, as you would call the distortion. The mind complex has inadequate oxygen in this distorted state and is weakened.

In this state the instrument, having the questioner's distortion without the questioner's strength of the distortion one might liken to the wearing of armor, began to enter into an acute psychotic episode. When the state of shock was past the symptoms disappeared. The potential remains as the empathic identity has not been relinquished, and both the questioner and the instrument live as entities in a portion of the mental/emotional complex of the instrument.

May we ask for one more full query at this working, and remind the instrument that it is appropriate to reserve some small portion of energy before a working.

106.23 **QUESTIONER** I would just ask if there's anything we can do to help the instrument and make her more comfortable or improve the contact? And what would be the soonest Ra would recommend the next contact? And we would certainly—I would certainly appreciate the return of the golden hawk. It gave me great comfort.

RA I am Ra. You have complete freedom to schedule workings.

We suggest the nature of all manifestation to be illusory, and functional only insofar as the entity turns from shape and shadow to the One.

I am Ra. We leave you, my friends, in the love and the glorious light of the One Infinite Creator. Go forth, then, rejoicing in the power and in the peace of the One Infinite Creator. Adonai.

EPILOGUE

In the fall of 1983 we moved L/L Research to Cumming, Georgia, just north of Atlanta where Don was based as a pilot for Eastern Air Lines. We thought that it would help him to actually live in the area so he wouldn't have to make the long commute from Louisville to Atlanta. But nothing much was going right for us then, and this was no exception. The traffic around Atlanta was heavy and slow. It took him just as long to drive to the airport from Cumming, GA, as it did for him to fly there from Louisville. On top of that, the water pipes in our house froze and soaked the carpet which created mold to which both Don and Carla were allergic. This was a most unfortunate move for us.

By the spring of 1984 we were able to get ourselves in good enough collective shape to have what would turn out to be the last session with those of Ra. It was in this session that we found out why Don and Carla were having such difficulties. Ra said that both were going through an initiation which is difficult enough by itself. But this initiatory process was made far more difficult by what Ra called a "deleterious energy exchange" between Don and Carla. Carla and I had noted Don's discomfort and decline over the last year. So she told Don that she would take over the worrying about how we were going to survive through the poor housing situation, through the threat of bankruptcy for Eastern Air Lines, and through the physical maladies that were building in both of them. Then she added that he could relax and be "small and foolish" like she was.

In all innocence that such an exchange of energies was possible, Don agreed, more to placate her than anything else. But Ra said that since both Don and Carla "had been as one since before time," the energy exchange was made. This action led to all their difficulties ramping up a few notches. Ra said this choice made it so that "a problem for one became the same, in sympathy, for the other." Now they had not only their own problems to work on but each other's as well. I am quite sure that our friend of negative polarity had no trouble finding ample targets of opportunity to further intensify their difficulties.

We were able to solve the housing problem by moving back to Louisville. Don had been able to find and purchase a wonderful old two-story bungalow with lots of trees and gardening spaces all around. While at that house during the last seven months of Don's life, he continued his physical and mental decline. This was exacerbated due to the deleterious energy transfer; he no longer had his normal armor of light to protect him. He began worrying more, eating less, losing weight, and could find no way to take Ra's advice to give praise and thanksgiving for all that was happening. Every day was worse than the last for him.

In June of 1984 Don checked himself into the psychiatric ward of a local hospital. He knew he needed help and he tried to get it, but, to make a long story short, it was not received from the hospital.

Throughout the summer and early fall Carla and I were unable to be of any real help to Don as he became increasingly mentally and emotionally dysfunctional. Though we tried everything we could think of, it seemed of no avail. Don took his own life on November 7, 1984. Thus the Ra contact came to an end.

Our grief at Don's death was overwhelming even though we saw it coming and could do nothing about it. Within the week following his death, however, Carla saw Don in waking visions on two occasions. He was surrounded by golden light, and he told her that all that had occurred happened as it should, and that all was well, but that we would not be able to understand until we, too, eventually passed through death's door.

The contact with those of Ra had been a mountain top experience for the three of us during those three years and three months. We had entered into this glorious adventure with a great desire to be of service to others, and we were able to complete 106 sessions with those of Ra by learning how to deal with a truly magical situation and, even more, by learning how to handle the most difficult and persistent of psychic greetings that we could imagine. Looking back on this situation now I am amazed at how we were able to continue for as long as we did with our great desire to serve being equaled by our magical naiveté. As Ra said it was necessary for us to wend our own way through the challenges and surprises that came our way by calling upon the light to be our shield and buckler.

So I give praise and thanksgiving to the One Infinite Creator for Don and Carla and Ra and all those whom it has been our honor to serve by offering *The Ra Contact: Teaching the Law of One*. It was a glorious beau geste, and I think that we made the Creator smile.

Jim McCarty
April, 2017

A NOTE ABOUT THE TAROT CARDS

The original deck that Don Elkins used for questioning was the work of C.C. Zain, founder of the Church of Light.

C.C. Zain's first deck was released in 1918. It was subsequently revised in the 1930s and issued as a monochrome deck in the 1960s. It is the 1960s deck that Don, Jim, and Carla used for questioning Ra about the archetypal mind. Unfortunately, those images are unavailable for reprinting.

In following pages, the first seven arcana in the series were those re-drawn by L/L Research according to Ra's suggestions.

Because L/L Research did not receive permission to publish the tarot images from the Church of Light deck, the remaining images, Arcana 8–22, come from a very similar deck made by George Fathman, printed in his book *The Royal Road*.

THE MAJOR ARCANA

MATRIX OF THE MIND

The Magician
Arcanum No. I

POTENTIATOR OF THE MIND

The High Priestess
Arcanum No. II

CATALYST OF THE MIND

The Empress
Arcanum No. III

EXPERIENCE OF THE MIND

The Emperor
Arcanum No. IV

SIGNIFICATOR OF THE MIND

The Hierophant
Arcanum No. V

TRANSFORMATION OF THE MIND

The Lovers or Two Paths
Arcanum No. VI

GREAT WAY OF THE MIND

The Chariot
Arcanum No. VII

MATRIX OF THE BODY

Justice or Balance
Arcanum No. VIII

POTENTIATOR OF THE BODY

Wisdom or The Sage
Arcanum No. IX

CATALYST OF THE BODY

Wheel of Fortune
Arcanum No. X

EXPERIENCE OF THE BODY

The Enchantress
Arcanum No. XI

SIGNIFICATOR OF THE BODY

The Hanged Man or Martyr
Arcanum No. XII

TRANSFORMATION OF THE BODY

Death
Arcanum No. XIII

GREAT WAY OF THE BODY

The Alchemist
Arcanum No. XIV

MATRIX OF THE SPIRIT

The Devil
Arcanum No. XV

POTENTIATOR OF THE SPIRIT

Lightning Struck Tower
Arcanum No. XVI

CATALYST OF THE SPIRIT

The Star or Hope
Arcanum No. XVII

EXPERIENCE OF THE SPIRIT

The Moon
Arcanum No. XVIII

SIGNIFICATOR OF THE SPIRIT

The Sun
Arcanum No. XIX

TRANSFORMATION OF THE SPIRIT

Judgment
Arcanum No. XX

GREAT WAY OF THE SPIRIT

The World
Arcanum No. XXI

THE CHOICE

The Fool
Arcanum No. XXII

GLOSSARY

Adept – One who devotes the self to seeking the Creator using the disciplines of the personality in the work of faith and spirit. After having adequately balanced the preceding energy centers, the adept proceeds into indigo-ray to make contact with intelligent infinity. The adept may bring intelligent energy through the indigo gateway in order to heal, teach, and work for the Creator in ways that are both radiant and balanced. Whatever the outer service, though, the adept's primary work is not that of doing, but of being.

Archetypal Mind – The architecture of the nature of the evolution of mind, body, and spirit, containing all facets which may affect mind or experience. It is a resource within the deep mind that is of great potential aid to the adept. The archetypal mind is not specifically a *plan* for evolution but is rather, when penetrated lucidly, a blueprint without distortion of the builded structure of all energy expenditures and all seeking.

Bodies (Seven) – One of the preconditions for space/time existence is some form of body complex. Each body offers a vehicle for learning, movement, and experience in a particular environment. Including the present physical body, there are seven basic bodies.

> **Red Ray:** The unconstructed material of the body, the elemental body without form, the chemical body. Not, however, the biological system of bone, tissue, organs, muscle, nerves, hormones, electrochemical impulses and so forth that is the human physical body. This basic unformed material body is important to understand for there are healings which may be carried out by the simple understanding of the elements present in the physical vehicle.

> **Orange Ray:** This purely physical body complex formed without self-awareness, the body in the womb before the spirit/mind complex enters. This body may live without the inhabitation of the mind and spirit complexes. However, it seldom does so.

> **Yellow Ray:** The body that is in activation within third-density incarnation; the physical vehicle as we now know it that is integrated with mind and spirit.

The following higher bodies—often referred to as subtle bodies—are available to the third-density entity, but there is skill and discipline needed in order to avail the self of the more advanced or lighter vehicles. They are not necessary for third-density work but are useful to the adept.

Green Ray: A lighter body packed more densely with life, called by some teachings the astral body. It is the body that will be activated and enjoyed by those in the fourth-density cycle of experience.

Blue Ray: A body of light which may also be called the devachanic body. There are many other names for this body, especially in the Indian Sutras as those of that culture have explored the regions available to the blue-ray body.

Indigo Ray: The etheric, or gateway, or form-maker body, described both as the "analog for intelligent energy" and "being intelligent energy." In this body, form is substance; it would be perceptible to our eyes only as light, as it may mold itself as it desires.

This is the first body activated upon what we call death (the cessation of the yellow-ray body). The indigo body also plays a critical role in health and healing, adopting the desired configuration and manifesting it in the yellow-ray body.

Violet Ray: The violet-ray body may perhaps be understood as what we might call the Buddha body or *that body which is complete.* It is also the body activated during the anomalous moment of harvest in order to gauge the harvestability of the entity.

Catalyst – A neutral instigator that, when used, offers learning (especially of pre-incarnatively chosen lessons), facilitates evolution, develops will and faith, precipitates experience, and polarizes the third-density entity. Essentially all that reaches the senses and everything that comes before the notice of an entity is catalyst, though other-selves are the primary mechanism of catalyst, serving as mirrors that offer reflections of the fruit of beingness.

The Choice – The primary function of the very intense, very short third-density experience is the making of the Choice: to choose and dedicate the self to the positive path of service to others or the negative path of service to self. If the catalyst of third density is successfully used to make the Choice, that is, to polarize and bias the consciousness (measured in vibratory rate of 51% for service to others and 95% for service to self), then, at the time of harvest, the entity will graduate from third to fourth density.

Complex – A term used by Ra essentially as a noun in the same fashion as Merriam-Webster defines it: "A whole made up of complicated or interrelated parts." Ra speaks of it this way in context of the archetypes: "A *concept complex* is a complex of concepts just as a molecule is a complex structure made up of more than one type of energy nexus or atom."

Some examples include: mind/body/spirit complex, mind complex, body complex, spirit complex, social memory complex, sound vibrational complex, and many more.

It may also mean a complex *of* something. When used this way, it may denote either a whole made of up interrelated parts (as in the above definition), or an assortment of multiple things, e.g.: "a complex of thought, ideas, and actions."

Confederation (of Planets In the Service of the Infinite Creator) – The Confederation of Planets (often called the "Confederation" for shorthand) is a group consisting of approximately fifty-three civilizations, comprising approximately five hundred planetary consciousnesses, along with entities from Earth's inner planes and graduates from Earth's third density. It is a true Confederation in that its members are not alike but are all allied in service according to the Law of One. In this Confederation each of the constituent social memory complexes voluntarily place their collective data in a central repository that becomes available to all members.

There are many Confederations in the galaxy, but in almost all cases this term refers to the one currently serving Earth.

Whereas their counterpart, the Orion Empire, calls itself to conquest, the Confederation of Planets awaits the call to service.

Crystallization (Crystallize, Crystallized Being) – Used in reference to energy centers or entities themselves. As Ra describes it, when a crystalline structure is formed of physical material, the elements present in each molecule are bonded in a regularized fashion with the elements in each other molecule. Thus the structure is regular and, when fully and perfectly crystallized, has certain properties. It will not splinter or break; it is very strong without effort; and it is radiant, traducing light into a beautiful refraction giving pleasure of the eye to many.

Through consistent work in consciousness over a period of time (aka: the "discipline of the personality"), energy centers themselves become crystalline, forming unique crystal structures described in 51.8.

Density – One of seven (or eight, depending on the perspective) dimensions or cycles of evolution in an octave of experience. It is called "density" because each successive density is more *densely* packed with light. Akin to a musical scale, seven densities are grouped together in an octave, where the eighth density begins the first of the next octave in an infinite string of octaves. Each density represents a quantum vibrational spectrum or portion of intelligent energy, and each density cycles, or moves to the next density, according to the predetermined clock-like rhythms of intelligent energy.

Designed by the Logos, each density of experience offers its own set lessons and parameters that must be learned and understood in order to cross the threshold and graduate from one density to the next. Each density has seven sub-densities. Each sub-density has seven sub-sub densities. And so on, infinitely. The core vibrations of the seven densities have correspondence to the seven true colors and the seven energy centers.

Disciplines of the Personality – The paramount work of any who have become consciously aware of the process of evolution. The heart of the discipline of the personality is threefold: One, know yourself. Two, accept yourself. Three, become the Creator.

The discipline of the personality results, eventually, in the whole knowledge of the self in micro- and macrocosm, and in a finely tuned compassion and love which sees all things as love.

Distortion – The second definition given for "distort" in Merriam-Webster is "to twist (something) out of a natural, normal, or original shape or condition." In a similar sense, Ra uses the term "distortion" to convey the twisting, modification, misrepresentation, or *concealment* of the un-differentiated, un-potentiated intelligent infinity in its pure form, i.e., the Creator.

Everything in the universe, then, is a distortion, beginning with the First Distortion of Free Will, moving to Love, then to Light, then to the created universe, including stars, planets, people, space, time, etc.

"Distortion" can have any value assigned to it ("good," "bad," "beautiful," "terrible,") but ultimately lacks positive and negative connation. It is used as a strictly neutral term to indicate that everything experienced within creation is a distortion of the One Creator.

Dual-Activated (Bodies, Entities) – Entities harvested from other third-density planets who have incarnated in Earth's third density to make the transition with this planet into fourth density. These entities are not wanderers in the sense that this planetary sphere *is* their fourth-density home planet. They are the pioneers or forerunners of Earth's fourth density.

They incarnate with a third-density/fourth-density double body in activation. This transitional body is one which will be able to appreciate fourth-density energies as the instreaming increases without the accompanying disruption of the third-density body. (If a third-density entity were electrically aware of fourth density in full, the third-density electrical fields would fail due to incompatibility.)

The purpose of such combined activation is that such entities are to some extent consciously aware of those fourth-density understandings which third density is unable to remember due to the forgetting. Thus fourth-density experience may be begun with the added attraction of dwelling in a troubled third-density environment and offering its love and compassion. It is a privilege to be allowed this early an incarnation as there is much experiential catalyst in service to other-selves at this harvesting.

At the time of the Ra contact, dual-activated entities were limited to those harvested from other planets. It is possible that entities harvested from Earth have since joined their ranks.

Energy Centers – The seven rays or centers of consciousness that filter and process the love/light energy of the One Creator, drawn in through both the south and north poles of the energy system. Each energy center (or ray, or chakra) represents a stage or modality of consciousness with its own expressions, lessons, and aspect of the overall identity of self.

Arranged sequentially in hierarchical, ROYGBIV structure, all life experienced is processed through the sequence of energy centers.

Harvest, General (Graduation) – The point of transition between the densities within an octave that operates according to what might be perceived as a three-dimensional clock-like face stretched across the entire galaxy. As the galaxy revolves or spirals, each constituent solar system and planet moves through the scheduled density of experience. The cycles move precisely as a clock strikes the hour. Upon completing a density, or cycle therein, those who have successfully learned the lesson of that cycle are harvested in order that they may ascertain whether they are ready to graduate to the next density. This is perhaps somewhat analogous to passing a final exam at the end of a grade in school in order to move onto the next grade.

Higher Self (Oversoul) – A being beyond polarity in the mid-sixth density that exists with full understanding of the accumulation of experiences of the entity. Operating from what we would consider our future, the higher self is you at mid-sixth density: the end result of all the development experienced by you up to that point. Every entity—whether positive, negative, or undecided—has a higher self. Whatever guidance is received from the higher self may be interpreted in a positive or negative light depending upon the polarity of the seeker, though the negative entity, separated from itself, is not likely to seek such guidance.

The higher self also works closely with the entity in between incarnations, aiding the entity in achieving healing of the experiences which have not been learned properly, and assisting in further life experience programming. Whatever its activity, though, the free will of the incarnate entity is paramount in the service it offers.

Honor/Responsibility, Honor/Duty, and vice versa – Each responsibility is an honor; each honor, a responsibility. Responsibilities and duties are not seen as chores or obligations to which one is shackled in a pejorative sense; rather, the seeker has the freedom to accept the responsibility or duty as an honor, and freedom to fulfill the responsibility or duty as a service. (It is Ra's honor/responsibility to stay with those of planet Earth to eliminate the distortions given to the Law of One.)

Initiation – A person will move through multiple initiations during the course of their incarnation. Each initiation may be characterized generally by stating that a threshold is crossed that delineates the former experience from the newer. This may transpire in a moment or over a long period of time. There is often a challenge or difficulty associated with the crossing of the threshold, and some measure of will and faith needed. For some this may manifest as a dark night of the soul.

Ra speaks of initiation as a process and means whereby the mind/body/spirit complex becomes a purified or initiated channel for the Law of One. The mind, the body, the spirit, or all of the above may move through an initiation. Such an initiated person may then channel the love/light of the One Infinite Creator through the gateway in order to be of service, whether that service be radiance of being alone, or the magical work of indigo ray, the communication of blue ray, or the healing of green ray.

Inner Light – The energy which dwells within an entity, that which is the entity's heart of being, the birthright and true nature of all entities. Drawn by the strength of the inner light, the upward spiraling light enters the red ray and moves northward through the energy centers of an entity to be met and reacted to by the inner light, indicating the level of an entity's progression. The strength of the inner light equals the strength of will to seek the light.

Inner Planes – Whereas humans in their physical bodies experiencing incarnation in the physical world are in space/time or *outer planes*, the non-physical portion of the third-density experience is in time/space, or *inner planes*. The inner planes are also experienced in between incarnations in the review and healing of the previous incarnation and the planning of the coming incarnation. They are also entered in the dreaming state and in other modes of non-ordinary consciousness.

Karma – Ra likens karma to inertia: those actions which are put into motion will continue using the ways of balancing until such time as the controlling or higher principle, which may likened unto braking or stopping, is invoked. This stoppage of the inertia of action may be called forgiveness. These two concepts are inseparable. In forgiveness lies the stoppage of the wheel of action, or what you call karma. Actions undertaken in a consciously unloving manner with other beings are those which may generate karma.

Law of One – Beyond the limitations of language, the Law of One may be approximated by stating that all things are one, that there is no polarity, no right or wrong, no disharmony, but only identity. You are every thing, every being, every emotion, every event, every situation. You are unity. You are infinity. You are love/light, light/love. You are.

To state that another way: All is one. That one is love/light, light/love, the Infinite Creator. This is the Law of One.

Law of Responsibility – A law or way which begins to be effectuated by the increasing ability of entities to grasp the lessons to be learned in this density. If a quickened or increased rate of learning is sought, the Law of Responsibility requires that the greater understanding be put into practice in the moment to moment experience of the entity. Likewise, the closer to the light one seeks to stand, the more the Law of Responsibility goes into effect. When in earlier cycles of this third-density experience the catalysts went unused, the lessons not learned, the fruits of learning not demonstrated, the life span became greatly reduced, for the ways of honor/duty were not being accepted.

Laws – Though the field of physics as it applies to the material realm (i.e., space/time) is a limited approach to understanding what Ra may mean by "Law," the definition can begin there. Scientific laws are understood to be fundamental operations of the physical universe that are not human-designed but human-discovered. Among their characteristics, scientific laws are verifiably empirically true, simple, absolute, stable, constant, and universal. Everything in the universe must in some way comply with or conform to or operate within these laws.

Ra indicates that there is actually only one law: the Law of One. Other so-called laws are *distortions of this law*, though some of them being primal and incredibly significant for evolutionary progress. Ra nevertheless does use the word "Law" when referring to the law-like *distortions* of the Law of One, such as Law of Confusion, Law of Love, Law of Light, etc. Ra indicates that the term "law" is interchangeable with "way."

Learn/Teaching (Teach/Learning) – Learn/teaching and teach/learning are inverse terms, one to the other. A teacher is a teach/learner; a student a learn/teacher. To learn is the same as to teach, unless you are not teaching what you are learning; in which case you have done you/they little or no good. One cannot learn/teach for another, but only teach/learn.

Logos (Logoi)Sub-logos – Logos is the Second Primal Distortion of the Law of One, the focusing of intelligent infinity through free will into intelligent energy, the Creative Principle, or Love. Each Creative Principle, Love, or Logos designs its own creation or system. Each Logos determines the paths of intelligent energy, designing the natural laws and ways of expressing them mathematically and otherwise. This energy is of an ordering nature which creates its patterns in holographic style.

The mind/body/spirit complex, or human being, once sufficiently awakened, is itself a Logos—or, more technically, a sub-sub-sub-Logos.

Sub-logos (Sub-Logoi) – The One Great Logos (Primal Logos, Great Central Sun) that creates the octave (universe, creation) is the Logos. Ra also commonly uses the term "Logos" to refer to the galactic Logoi, thus using the term "sub-Logos" to refer to the solar Logoi (sun body) and "sub-sub-Logos" to refer to mind/body/spirit complexes. All levels of sub-Logoi, like the Logos, are possessed of free will. Within the guidelines or ways of the senior Logos, the junior sub-Logos may find various means of differentiating and refining experiences without removing or adding to these ways. Every entity that exists is a sub-Logos of some order down to the limits of any observation, for the entire creation is alive. Each is also a co-Creator which, in holographic style, contains the whole.

Ra may, at times, use the "sub" prefix inconsistently, though it is always used to indicate a hierarchical architecture of the Logoi. If the one Primal Logos of the octave is seen as the first or original tier in the Logos hierarchy, and if it is thereby used as the basis for the "sub" prefixes, then *sub-Logos* could refer to the next tier (galactic Logoi), *sub-sub-Logos* to solar Logoi, and *sub-sub-sub-Logoi* referring to mind/body/spirit complexes. (92.22 may be an example of this nomenclature.)

Love/Light (Light/Love) – In the infinite universe there is only one energy: love/light or light/love or intelligent energy—the universe is made from and of love/light, light/love. It is that energy which heals, builds, removes, destroys, transforms, and forms the pathways or so-called natural laws of any particular universe. This energy comes into being as Love (the Second Primal Distortion), using Free Will, creates Light (the Third Primal Distortion), thus becoming love/light.

Love and light (like love and wisdom), are not black and white, but faces of the same coin. There is the same difference between love/light and light/love as there is between teach/learning and learn/teaching. Love/light is the enabler, the power, the energy giver. Light/love is the manifestation which occurs when light has been impressed with love.

Magic – The ability to create changes in consciousness through will, or the ability to consciously use the unconscious. Magic is the work of the adept; it is a sacramental connection undertaken at the level of the gateway, or indigo ray, which is fed by the disciplines of the personality. The heart of white magic (the positive use of magic) is an experience of the joy of union with the Creator that joins body, mind, and spirit with the One Infinite Creator and radiates throughout the life experience.

Magical Personality – When the higher self is properly and efficaciously invoked for the purpose of a working, it is called the *magical personality*. Upon this invocation, a bridge is made between space/time and time/space. As consequence, the higher self directly experiences the third-density catalyst for the duration of the working. And the third-density self takes upon itself something of a vestment of a personality of consciousness that bestows magical perception and power.

Master & Major Cycles – Third density begins and ends in the span of a master cycle, ours being approximately 75,000–76,000 years. At the end of the master cycle, all are harvested regardless of their progress. Those who have successfully polarized will transfer to a polarized fourth-density home. Those who have not made the Choice will repeat third density elsewhere. Within the master cycle are three major cycles of approximately 25,000 years.

Maldek – What we know as the asteroid belt is the remains of a former planet which was home to active first, second, and third densities. There are various names by which this planet has been identified, but in certain quarters of Earth's history (perhaps some of which have been lost) it apparently had the name of Maldek. The third-density population of Maldek had a civilization that gained much technological information and used it without care for the preservation of their planet, following the ways of warfare and service to self which was sincerely believed to be service to others. The escalating devastation wracked their biosphere and caused its disintegration.

Mars – Was once home to active first, second, and third density vibrations. The tendencies of the native third-density population toward warfare caused the atmosphere to become inhospitable before the end of its cycle. The Confederation aided these entities by transferring them at the start of Earth's third-density experience 75,000 years ago. This transfer was unusual in that their genetic material was preserved, adjusted, and, through a sort of cloning process, transferred to Earth. Consequently, the quarantine of planet Earth was instituted due to the assessment of the Guardians that the free will of those of Mars had been abridged.

Meditation – Ra describes meditation as a foundational prerequisite of the path of the spiritual seeker, for without such a method of reversing the analytical process, one could not integrate into unity the many understandings gained in such seeking. They would not endorse a best way to meditate, but described broad categories:

1. The **passive meditation** involving the clearing of the mind and emptying of the mental jumble which is characteristic of the human mind complex. This is efficacious for those whose goal is to achieve an inner silence as a base from which to listen to the Creator. It is by far the most generally useful type of meditation as opposed to contemplation or prayer.

2. **Contemplation** or the consideration in a meditative state of an inspiring image, text, or spiritual principle.

3. The faculty of will called **praying**. Whether it is indeed an helpful activity depends quite totally upon the intentions and objects of the one who prays.

4.   The type of meditation which may be called **visualization** is the tool of the adept. When the ability to hold visual images in mind has become crystallized in an adept, the adept may then, without external action, do polarizing in consciousness which can affect the planetary consciousness. Only those wishing to pursue the conscious raising of planetary vibration will find visualization to be a particularly satisfying type of meditation.

Mind Complex – That aspect of an entity which contains feelings, emotions, intellectual thoughts, ideation, imagination, conceptualization, dreaming, etc. It reflects the inpourings of the spirit and the up-pourings of the body complex. The mind is referred to as "complex" due to the veiling that partitions the conscious from the unconscious mind.

Ra describes the mind as having a configuration of layers or deeper natures. The intuition conveys information to the individual mind from the deeper aspects of the racial mind, the planetary mind, the archetypical mind, and the cosmic mind. The spirit complex then funnels these roots of mind into contact with intelligent infinity.

Mind/Body/Spirit Complex – A term Ra uses to refer to entities (aka: people) of third-density or higher. (Second-density entities are referred to as mind/body complexes.) Mind, body, and spirit are inextricably intertwined and cannot continue, one without the other. The work of third density is done through the interaction of these three components, not through any one.

The nature of the mind, body, and spirit as *complex* (consisting of seemingly separate and distinct components or parts) is a result of the veiling. Pre-veil entities were simply mind/body/spirits (non-complex).

Mixed Contact – It is possible for a positively oriented but un-tuned and confused channel to receive both positive and negative communications. If the channel at the base of its confusion is oriented towards service to others, negative sources may impress messages which speak of coming doom and offer reason to fear. Many channeling contacts have been confused and self-destructive because the channels were oriented towards service to others but, in the desire for proof, were open to the deceptive information of the crusaders who were then able to neutralize the effectiveness of the channel. Tuning and challenging are always counseled for positively oriented channels.

Octave – The system of densities that the evolving entities and social memory complexes move through takes place within a larger cycle known as an octave. Each octave contains seven densities with the eighth density being the first density of the following octave. Each octave is a heartbeat that births a new universe which begins with first density and is absorbed again at the eighth density. That which is learned in one octave is carried forward in the next. Acknowledging limitations upon their knowledge, Ra assumes that there are an infinite number of octaves, the ways of the octave being without time; that is, there are seven densities in each creation, infinitely.

As the creation can be seen to have some fractal characteristics, Ra sometimes refers to individual densities, sub-densities, or even certain cycles of experience, as octaves. Octave is also synonymous with the terms *universe* and *creation*.

One Original Thought/Original Thought – All things, all of life, all of the creation is part of One Original Thought. In each octave this Original Thought contains the harvest of all experience of the Creator by the Creator from the preceding octaves. For instance, the harvest of the previous octave into our present octave was the efficiency of the male/female polarity, and the Creator of Love manifested in mind, body, and spirit.

Orion – An empire of entities and social memory complexes who have chosen the negative path. Whereas the Confederation of Planets is organized as a confederation of alliances which share power and service on the basis of the oneness of all things, the Orion Group organizes itself on the basis of power against power, establishing a pecking order with the more powerful controlling the less powerful. The Confederation teaches unity and service to others; the Orion Empire teaches separation and service to self. They do this by calling themselves to conquest, attempting to bring third-density entities and planets into their fold using various means of manipulation and enslavement. This is done by finding and establishing an elite and causing others to serve the elite. Due to the problems inherent in pitting power against power, spiritual entropy causes them to experience constant disintegration of their social memory complexes, thus their numbers are perhaps one-tenth of the Confederation's at any point.

They are referred to as Orion because social memory complexes from the Orion constellation have the upper hand and thus rule the other members. It is unclear whether there are also positive beings from the stars within the Orion constellation.

Other-Self – The term Ra uses to refer to entities other than the self, i.e. I am your other-self, and you are my other-self. It is also a term that acknowledges the unity of all things, for each is a self, and each is an other-self to a self, and each is part of one self: the One Infinite Creator.

Polarity (In Consciousness) – In order to successfully graduate from the third density, consciousness can and must become polarized toward one pole or the other: "service to others" or "service to self." The purpose of polarity is to develop the potential to do work. This work drives evolution forward and galvanizes the development of will and faith, creating a more vivid and intensive experience of the Creator knowing itself. Called the axis upon which the creation turns, the higher densities do their work due to the polarity gained in this choice until sixth density when the polarities are released.

The Law of One blinks neither at the light or the darkness, but is available for service to others and service to self. In sixth density, the density of unity, the positive and negative paths must needs take in each other for all now must be seen as love/light and light/love. This is not difficult for the positive polarity, which sends love and light to all other-selves. It is difficult enough for service-to-self polarized entities that at some point the negative polarity is abandoned.

Possibility/Probability Vortex – A term used by Ra to describe possible experiences and scenarios in the future (as we understand it). Some vortices or possibilities may be stronger than others, having a higher probability of unfolding based upon the free will choices of the entities involved and existing patterns of momentum and energy. Any possibility/probably complex has an existence due to infinite opportunity. Prophecy can be considered a viewing of various possibility/probability vortices, with the stronger vortices being more readily perceivable. The value of prophecy must be realized to be only that of expressing possibilities.

Programming (Incarnational) – Prior to an entity becoming consciously aware of the path of spiritual evolution, incarnation is automatic and catalyst is generally of a random nature. When the entity becomes aware of the mechanism for spiritual evolution (upon the activation of the green-ray energy center), the entity itself will, prior to incarnation, arrange and place those lessons and entities necessary for maximum growth and expression of polarity in the incarnative experience. Such programming may include: genetic predispositions, selection of parents and family, life circumstances, time period in which the incarnation will take place, personality characteristics, lessons of polarity, balance between love and wisdom, etc.

Psychic Greeting (Psychic Attack) – The energizing of pre-existing distortions of a third-density seeker by higher-density entities. A negative greeting may consist of the tempting of the entity or group of entities away from total polarization towards service to others and toward the aggrandizement of self or of social organizations with which the self identifies. Depending upon the vibratory nature and purpose of the greeting, the third-density entity may be energized, blocked, or its imbalances accentuated.

Quarantine – Approximately 75,000 years ago, those who Ra calls the Guardians transferred the genetic material of the third-density Mars population from its destroyed home to Earth. This was deemed to be an abridgement of free will, so a quarantine was placed around Earth by the Guardians at the start of the 75,000 year master cycle of third density. The quarantine prevents interference from entities of other densities except in two circumstances: one, the Council grants permission to break quarantine, or two, a negative entity takes advantage of the window effect.

Ra – A social memory complex that evolved upon the planet Venus, experiencing the third-density there 2.6 billion years ago, they have since left the planet and are presently at the sixth-density level of evolution. Their primary purpose is to teach the Law of One in response to the call for service issuing from this planet. They have made historical attempts of this, including interacting with the Egyptians. Their teachings, however, were distorted by the peoples of the time, thus their primary present goal is to heal those distortions given to the Law of One.

Seniority of Vibration – The preferential treatment that gives priority of reincarnation to entities who are aware of the need to bend mind, body, and spirit toward achieving harvestability. It can be likened to placing various grades of liquids in the same glass: some will rise to the top, others will sink to the bottom. Layers and layers of entities will ensue, and, as harvest draws near, those filled with the most light and love will naturally, and without supervision, be in line for the experience of incarnation.

Service to Others (Positive Path) – One of two paths of polarity chosen in third-density experience. Also called the *path of that which is*; love, acceptance, and radiance are the hallmarks of the positive path. The positive path seeks to understand the unity of all things and revolves around the understanding, experiencing, accepting, and merging of self with self and with other-self, and finally with the Creator. In the desire to serve others is the fundamental respect for the free will of all beings and thus the positive entity awaits the call to service, serving only insofar as it is requested. The best way of service to others is the constant attempt to seek to share the love of the Creator as it is known to the inner self. This path attempts to open and balance the full spectrum of energy centers.

Service to Self (Negative Path) – One of two paths of polarity chosen in third-density experience. Also called the *path of that which is not*; control, manipulation, and absorption are the hallmarks of the negative path. This path is predicated upon separation and the manipulation, infringement, and enslavement of the free will of all other selves for the benefit of the self. This necessitates an omission and denial of universal love, or the green-ray energy center. Thus lacking empathy, the service-to-self entity does not await the call to service but calls itself to conquest.

Sexual Energy Transfer – Energy transfer in general is the release of potential energy differences across a potentiated space. *Sexual energy transfer* is the transfer of energy during sexual intercourse between two sexually polarized entities depending upon the male/female principle ratio. Both positive and negative sexual energy transfers are possible. Positive energy transfer requires both entities to be vibrating at a green-ray level. In the positive transfer, the male will have offered the discharge of physical energy to the female, and the female discharges its stored mental and emotional energy. The transfer is mutually uplifting and enhancing, and offers possibility of polarization and service. With careful development this transfer also holds the possibility of opening the gateway and experiencing sacramental communion with the Creator.

Sinkhole of Indifference – The spiritual path being predicated on the choice between the positive and negative polarities, the sinkhole of indifference is the state of remaining unpolarized and not achieving the transformation afforded by making the Choice. It is a state of being less-than-conscious and without power, a blind repetition of patterns. When neither path is chosen, the entity will continue to receive catalyst until it forms a bias towards acceptance and love or separation and control.

Social Memory Complex – When a collection of related entities, called a social complex, reaches a point of one orientation or seeking, it becomes a *social memory complex*. In a social memory complex, the experience of each entity is available to the whole, this forming a group memory that becomes available to the entire social complex. This is generally achieved in fourth density by positive and negative groups. The advantages of this complex are the relative lack of distortion in understanding the social beingness and the relative lack of distortion in pursuing the direction of seeking.

Negative social memory complexes are organized in a strict pecking order on the basis of relative power, those more powerful controlling and enslaving the less. Positive social memory complexes are organized on the basis of unity, or the Creator in all things. In this arrangement, power and love are shared and free-will-respecting service is freely given.

Space/Time and Time/Space – **Space/time** is the visible, physical realm that we now experience as conscious, incarnate beings. This is the realm of physics and the proverbial five senses. **Time/space** is the invisible, metaphysical realms, also known as the inner planes. This is the realm of intention and the unconscious. The terminology is likely based upon the theories of physics of Dewey Larson, used by Don and Ra to integrate this scientific understanding with the spiritual understanding.

Space/time and time/space are complex and complete systems that form fundamental aspects of our illusion. They share an inverse relationship due to the inequality between time and space. In space/time, the spatial orientation of material causes a tangible framework for illusion. In time/space, the inequality is shifted to the property of time.

These space/time and time/space distinctions, as we understand them, do not hold sway except in third density. However, fourth, fifth, and to some extent, sixth densities, work within some system of polarized space/time and time/space.

Note: Ra also uses the term "time/space" to indicate the passage of clock and calendar time as we know it.

Spirit Complex – The fields of force and consciousness which are the least distorted of the mind/body/spirit complex (but which can be realized in many distorted and unintegrated ways by the mind and body complexes of energy fields). When the intelligent energy of mind and body are balanced, the spirit complex acts as a two-way channel, pathway, shuttle or communicator whereby 1) the inpourings from the various universal, planetary, and personal sources may be funneled into the roots of consciousness, and 2) consciousness may be funneled to the gateway of intelligent infinity. Healing is the realization and undistorted opening of the mind and body to these spiritual instreamings.

The apparent addition of the spirit complex happens as second-density entities (mind/body complexes) become self-aware, thus becoming mind/body/spirit complexes and entering third density, the first density of consciousness of spirit. This addition is *apparent* rather than real as it is simply a realization of the spirit complex which was always available in potentiation.

Spiritual Entropy – A type of loss of polarity and cohesion. This is particularly experienced by negative social memory complexes due to their tendency toward inability to act totally as one being, thus causing them to experience constant disintegration of their social memory complexes.

Tarot – A system of 22 images (The Major Arcana) first developed by Ra during their third-density experience and later passed to the Egyptians by Ra, it is used as a tool to study the archetypal mind and develop the magical personality. Ra suggests that the Major Arcana not be used as a method of divination but instead used as a means to study the archetypal mind, and to gain knowledge of the self by the self for the purpose of entering a more profoundly, acutely realized present moment.

Thought Form – A pattern or persistence of thought that in some cases can exhibit persistent metaphysical or physical characteristics separate from the original thinker. Physical characteristics may include visual or material beingness. Thought forms can be created by entities consciously (typically higher-density beings) or unconsciously, particularly by the collective unconscious mind.

Trance State/Channel – In the context of the Ra contact, the state in which the instrument's mind/body/spirit complex left the physical body and allowed Ra to speak through it in a way supposedly undistorted by the presence of the instrument's own biases. In this state the instrument was unconscious and awoke with no memory of the information which was passed through her.

Transient Information – In the context of the Ra contact, information that is of a specific nature and lacks metaphysical principle or relevance, or is not directly related to the evolution of mind, body, and spirit. The level and purity of the contact was dependent on the level and purity of the information sought. Transient and specific information, especially if emphasized, was deleterious to the working.

True Color – The frequency that is the basis of each density, every color having specific vibratory characteristics both in space/time and in time/space. It is the basic vibration of a density which is then overlaid and tinged by the various vibratory levels within that density, and the attraction to the vibrations of the next true color density.

Tuning – To bring into harmony, reminiscent of tuning a musical instrument. Includes activities such as bringing the energy centers into a harmonious balance or tuning of the self in order to match the vibration of a contact for channeling.

Unconscious – A portion of the mind complex which is outside the perception of the entity's conscious awareness. It has various levels and depths ranging from the personal mind to the cosmic mind, and may contain a differing configuration, awareness, or will than the conscious mind. The nature of the unconscious is of the nature of concept rather than word. It corresponds to the female archetypal energy, is represented by the archetype of the High Priestess, and is the Potentiator of consciousness. Ra describes the nature of penetrating the veil to the unconscious mind as being "likened unto the journey too rich and exotic to contemplate adequate describing thereof."

Unmanifested Self – The self which does not need other-self in order to manifest or act; that being which exists and does its work without reference to or aid from other-selves. Meditation, contemplation, and internal balancing of thoughts and reactions are those activities of the unmanifested self, while things such as pain or disease are the catalyst of the unmanifested self. In magic, one is working with one's unmanifested self in body, in mind, and in spirit; the mixture depending upon the nature of the working.

Upward Spiraling Light – Commonly called "prana," this light is the ever-present energy of the Creator which radiates outward from all points in space. The term "upward" is not an indication direction, but an indication of the concept of that which reaches towards the source of love and light (the Creator). It is through this light that we progress in evolution towards the Creator, and it may be called upon and attracted by use of the will to seek the light. Different geometric shapes, such as the pyramid, can harness this light for various purposes.

Veil – An aspect of consciousness and experience that could be described as the separation of the conscious and the unconscious mind, which also results in a veiling of our awareness from the true nature of the Creator. The veil exists as the result of an experiment of the early creations of the sub-Logoi. This is referred to "extending free will" and resulted in such a significant increase in free will that non-veiled entities were seen as not having free will. Prior to this implementation, non-veiled entities progressed along the path of spiritual evolution very slowly, the non-veiled condition being unconducive to polarization. The veiling was so effective at increasing polarization that it was adopted by all subsequent sub-Logoi. The conditions created by the veil resulted in what Ra refers to as the Choice, the central purpose of third-density experience.

The veil is semi-permeable, and while progressive lifting of the veil is third-density work, completely lifting the veil is not.

Vibration – A term used to refer to: densities or sub-densities; to sounds, or speaking, or names; to state of mind; to channeling contact; an entity's overall beingness, or pattern of behavior, or pattern of distortions, or progress of spiritual evolution, or thought-processes; the metaphysical state of a place; the metaphysical state of a planet and the peoples on the planet; vibration or movement in physics, particularly Dewey Larson's Reciprocal Theory. Ra indicates that everything which is manifest is a vibration, beginning with the photon itself.

Vibratory Sound Complex (Sound Vibration Complex) – Occasionally used by Ra as a term for "word," often used when referring to names.

Vital Energy – The complex of energy levels of mind, body, and spirit. Unlike physical energy, it requires the integrated complexes vibrating in an useful manner. It may be seen to be that deep love of life and the appreciation of other-selves and of beauty. Without this vital energy, the least distorted physical complex will fail and perish. With this love, or vital energy or élan, the entity may continue though the physical complex is greatly distorted. Vital energy may be used, or reserved, depleted or increased.

Wanderer (Brothers and Sisters of Sorrow) – Entities from the fourth, fifth, and sixth densities who respond to a calling of sorrow by incarnating into a third-density environment in order to be of service to others by radiating love of others. In performing this service, the wanderer becomes completely the creature of third density, and thus is subject to the forgetting which can only be penetrated with disciplined meditation and working. This decision carries the risk the wanderer will forget its mission and become karmically involved, thus needing to continue reincarnating within third density in order to balance the karma.

White Magic – Magic in general being ritual dedicated to working with the unmanifested being, white magic is directing this working toward experiencing the love and joy of union with the Creator for the purpose of service to others. This love or joy then may be both protection and the key to the gateway to intelligent infinity and will radiate throughout the life experience of the positive adept. White magic is best undertaken in a group, but it may be performed by an individual so long as it is done in the knowledge that to aid the self in polarization towards love and light is to aid the planetary vibration.

Will – Pure desire; the motivation, or impetus within an individual that becomes awakened and harnessed when directed towards service and spiritual seeking. Will could also be seen as the attraction to the upward spiraling line of light guiding spiritual evolution. It is the single measure of the rate and fastidiousness of the activation and balancing of the various energy centers. The will can be conscious or unconscious, the unconscious utilization of will possibly depolarizing the individual in their seeking. The faculty of will has been greatly enhanced by the veiling. In conjunction with faith, the seeker's will is a vital aspect of many aspects of service and seeking, from the simple utilization of catalyst for evolution to the opening of gateway to intelligent infinity.

Work – A term that generally refers to action, experience, or service done in a spiritually significant and effective sense. Such work requires polarity in consciousness, thus it is done far more efficiently—with greater purity, intensity, and variety—when an entity continuously makes the Choice, polarizing in either service to others or service to self. Examples can range from the subtle work of mental balancing to the great work of offering one's life in service as a healer.

Glossary created by Austin Bridges and Gary Bean.

These definitions are not intended to be final or authoritative.

For a more in-depth examination of these terms, see the Concept Guide in the Resource Series.

NOTES ABOUT THE INDEX

The following index is uniquely designed to enable an in-depth study of
The Ra Contact material, and as such it departs from standard index
formats in several ways.

- The reference numbers point to the particular *session* and *question*
  number in which the relevant information can be found rather than
  the page number.

- The entries are listed in alphabetical order, though some of the sub-
  entries are ordered based on their conceptual context presented in
  the material. (For instance, energy centers are listed from Red, to
  Orange, to Yellow, etc. within the Energy Center entry.)

- The listed references are not limited to only Q&As where the term
  was mentioned, but also Q&As that may not contain the term yet
  speak to the concept.

- This particular index is specific to Volume 2 of *The Ra Contact*,
  containing only references to the sessions contained within these
  pages. Volume 1 includes a similarly split index. Any entry with
  references contained only in the other volume are still included with
  pointers to that volume. A complete and unified index listing
  references to all 106 sessions of the Ra contact is available as an
  independent booklet.

This index is as comprehensive as possible within the capabilities of the
many individuals who have contributed to its creation and refinement. It
contains 590 total terms (including primary, secondary, and tertiary), 81
alternative wordings, 114 "see also" associated terms, and 60 "see"
references, with over 9,000 total Q&A listings. As comprehensive as it is,
this index should be considered a constant work in progress and will
receive subsequent updates in future editions.

Along with the volunteers, we discovered that reading every Q&A for a
given term is one of the richest ways to deepen one's study of this
material. We hope you find this index a useful tool in your own study of
the many and varied topics discussed within the material.

INDEX

Activate

58.3	65.18-19	83.18
62.29	66.7	86.7
63.8	66.14	91.35
63.14	72.17	92.17
63.17	74.3	95.19
63.19	75.19	97.15
63.24-25	75.24	83.18
63.32	79.20	86.7

Acupuncture

See Volume 1

Adept

57.24	74.6	85.16
59.17	74.8-11	86.7
61.3	74.13	88.12
61.13	74.16	89.19
64.10-13	75.23-24	89.29
65.20	75.27-29	90.29
67.28	75.31-32	91.34-37
69.3	75.38	92.8
69.10	76.4	92.12
69.18	78.32	93.10
69.20	80.4	93.14-18
71.15-17	80.8-15	95.27
72.17	80.18-20	97.9
73.2-10	83.16	99.7
73.14	83.18	99.10
73.19-20	84.20	100.13
74.4	85.11	

Cycle of the Adept

61.2-4	64.10-13

Rituals of the Adept

73.7-8	74.4	89.44
73.10	89.19	

Services of the Adept

74.9-11	74.16

Tools of the Adept

58.3	88.24	91.35
76.9	90.29	97.9

Aging

59.20	105.19-20	106.12

Akashic Records

Hall of Records

91.7

Akhenaten

Ikhnaton

See Volume 1

Allergy

63.3	98.3-5	105.2
83.2	98.15	105.11
84.2-3	99.1-2	106.3-5
97.15	101.4	
97.20	102.16	

Allopathic Healing

See "Healing, Allopathic"

American Indians

See Volume 1

Anak

See Volume 1

Angels

69.5	90.4	106.7

See also "Guides"

Anger

59.3	98.15	105.17
66.32	99.5	
98.9	101.4	

Ankh

Crux Ansata

63.32	93.24	96.16-17
92.24	94.26-27	96.19
92.29-30	95.27	96.21

Archetypes

Concept Complexes

See also "Mind, Archetypal"

1) Matrix

Matrix of the Mind

74.4	79.42	91.17-34

Banishing Ritual of the Lesser Pentagram

67.16	73.2	79.5
72.2	74.14	80.2
72.8	75.3	95.4
72.13-14	75.5-7	103.18-19
72.17	76.4-5	

Battle Beyond the Stars (movie)

See Volume 1

Beingness

58.23	92.3	95.16
66.13	92.11	97.17
74.4	92.13	
86.18	94.9	

Bermuda Triangle

60.11

Bible

87.3

Bid

See Volume 1

Bigfoot

64.17	64.19

Biology

See "Sciences, Biology"

Biorhythm

61.2-4	64.10-14	89.4-5

Birth Defects

See Volume 1

Black Hole

See Volume 1

Body Complex

Physical Complex

58.3	59.17	61.2
58.19	60.20	(Cont. ...)

(... Cont.)	77.9	86.20
61.6-7	77.17	87.22-23
61.10-11	78.5	88.17
62.5	78.10-12	90.11-12
62.28	78.19	90.18
63.25	81.14	91.11
63.27	82.12	92.19
65.19	82.14	94.3
65.22	83.2	94.10
66.32-34	83.5-6	97.10
67.23	83.19-20	99.10
68.6	83.22-23	105.14
69.5	84.17	105.16
73.22	86.12	105.19-21
76.20-21	86.18	106.4

Red Ray Body Complex
See Volume 1

Orange Ray Body Complex
See Volume 1

Yellow Ray Body Complex

68.6	75.24	103.2-3
74.3	79.9	

Green Ray Body Complex

63.25	63.27

See also "Astral Body"

Blue Ray Body Complex

67.6	67.15

See also "Devachanic Body"

Indigo Ray Body Complex

66.14	70.17	71.6
70.14		

See also "Etheric Body"

Violet Ray Body Complex
See Volume 1
See also "Buddha Body"

Body Relationship with Mind and Spirit

61.6-7	77.9

Sacramental portion of the Body

86.20	95.5

Children

63.16	66.14	90.13
63.18		

China

See Volume 1

Choice, The

60.16	78.24	89.33-34
67.11	78.26	91.16
69.11	79.31	92.22
76.15-17	85.9	92.33-34
77.12-16	85.11	95.27
77.19	87.11	
78.21	87.25	

See also "Polarity (in Consciousness)"

Choice, The (Archetype)

See "Archetypes, The Choice"

Christianity

88.19

Cleanliness

95.7	95.16	96.4

Cleansing Ritual

95.4-5	96.4-5	105.11
95.10	101.6-7	106.9
95.15-17	105.6-8	106.21

Colors

57.12	67.11	93.8
58.20	74.4	94.16
59.23	77.17	94.18
62.29	78.18	94.23
63.25	81.3	97.12-13
63.28	85.11	97.17
64.4	92.22	99.11
67.6	92.34	

Compassion

Loving, Green Ray Love, Unconditional Love, Universal Love, Vibration of Love

59.3	64.6	83.18
60.3	65.11	84.4
60.8	67.11-13	85.11
61.6	70.22	85.16
61.11	75.2	86.7
62.26	75.14-15	89.29
63.5	75.32	89.35-39
63.8	75.39	99.5
63.14	81.23	

Complex

79.42	83.19-20	89.20

Body Complex
See "Body Complex"

Consciousness Complex

61.2	78.11	82.11-12
67.6	78.33	84.8
67.13-15	78.37	87.7
68.6-7	79.20	91.33
74.4	80.20	
75.24	82.7	

Mind Complex
See "Mind Complex"

Mind/Body/Spirit Complex
See "Mind/Body/Spirit Complex"

Physical Complex
See "Body Complex"

Social Complex

64.15	71.14	83.14
70.7	83.10	

Social Memory Complex
See "Social Memory Complex"

Sound Vibration Complex
See "Sound Vibration Complex"

Spirit Complex
See "Spirit Complex"

Defense, Magical

See "Magical Defense"

Deleterious Energy Exchange

106.13	106.22

Deneb

See Volume 1

Density

See also "Dimension"
See also "Sub-Density"

57.33	65.18	78.17-18
60.12	70.15	78.24-25
62.27-29	71.10	78.30
63.8	71.13	82.12-13
63.25	75.24	82.29
63.29	77.17	89.13
63.32	77.24	90.24-26

First Density

76.13	78.29	90.11
76.16		

Second Density

76.13	90.5-6	94.16
76.16	90.10	98.6-7
76.20-21	90.12	99.10
77.24	90.21-22	101.5
89.9	91.12-13	

Third Density

See "Third Density"

Fourth Density

57.33	65.6	82.29
58.19-21	65.10-12	85.9-13
60.20	65.17-19	87.7-13
61.13	66.7	87.9
62.18-23	66.29-32	87.25
62.28-29	66.30-31	90.3-5
63.8-32	67.7	90.4-5
63.25	77.15-17	90.9
63.28	78.24-25	
64.8	79.32-33	

Fifth Density

57.33	67.19	80.5-6
62.18-23	67.26	85.9-13
62.21	68.5-7	87.6-9
63.17	68.15-16	87.9
65.12	71.2-3	89.6
66.6	75.17-19	90.3-7
67.6-15	77.24	90.5
67.14	78.24-25	90.7

Sixth Density

57.33	66.6	75.32
59.3	67.27	75.36
60.13-16	68.10	77.24
63.17	69.11	78.25
64.6	70.6	81.16
65.12	70.9-12	

Seventh Density

See Volume 1

Eighth Density

See Volume 1

Devachanic Body

See also "Body Complex, Blue Ray"

Devachanic Planes

See Volume 1

Diaspora

See Volume 1

Diet

83.28	102.5	102.21
84.3	102.12	103.3
102.2	102.17	105.2

Dimension

57.33	62.20	65.9
59.14	63.24	76.17
61.9	64.4	

See also "Density"

Dinosaur

See Volume 1

Local Sub-Logos

65.17	77.24	90.23-26
74.4	78.20	91.2-3
76.8	78.22	91.6
76.10	78.33	93.13-14
76.21	81.25	94.13
77.11-17	90.11-14	99.8
77.21	90.16-21	99.10

Milky Way (Galactic) Logos

63.27	78.22	82.8-9
63.29-30	80.22	82.12
65.17	81.24	93.5
71.11	81.32-33	93.7
78.8-10	82.5-6	

Sub-Logos/Logoi

65.17	81.33	90.11
71.11-12	82.7-10	90.13-17
77.17-22	82.12	90.23
78.19-20	82.21	91.2-3
78.26	82.24	91.12
79.11-14	82.29	91.14-17
79.20	83.6	92.10
79.24	83.21	92.13
79.28	83.26	92.18
81.23-25	84.9	92.22
81.30	84.22	93.13-14

Logoic Bias

84.22	92.33	100.8
86.20	94.20	100.13
90.20-23	99.8	
90.25-26	99.10	

Local Sun Body (physical)
See "Solar System, Sun"

Love

See "Compassion" and "Distortion,
Second" and "Logos"

Love/Light

64.6	78.25	87.6
65.12		

See also "Light/Love"

LSD
See Volume 1

Magic

61.3	73.7-8	85.4
61.12	73.10	85.6-7
62.6	73.12	87.2-3
64.4	73.14	88.10
64.10	73.22	88.19
64.12	74.11-16	89.44
67.7-9	75.2-7	91.19
67.13-15	75.11	91.35
67.19	75.16	92.25
68.11-12	75.28-29	93.18
68.16	75.36-37	93.21
69.17	76.4-5	93.24
69.20	78.33	94.20
69.22	79.5	95.3-5
71.15-18	79.32-33	95.7
72.7-8	80.2	95.24
72.14	80.4	96.4-5
73.2-3	80.10	96.14

White Magic

64.4	72.11-14	75.3-7
67.16-17	73.2-11	75.10-11
69.22	73.13-15	75.26-31
71.16-18	74.4-8	87.6
72.7	74.11-19	98.2

See also "Magical Defense/Protection"

Magical Defense/Protection

64.4	74.12-14	101.7
68.11-12	75.2-4	103.16-19
69.3	76.2	105.6
69.5	91.38	105.8
72.7-8	95.4-8	106.9
72.13-14	95.14-15	
72.17	96.4-5	

Magical Personality

73.7	74.16	86.7
73.10-11	75.32	88.14
73.17	75.36-39	89.19
73.22	79.5	

Planetary Mind
Racial Mind, Mass Mind

Roots/Trunk of the Mind

Unconscious/Subconscious Mind

Mind Complex

Mind

Mind/Body

Mind/Body/Spirit Complex

Mind/Body/Spirit Complex Totality

Mind/Body/Spirits

Mind/Spirit (Spirit/Mind)

Mixed Contacts

Money
60.16

Mu
See "Lemuria"

Muhammad
See Volume 1

Mummies
60.29

Mystery, The
See also "Intelligent Infinity"
See also "One Infinite Creator"
See also "Unity"
97.9

Third-Density Variety

78.33	79.40	84.20
79.21	80.10	86.20

Nagasaki
See Volume 1
See also "Hiroshima" and "Nuclear Energy"

Narrow Band Channel
See "Channel, Trance"

Narrow Band Vibration

59.23	65.4	85.20
61.12	72.17	88.10
64.5	74.2	

Natural Laws
See "Laws, Natural"

Nazca (Lines of)
See Volume 1

Negative Contact with Intelligent Infinity
See "Intelligent Infinity, Negative Contact With"

Negative Path
Left-Hand Path

62.16	78.25	94.11-12
62.20	80.8	94.19
64.5	80.10	94.29
64.16	85.9	95.21
67.8	86.22	95.26
68.6	87.7-16	97.13
68.15-18	89.27	99.8
69.11	90.4	100.9
71.8	90.20-23	
73.4	93.8	

See also "Service to Self"

Ninety Degree Deflection (tesseract)

94.18	103.11	103.14
95.27		

Nothingness
See "Plenum"

Nuclear Energy
Nuclear War, Nuclear Device
See Volume 1
See also "Hiroshima"

Oahspe (book)
See Volume 1

Octave

71.11-13	78.22	82.4-5
77.13	78.30	82.11-12
78.10	81.16-18	91.15
78.14-15	81.28	97.17
78.18	81.33	

One Infinite Creator

60.18	80.8	88.17
67.7	80.17	88.19
67.28	80.20	92.24
71.17	81.7	94.9
72.17	81.33	95.24
73.8	82.10	97.9
74.4	82.29	100.4
75.2	87.6	105.11
75.23	87.23	
78.9	88.6	

Responsibility

61.7	80.5	94.9
66.10		

See also "Honor/Responsibility"

Responsibility, The Law or Way
See "Law of Responsibility"

Rhythm of Reality

See Volume 1

Robot

See Volume 1

Roosevelt, Eleanor

See Volume 1

Roosevelt, Franklin

See Volume 1

Russia

65.8

Sacrifice

69.5	93.24	103.8

Human Sacrifice
See Volume 1

Price

61.12	72.10	84.20
62.26	81.8	94.26
71.1	83.2	

Saints, Teresa, Augustine, Francis

See Volume 1

Salt Cleansing

95.4-8	101.7	106.21
96.5	105.6	
96.14	106.9	

Sanskrit

74.17-19	75.26-31

Sasquatch

See "Bigfoot"

Schweitzer, Albert

See Volume 1

Sciences

Astronomy

71.9-10	81.28-31	82.13
78.8-9	81.33	
81.19	82.6-10	

Biology

63.7	66.25-28	90.5-12
66.13		

Evolution

63.27	78.19-22	90.15
65.17	78.33	90.18-19
70.22	81.30-32	90.24-26
71.6	82.4-5	90.29
71.11-13	82.10-13	91.35-36
77.10	83.25	92.11
78.8	88.16	92.19
78.10	89.26	93.14-16
78.13	90.5	105.14-16
78.16	90.11-13	

Physics

70.22	75.33-34	78.9
75.26		

Scientists

See Volume 1

Scribe, The

59.3	85.16	101.2
59.21	89.7	101.5
61.7	96.3	105.4
67.23	99.5	105.11

Seeker

57.33	75.23	94.9
60.18	76.9	95.24
66.5	83.16	97.9
66.9	84.20	99.8
66.12-13	85.19	
67.30	88.17	

See also "Seeking"

Seeking

57.14	70.4	84.7
57.24	72.17	84.18
57.33	73.10	84.20
58.23	73.22	86.18
60.26-27	74.8	86.20
62.4	74.13	87.22
62.20	75.15	88.12
64.6	75.23	89.7
64.16	75.24	89.35
65.2-7	75.31-32	89.39
65.11-12	76.8-9	91.37
65.15	76.21	93.10
66.4	79.37	94.9
66.11-12	79.42	95.26
66.14	80.8	97.9
66.16	82.29	98.7
68.5	83.3	99.11
68.12	83.14	
68.16	83.17	

See also "Seeker"

Self

57.33	70.11-12	75.25
58.23	71.5-7	75.32
65.20-22	71.16	92.18
66.32	73.22	
70.9	74.11	

Self-Acceptance

57.33	66.9	82.3
60.4	74.11	85.16
60.8	75.13	

See also "Self-Worth"

Self-Conscious

Self-Consciousness, Self-Aware, Self-Awareness

75.23	82.12	92.10-11
78.33	83.10	
79.20	90.9-10	

Self-Worth

103.8

See also "Self-Acceptance"

Seniority of Vibration

57.12	61.2	65.5

See also "Reincarnation"

Service to Others

57.33	71.16-17	82.28-29
60.27	71.20	83.11-13
60.29	72.7	83.17-18
62.23	72.8	84.18
63.14-15	73.3-4	85.4
64.2	73.2	85.7
64.4	73.12	85.9-11
64.15	74.12	85.13
65.14	74.15	87.12
65.21	75.23	87.22
66.18	77.19	88.12
66.33	78.14	89.30
67.3	78.16	89.38
67.7	78.25	89.44
67.11	79.28	90.3
67.21	79.33	90.20-23
67.26	79.7	92.2
68.16	80.1	93.3
68.17	80.5	93.4-6
69.7	80.11	94.12
69.9	80.12	95.23-25
69.11	80.15	97.16
69.15	80.17	99.8
70.5	81.29-30	100.9
70.7	82.18	
71.14	82.22	

See also "Positive Path"
See also "Polarity (in Consciousness)"

Service to Self

62.17	69.15	78.25
62.20	70.7	80.5-8
65.14	70.23	80.11
66.29-33	71.7	80.15
67.7	71.14	80.17
67.26	72.8	85.4
68.6	73.4	85.7
68.16-18	75.19	85.9
69.9	75.23	85.11
69.11	77.17	(Cont. ...)

Understanding

Vibration of Understanding

See also "Density, Fourth"

Unity

See "Intelligent Infinity" and "One Infinite Creator"

Unmanifested Self

Unmanifested Being

Upward Spiraling Light

See "Light, Upward Spiraling"

Ur

Urantia Book

See Volume 1

Uranus

See "Solar System, Uranus"

Van Tassel, George

See Volume 1

Veil of Forgetting

Pre-veil Conditions

Venus

See "Solar System, Venus"

Vibration

See also "Narrow Band Vibration"
See also "Sound Vibration Complex"

General

Basic or Core Vibration

For Energizing

Vibration of Density

57.28	70.14	81.13
59.24	77.24	
68.6	78.15	

Vibration of One's Being

57.12	73.20	87.17
57.33	86.23	

See also "Seniority of Vibration"

Planetary Vibration

65.11-12	71.16

See also "Planetary Consciousness"

Visions

Visionary Information

58.3	86.12	88.17
84.8	86.15	89.16

Visualization

61.12	73.10	75.39
67.13-14	74.16	88.19-21
68.14	75.4-5	88.24
73.5	75.11	98.6

Vital Energy

Vitality, Vital Force

63.3	72.1	86.23
63.6-7	72.10	88.6
64.4	75.1	92.2
65.4	75.10	96.1-2
68.2	76.1-3	100.12
70.2	83.2	103.1
70.4	86.1-3	

Wanderer

58.20	65.11-12	70.15-17
59.3-5	65.19	75.24
63.10	66.6-8	81.27
63.15-18	66.34	85.16
65.3	68.10-11	89.33-39
65.5	69.10-12	

See also "Brothers and Sisters of Sorrow"

War

Bellicose Action

65.6-8	66.31

Water

57.9	60.11	89.20
58.15	78.29	106.4-5
59.7	88.23	

Blessed Water (for Cleansing or Drinking)

95.4-7	101.7	106.21
96.14	106.9	

Swirling Water

75.9	91.38	100.2-3
80.0	92.3	104.2
82.2	93.24	106.22
84.5	95.28	
89.45	99.11	

Weapons (Particle Beam and Psychotronic)

65.8

White Magic

See "Magic, White Magic"

Will

57.14	74.4	87.7
58.18	74.12-13	87.16
60.3	74.16	88.6
60.18	75.35	90.26
63.2-3	76.1	90.30
63.6	77.9-10	91.19
66.14-15	77.17	92.2
66.22	79.32	92.11
67.2	79.42	94.7
67.21	80.20	95.16
67.28	81.8	96.2
68.2	82.19	97.9
70.4	82.29	99.9
72.7	84.4	100.3
72.10	84.13	101.2
73.4	84.21	102.1
73.8	85.4	103.1
73.10-12	85.19	104.3
73.22	86.18	105.1

Williamson, George Hunt

See Volume 1

Window Effect

67.19-20	72.8

Wisdom

59.3	67.20-21	85.4
60.3	70.22	85.16
60.8	72.10	87.6-7
61.6	75.14	89.29
61.11	75.32	89.35
62.20	75.39	89.38-39
64.6	77.24	90.5
64.15	78.11	93.21
65.11-12	78.24	99.5
67.11	81.8	101.2
67.13	84.4	

Work

59.11	73.22	95.23
63.17	75.16	97.5
68.3	75.23	97.7
69.5	76.16	97.9
71.22	78.11	103.8
73.10	78.24	
73.12-14	94.9	

Wrong

57.12	77.17	103.8

Yahweh

60.17	74.19

Zeta Reticuli

81.24

AFTERWORD

The 106 sessions of the Ra contact represent an extraordinary subset of channeling in L/L Research's long history. During those 106 sessions the instrument was completely unconscious and, according to Ra, removed from her body. This is in contrast to the great majority of L/L's channeling undertaken with a conscious vocal instrument, awake and aware of the information coming through. That conscious channeling continues unbroken into the present day.

L/L Research makes this book, every channeling transcript, and much more available for free in its online library at the archive website www.llresearch.org.

Other recommended resources for further study of *The Ra Contact: Teaching the Law of One* include:

- The world's best Law of One study tool: www.lawofone.info
- *The Ra Contact* audiobook narrated by Jim McCarty, available at Audible.com.
- The actual recordings of the conversation with Ra, available for free listening at www.llresearch.org and www.lawofone.info, and combined with text at https://www.youtube.com/LLResearch.
- The Resource Series.
- Book V of the original published *Law of One* series containing Commentary of the journey of conducting the Ra contact.

We do this work for L/L Research keenly aware of the worldly context. It can sometimes seem to the sensitive seeker that the circumstances on our planet are tinged by chaos, disharmony, and suffering. But if you know where to look, and how to tune your senses, you'll see that a consciousness of love is growing all the time, inside of you, inside of others.

Our message for each wanderer we meet is the same: You are not alone. You are loved. You are here to assist with the transition to fourth density, first and foremost simply by being your truest most authentic self.

We are honored to play a small part in contributing to that blossoming awareness of love. We are grateful to help heal this planet alongside you, one open heart at a time.

ADDITIONAL L/L RESEARCH PUBLICATIONS

Living The Law of One 101: The Choice

Written with the intent of creating an entry–level, simple to read report concerning the core principles of the Law of One and Confederation philosophy in general, this book takes the reader through a discussion of Law of One principles such as unity, free will, love, light and polarity.

A Wanderer's Handbook

A reference manual for spiritual outsiders. It explores the alienation that seekers experience, the varieties of the pain of living, the healing of the incarnation, the discovery of the life's mission, and how to live a devotional life in a busy world.

Secrets of the UFO

A summary of the 25 years of philosophical study that preceded the Ra contact. The progression from physical sightings to metaphysical implications is carefully traced and, in some respects, serves as an introduction to the *Law of One* series.

A Channeling Handbook

Written for channels and those who would like to improve their channeling. Topics include: What is channeling? Why channel? Psychic greetings/attacks. Temptations and the ethics of channeling. Channeling and Christianity.

Tilting At Windmills: An Interview with Carla & Jim

The transcripts of a seven-day interview with Carla Rueckert and Jim McCarty that includes exploration of the Ra contact, the life story of L/L Research, personal biography of its three founding members, and examination of spiritual principles and philosophy.

On the L/L Research Website:

- More publications not listed above
- Over 1,500 channeling transcripts from 1974–Present
- A collection of interviews and speeches including rare gems with Don Elkins.
- The *Light/Lines* and *Gatherings Newsletter*s
- Information from various past L/L Research gatherings and workshops
- An *Origins* section including the *Brown Notebook* which opened Elkins to Confederation channeling.
- Transcripts and audio of L/L Research's podcast *In the Now*.
- Over twelve translations and more being added.
- Forums, Blogs, Chatrooms, Seeker Connector, and more.

Hardcopy versions of L/L publications are available through the online store.

Made in the USA
Columbia, SC
30 August 2024

40761218R00293